WILLIAM STANLEY JEVONS AND THE MAKING OF MODERN ECONOMICS

The Victorian polymath William Stanley Jevons (1835–1882) is generally and rightly venerated as one of the great innovators of economic theory and method in what came to be known as the "marginalist revolution". This book is an investigation into the cultural and intellectual resources that Jevons drew upon to revolutionise research methods in economics. Jevons's uniform approach to the sciences was based on a firm belief in the mechanical constitution of the universe and a firm conviction that all scientific knowledge was limited and, therefore, hypothetical in character. Jevons's mechanical beliefs found their way into his early meteorological studies, his formal logic, and his economic pursuits. By using mechanical analogies as instruments of discovery, Jevons was able to bridge the divide between theory and statistics that had become institutionalised in mid-nineteenth-century Britain. For better or worse, Jevons, thus, transformed political economy into social physics and irrevocably changed the domain of discourse of economics.

Harro Maas is Lecturer in History and Methodology of Economics at the University of Amsterdam. He is an associate researcher of the Centre for Philosophy of the Natural and Social Sciences at the London School of Economics. Dr. Maas's research has been published in the *History of Political Economy*, *Studies in History and Philosophy of Science*, and the *Revue d'Histoire des Sciences Humaines*.

Historical Perspectives on Modern Economics

General Editor: Craufurd D. Goodwin, Duke University

This series contains original works that challenge and enlighten historians of economics. For the profession as a whole it promotes better understanding of the origin and content of modern economics.

Other books in the series:

William J. Barber, *From New Era to New Deal: Herbert Hoover, the Economists, and American Economic Policy, 1921–1933*

William J. Barber, *Designs within Disorder: Franklin D. Roosevelt, the Economists, and the Shaping of American Economic Policy, 1933–1945*

M. June Flanders, *International Monetary Economics, 1870–1960: Between the Classical and the New Classical*

J. Daniel Hammond, *Theory and Measurement: Causality Issues in Milton Friedman's Monetary Economics*

Lars Jonung (ed.), *The Stockholm School of Economics Revisited*

Kyun Kim, *Equilibrium Business Cycle Theory in Historical Perspective*

Gerald M. Koot, *English Historical Economics, 1870–1926: The Rise of Economic History and Mercantilism*

David Laidler, *Fabricating the Keynesian Revolution: Studies of the Inter-War Literature on Money, the Cycle, and Unemployment*

Odd Langholm, *The Legacy of Scholasticism in Economic Thought: Antecedents of Choice and Power*

Philip Mirowski, *More Heat Than Light: Economics as Social Physics, Physics as Nature's Economics*

Philip Mirowski (ed.), *Natural Images in Economic Thought: "Markets Read in Tooth and Claw"*

Mary S. Morgan, *The History of Econometric Ideas*

Takashi Negishi, *Economic Theories in a Non-Walrasian Tradition*

Heath Pearson, *Origins of Law and Economics: The Economists' New Science of Law, 1830–1930*

Malcolm Rutherford, *Institutions in Economics: The Old and the New Institutionalism*

Esther-Mirjam Sent, *The Evolving Rationality of Rational Expectations: An Assessment of Thomas Sargent's Achievements*

Yuichi Shionoya, *Schumpeter and the Idea of Social Science*

Juan Gabriel Valdés, *Pinochet's Economists: The Chicago School of Economics in Chile*

Karen I. Vaughn, *Austrian Economics in America: The Migration of a Tradition*

E. Roy Weintraub, *Stabilizing Dynamics: Constructing Economic Knowledge*

WILLIAM STANLEY JEVONS AND THE MAKING OF MODERN ECONOMICS

HARRO MAAS
University of Amsterdam

CAMBRIDGE
UNIVERSITY PRESS

CAMBRIDGE UNIVERSITY PRESS
Cambridge, New York, Melbourne, Madrid, Cape Town, Singapore,
São Paulo, Delhi, Dubai, Tokyo, Mexico City

Cambridge University Press
32 Avenue of the Americas, New York, NY 10013-2473, USA

www.cambridge.org
Information on this title: www.cambridge.org/9780521154734

First published 2005
First paperback printing 2010

A catalog record for this publication is available from the British Library

Library of Congress Cataloging in Publication data
Maas, Harro.
William Stanley Jevons and the making of modern economics / Harro Maas.
p. cm. – (Historical perspectives on modern economics)
Rev. version of the author's thesis (doctoral).
Includes bibliographical references and index.
ISBN 0-521-82712-4 (alk. paper)
1. Jevons, William Stanley, 1835–1882. 2. Neoclassical school of economics – History –
19th century. 3. Marginal utility – History – 19th century. 4. Economics – History – 19th century.
I. Title. II. Series.
HB103.J5M33 2005
330.15′7′092–dc22   2004052546

ISBN 978-0-521-82712-6 Hardback
ISBN 978-0-521-15473-4 Paperback

To Geerte, Timo, and Jonne

CONTENTS

Illustrations

Abbreviations

Archival Materials

JA = Jevons Archives, John Rylands Library, Manchester.
TCC = Trinity College Cambridge Archives, Trinity College, Cambridge.
ULL = University Library London at Senate House.

Works Frequently Cited

Babbage = 1989. *The Works of Charles Babbage*. Edited by M. Campbell-Kelly and P. M. Roget. London: William Pickering.

Inoue = 2002. *W. Stanley Jevons: Collected Reviews and Obituaries*. 2 Vols. Edited by Takutoshi Inoue. Bristol: Thoemmes.

LJ = 1886. *Letters and Journal of William Stanley Jevons*, edited by Harriet A. Jevons. London: Macmillan.

Mill = 1963–1991. *Collected Works of John Stuart Mill*. 33 Vols. Edited by J. M. Robson. Toronto: University of Toronto Press.

MSR = 1883. *Methods of Social Reform*, by William Stanley Jevons. London: Macmillan.

PC = 1972–1981. *Papers and Correspondence of William Stanley Jevons*, Vols. 1–7. Edited by R. D. C. Black and R. Könekamp. London: Macmillan.

PL = [1890] 1971. *Pure Logic and Other Minor Works*, by William Stanley Jevons. New York: Burt Franklin.

PS = [1874] 1958. *The Principles of Science: A Treatise on Logic and Scientific Method*, by William Stanley Jevons. Introduced by Ernst Nagel. New York: Dover.

Ruskin = 1903–1912. *The Works of John Ruskin*. 39 Vols. London: Allen.

Stewart = 1994. *The Collected Works of Dugald Stewart*. 11 Vols. Edited by W. Hamilton and K. Haakonssen. Bristol: Thoemmes.

TMS = [1759] 1976. *The Theory of Moral Sentiments*, by Adam Smith. Oxford: Oxford University Press.

TPE1 = 1871. *The Theory of Political Economy*, by William Stanley Jevons. London: Macmillan.

TPE2 = [1879] 1970. *The Theory of Political Economy*, 2nd edition, by William Stanley Jevons. Edited and introduced by R. D. C. Black. Harmondsworth: Penguin.

Whewell = 2001. *Collected Works of William Whewell*. Edited by R. Yeo. Bristol: Thoemmes.

Preface

This book dates back to one of the many pleasant evenings I enjoyed with two of my friends, Peter van der Veer and Janneke Plantenga, some twenty years ago. They will not remember and, perhaps, I would not have either, if it were not for some lucky turns of fate that put me in the position to gradually unfold the consequences of an idea I then only vaguely conceived of. That evening, we discussed the image of man as depicted in what is commonly referred to as neoclassical or marginalist economic theory.

To many non-economists, the image of man depicted in neoclassical economics is considered so meagre that it hardly needs to be taken seriously. Yet, this image has proved persuasive to economists – its parsimony is even considered by economists, such as Nobel laureate Robert Lucas, as its prime virtue. It is not just the focus on self-interest that bothers non-economists. When turning to Scottish Enlightenment philosophers such as Hume and Smith, the very notion of self-interest was analysed as a multifaceted and complex concept. That evening, my hunch was that the marginalist revolution radically changed the way man's mind was analysed. This change did not so much result from the adoption of utility theory per se, but more importantly from the change in the methods of research that went with it. Pressed for details, I did not have much to add.

At that time, I only had scattered knowledge of the history of economics (like many trained economists) and had no specific economist in mind to substantiate my thoughts. This book now explicates these thoughts, calling on one of the founders of the marginalist revolution, William Stanley Jevons. Bluntly stated, my message is that this Victorian polymath introduced a specific style of reasoning into economics. This British style of reasoning heavily relied on mechanical analogies to uncover the laws governing nature.

Trained in the natural sciences, Jevons naturally took this style of reasoning with him when he turned his attention to political economy. Jevons leveled down the categorical distinction between matter and mind – between the natural and the moral sciences – that had haunted Victorian intellectual discourse. In so doing, Jevons transformed the tools and instruments used by economists to unravel the complex regularities of the social realm and, of consequence, the universe of the economic discipline's discourse.

The fortunate circumstance that gave me the opportunity to explore these ideas was a telephone call in the early 1990s from my present colleague Geert Reuten to the secondary school in Amsterdam where I then taught economics. His question was whether I would be willing to teach a class in the philosophy of science to undergraduates. This opportunity introduced me to an extremely versatile and inspiring group of researchers who, one way or another, investigated economic methodology in a history of science–type of approach – something that was not regularly done at other places in the world at that time.

This book, a thoroughly rewritten version of my thesis, examines the intellectual and scientific resources Jevons drew upon. Though Jevons's mechanical image of the human mind was central to his new endeavours, his investigations proved, as we will see, of far broader scope – a fact that undoubtedly added to its persuasiveness for later generations of economists. The emerging discourse of reflex theory in (psycho-)physiology and the emergence of formal logic were, beyond doubt, two of Jevons's most important resources in rethinking the theory and methods of political economy. Formal logic, with its easy link to notions of rationality, carried the day in economics in the twentieth century. Interestingly, with the challenges set to the notion of rationality in economics, this other resource of Jevons – psychophysiology – recently gained increasingly in importance, and has led to renewed boundary crossings between physiology and economics. My story about Jevons may well be seen as a prehistory to these recent developments.

Acknowledgements

The help of many friends, colleagues, and institutions was of immense value in writing this book. At a very early stage, Margaret Schabas encouraged me to pursue my research interests in Jevons, as did Sandra Peart at a later stage. Neil De Marchi's persistent and constructive encouragements deserve a separate mention as well. Mike White's incredibly detailed knowledge of Jevons's work, of his social environment, and of the intellectual resources he drew on proved indispensable in helping me to sort out holes in my argument and to add historical detail. Also, Bert Mosselmans gave helpful advice and encouragements. I encountered the same academic spirit with many others who helped me over time. William Ashworth, Philippe Bazard, Anne Beaulieu, Mark Blaug, Nancy Cartwright, Nicolas Chaigneau, Annie Cot, John Davis, Trudy Dehue, Philippe Fontaine, Philippe Le Gall, Henk de Gans, Ivor Grattan-Guinness, Craufurd Goodwin, James Henderson, Kevin Hoover, Ian Inkster, Albert Jolink, Judy Klein, Robert Leonard, Uskali Mäki, Karel Markus, Sybilla Nikolow, Bernike Pasveer, Marcia Pointon, Ted Porter, Julian Reiss, Adrian Rice, Ida Stamhuis, and Jo Wachelder all commented on my writing, provided me with additional information, or gave me the opportunity to clarify my thoughts. Special thanks go to Fabrice Thierry, who, at a very late stage, read all of the manuscript.

I would like to thank my colleagues Hsiang-Ke Chao, Edith Kuiper, Geert Reuten, Peter Rodenburg, and Jack Vromen for their constructive comments. The joint meetings on measurement in economics and physics that our Amsterdam group enjoyed with colleagues at the Centre for Philosophy of Natural and Social Sciences at the London School of Economics were particularly productive in speeding up my research. I would like to thank Hasok Chang and Sang Yi for their comments and encouragement.

Of my colleagues, Adrienne van den Bogaard and Marcel Boumans have been indispensable in teaching me how to do research. Marcel's comments on large parts of the manuscript were always welcome and always to the point. Most notably, however, my thanks go to my former thesis supervisor Mary Morgan, who encouraged me to turn my thesis into a book and who was willing, yet again, to comment on many parts of the manuscript. It was a great pleasure to have had the opportunity to engage in conversation with such an extraordinary historian, economist, and philosopher.

In rewriting my thesis into a book, I greatly benefited from a stay at Clare Hall, Cambridge, for additional research in the Whewell and Sidgwick papers at the Wren Library, Trinity College. My thanks go to the staff of Clare Hall for the perfect research environment they provided for me and to the Netherlands Organisation for Scientific Research (NWO) for financially supporting my visit. I would like to thank Jonathan Smith, librarian at the Wren, for his help and support. In addition, my home faculty at the University of Amsterdam should be thanked for enabling me to spend the Autumn of 2002 at Cambridge. I would like to thank Charles Baden-Fuller for his hospitality on all occasions I was in London visiting yet another library or archive.

Scott Parris and Simina Calin of Cambridge University Press and Eleanor Umali of TechBooks are to be thanked for their encouragement at various stages in the production process of this book, and are to be admired for their professionalism. Robert Helmink, Loes Lotze, and Sebastine Postma greatly helped me with making the index. Hannie Pijnappels gave helpful comments on the design of the book.

The cooperation of many libraries and archives was indispensable in the making of this book. I would like to thank Peter Nockles, Peter McNiven, and John Hodgson of the John Rylands Library in Manchester, where the Jevons Archive is located, for their invaluable help. Stephen Johnston of the Oxford Science Museum answered many of my queries on Jevons's Logical Machine and provided me with information I would not have been able to obtain otherwise. Tom Freshwater gave me the opportunity to visit the Science Museum at Oxford and to inspect the Logical Machine in its possession. I would also like to thank Doron Swade and the staff of the British Science Museum for giving me a demonstration of the working of Babbage's *Difference Engine II*. This demonstration and discussions with Doron on Babbage's work were extremely helpful in framing my argument in Chapters 5 and 6. Keith Austin, then affiliated with the special collections at Senate House, University of London Library, kindly guided me through the De Morgan papers. Adrian Byrne of the Royal Society Archive helped me resolve my queries on the Herschel-Jevons correspondence located there. I would like to thank Ngadi Kponou of the Beinecke Library, Yale University, for providing additional information on the Lewes-Jevons correspondence in their possession. Many thanks go to the staff of the Central Library, the Library of Science Dynamics, and the Pierson Library – all at the University of Amsterdam – and especially, to Jacob Tiesinga.

Acknowledgements for permission to use archival materials and images go to the following institutes. My first thanks go to the Director and University Librarian of the John Rylands University Library of Manchester for permitting me to quote extensively from the Jevons Archives. Thanks go to University Library, London, at Senate House, for permission to quote from the De Morgan papers. I thank the Master and Fellows of Trinity College, Cambridge, for their permission to quote from the Whewell and Sidgwick papers in their possession. The Beinecke Library, Yale University, is acknowledged for its permission to quote from the Lewis-Jevons correspondence; the archives of the Royal Statistical Society, London; the University Libraries at Amsterdam, Groningen, Leiden; and the Teylers Museum, Haarlem, for permission to reproduce images in their possession. Thanks also go to Palgrave/Macmillan for permission to reproduce images from Jevons's original publications; to *Nature* to reproduce an image relevant to Jevons's early labour experiments; and to Rowman & Littlefield to reproduce a table from James Henderson's 1996 book on Whewell. I would like to thank the *Manchester Guardian* and its photographer for giving me permission to reproduce the image of the Jevons exhibition that was held in 1952 at Christie Library, Manchester.

Several chapters have appeared earlier in a somewhat different form as separate articles. I would like to thank the editors for permission to use these materials in this book. Chapters 5 and 6 expand on an article that appeared in volume 30A of *Studies in History and Philosophy of Science*, 1999. Chapter 8 appeared in *Economic Engagements with Art* (annual supplement to volume 31 of *History of Political Economy*, Duke: Duke University Press), edited by Neil De Marchi and Craufurd Goodwin. Chapter 9 appeared as a joint article with Mary Morgan in *Revue d'Histoire des Sciences Humaines*, 2002, and Chapter 10 in *The Age of Economic Measurement* (annual supplement to volume 33 of *History of Political Economy*), edited by Judy Klein and Mary Morgan.

There remains the category of those who predominantly suffered – my friends, my family, and my beloved. And, if they did not suffer, I suffered sometimes from the lack of their company, which one inevitably seems to deny oneself when writing a book. Most notably, my childhood friend Matthijs Engelberts and his wife Julia Koopmans should be thanked for their stubborn attempts to keep me in touch with the world. In my opinion, friends like them form an indispensable part of the laws of human enjoyment. It is commonly known that those who suffer most are often those one loves the most. Unfortunately, this is true in this case as well. I thank my wife Geerte Wachter and my children Timo and Jonne for the stoic way in which they endured the gestation of this book. I hope they accept this book in return.

~

ONE

THE PRYING EYES OF THE NATURAL SCIENTIST

William Stanley Jevons (1835–1882) is unquestionably one of the great minds in the history of economics. Today, he is remembered as one of the "fathers" of the so-called marginalist revolution in economics. With his *Theory of Political Economy* (1871), decisions of economic agents came to be analysed by means of the calculus, in terms of deliberations over marginal increments of utility. In this "mechanics of utility and self-interest" (*TPE2* 90), economic agents – whether in their role of consumers, workmen, or other – came to be seen as maximising utility functions. The marginalist revolution was a definitive break with the labour theory of value – value came to be identified with exchange value, and this was identified with marginal utilities, not with the costs of production. Jevons is also remembered for his innovative contributions to the empirical, statistical study of the economy. He ardently propagated the use of graphs to picture and analyse statistical data. He introduced index numbers to make causal inferences about economic phenomena. In short, there is no particle of economic science, theoretical or empirical, to which Jevons did not make important contributions that are, today, considered revolutionary. Jevons is one of the fathers of modern economics, indeed.

This summary evaluation of the importance of Jevons's contributions to economics contrasts starkly with the image we gain from a superficial glance at his contemporaries. In his lifetime, Jevons was well valued as an able statistician, but many of the leading contemporary political economists considered his pursuits in mathematical economics as obscuring the subject. It was only the younger generation of scientists and economists – like George Darwin and Francis Ysidro Edgeworth – who appreciated the novelty and

fruitfulness of his ideas.[1] It is worth quoting from John Stuart Mill's famous letter to Cairnes on Jevons's *Theory* to illustrate his reservations (*Mill*
17:1862–3):[2]

> I have not seen Mr. Jevons's book, but as far as I can judge from such notices
> of it as have reached me, I do not expect that I shall think favourably of it.
> He is a man of some ability, but he seems to have a mania for encumbering
> questions with useless complications, and with a notation implying the
> existence of greater precision in the data than the questions admit of.

Mill (1806–1873) was not alone in his judgement. Reviews of the book –
from, amongst others, Alfred Marshall (1842–1924) and John Elliot Cairnes
(1823–1875) – were quite sceptical.[3] Henry Sidgwick (1838–1900), the great
utilitarian philosopher, downplayed the importance of Jevons's use of the
calculus while acknowledging the importance of his new utility theory of
value.[4] In the 1875 re-edition of John Elliot Cairnes's influential *Lectures on
the Character and Logical Method of Political Economy*, Cairnes even wrote
that the work of his "able friend" did not give him any reason to alter the
views on method he had expressed as early as 1857. Reservations to the *Theory*
were made not only by those whom Jevons explicitly attacked – the classical
economists – but also by political economists of the historical school, such
as Cliffe Leslie (1825–1882) and John Kells Ingram (1823–1907), who favoured
detailed historical explanations over theory abstracted from historical detail,
whether expressed verbally or mathematically.

These conflicting appraisals from past and present leave us with an enigma
of how to evaluate Jevons's place in the history of economics. Using Roy
Weintraub's recent distinction between the body and the image of a science

---

[1] See also Schabas (1990), Chapter 7.

[2] Mill, Letter 1698, 5 December 1871, to Cairnes.

[3] In later years, Marshall admitted that he was angry about the book for two reasons. Firstly,
he had been thinking along the lines of Jevons; secondly, being an ardent admirer of Ricardo
and the Classical School, he felt that injustice had been done to them in the *Theory*. See
Schabas (1989). A more general account of the reception of the *Theory* is to be found in
Schabas (1990). Inoue's recent collection of reviews of Jevons's work corrects the impression
that the *general* response to the *Theory* was negative. This was far from the full picture. See
Inoue (2002, 2:187–297).

[4] Sidgwick fully acknowledged the additional challenge Jevons's theory of utility posed to
classical political economy that had come under severe pressure with William Thornton's
On Labour and John Stuart Mill's subsequent "recantation" of the wage fund theory. For
Thornton's influence on economic theory, see, for example, Chaigneau (1997), Donoghue
(1998), Ekelund and Thornton (2001), Vint (1994), and White (1994b).

(2002, 1–2) – that is, between its substance and its perceived methods and history – this book traces these conflicting appraisals of Jevons back to the contrasting images of political economy that were defended by Jevons himself and his contemporaries. From an evaluation of these contrasting images, it may be understood why and to what extent Jevons can be seen as one of the fathers of modern economics. Hence, my focus is on the changing methods of political economy, not on the changes in its theoretical content. Before going into any detail, it will be useful to briefly review existing appraisals of Jevons's work.

Jevons's Place in the History of Economics

Much has been written about Jevons's place in the history of economics. Starting with Keynes's and Robbins's centenary appraisals of Jevons, these studies have considerably deepened our knowledge and understanding of Jevons's work and the context in which it was produced. In his beautiful and dense essay on Jevons, Keynes paid equally high tribute to the *Theory* and to Jevons's statistical studies. At home as well in abstract theory as in the "black arts of inductive economics", Jevons was, according to Keynes, "the first theoretical economist to survey his material with the prying eyes and fertile, controlled imagination of the natural scientist" (Keynes [1936] 1988, 66). Robbins even went to the extreme when he noted that the "sheer genius" of Jevons's "capacity in handling facts", more than the *Theory*, was perhaps his "most conspicuous claim to fame" (Robbins [1936] 1988, 101).

Keynes's portrayal of Jevons – as scrutinising the data, spending "hours arranging his charts, plotting them, sifting them, tinting them neatly with delicate pale colours like the slides of the anatomist, and all the time poring over them and brooding over them to discover their secret" ([1936] 1988, 66) – rightly describes him as pursuing an anatomy, or physiology, of society, although Keynes's account is more imaginative than informative. Scientists use instruments and experiments to let the data speak, and this might be only vaguely inferred from Keynes's description. Moreover, Keynes seems to have meant this description only for Jevons's empirical studies, whereas it was generally considered that his most important innovation was the introduction of a specific instrument – the calculus – into economics.

Collison Black delivered his centennial commemoration of Jevons's first airing of his marginalist ideas in his "Notice of a Mathematical Theory of

Political Economy" (read in 1862 to section F of the British Association for the Advancement of Science (BAAS)). In 1962, Black had just recently discovered a wealth of material in the possession of Jevons's granddaughter, Mrs Könekamp, which provided new insight into Jevons's life and work. Contrary to what might perhaps be expected from Black's modesty with regard to his eminent predecessors, his and Könekamp's edition of these papers, from 1972 through to 1981, have greatly contributed to a renewed interest in Jevons's work. Various detailed studies appeared regarding exactly what Jevons's contribution was to the so-called marginalist revolution (see, especially, Black et al. 1973). His contribution to the development of statistics and econometrics is discussed in detail in several highly valuable studies (e.g., Stigler 1982; Aldrich 1987, 1992; Morgan 1990). His relation to his predecessors and successors has also been extensively examined (e.g., Bostaph and Shieh 1986; Schabas 1989, 1990; Kim 1995; Peart 1993, 1995a, 1996; White 1989, 1991b, 1994a, 1994b, 2004b). From these in-depth studies, a much richer image emerges of Jevons as one of the founders of "modern economics" – as in the title of Black's contribution to the Bellagio conference on the marginalist revolution in economics (Black et al. 1973). The term echoes Robbins's depiction of marginalist economic theory as the unifying core of modern economics (White 2004).

The Bellagio conference on the marginalist revolution deserves some special attention. Obviously, not only was Jevons's work addressed, but also the more general issue of whether there was any unifying core at all in the work of the three founding fathers of the "marginalist revolution", as was once claimed by Schumpeter. Was it sheer coincidence that Jevons, Menger, and Walras all published their tracts in the first half of the 1870s, or were these different authors, unknowledgeable about each other's work, nevertheless working on the same project: the introduction of a marginalist theory of choice in which actors maximised their utility in light of given means? It is certainly not my purpose to repeat this discussion; I will summarise it briefly.

Though to a considerable extent Jevons and Walras were in agreement with their approach to economic theory, this was certainly not the case for Menger.[5] It was argued that most of Jevons's theoretical innovations – such

---

[5] Jaffé's 1976 de-homogenisation of the "fathers" of the marginalist revolution has been recently discussed in a special issue of the *American Journal of Economics and Sociology*. See Comim (1998), Fontaine (1998), Hébert (1998), and Peart (1998).

as marginal utility, maximising behaviour, and emphasis on consumption theory – were present in the work of other economists long before Jevons, though not in the Ricardian mainstream. Upon closer inspection, Jevons proved more tied to the classical cost of production theory than was suggested by his vehement rejection of the "wrong-headed" doctrines of Ricardo and Mill. The only thing that most authors agreed upon as being Jevons's genuine contribution to modern economics was his insistence on the use of mathematics, especially the calculus, in framing economic theory. This is despite the fact that it was evident – as indeed Jevons himself had pointed out in the second edition of the *Theory* (1879) – that Jevons had many precursors, especially in France, some of whom had shown considerably more skill in handling the calculus than Jevons (see Ekelund and Hébert 1999). Instead of placing the emphasis on a continuity or discontinuity with his predecessors in terms of theoretical content, the attention shifted to Jevons's methodological contribution. His use of the calculus seemed to concur with the unity in method he defended with regard to all of the sciences – the natural and the social – including economics.[6]

From very different perspectives, Mirowski's highly influential *More Heat than Light* (1989) and Schabas's 1990 monograph on Jevons investigated this thesis more closely. Schabas explicitly addressed Jevons's use of the calculus in light of his philosophy of science as set out in *The Principles of Science* (1874). The *Principles* is a book which, until then, had hardly been noticed outside the realm of the natural sciences – a fact which was explained by the philosopher of science Ernst Nagel in his introduction to the 1958 Dover edition as being due to its lack of discussion of the distinct methods of the natural and the social sciences. Schabas forged this alleged defect of the book into its very strength. From her discussion, it transpired that there are good grounds for defending the thesis that Jevons foreshadowed the so-called hypothetical deductive method as the unifying approach to the sciences (which was distinctly one of the reasons for Nagel's enthusiasm for the *Principles*), and she approached Jevons's *Theory of Political Economy* from this perspective.

---

[6] As had been argued as early as 1962 by the logician Wolfe Mays, "there is a close relationship between Jevons's philosophy of the natural sciences and his methodology of the social sciences" (Mays [1962] 1988, 212).

Granted that this is the case, it unfortunately does not explain why the calculus can be of use in economics, nor why a subjective theory of value should be preferred to a cost of production theory. Even more pressing, such a unified method of inquiry does not entail that the subject matter of political economy be quantitative in nature – Jevons's main argument for treating economics mathematically. As Schabas (1990, 80–1) contends, Jevons's "appeal to the quantitative complexion of economics" was "perhaps the most simplistic of [his] arguments" even though it might have been "to Jevons and his contemporaries . . . perfectly cogent". It enabled the economist to freely "explore analogies to the natural sciences", especially "to mechanics" (80, 84).

As we will see in more detail in this book, Jevons's "appeal" to mechanical analogies was not at all "cogent" to his contemporaries. Far from unequivocally agreeing with Jevons's appeal to the "quantitative complexion of economics", contemporary economists reacted dismissively or with puzzlement to Jevons's use of mathematics in political economy. Even though they would have agreed with the *complexion* of political economy, this did not make the subject fit the use of mathematics to unravel its secrets, nor did this make analogies legitimate with mechanics – quite the contrary. Hence, Mirowski's penetrating and, as it happened, highly provocative thesis that early marginalists like Stanley Jevons modelled their new theories and method on a specific brand of physics that rose to the fore in mid-century Europe, thermodynamics, seemed a much more promising route than that of Schabas to explain the rift between classical economists and the newly emerging marginalist theory. However "totalising" Mirowski's narrative may be (Weintraub 2002, 6), it clearly opened new vistas within the history of economics.

But Mirowski's strong language was not particularly helpful to make his case, depicting early marginalists like Jevons as incompetent engineers who lured economists into the wrong theory because of their lack of understanding of the new physics and the mathematics that went with it. In her own account of Jevons, Schabas (1990, 6) clearly showed herself annoyed with such a "conspiracy thesis", and she was not alone in this. If we look through Mirowski's normative language, however, it remains undeniable that there were moves between physics and economics in nineteenth-century Europe in which thermodynamics played a significant role.

In relation to Jevons, these exchanges have recently been detailed by Michael White (2004b). White argues that Jevons's summary statement of the fundamental "problem of economics"[7] and his reworking of his original outline in between its presentation to the BAAS in 1862 and the *Theory* in 1871 are to be understood in relation to his engagement with the debates over the conservation of energy in the 1860s. Jevons's *Coal Question* (1865), which was somewhat of a hit in his own day, serves as a major source in this regard. But even without such a detailed analysis, it might seem obvious that Jevons's energy came from energy physics. In the preface to the *Theory* we read:[8]

> The nature of wealth and value is explained by the consideration of an indefinitely small amount of pleasure and pain, just as the theory of statics is made to rest upon the equality of indefinitely small amounts of energy.
> (*TPE2* 44)

This obvious relation between Jevons's program in economics and energy physics produces a serious problem. White's investigations into the context of the alterations Jevons's program underwent in the 1860s and onwards reveal that its initial impetus lay not in his engagements with debates over the conservation of energy, but elsewhere. After all, Jevons's first airing of his new mathematical theory to the BAAS in 1862, published in 1866 as the *Brief Account*, certainly did not rely on notions of energy. Jevons used mechanical metaphors well before he recast some (not all) of them in terms of energy. More importantly, as White notes, Jevons's references to the "energy framework...left no mark on the formal mathematics (i.e. calculus and geometry) of TPE" (2004b, 242). Referring to his 1862 paper, Jevons wrote in the introduction to the *Theory*: "All the chief points of the theory were sketched out ten years ago" (*TPE2* 77). Neither Schabas's recourse to Jevons's *Principles* nor Mirowski's narrative about the transfer of energy physics to economics is thus sufficient to explain the rift in method between Jevons and the classical economists.

---

[7] Jevons stated this problem in the concluding remarks of the *Theory*. It reads: "Given, a certain population, with various needs and powers of production, in possession of certain lands and other sources of material: required, the mode of employing their labour which will maximize the utility of the produce" (*TPE2* 254).

[8] The phrasing is an allusion to White (1991d).

Perhaps because of these difficulties, Sandra Peart, in her monograph on Jevons (1996), approached the differences between the classical economists and Jevons from a more pragmatic perspective. While emphasising theoretical continuity between Mill and Jevons, she aimed to locate their differences in perspective in their widely diverging approaches to empirical research. Turning to the methodological writings of classical economists like Mill and Cairnes, it is easily seen that differences in their opinions on the fitness of political economy to mathematics did not reside in an agreement or disagreement about the similarity between political economy and the natural sciences per se. Whatever may have been the differences between the methodological views of these classical economists and Jevons – and there were many – there was no dispute about the laws of political economy appealing to the same status as the laws obtained in the natural sciences, though this status as such met with radically different appraisal by Mill and Cairnes on the one hand and Jevons on the other. Indeed, one of the main purposes of John Stuart Mill's famous 1836 essay on the proper definition and method of political economy had been to secure for the laws of economics the same status as natural laws.

Peart argues that what economists like Mill and Cairnes on the one hand and Jevons on the other did not agree on was how to assess these laws. Jevons's distinction between the mathematical character of political economy and its exactness is relevant here. Peart scrutinised this distinction even more incisively in her article on Mill and Jevons (1995a). She pinpoints the disagreements between Mill and Jevons in their different attitudes towards the problem of multiple causation, a serious conundrum in those days. According to Mill, the "abstract truths" of political economy could not be perceived empirically due to the interference of disturbing causes. Jevons, in contrast, treated these disturbing causes as "noxious errors" which would average out on the whole. As a consequence, Mill resisted the introduction of statistical tools and techniques that in Jevons's perception formed the alpha and omega of the toolbox of the social scientist.

Peart reinterprets Jevons's *Principles of Science* in this light. Jevons's extensive discussions in the *Principles* of methods for correcting measurement errors naturally concur with his statistical innovations. Peart's account of Jevons enforces the image one forms from the detailed studies on his empirical work mentioned earlier, in which Jevons is depicted as a forerunner of the probabilistic revolution (Aldrich 1992), or at least one of those paving the way for the rise of econometrics in the thirties (Morgan 1990).

On Peart's reading, what had been considered *the* distinguishing feature of Jevons's work at the Bellagio conference – the introduction of the calculus – typically enough turns out to be of far less importance than is commonly thought. In her view, the distinguishing contribution of Jevons to economics did not reside in treating political economy mathematically, but where it was located by Keynes and Robbins: in his scrutinising an avalanche of numerical data to unravel their hidden secrets. On Peart's reading, research on Jevons seems to be thrown back to Robbins's statement at the very beginning of his 1936 essay on Jevons's place in the history of economics: "It is not easy... to define the exact nature of his achievement.... He formed no school. He created no system". His summary statement seems to be the most that can be said of Jevons: "The totality of his achievement, the wide range of his activities, the fertility of his imagination, the marvellous lucidity and attack of his expository style, rather than the perfection of any one of his constructions... gives him his place in history" ([1936] 1988, 94).

THE DISTINCTION BETWEEN MIND AND MATTER IN VICTORIAN BRITAIN

Maybe we should acquiesce, like Robbins, in appraising Jevons's lively and fertile imagination as his main claim to fame. Unity is not always found. In Jevons's case, however, there is a firm reason to dig deeper. Why else would he have proclaimed in the *Theory* that there is but one method for all of the sciences and threw up his hands in dismay at those who thought otherwise:

> There exists much prejudice against attempts to introduce the methods and language of mathematics into any branch of the moral sciences. Most persons appear to hold that the physical sciences form the proper sphere of mathematical method, and that the moral sciences demand some other method, I know not what.
>
> (*TPE1* 3)

The most notable distinction in this quotation is that between the "natural" and the "moral" sciences. The question that may be raised is why Jevons denied a distinction between different fields of the sciences that apparently was so obvious to "most persons"? Neil De Marchi's 1972 short, but still extremely complete, survey of the differences and agreements between Jevons and his predecessors is very helpful in searching for an answer.

Mathematics, De Marchi (1972, 350) notes, "was not essential to the concept of marginal utility nor to the principle of diminishing (marginal) utility". De Marchi argues that for someone like Mill or Cairnes, an explanation of diminishing marginal utility would have to be given in terms of the association psychology, and this type of psychology ran counter to "a clear conception of marginal satisfaction" (1972, 352). According to De Marchi, adherence to this type of psychology might explain why political economists such as Mill, Cairnes, and Cliffe Leslie were "blinded . . . to the clarity of expression which Jevons' mathematics imparted to the notion of the margin".

De Marchi modifies his statement on the relationship between the association psychology and mathematics when he writes that the association psychology did not constitute an "absolute barrier" to "a clear conception of marginal satisfaction", and he refers to Richard Jennings's *Natural Elements of Political Economy* (1855) as a case in point. But was it really only a matter of clarity of conception? Without exploring the theme any further, De Marchi implicitly locates the distinction between Jevons and his adversaries – Mill, Cairnes, and Cliffe Leslie – in developments in psychology that came to blur a distinction that provoked vehement debates in Victorian England: the distinction between the phenomena of mind and matter.

White's incisive essay on the relation of Jennings to Jevons (White 1994a) serves as a hallmark on this issue. White makes it sufficiently clear that the gist of Jennings's arguments were not derived from the association psychology, but from so-called psychophysiological theories, such as those of William Carpenter and Thomas Laycock in which man's actions are seen as the offspring of his neurophysiological constitution. With regard to this type of argument, Cairnes remarked that, if "Political Economy is to be treated in this way, it is evident it will soon become a wholly different study from that which the world has hitherto known it" (1857, 181).

And that is just what happened. Developments within psychophysiology in Victorian Britain tended to blur the notorious distinction between mind and matter. When this distinction lost its relevance in the course of the nineteenth century, it became increasingly unclear wherein the difference between the physical and the moral sciences resided. As is argued at length in this book, it is these very different attitudes towards the distinction between mind and matter that help to explain the different views on the method of political economy that were maintained by Jevons on the one hand and by contemporaries like Mill and Cairnes on the other.

In her article on Victorian economists and psychology, Schabas rightly considers the "short-lived enthusiasm" for psychology a distinguishing characteristic of Victorian economists (1997, 77). This enthusiasm can be traced from Mill's 1836 essay up to Marshall, and then it fades away. However, covering the distance from Mill to Marshall, the very different conception of what psychology stood for should not have been left unnoticed. John Stuart Mill's reluctance to think of the mind in mechanical terms and Marshall's description of the mind as a machine are particularly striking. For Marshall, "the most important machine is man, and the most important thing produced is thought" (Raffaelli 1991, 52, quoting Marshall; see also Raffaelli 2003). Somewhere between Mill and Marshall, it became fashionable to conceive of the mind in mechanical terms and to use the instruments of the natural sciences to analyse its workings. My contention is that, with regard to economics, this turn of mind gained ground with Jevons's work.

The importance of the distinction between mind and matter in Victorian discourse may be read from a review by Henry Sidgwick of the second edition of Herbert Spencer's *Principles of Psychology* (1870–1872) in the *Spectator* on 21 June 1873 (TCC Add.Ms.c.97.1(10)). Sidgwick states that "the first question . . . we ask of any philosopher is, what does he hold of Mind and Matter?" (798). Against Spencer's identification of "mind with motion", he argues (in line with the Scottish common sense school of philosophy of Thomas Reid and Dugald Stewart) that "I have an immediate intuitive knowledge of the extended material world, as somewhat totally distinct from the feelings of my own mind" (799). Sidgwick concluded that the "introspective and hypothetical" methods of research are totally "confounded" in Spencer's book. For this reason, he considered "Mr Spencer's philosophy . . . fundamentally incoherent" (798).

The distinction between the realms of mind and matter, and the appended distinction between the "introspective" and "hypothetical" modes of enquiry, will prove to be of fundamental importance to understanding the puzzled or straightforwardly dismissive reactions to Jevons's transgression of the fields of the natural and moral sciences. This distinction, with a slightly different emphasis as we will see, motivated Mill to his separate treatment of the methods of the moral sciences in book VI of the *Logic* (1843), to "prove" that the phenomena of both mind and matter obey the reign of law. Though both phenomena were lawlike, these laws were for Mill of a categorically different nature.

Mill's "proof" of the scientificity of political economy was about the certainty of the laws, and these were equally certain for the mental and natural sciences. For Mill, the claim to certainty of political economy was guaranteed by its deductive method and its introspectively ascertained first principles; in this sense, the moral sciences fully equalled the natural sciences. But this did not make the phenomena of the mind suited to be analysed by means of the same tools and methods as those of matter. Mind and matter were considered categorically distinct phenomena. To invoke mechanical analogies thus at no point forced the political economist to investigate the mind with the same tools of research as nature. Indeed, Mill regarded mechanical analogies for mental phenomena with distrust.

For Jevons, however, the very idea of certain laws was a misunderstanding of science itself. The world could always turn out to be different from what science considered it to be. Mill's idée fixe that observation and experiment led in the natural sciences to certain laws, and his emphasis on "disturbing causes" in the social realm, was, for Jevons, simply nonsense. There was no experimental law in the sciences, nor any law in astronomy – itself a nonexperimental science – that was not plagued by disturbing causes, yet this did not prevent those sciences from attempting to search for the mathematical laws governing the (experimental) observations. For Jevons, it was no different in political economy. Mill's recourse to introspection was a nonstarter, which Mill effectively obscured by claiming that laws in the mental sciences were obtained by the very same procedures of "observation and experiment" as used in the natural sciences. But Jevons's argument assumed that there was no relevant distinction between the phenomena of mind and matter in the first place.

Halfway through the nineteenth century, the categorical distinction between the phenomena of mind and matter vanished under the influence of developments within psychophysiology. This enabled economists such as Jevons to transgress the boundaries traditionally set to the tools of investigation with regard to the mind and to explore how the tools of the natural sciences might be used to disclose the laws of the mind. De Marchi (1972, 350) refers to this last mode of reasoning as "mechanical reasoning", a term I consider completely apt to pinpoint Jevons's specific contribution to the formation of modern economics. De Marchi apparently used it to refer

1-1. Geometry of the lever. From Simon Stevin, *De Beghinselen der Weeghconst*, 1586, 20. UBA 275 D 11 (1). Courtesy of University of Amsterdam Central Library.

only to Jevons's use of mathematics in economics. It will be useful to briefly expand on the rich history of this term before we can see its meaning in the Victorian context.

MECHANICAL REASONING

Originally, mechanical reasoning referred to the use of simple machines to disclose the wonders of the universe. It had its origin in the mixed mathematics tradition that went back to Archimedes, and that was very important in the scientific revolution of the sixteenth and seventeenth centuries.

In mixed mathematics, geometry was used to understand the working of simple machines like the balance, the inclined plane, and the pendulum. A woodcut from Simon Stevin's *The Elements of the Art of Weighing* (*De Beghinselen der Weeghconst*, 1586, 20) may serve as an example (Figure 1-1). We see a stylised lever, containing a (heavy) weight, and a workman – a "mechanic" – who holds the lever at its end. Directly mapped on the machine, we see the geometry of the lever, indicated with lines, triangles, and capitals, explaining how the mechanic can lift the weight with the help of this simple machine. Geometrical principles of the lever explain how work can be done by the mechanic. The representation of the lever and its geometry is stripped down to its essentials, while the image of the workman is left to the artistic freedom of the woodcutter. Also, the external world is indicated with some sketchy lines – some loose stones are laying in front of the mechanic. The simple machine, not the workman or nature at large, is the subject of the analysis, as is clear from the accompanying text and from the woodcut itself.

Among economists, Stevin's book is most well-known for the wonderful engraving of the inclined plane he used to refute any attempts to construct a *perpetuum mobile*. Stevin was so pleased with his result that he used this woodcut as the frontispiece of his book, adding the words "Wonder, en is gheen wonder", which Herbert Simon somewhat dryly translated as "wonder, but not incomprehensible". An entry in Chambers' *Cyclopaedia* for 1741 shows a plate of such simple machines (Figure 1-2), and one can see the close connection between the actual contrivance and the geometry used to describe its working.[9]

This entry was about mechanical reasoning, however, not just about mixed mathematics. It was about the extension of mixed mathematics to understand those domains that were only sketched in Stevin's woodcut of the lever, the physiology of mankind, and the physical laws governing the world at large. To summarise a much more complex history too briefly: That extension was what the scientific revolution of the sixteenth and seventeenth centuries was all about. The entry read (Figure 1-3):

> MECHANICAL is also applied to a kind of *reasoning*, which of late has got great ground both in physics, and medicine; thus denominated, as being conformable to what is used in the contrivance, and accounting for the properties and operations of machines.
>
> This manner of thinking and arguing, Dr. Quincy insists, is the result of rightly studying the powers of a human mind, and the ways by which it is only fitted to get acquaintance with material beings: For considering an animal body as a composition out of the same matter, from which all other bodies are formed, and to have all those properties which concern a physician's regard, only by virtue of its peculiar make and constructure; it naturally leads a person to consider the several parts, according to their figures, contexture, and use; either as wheels, pullies, wedges, levers, screws, chords, canals, cisterns, strainers, or the like; and throughout the whole of such enquiries, to keep the mind close in the view of the figures, magnitudes, and mechanical powers of every part or movement; just in the same manner, as is used, in enquiring into the motions and properties of

---

[9] We see Stevin's inclined plane and its geometry in this image as Figures 59 and 60.

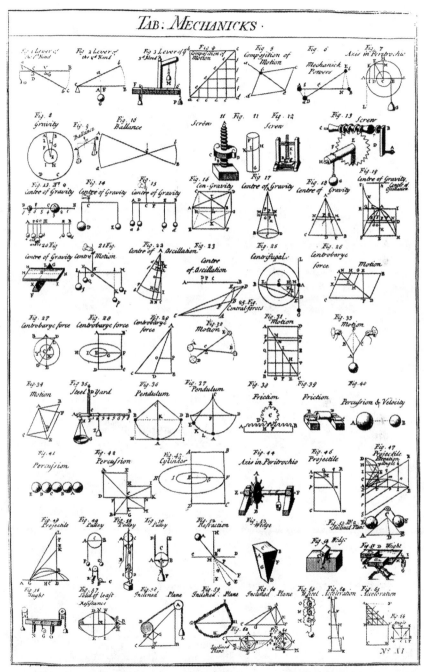

1-2. Plate of engravings of simple machines, opposite to lemma on mechanical reasoning. From Chambers' *Cyclopaedia*, Vol. 2, 1741–43. ET M–8. Courtesy of University Library Groningen.

> MECHANICAL is also applied to a kind of *reasoning*, which of late has got great ground both in phyfics, and medicine; thus denominated, as being conformable to what is ufed in the contrivance, and accounting for the properties and operations of machines. See PHYSICS.
>
> This manner of thinking and arguing, Dr. Quincy infifts, is the refult of rightly ftudying the powers of a human mind, and the ways by which it is only fitted to get acquaintance with material beings: For confidering an animal body as a compofition out of the fame matter, from which all other bodies are formed, and to have all thofe properties which concern a phyfician's regard, only by virtue of its peculiar make and conftructure; it naturally leads a perfon to confider the feveral parts, according to their figures, contexture, and ufe; either as wheels, pullies, wedges, levers, fkrews, chords, canals, cifterns, ftrainers, or the like; and throughout the whole of fuch enquiries, to keep the mind clofe in view of the figures, magnitudes, and mechanical powers of every part or movement; juft in the fame manner, as is ufed, in enquiring into the motions and properties of any other machine. For which purpofe it is frequently found helpful to defign, or picture out in diagrams, whatfoever is under confideration, as it is cuftomary in common geometrical demonftrations.
>
> The knowledge obtained by this procedure is called *Mechanical knowledge*. See KNOWLEDGE.

1-3. Entry on mechanical reasoning. From Chambers' *Cyclopaedia*, Vol. 2, 1741–43. ET M–8. Courtesy of University Library Groningen.

any other machine. For which purpose it is frequently found helpful to design, or picture out in diagrams, whatsoever is under consideration, as it is customary in common geometrical demonstrations.

   The knowledge obtained by this procedure is called *Mechanical knowledge*.

Mechanical, as "applied to a kind of *reasoning*", the lemma says, is a "manner of thinking and arguing"; it is the "result of rightly studying the powers of a human mind, and the ways by which it is only fitted to get acquaintance with material beings". Mechanical reasoning, in short, is presented as a package that includes specific modes of arguing as well as distinct procedures to establish evidence for the arguments put forth.[10] These procedures are

---

[10] Van den Bogaard (1998) takes a "package" as a three-dimensional concept: It structures scientific activity on (1) conceptual, (2) institutional, and (3) practical level. This study will focus on the first and third levels, though one might argue that the introduction of mechanical reasoning within economics was important in the institutional formation and stabilisation of economics as a scientific discipline.

enumerated: It is "helpful" to make use of diagrams, just as in "geometrical demonstrations". The diagrams fulfil a specified role, namely to inquire to what extent the mechanical powers of a "material being" can be compared with "any other machine". On the presupposition then, that material beings can be considered to be some sort of machine, one investigates the extent to which this analogy holds good and thus derives so-called *mechanical knowledge.*

This lemma on mechanical reasoning brings out the epistemic claim that went with the extension of mixed mathematics to other domains. Geometry was not merely used to understand simple machines, as had been Stevin's purpose; rather, simple machines and their geometry were used to understand the material world. By using simple machines as analogies for natural phenomena, they became paradigms of intelligibility. It is well-known that the famous Dutch professor of medicine, Herman Boerhaave, recommended just this mode of reasoning in his inaugural address at Leiden University in 1703,[11] as he practised it in developing his model of the human body as a hydraulic machine. The Italian mixed mathematician Borelli, a disciple of Galileo, might equally serve as an example in his framing of the human body as a compound of levers. The poetically pictured mechanic in Stevin's woodcut himself became the subject of mechanical analysis. Most famously, as Peter Machamer (1998, 16) recently argued, did Galileo Galilei install this mode of reasoning in physics:

> Knowledge of any thing could be modeled by real machines or real bodies, for the world was constructed as a machine was. The world was merely a set of Archimedean simple machines hooked together or a set of colliding corpuscles that obeyed the laws of mechanical collision (i.e. the laws of the balance). . . . This was Galileo's vision, and from him it swept around Europe and even across the seas into China.

In Machamer's reading, mechanical reasoning might equally well be labelled the Galilean approach to science. Machamer compares the role of Galileo's simple machines to Kuhnian exemplars. An explanation of a natural phenomenon can, by analogy, be deduced from the mechanical principles embodied in these contrivances, and this is what Galileo consistently

---

[11] *De usu ratiocinii mechanici in medicina.* Address, Leyden ([1703] 1964). On Boerhaave, see Lindeboom (1968). On the general context of Boerhaave's work (and much more), see Jonathan Israel's provocative work (2001).

attempted to attain. Without any doubt, in his view, Galileo's training in mixed mathematics played an important role in this new approach of how to gain knowledge of nature. Members of the "mixed sciences" (*scientia media*) came to denote themselves as mechanical philosophers.

The use of simple contrivances like the balance as a mode of comprehending nature – in a similar fashion as a Kuhnian exemplar – also involved shifting criteria of proof and evidence. It was easily observable when a problem had been solved; any individual could judge whether the balance was in or out of equilibrium. Another important element in Galileo's use of the balance was that it emphasised reproducible and constructive evidence. The visibility of the solution also related to the mathematics used. Mathematics, for Galileo, was geometry. It involved a visual display of the geometry of the balance (or any other simple machine). These ingredients for Machamer add up to a "clear moral": "To get at the true cause, you must replicate or reproduce the effects by constructing an artificial device, so that the effects can be seen" (69).

MIXED MATHEMATICS IN VICTORIAN BRITAIN

Jumping from the sixteenth or seventeenth century into the nineteenth century, things did of course change considerably – especially in Britain. Bacon and Newton reigned supreme and Newton's *Principia* was the most important "course book" for studying physics and mathematics. Mathematics, in late Georgian Britain, was geometry and Newton's theory of fluxions. The close correspondence in teaching between physical questions and mathematics had its roots in the earlier mixed mathematics, however, and is typical of Britain throughout the nineteenth century. It is typified in the famous and notorious Cambridge Mathematical Tripos.

In his recent book on the relation between mathematics and economics in the twentieth century, Roy Weintraub images the Cambridge Tripos in highly negative terms, if not as straightforwardly obsolete (2002, Chapter 1). Weintraub's austere judgement would have certainly been shared by no lesser a scientist than Pierre Duhem, who famously distinguished between the "deep" and the "ample" mind, between the "French" and the "English" mind, in *La Théorie Physique: Son Objet et sa Structure* (1906, first translated 1954).

Duhem complained that the "English mind" time and again took recourse to "strings which move around pulleys, which roll around drums, which go through pearl beads", rather than aiming to understand the "purity of abstract theory which it is claimed the model embodies". With an annoyance that fairly spatters the page, Duhem observes that "we thought we were entering the tranquil and neatly ordered abode of reason, but we find ourselves in a factory" (Duhem 1981, 70–1). Duhem would have assented indeed to Weintraub's verdict that this mathematics, taught in the Cambridge Tripos, was long overdue at the end of the century and retarded the development of "what we now think of as rigorous mathematics" in England (Weintraub 2002, 16). It may have been obsolete in mathematics, but was it obsolete in science?

One of Weintraub's examples of "absurd" questions asked at the Tripos examination for 1878 serves as a case in point. The examination question that he quotes at length (2002, 16), begins as follows: "Describe the theory of Atwood's machine, and explain how it is used to verify the laws of motions". Weintraub uses his more extensive quotation to exemplify "how contrived, unreal, and even bizarre the Mathematical Tripos had become by the late nineteenth century". By this, he means how "insulated" Cambridge mathematicians had become from the "concerns of continental mathematicians" (16). At the risk of doing Weintraub injustice by cutting his longer quotation so short, the example of Atwood's machine is highly revealing about the close correspondence that existed throughout the nineteenth century in Britain between mathematics and real problems, if "real" does not refer to mathematical concerns but to physical problems. George Atwood constructed his machine around 1770. It can be looked at as no more than a pulley with two different weights, a clock, and a measuring rod that was used to demonstrate Newton's laws of motion (Figure 1-4). It thus converted "a rather conventional pulley... into a careful scaled device capable of being subjected to mathematical analysis" (Schaffer 1994, 160). Norwood Hanson used Atwood's machine, a machine "every physics student knows" (1965, 100), to question the relation between empirical testing and analytical truth.[12] Widely used in Georgian Britain, it was a typical example of how mixed mathematics was used to study the laws of nature, and thus an instance of the "curious feature" of the Cambridge Tripos to take "'applied mathematics', or actually rational mechanics" for mathematics (Weintraub 2002, 13). The relation between mathematical certainty and empirical

---

[12] See Hanson (1965, especially 99–103).

1-4. Atwood's Machine constructed by the instrument maker George Adams, 1790, London. It is slightly more than 2 meters in height and intended to show the laws of motion of bodies uniformly accelerated or retarded, as well as those undergoing uniform motion. Both sides of the cord that runs over the central pulley wheel are loaded with equal weights to balance the gravitational force. As this load descends, it passes through a perforated stage which lifts off the bar weight, leaving the remainder to travel downwards with constant velocity. The time of the fall is taken by listening to the bell attached to the pendulum. On top of the machine, the pulley wheel is carried by a set of friction wheels to minimise friction (see Turner and Levere 1973, 161). Courtesy of Teylers Museum, Haarlem, the Netherlands.

evidence has never been an easy one, however. Schaffer shows how Atwood's machine may serve as an instance where simple machinery "did not simply transmit rational mechanics, [but] also helped to make it" (Schaffer 1994b, 159).

Rather than being obsolete, as suggested by Weintraub, this mode of understanding in physics proved astonishingly successful in the second half of the nineteenth century, as witnessed by the pathbreaking discoveries of William Thomson and James Clerk Maxwell in particular. Following such research, Britain was, at the end of the century, praised for its telegraph rather than for its contributions to abstract mathematics.

The French emphasis on definitional rigor and internal consistency that became even stronger in the work of Gauchy and Lacroix never fitted well with the British. The initial turn of the short-lived *Analytical Society* at Cambridge to the French mathematics of Lagrange and Laplace has been the topic of an extensive literature.[13] Mathematicians and scientists like George Peacock, William Whewell, Charles Babbage, John Herschel, and Augustus De Morgan in early Victorian Britain all struggled with the relationship between their mathematics and its concrete interpretations. However different their approaches, someone like Whewell, who was important in re-forming the Cambridge Tripos in mid-century Britain (Becher 1981), and Augustus De Morgan, whose mathematics course was by far the most demanding of his day, both (re-)emphasised the relation of mathematics to practical problems in physics or its "use to any one in the business of life" (Smith and Wise 1989, 172, quoting De Morgan). As Fisch (1994, 226) argues, all of the Cambridge reformers "retained a traditional commitment to a Baconian view of the natural sciences – i.e. inductivist, reductionist, realist, causal and explanatory", that fitted poorly with the formalism that was increasingly taking hold in mathematics on the Continent.

For Duhem, this British approach to science and mathematics was exemplified by William Thomson. Indeed, his approach to physics staggered Duhem. When "two electrically charged bodies are before us", the "French

---

[13] For mathematics at Cambridge in the early nineteenth century, see Becher (1980, 1992), Enros (1983), Richards (1991), and Wilkes (1990). For the subsequent development of British mathematics, see Ashworth (1996), Fisch (1994), Dubbey (1978), Pycior (1981, 1984), Rice (1996a), Richards (1980), and Smith and Wise (1989). On Whewell's role, see Becher (1981) and Fisch (1994). On Augustus De Morgan, see Pycior (1983), Rice (1999), and Richards (1987, 1991, 2002).

Mind" moves to abstract mathematics and deduces consequences from his abstract formulae. This was not so for Thomson, the later Lord Kelvin. He considered the possibility of making a "mechanical model" as the ultimate test of intelligibility. In retrospect, Machamer's moral of the Galilean approach to science reads like a liberal transcription of William Thomson's famous expression in his Baltimore lectures that would annoy Pierre Duhem to the point of ridicule: "It seems to me that the test of 'Do we or do we not understand a particular object in physics?' is, 'Can we make a mechanical model of it?'". It would be a mere shortcut to identify William Thomson's approach to physics with the sort of examination questions asked at the end of the nineteenth century at Cambridge, yet his "engineering approach" to mathematics and physics that emerges from Smith and Wise's monumental 1989 biography still reflects the same inductive spirit. To use "Atwood's machine" (a pulley with two different weights) "to verify the laws of motion" (Weintraub 2002, 16) came very close to William Thomson's test for understanding the natural world: "As long as I cannot make a mechanical model all the way through I cannot understand" (Duhem 1981, 71–2, quoting Thomson). From this, Duhem concluded that for the "English mind" to understand a phenomenon was "the same thing as designing a model imitating the phenomenon . . . the English school is completely committed to the purely mechanical explanation of physical phenomena" (Duhem 1981, 72). For Duhem, this reliance on mechanical models as a mode for understanding more or less embodied the vices of the English mind, that "we shall have to combat" (57). This "English mind", adhering to Bacon's *Novum Organum* rather than Descartes's "clear and distinct" rational universe, proved highly successful in unravelling the laws governing the universe by building mechanical analogies.

Formal Logic and the Mechanics of Utility and Self-Interest

It is my argument that Jevons introduced this British style of science into economics by similarly using mechanical analogies as modes of intelligibility. In this context, Jevons's pursuits in formal logic and British foundational debates over algebra find their place. Bert Mosselmans recently noted how "particular" Jevons's position is in the history of logic (see Mosselmans 1998; the quote is from Inoue 2002, 1:67). Like his successors, Peano and Russell, he attempted to derive mathematics from logic; but in his logical system, Mosselmans argues, he stayed close to Boole and De Morgan (1998, 96). Jevons, it should be noted, was not a mathematician and never considered himself as such. He figures in Adrian Rice's list of "principal UCL students" (1996a, 383) but does not appear in Rice's "London network of mathematicians" (414). Jevons was not a mathematician like Sylvester or Cayley.

When Jevons moved to University College, London, in the 1870s from Owen's College, Manchester, he did so to take up the post in political economy.[14] He had been professor of logic and political economy at Owen's College. Logic, in earlier days, had been a branch of the moral sciences rather than of mathematics. As an outcome of Victorian foundational debates over the nature of algebra, algebra no longer merely served as a form of generalised arithmetic, but developed into a "science of operations". It thus gained the status of reasoning as such. This is the context in which George Boole and Augustus De Morgan developed their formal approaches to logic, which moral philosophers protested as stretching formalism too far (Richards 2002).[15] This was also the context in which Charles Babbage designed his calculating engines as material embodiments of algebra. With Boole's algebraic approach to logic, logic gained a meaning and significance that could not have been attributed to it in its traditional interpretations.

As will be detailed in this book, this is where Jevons's work in formal logic finds its place. But Jevons's outstanding experimental skills and training rather than his skills and knowledge of mathematics would serve him as a guide in his logical investigations. Jevons explicitly designed mechanical analogies to clarify and illustrate questions of logic – his was not the approach of a mathematician. In Jevons's approach to science, a material mechanism served to unlock the secrets of the world: the material and the mental. I have already indicated the importance of psychophysiology in relation to the notorious divide between the realms of mind and matter. From a very different angle did the intimate links between calculating engines, algebra, and formal logic serve to bridge the gap between the natural and the mental realm.

---

[14] A more systematic account of Jevons's work and life will be provided in Chapter 2.
[15] Richards (2002) discusses Henry Longueville Mansel's criticism of De Morgan as an example. Mansel was, with Sir William Hamilton (no family link with Rowan Hamilton, the mathematician), severely criticised for his adherence to a particular blend of common sense and Kantian philosophy. See Mill (*Mill*, 9). See also Chapter 6 of this book.

It was certainly not by accident, then, that Jevons referred to Galileo as his authority, in the introduction to the *Theory*, to justify his new mathematical theory of political economy and to argue against those "uninquiring and unhoping spirits" who never tried to measure, and thus never succeeded. "Had physicists waited until their data were perfectly precise before they brought in the aid of mathematics, we should still have been in the age of science which terminated at the time of Galileo" (*TPE1* 7). Where Galileo had used his famous *Discorsi* to convince a sceptical audience that the book of nature was written in the language of mathematics, Jevons aimed to do so for the moral realm: "it is clear that economics, if it is to be a science at all, must be a mathematical science" (*TPE2* 78). To those who thought otherwise, he said: "I know not what".

It is clear whom Jevons had in mind. John Stuart Mill and John Elliot Cairnes, in particular, denied political economy the tools and methods that were used with so much success in the physical sciences. Their denial was based upon a division of the sciences that served as a roadblock to the use of quantitative tools of inquiry into the domain of the moral sciences, including political economy – the notorious distinction between mind and matter. Jevons straightforwardly denied the relevance of any such distinction and advocated a unified approach to the sciences instead. But Jevons's approach to the moral realm only made sense once psychophysiology and formal logic gained ground.

Outline of the Book

Let me briefly say something on what the reader is to expect from this book. For reasons that will become clear, I will, after a short introduction to Jevons's life and work, turn to William Whewell's and John Stuart Mill's respective views on the method of political economy. The views of Whewell and Mill form two opposing reactions to Dugald Stewart's influential classification of the sciences: that of mind and matter. Their initial antagonism determines to a large extent the mode in which political economy was practised in Victorian England and the manner in which quantitative methods of enquiry, like statistics, were relegated outside the margins of the field. Then, I turn to the early and largely forgotten research of Jevons on cloud formation, not so much for its own sake, but to show how Jevons – from a very young age – used mechanical analogies to search for stability in an otherwise unstable environment. This attitude was no different in the case of his meteorological studies than in his approach to social statistics. The next two chapters examine how Jevons's involvements in formal logic framed his general philosophy of science. Rather than moving away as quickly as possible from Jevons's "obsolete notations" in logic and from his logical machine made of "baywood and brass rods", as Mirowski advises us to do (2002, 38), we will ponder upon this machine and its "baroque principles" to fathom its importance in razing the distinction between the spheres of mind and matter. We are then in a position to see what Jevons's project of a unified science implies for his "mechanics of utility and self-interest". Though there is an important linkage between Jevons's interests in mechanising logic and in approaching economics mathematically, the missing element to move from one to the other is the idea of functional form that Jevons derived from psychophysiology. Having arrived at that point, we can probe the distance between the views of Mill and Jevons on the method of political economy.

Subsequent chapters detail how Jevons brought his method into practise through his theory of labour, his statistical studies, and his theory of exchange. In all these cases, Jevons took recourse to mechanical analogies to frame his investigations. To give an example here of what is argued extensively in the book, one may, for example, depict Jevons's famous study into the fall in value of gold in terms of his adherence to a quantity theory of money. Thus, one will never see that it was not the quantity theory, but a mechanical balance, that helped him to introduce an index number to make a causal claim on the relation between inflation and the gold discoveries.

My treatment of Jevons's work is far from comprehensive, as is easily seen, and it would only be a pointless repetition of the existing secondary literature if I tried to be so. Even without full coverage, it transpires that using mechanical analogies to structure investigations in political economy involved a radical reshuffling of what was meant with theory and data in the social realm, and a radical transformation of the methods and goal of explanation in economics. In all these regards, Jevons radically changed the image of modern economics.

TWO

~

WILLIAM STANLEY JEVONS: VICTORIAN POLYMATH[1]

William Stanley Jevons was born in 1835 into a well-to-do middle-class family of iron traders in Liverpool. His father, Thomas Jevons, was a man with utilitarian sympathies said to have invented the first floating iron ship. Jevons's mother, Mary-Ann Roscoe, was the daughter of William Roscoe, who was considered one of the great men of his time – a Liverpool banker and art connoisseur who rediscovered and ardently collected neglected Italian and Flemish masters.[2]

The Jevonses and Roscoes were Unitarians. Closely related to the Huttons and the Martineaus among others, the two families formed part of the intellectual Unitarian circle in Lancashire that was instrumental in promoting the natural sciences. They shared the "superb confidence of the Victorian middle-class" (Thompson 1978, 264) in the promises of rational argument and the advancement of science for the public good. Middle-class Unitarians, for example, greatly contributed to the establishment of Mechanics' Institutes designed for the education of the higher working class in the principles of the natural sciences, as well as the formation of the various literary, philosophical, and statistical societies (Kidd and Roberts 1985, 10–11). The advancement of society was the goal; the progress of science, the means.

---

[1] Jevons's life and work are covered in greater detail in Könekamp (1962) and Schabas (1990); Black and Könekamp's edition of the *Papers and Correspondence* (*PC*) is an indispensable source. The development of Jevons's life in his own words is still most vividly to be gathered from his wife's choice from his *Nachlass* in the *Letters and Journals* (*LJ*).
[2] George Chandler, William Roscoe's biographer, described him as late as 1953 as "one who has been called Liverpool's greatest citizen" (Chandler 1953, vii).

It is therefore not surprising that education, especially in the natural sciences, was considered of utmost importance by Jevons's parents, although the boy was also naturally well-acquainted with various aspects of culture through his mother. Stanley took to music in particular and became a competent organ player.[3] When he was eleven years old, he attended Liverpool Mechanics' Institute School. After an interlude of two years at a grammar school, Jevons was sent to London University College's preparatory school, entering the college itself one year later at the age of sixteen. His studies in the natural sciences were distinctly more to his liking than the humanities.

For Unitarians and other dissenters of the Anglican Church, University College, London, was one of the few places to receive a higher education. The college was founded in the 1820s by the circle of philosophical radicals allied to Bentham to break the Oxbridge exclusion of dissenters from higher education (Bellot 1929).[4] Jevons progressed well at the college, especially in chemistry and experimental philosophy, in which he won gold medals. However, he derived most enjoyment from the teachings of one of the permanent influences of his later life: the first professor of mathematics at University College, Augustus De Morgan.[5]

Jevons received his education despite the enormous distress suffered by the family; first, the death of his mother when he was only ten and, soon after, the 1848 bankruptcy of his father's iron trading business in the aftermath of the great railway crisis of 1847. As a result, the family was forced to move to Manchester. The family's financial straits were instrumental in Stanley's sailing to Australia in 1854 to take up a position as one of the two gold assayers at the newly established Mint in Sydney. Jevons went to Australia before finishing University College, and it is sometimes thought that this was because of the Australian job offer. However, Stanley Jevons was not planning to complete his college education in any event (Könekamp [1962] 1988, 236) because he wished to return to Manchester to pursue a career in business, reserving his scientific interests for pleasure in his spare time. In a diary

[3] He also showed a theoretical interest in music and at one stage prepared a book on musicology. For more on this manuscript, see Mosselmans and Mathijs 1999.
[4] As is well-known, to enter Oxbridge, one had to subscribe to the thirty-nine articles of faith of the Anglican Church.
[5] On De Morgan's qualities as a mathematics teacher, see Rice (1999).

entry of 16 January 1853 (*PC* 1:78, original emphasis), where he considered the possibility, Stanley wrote:

> I shall however as soon as I am home, begin to work a little at French and German. . . . I shall also *amuse* myself, down in the cellar, with chemical experiments, making instruments which however I think are not altogether useless amusements.[6]

Only two weeks after this diary entry was made, his cousin Harry Roscoe, with whom he shared rooms in London, talked to Stanley about the job offer at the Mint in Sydney – an offer which he fretted about for at least a week. The position of gold assayer had first been offered to Harry, who would later become professor of chemistry at Owen's College, Manchester, and who was Stanley's elder by a few years. However, Harry Roscoe decided to pursue his studies in chemistry in Heidelberg, Germany, instead of taking the job.

Roscoe proposed Stanley as an alternative and Thomas Graham, their chemistry teacher at University College, agreed. Having received gold medals in chemistry and experimental philosophy, Stanley Jevons was an excellent replacement. Because of his strong attachment to his family, Jevons was initially reluctant to accept the job, but his father urged him not to refuse in order to lessen some of the financial burden on the family. Stanley's salary, at the tender age of nineteen, was £675, a high salary in those days which enabled him to make substantial savings.[7] After undertaking some training in gold assaying with Graham and an additional course in Paris when it became clear that there was some delay in the opening of the Mint in Sydney, Jevons finally sailed to Australia in the summer of 1854 for a

---

[6] Jevons did not enjoy studying languages. An important reason for his plan to study French and German must have been that these were the dominant scientific languages at that time in the natural sciences. An example of his prime interest in technical solutions when a problem presented itself can be found in a letter to his sister Henrietta of 3 May 1856 on music, when Jevons was already in Sydney. Jevons explained his difficulty in playing trioles correctly. After having shown in notation how he did play them, he continued: "Am I not wrong. How stupidly contrived the *notation* of music is, is it not. I should improve it I think if I had much to do with it" (*PC* 2:227). Jevons considered the difficulty of trioles not so much a problem of his own skills and understanding, but as a problem that could be solved, in principle, by improving notation. Jevons's thinking here is in keeping with his more general utilitarianism: Improving notation is to the benefit of all, but improving one's own playing can be regarded as an "altogether useless amusement".

[7] Initially, the salary consisted of a fixed amount of £100 that was to be supplemented by private assaying. Not long after Jevons arrived in Sydney, the arrangement changed to a fixed-salary payment only, which gave Jevons more time to pursue his scientific interests.

five-year stay in the colony. Meteorological observations made by Jevons en route eventually would lead to his experiments on cloud formation, which he published in the *Philosophical Journal* in 1857 and 1858, among others.

Jevons planned to go to Australia for only a limited period of time and "to be at home again from five to ten years", something that was clear to his family from the start (*LJ*, e.g., 38, 49).[8] The romantic myth of Jevons becoming enlightened about his true mission in life and then deciding to return to England to found political economy on a sound scientific basis is without merit. It is equally misleading to portray Jevons as someone who spent his time in Australia in isolation, although it is true that his scientific work in those days at times lacked the input of developments that were going on in other parts of the world.[9] The image does not hold, even for his actual living circumstances: In the first years in Australia, he shared a house with the second official gold assayer, Charles Miller. Initially, they had their assaying office at home, assaying for both private individuals and the Mint.

Despite his youth, Jevons actively participated in the Australian literary and scientific circles, devoting most of his spare time to the study of meteorology as well as social and economic issues. Jevons ingeniously attempted to get a grip on the Australian climate by superimposing a map of the Northern Hemisphere on its southern counterpart (Nicholls 1998). But also worth mentioning are his experiments on clouds (1857, 1858a,b); his contribution to Waugh's *Almanac* (1859), which provided the first systematic collection of data on the Australian weather; his social survey of Sydney, following up an interest in the "industrial mechanisms of society" in his early London years; and contributions to the railway controversy.[10] On the whole, Jevons's

---

[8] The best information on Jevons's private circumstances in Australia can be found in Burke ([1955] 1988).

[9] The idea of a solitary existence also comes to the fore in accounts in his diaries about his journeys to the Australian gold diggings. These journeys were considered so arduous and dangerous that Jevons was unable to find anyone willing to travel with him. The solitary image is further enforced by Jevons's notorious fear of speaking in public, as witnessed by the fact that Jevons's early papers to the BAAS were read in absentia. Although there are other such examples, it was certainly not the standard practice (Morrell and Thackray 1981; Grattan-Guinness 2002).

[10] Historians of economics have extensively discussed the possible influence of the Australian railway controversy on the development of Jevons's economic thinking, mostly in relation to Lardner's *Railway Economy*. See, for example, White (1982), Bostaph and Shieh (1986), and, critical of White, Hutchison ([1982] 1988). For an early account of Lardner's influence on Jevons, see Robertson ([1951] 1988). From a doctrinal point of view, it is interesting

writings were very well-received. When he left Australia for England in 1859, the editors of the *Sydney Magazine of Science and Art* wrote admiringly that "Australia is about to lose this laborious and unassuming yet most promising natural philosopher. We fear it will be long ere we shall find another observer so industrious, so talented, and so modest" (La Nauze [1941] 1988, 113).

Despite the fact that Jevons would have returned to England anyway, one does get the impression from his letters and diaries that the shift in his mind from pursuing research in the natural sciences to political economy made this decision more pressing (Schabas 1990, 16–17). Back in London, Jevons resumed his studies at University College from 1860–1863, first completing his B.A. and then obtaining his Masters. As previously described, his job as a gold assayer had paid well, and he was able to finance those years in London with the money he had saved. He did not particularly enjoy the classes in political economy, which he found completely outdated, but, as had been the case in the early 1850s, De Morgan's mathematics classes were his favourite. Jevons was most upset when he was ranked only fourth in political economy in an exam at the end of the summer term in 1860, something he attributed to differences of opinion with his teacher Jacob Waley. An ardent defender of Mill, Waley was reputedly "prejudiced" against contrary or innovative opinions (*LJ* 154; Checkland [1951] 1988, 139).

why Jevons referred favourably to Lardner in the *Theory*, but did not make use of his mathematical analysis which stemmed from Cournot. With regard to Cournot, in my view Schabas (1990, 92) convincingly argues that "Jevons did not regard Cournot as a full-fledged precursor", because he "failed to reduce economics to the more fundamental theory of utility and thus to establish a mechanical scheme that demonstrated the indispensability of mathematics in economics". The same holds true, by implication, for Lardner's work. As far as Cournot is concerned, Ekelund and Hébert's (1999) important book pinpoints the same issue when they state that Cournot rejected utility as unscientific, thus failing to offer an explanation for the motivation of individuals to engage in acts of exchange: "Cournot's demand analysis remained without an anchor in economic theory" (1999, 13). Jevons does not seem to have been familiar with Cournot's work before the publication of the *Theory* in 1871. Cournot's logical writing is mentioned at least twice in the correspondence between Boole and De Morgan. Boole first writes, in a letter of 28 June 1852, about "a work on the laws of thought (mathematical)" that "has been presented to the French Academy by a M. Courtois (or some such name)". Boole returns to this topic in a letter of 8 December 1852: "De Vericour tells me that he saw six months ago a notice of a report to the Institute by Cournot on some paper on Mathematical Logic. I mentioned this to you but did not remember then the name Cournot". De Morgan referred to Cournot in his vast *Differential and Integral Calculus* (1842). There is no indication that De Morgan picked up on Cournot's epistemological writings. In the late 1840s, Cournot's name also circulated in the correspondence between J. T. Graves, professor of law at University College, and William Whewell. See Rashid (1977, 388).

In these early years back in London, Jevons was clearly making strides in new directions. Shortly before he experienced this "sad reverse" at the exam, we find the first allusions to his new theory of political economy in a letter to his brother Herbert (*LJ* 151, letter of 1 June 1860). Many of the elements of the *Theory* are hinted at in this letter. He clearly states "the most important axiom" of the declining degree of what he then called the "*ratio of utility*", and he also makes it clear that he "assume[s] that on an average" this ratio of utility "is some continuous mathematical function of the quantity of commodity"; a "law" that, according to Jevons, had been assumed by political economists "under the more complex form and name of the Law of Supply and Demand" (*LJ* 151).[11] We can easily imagine Waley's dismissal of these kinds of innovations in an oral exam. Jevons wrote to his brother Herbert that he would "avenge" himself for this setback as soon as "I bring out my *Theory of Political Economy*" (*LJ* 154). When his "Notice of a General Mathematical Theory of Political Economy" was read two years later in his absence to section F of the British Association for the Advancement of Science (BAAS) at the beginning of October 1862, however, it was greeted with similar reservations. Only an abstract, presumably made by the secretary of the section (Grattan-Guinness 2002), was published.[12]

---

[11] This episode is extensively discussed in Schabas (1990, 21–4). Schabas wrongly infers from Jevons's diary that Jevons conceived of his mathematical theory more to "the format of Newton's *Principia* (1687) than to the model of constrained maximization found in Lagrange's *Mécanique Analytique* (1788)". De Morgan's teaching – Jevons's major source for mathematical knowledge and one of the most demanding courses in mathematics available in Victorian England – provided an extensive training in the calculus rather than in the Newtonian theory of fluxions, and Jevons's invocation of the principle of virtual velocities clearly stems from French rational mechanics. In effect, the issue involves a clear answer to the question of what version of mechanics was on Jevons's mind at that time. Schabas (1990, 91) dates Jevons's beliefs "directly back" to a course he took in natural philosophy from Richard Potter at University College from 1852–1853. Rice relates, however, that Potter "turned out to be quite incompetent as a lecturer, and how in the early 1860s his course had become a 'laughingstock'" (Rice 1996a). It is clear from Jevons's diary as well that his enthusiasm for De Morgan's mathematics classes hardly make a convincing case for any influence of Potter on Jevons.

[12] His statistical "Study in Commercial Fluctuations" that was read at the same meeting of section F did meet with approval, however. The "Notice" was published in 1866, with minor changes, in the *Journal of the Statistical Society* under the heading "Miscellanea" and with the title changed to "Brief Account of a General Mathematical Theory of Political Economy". The history of the "Notice" turns out to be more complex than is suggested from Jevons's papers, however. Ivor Grattan-Guinness recently discovered an earlier different version of the "Notice" in the archives of Taylor and Francis, the editors of the *Philosophical Magazine*, where it was submitted by Jevons shortly before the "Notice" was read to section F of the

At the time, his new economic theory was far from the only thing on Jevons's prolific mind. He contributed a paper, "On the Deficiency of Rain in an Elevated Raingauge as Caused by Wind", to the mathematics and physics section of the BAAS meeting in September 1860 in Manchester; started work on his so-called Statistical Atlas project, an ambitious plan to display the commercial movements in the economy by means of an extensive set of diagrams;[13] and, during the winter, wrote various articles on measurement instruments for A Dictionary of Chemistry and the Allied Branches of Other Sciences (1868), edited by Henry Watts.

Soon afterwards, Jevons became absorbed by his studies in formal logic, triggered especially by his reading of Boole's Laws of Thought (1854), on which he published a short critical book in 1863.[14] Jevons pursued his studies in logic throughout the 1860s and constructed a mechanical contrivance to prove to the eye the power of Boole's logical system. Indeed, Jevons once described his well-received Principles of Science (1874) to his brother Herbert as a study in logic in disguise.

BAAS. At that time, Jevons regularly chose the Philosophical Magazine as a medium for his studies in the natural sciences, most notably meteorology. The paper was not accepted for publication. See Grattan-Guinness (2002).

[13] Jevons finally managed to get two of his charts published with his own funds.

[14] Jevons's tract on Boole was reprinted in Pure Logic and Other Minor Works (1890). Jevons's logic merits better than George Stigler's reference to John Venn's criticism of it (Stigler [1983] 1988, 279). According to Stigler, "Jevons's work on logic and scientific method . . . soon received severe criticism from the professional logicians" ([1983] 1988, 279). The implicit suggestion that Jevons was not a professional logician is plainly odd, given the fact that Jevons was appointed Professor of Logic at Queens College, Liverpool, in 1865 and Professor of Logic and Political Economy one year later at Owen's College, Manchester. John Venn was a fellow of Caius College, Cambridge, where he lectured on moral philosophy. His criticism of Jevons's logic, which is far from fair, fits in the more general animosity of Cambridge academia towards Jevons's work, as exemplified by Sidgwick and Marshall in particular. Jevons distinctly hurt his own case with his quixotic battle against John Stuart Mill's "illogicalness", as Mill for someone like Sidgwick was the Locke and Bacon of nineteenth-century Britain. Jevons's "exaggerated and violent" (Sidgwick) attacks on Mill certainly helped to mobilise Croom Robertson, the successor of Alexander Bain as the editor of Mind, to write an overtly hostile review (Mind, 1876, reprinted in Peart 2003 4: 12–26) of Jevons's Principles of Science. Some awareness of this context might have prevented Philip Mirowski (2002, 38) to simply write that we had better not become "embroiled in [Jevons's] obsolete notation and baroque principles". More justice has been done recently to the merits and demerits of Jevons's logic by Sánchez Valencia (2001) in a discussion of De Morgan's reviews of both Boole's and Jevons's logical systems. A balanced view on Jevons's logic is also provided in Schabas (1990) and Mosselmans (1998). For Cambridge criticism of Jevons's work, see White (1996).

His first successful publication came in 1863 with his study on the fall of the value of gold, the first to systematically make use of index numbers. It was immediately and widely recognised as a remarkable piece of work. From then onwards, Jevons became quickly acknowledged as one of the leading statisticians of the day.[15] Although his early complaints in his diaries as well as in his correspondence about lack of recognition were to some extent justified, this was not so from 1863 onwards as his professional career flourished (see also De Marchi 1973).

His cousin Harry Roscoe proved helpful a second time in securing Jevons a position as tutor at Owen's College, Manchester. Jevons shortly thereafter combined his tutorship with a part-time professorship in logic and political economy at Queen's College, Liverpool, in 1865. By this time the clouds of the early 1860s seem to have lifted, and Jevons noted proudly in his diary that he was considered "by reviews of authority, a *competent statistician*". He had effectively been elected a member of the London (now Royal) Statistical Society in November 1864 (*PC* 1:197–8).[16]

His definitive breakthrough came with the publication of *The Coal Question* in 1865, which predicted a decline of Britain's prosperity due to the future exhaustion of cheaply extractable coal. An outstanding success, the book prompted John Stuart Mill to ask questions in Parliament and Gladstone to invite the author to Downing Street. Allegedly, the book was used to plea for a reduction of government debt.[17] Without doubt, the success of the book contributed to Jevons being appointed to the newly established Cobden Chair in logic and political economy at Owen's College, Manchester. For someone who had just reached the age of thirty, this was hardly regarded as a weak professional record!

His major publications were, of course, *The Theory of Political Economy* (1871) and *Principles of Science* (1874). Jevons considered the latter a well-written synthesis of much of the philosophical disputes on the methods of the sciences, his most important work. It was to be of some influence on the early Wiener Kreis, and in particular on Otto Neurath.

[15] See the previous note.
[16] It has been suggested that the negative response to the *Theory* can be partly explained because Jevons was predominantly known for his statistical work.
[17] White (1991a) argues that in terms of its content, Jevons's book was far less influential than is commonly assumed.

From the mid-1870s, Jevons's mathematical economics gained ground in Victorian economics, most notably through the work of Edgeworth, Marshall, and Wicksteed.[18] Even Henry Sidgwick's *Principles of Political Economy* (1883), an apologetic restorative tract in the tradition of Mill and Ricardo and consequently far from enthusiastic about Jevons's mathematical pursuits, stated that "the leading ideas" of Jevons's *Theory* had been "continually on his mind". In the 1880s, Wicksteed's crushing criticism of Bernard Shaw's complacent discussion of Jevons's utility theory made Shaw quickly shift sides. If really more a matter of rhetorics than of substance, Shaw managed to base the Fabian social reform movement on Jevons's theory of value instead of Marx's in the Fabian manifesto *Fabian Essays*, combining Jevons's theory of value with Ricardo's theory of rent. By the turn of the nineteenth century, Jevons's utility theory of value had a firm basis in economic theory as well as in by then the most important movement for social reform in Britain (Schabas 1990, Chapter 7).[19]

The publications dating after the *Theory* and the *Principles* are generally considered to be of much lesser importance. His sunspot studies, in which he attempted to establish a causal nexus between solar activity and commercial crises, though not as absurd as they are sometimes described (Sheenan and Grieves [1982] 1988), are generally thought of as a failure and as having contributed to the bad name associated with the analytical use of statistics at the turn of the nineteenth century (Mirowski [1984] 1988; Morgan 1990). Jevons also worked on an encompassing *Principles of Economics*, the manuscript of which was published by Henry Higgs in 1905. From what can be judged from this unfinished material, the end result would not have been too promising. He wrote four vehement articles directed against John Stuart Mill, which did not have the effect for which Jevons must have hoped. And he worked on a second edition of the *Theory* (1879), containing the first bibliography of all the mathematical precursors in economics that Jevons had been able to trace. Jevons substantially reworked his argument in an attempt to answer

---

[18] This is shown convincingly in Schabas (1990), especially in Chapters 6 and 7.

[19] On the continent, Walras was, of course, of the greatest importance in the breakthrough of mathematical economics. The similarity between Walras's results and his own strengthened Jevons's "belief in the correctness of the theory". See Jevons's letter to Walras, 12 May 1874, in which he asked Walras to grant him priority of discovery, something Walras promptly and on several occasions acknowledged (*PC* 4:41). The original letter was rediscovered by Heertje in 1981. For further discussion, see Heertje ([1982] 1988).

criticism raised to the first edition of the *Theory* and rephrased difficulties he perceived himself in the initial argument. But many difficulties remained.[20] In *The State in Relation to Labour* ([1882] 1968) and a posthumous collection of essays on social reform (1883), Jevons turned more explicitly to the social and political issues of the day, issues that were never far from his mind.[21] These essays undeniably lack the sharpness and innovative force of his early statistical studies and of his *Theory*. For all its bluntness, there is something to be said for Keynes's horrifying remark that when Jevons so untimely drowned in 1882, leaving his wife and three young children, "his work was done" ([1936] 1988, 85).

From this short account of Jevons's life and work, the image arises of a genuine Victorian polymath. Throughout his life, Jevons contributed to what we now consider to be distinct fields of enquiry. If we take Inoue and White's 1993 bibliography of Jevons's published works at hand,[22] we see that his writings range wildly from contributions to the study of Brownian motion in molecules via his meteorological studies to empirical and theoretical work in political economy. The emphasis distinctly shifts from his work and interest in the natural sciences to economic theory and statistics. But whatever the emphasis was, Jevons was clearly not deterred by nature's complexity. His ingenious use of an inverted world map to compare the climate of Australia with that of North Africa, his conscious use of averaging techniques to bring out the general course of the Australian climate from his carefully collected data, his experimental search for a uniform mechanism of cloud formation, his experiments on work and fatigue to gain insight into the "physical groundwork" of political economy, his use of index numbers to flesh out a causal relationship between price rises and the gold influx following the Australian and Californian gold discoveries – all are cases in point.

Most of these examples are treated in more detail in a later chapter. In retrospect not all of them proved equally successful, and some, as was

---

[20] Jevons's reformulations have been the subject of intensive scrutiny by Michael White. See, for example, White (2004b).

[21] During his time in Australia, Jevons had commenced work on a *Social Survey of Sydney*. Portions of this manuscript were published as "The Social Cesspools of Sydney" in the *Sydney Morning Herald*, 7 October 1958. Jevons envisaged a similar study on the working men's districts in London.

[22] An improved and considerably extended version appeared as an appendix to Inoue (2002).

not uncommon for scientific endeavours of the nineteenth century, are now considered almost stupefyingly off the mark. But whatever their merits from our vantage point, they demostrate the contrary of the "unenquiring and unhoping spirit" that Jevons so criticised in his battles with political economists and statisticians of his day. It is to the background of these battles that we now turn to measure the distance that had to be bridged – and the steps Jevons made – to alter the image of political economy.

~

THREE

THE BLACK ARTS OF INDUCTION

DUGALD STEWART: HISTORY AND POLITICAL ECONOMY AS INDUCTION BY REFLECTION

At the turn of the eighteenth century, the distinction between the sciences of nature and history, including political economy, was made most forcefully in Britain by the professor of moral philosophy at Edinburgh, Dugald Stewart. Stewart's influence was great. He was the only professor in moral philosophy lecturing in political economy. John McCulloch and James Mill were among his audience, and his work was carefully read by Richard Whately and Nassau Senior, amongst others. He entertained a wide range of international contacts (Coleman 1996, 219). Stewart thus provided, in John Stuart Mill's words, an "important stimulus to the national intellect" (quoted from Coleman 1996, 219).

A student of the Scottish "common sense" philosopher Thomas Reid (1710–1796), Stewart was a pivotal figure in canonising the nineteenth-century view of the Scottish Enlightenment's contribution to the sciences as mainly consisting of its invention of political economy and history – an image that is defended to this day.[1] For Stewart, political economy inextricably belonged to the science of history; indeed, it was its most advanced branch.

---

[1] The standard reference here should be to Gladys Bryson's seminal 1945 *Man and Society: The Scottish Inquiry of the Eighteenth Century*. Following up on Dugald Stewart, the claim that the heritage of the Scots consisted predominantly of their "invention" of history and political economy was preluded in James McCosh (1875) and made most forcefully by Hugh Trevor-Roper – Lord Dacre – and in our day by John Robertson (e.g., in P. Wood 2000b). It underlies the influential collection of essays of Hont and Ignatieff (1983), though the emphasis here is the humanist context of much of Scottish writing, which came to be acknowledged through the work of Andrew Skinner, Roy Campbell, and John Pocock.

The notion of "conjectural history", which stipulates an ideal type of development of history through various types of society, originates from Stewart, who thus influentially summarised the endeavours of the various Scottish philosophers and literati in historical enquiry. This term is not to be found in any of the original writings of the Scots, who took their work in the tradition of natural histories of nature and society (Wood 1990). Like natural histories, however, Stewart's notion of conjectural history enabled him to combine the view of a universal nature of man with the alterations of concrete historical circumstances in which Providence, God's universal order, manifested itself in different ways.

Stripped from Providence or any reference to the natural order in nature and society, a universal nature of man remained that manifested itself in concrete historical circumstances. In the combination of Hartley's (or rather Priestley's) association psychology, Benthamite utilitarianism, and Ricardian political economy, this would become the dominant view of man and history as propagated by the political radicals like James and John Stuart Mill. For the Mills, as for Stewart, this view essentially rested on a distinction between the sciences of nature and man and a methodologically privileged access to the latter by way of introspection.

Stewart defended this distinction in his *General View of the Progress of Metaphysical, Ethical, and Political Philosophy, Since the Revival of Letters in Europe*, of 1824.[2] Contrasting his views with earlier classifications of the sciences – by Bacon, Locke, and the famous one by d'Alembert in his foreword to the equally famous *Encyclopédie* – Stewart used the two "diametrically opposite" fields of "observation" and "reflection" to distinguish between the sciences of mind and matter. Stewart emphasised that this division of the sciences did the most justice to common sense usage: "the word *Physicks*,

---

See Campbell and Skinner (1982) and Pocock (1975). Trevor-Roper's view has been most forcefully rejected by Roger Emerson (e.g., 1988) and Paul Wood (1990, 2000a), who emphasise in contrast the importance of the developments within natural philosophy to characterise the Scottish Enlightenment. Emerson's challenge also finds support in the many recent contributions of Richard Sher and Nicolas Phillipson. The literature on this issue is obviously too vast to be done justice to in any detail. For a recent overview and further references, see Wood (2000).

[2] The first part of Stewart's essay was published in 1815; the second, in French, in 1821. The full essay, together with John Playfair's (the elder brother of William and professor of mathematics at Edinburgh) two essays on the progress of the mathematical and natural sciences, was printed in 1824 as a preliminary dissertation to the supplement of the 4th edition of the *Encyclopaedia Britannica*. See Stewart and Playfair (1975).

in particular, which, in our language, long and constant use has restricted to the phenomena of Matter, cannot fail to strike every ear as *anomalously*, and therefore *illogically*, applied, when extended to those of Thought and Consciousness" (Stewart and Playfair 1975, 26). Stewart criticised Turgot, who included "under the name of Physics . . . even History". In contrast, Stewart noted approvingly, Descartes had "perceived the necessity, in studying the laws of Mind, of abstracting entirely from the analogies of Matter" (167).

History formed part of the sciences of the mind, as political economy did also by implication. In contrast with natural philosophy, the study of history involved the constant use of memory. Its aim was "to treasure up particular facts" as opposed to the establishment of "general conclusions" (15). The word "history" should be understood "to comprehend all our knowledge of particular facts and particular events" (19). This did not mean there were no general laws governing these "particular events". Indeed, Stewart singled out the work of political economists as having contributed much to their discovery. But these laws were found not by the means of the natural philosopher – that is, by observation with the eye, but by the means of the philosopher of the mind – by internal reflection. Stewart offered the example of Adam Smith to elucidate how economists explain. Political economists appealed to "the maxims upon which men act in private life". Thus, Smith "indulged in theory" by simply exposing the "common sense which guides mankind in their private concern" (*Stewart* 2:235). A "particular event" was explained when it was shown how individuals, acting on their motives and passions, brought about the event.

Stewart equated this explanatory strategy with induction.[3] Indeed, on many occasions, he paid tribute to the "father of induction", Francis Bacon. But, he was careful to point out that the inductions of the political economists should not be identified with the false inductions of the political arithmeticians, or "statistical collectors". Stewart shared Adam Smith's low opinion of political arithmetic. Statistics, in his view identical to the "collection of facts", provided only delusory information. "The facts accumulated by the statistical collector are merely *particular results*, which other men have seldom an opportunity of verifying or of disproving; and which, to those who consider them in an insulated state, can never afford any important information". Even when a fact was "accurately" observed and described by the

---

[3] See especially Rashid (1985). See also Coleman (1996).

statistician, it did not give us "the combination of circumstances whereby the effect is modified". The "particular results" of the political arithmetician of consequence did not add up to something "important" (all quotes from *Stewart* 2:331).

Stewart's criticism of political arithmetic is striking for several reasons. It shows that exceedingly more trust can be put in the observations of the inner mind than in those made by external observation. It shows that historical explanations in his view were only to be gathered from knowledge of all the contributing causes to an essentially complex event. To consider part of such an event – that is, a "fact" in an "insulated state" – as helpful for explanatory purposes was not even considered by Stewart, let alone to *construct* an event or phenomenon (e.g., a seasonal fluctuation) by connecting different insulated facts as it is done, for example, in a time-series graph. A graph typically does away with the presentation of a "particular result" in an "insulated state", but brings out the general course of these particular results. However, having his inductive route to certain and infallible laws within the reach of the mind, Stewart never even considered visual devices like graphs as relevant to history. Neither did political economists who, as did Stewart, relied on introspection as the road to truth, as we will see. In Stewart's view, statistics – or political arithmetic – coincided with the collection of individual facts. That is, statistical data were senseless units when searching for an explanation of historical events. They did not indicate motives for action. It was therefore wiser, in Stewart's view, to have recourse to political economy as a check on the "extravagancies of political arithmetic", instead of the other way around (*Stewart* 2:331–2).

In early Victorian Britain, two opposite reactions dominated the reception of Stewart's views on the methods of the sciences: that of the Cambridge omniscientist William Whewell and that of John Stuart Mill. Reversing historical order of appearance, I will first discuss John Mill's views on the method of political economy, described ad nauseam over the past decades, yet impossible to pass over in silence, and then turn to Whewell. Mill's so-called a priori method served as a benchmark for all writing on methodology in political economy in Victorian England, while Whewell's *Philosophy of the Inductive Sciences* (1840) competed with Mill's *Logic* (1843) to serve as a similar benchmark for the natural sciences. The debate between Mill and Whewell on the nature and proper methods of induction not only permeates Victorian intellectual debate, but is also heavily important for the more or less institutionalised division of labour that emerged between political economy as solely devoted to theory, and statistical research as devoted to naïve Baconian fact-gathering only. Mill's and Whewell's views thus set the stage for all subsequent skirmishes over the proper method of enquiry in political economy.

JOHN STUART MILL: SHIELDING POLITICAL ECONOMY FROM HISTORY

We have seen how Dugald Stewart based his plea for introspection on the categorically distinct character of the sciences of mind and matter. History was the umbrella science to which all other sciences of mind, like political economy, were subjugated. The difficulty of history – and of consequence to political economy – was that concretely, so many causal factors interacted that it looked liked sheer impossibility to explain historical events in their full complexity. As Neil De Marchi (2002) convincingly argued, John Stuart Mill's views on the method of political economy, especially those developed in his famous essay on the definition and method of political economy of 1836, were designed to overcome this difficulty and so to preserve the scientific character of the subject.[4]

In his 1836 essay, Mill effectively separated political economy from the other moral sciences, including history.[5] The study of history, Mill lamented elsewhere, had "not passed that stage in which its cultivation is an affair of mere literature or erudition, not of science. It is studied for the facts, not for the explanation of the facts" (*Mill* 20:260). Even though this was an important departure from Dugald Stewart, who considered political econ-omy part of history, Mill agreed with Stewart in an important number of other respects. Like Stewart, Mill considered the split between the realms of mind and matter the most natural to be made and the "foundation" for all classifications of the sciences. Like Stewart, Mill considered the collection

---

[4] The controversies on the exact import of John Stuart Mill's views on the method of political economy and their implication for his economic work continue. In the history of economics, now standard interpretations can be found, amongst others, in Blaug (1992), De Marchi (1986), Hirsch (1992), and Hands (2001). Important recent interpretations in the philos-ophy of science are Cartwright (1989), Hausman (1992), and in the history of economics De Marchi (2002). An earlier version of this last paper provoked a challenge of the empirical adequacy of the standard interpretation of Mill by Hollander and Peart (1999).

[5] On Mill's early struggles with history, see especially De Marchi (2002).

of "isolated historical facts" of no help in getting at general, lawlike explanations. Historical facts might give evidence for general laws, but the complexity of these facts themselves forbid the inference to causes or lawlike relations from them.

The distinction between the realms of mind and matter opened up the route of introspection as a legitimate route of observation. Thus, Mill essentially agreed with Stewart that the laws of society were to be established introspectively, not by external observation. Causes were to be sought in the inner province of the mind. Mill diverged from Stewart in that he refrained from explanations of man "in the social state". That is, Mill retained a universal theory of human nature as the basis of political economy, but harnessed political economy to the concrete complexity of history, which political economists – according to Stewart – dealt with by means of conjectural history.

For the purpose of political economy, Mill narrowed down human nature to just three motives of action: the desire for wealth, the strive for luxury, and the aversion to labour. By focussing on just these motives of action, political economy was able to derive lawlike relations or *tendencies*. In doing this, political economists circumvented the problem facing history: that the explanation of an event involved knowledge of all contributing causes to it. This last problem was to be solved by the concrete deductive method, which – in the case of social explanations – was a bridge too far. In contrast with Stewart, it was no longer the purpose of political economy to explain the complexity of historical events by examining all its *contributing* causes. Rather, Mill considered these contributing causes as *disturbing* causes, obfuscating the laws of political economy, which were rooted in human nature.

Mill took great pains to point out that the route of reflection – introspection – followed by the political economists was no more than the ordinary route of "observation and experiment" of the natural sciences. The "inner" and the "outer" eyes were equally able to make controlled experiments. In psychology, experiments could be carried out by each individual in his or her own mind. Mill drew upon his father's version of association psychology. The main claim of association psychology was that mental phenomena, such as ideas, were complexes produced by the regular association of ideas or their more simple constituents – sensations. Sensations, in turn, were derived from perceptions or sense impressions. Sensations, and the phenomena of the mind in general, were also referred to as "feelings". Whatever label they had, they were *conscious* states of mind, in which consciousness itself was considered as a "feeling". The goal of the analysis was to show how complex mental phenomena could be decomposed into sensations, from which the original complexes were formed by the mental laws of contiguity and succession. Since psychology, in Mill's view, was "a science of which Ideas or Conceptions are avowedly (along with other mental phenomena) the subject matter", introspection was in fact its only appropriate method to obtain any truths (*Mill* 7:89 g-g).

Political economy thus combined the inductive method of association psychology (introspection) and the deductive method of Ricardian economics. Mill labelled this combination the a priori method, to distinguish it from naïve Baconian fact-gathering as pursued in statistical research, which he labelled the a posteriori method. The tendency laws political economists deduced from this psychological basis were as certain as the best laws of physics. By further distinguishing between the *science* and the *art* of political economy, Mill relegated the application of the laws, or tendencies, political economists deductively derived to the wisdom of "practical men" or politicians.

Mill thus brilliantly solved and summarised discussions in the early decades of the nineteenth century on the nature and status of political economy vis-à-vis history and the natural sciences. In divergence from Stewart, Mill separated political economy from history by focussing on a select list of motives of action only. He relegated the examination of the different institutional settings in which these motives expressed themselves differently (i.e., "man in the social state") to history, or, in the *Logic*, to his so-called science of ethology, which he never made much of. Political economy was also separated from the natural sciences due to its privileged access to the mind that Mill equated with experiment and observation.[6]

---

[6] In economics, Mill's recourse to "mental experimentation" played a role in the disputes on the status of "as if" claims that were provoked by Friedman (1953). The extent to which modern commentators still accept Mill's phrasing of introspection in terms of experiments is, in my view, simply astonishing. Referring to Mill's "introspective experimental" method, Daniel Hausman (1992, 146) argues, for example, that "every day experience and introspection are sufficient to establish that some of these laws [of equilibrium theory], such as diminishing marginal rates of substitution and diminishing returns, are reasonable approximations" (210). Hausman even claims that "introspection provides evidence that consumerism is a significant causal factor affecting economic phenomena" (216). In my opinion, Hollander and Peart (1999) also accept Mill's account that the "empirical laws of

Cambridge Opposition to Ricardianism

Dugald Stewart offered another reason to show blind faith in the theories of political economists and to distrust the studies of political arithmeticians. In his eyes, these last studies invariably offered the wrong policy advice on the basis of their illegitimate inductive inferences. Where political economists in Stewart's view rightly argued for the importance of free trade to improve the wealth of nations, political arithmeticians – like William Petty, John Graunt, and Gregory King – in earlier days "invariably encourag[ed] a predilection for restraints and checks, and all the other technical combinations of an antiquated and scholastic policy" (*Stewart* 3:334).[7]

This political statement was of course grist to the mill for someone like James Mill, Stewart's former student at Edinburgh, who combined Stewart's methodological message with Bentham's utilitarianism and Ricardian political economy. This fusion would dominate debates over political economy and statistics in the first half of the nineteenth century and found its most eloquent defence in John Stuart Mill's methodological writings in political economy as well as his *Principles of Political Economy* (1848). Mill's stance was for political and methodological reasons completely unacceptable to William Whewell, who formulated another approach to induction in the first decades of the nineteenth century.

William Whewell (1794–1866) was, beyond any doubt, one of the great minds of his age. Son of a master carpenter, he became Master of Trinity College, Cambridge, one of the most powerful positions in the Victorian scientific community. He held professorships in mineralogy and moral philosophy and had an ardent interest in political economy. There is simply

human nature" are established by "specific experiments", that is, introspectively. Recently, Neil De Marchi (2002) suggested that, "to keep things manageable Mill selected a few undeniable active and common desires". These desires are "undeniable"; "since we know ourselves under various circumstances, it is also a sort of experimental knowledge" (2002, 30). Nowhere is the question posed about the experimental nature of Mill's introspective investigations.

[7] When statistical enquiry took off in Victorian England, this was, of course, no longer so. Indeed, Tooke and Newmarch, two of the most outstanding statisticians of their day, highly welcomed the benefits of free trade, which Newmarch compared in importance with the discovery of a new continent. Theodore Porter (1986, 5–6) emphasises how statistics as the "calculus of nature" was embraced by nineteenth-century liberalism. The relation of statistics to political economy seems to have been easier on the Continent. On political economists and statisticians in Germany in the early nineteenth century, see Nikolow (1999, 2001). On the reception of statistics in France, see Desrosières (1993), and Ménard (1980).

no subject one might think of to which he did not make a significant contribution, as witnessed from the overused expression that "science was his foil, omniscience his foible".[8] The historian of science Susan Faye Cannon pictures Whewell as one of the dominating voices in the "Cambridge network" of liberal (Whig) Anglican scientists and clericals.[9] Some of the other "members" of the Cambridge network (the term was Thomas Arnold's) included mathematic reformers like John Herschel, George Biddell Airy, George Peacock, and the "scientific gadfly" of the period, Charles Babbage; most of them were part of the short-lived Analytical Society at Cambridge.

This same group of scientists plays an important role in Jack Morrell and Arnold Thackray's superb book on the early history of the British Association for the Advancement of Science (BAAS) (1981). Present-day accounts of the period rightly take Cannon's and Morrell and Thackray's work as their point of departure, as, for example, in James Henderson's recent book on Whewell and early mathematical economics at Cambridge (1996), and so it is done here as well.

For the Cambridge network and the "gentlemen of science" more broadly, science was a source of both objective knowledge and social stability. They considered this to clearly separate them from the rioteers that were, in their eyes, part of the political radicals of the Benthamite–Ricardian brand. In contrast with the agnosticism of political radicalism, the gentlemen of science firmly believed that the Anglican Church fulfilled an important role in stabilising English society, and equally believed that one of the important, if not *the* important, tasks of the sciences was to reveal the providential order in nature and society. Whewell addressed the conformity of science and religion in his well-received Bridgewater treatise *Astronomy and General Physics, Considered with Reference to Natural Theology* (1833).[10] Science and religion were the cement of society. Morrell and Thackray's image of the early circular movement of the meetings of the BAAS makes clear (perhaps better than anything else) how much the advancement of science in Britain

---

[8] For recent examinations of Whewell, see Fisch (1991, 1994), Fisch and Schaffer (1991), Yeo (1993), and Henderson (1996).

[9] See her incisive collection of essays *Science in Culture, the Early Victorian Period* (1978); also Cannon (1964a,b).

[10] As is well-known, the Bridgewater Treatises were commissioned by the Reverend Francis Henry Egerton, Earl of Bridgewater, to show the conformity of science with natural religion.

in these early decades of the nineteenth century was not just a neutral matter; it shows the important integrative role of science and science's claimed place in British society.

Whewell's vehement anti-Ricardian and anti-Benthamite stance has sometimes been considered as a matter of personal interest. This is stretching an obvious thought too far, however. The argument goes that Whewell, as Trinity College incarnate, seriously objected to the Ricardians because they pinpointed the landlord's utterly uselessness for society and in line with this proposed a heavy tax on rent. This, of course, would seriously affect the means and position of Trinity College, one of the greatest landowners in Cambridgeshire. It has been repeatedly pointed out that there is no textual evidence for this allegation (see, for example, Yeo 1993).

More importantly, and depersonalising this argument, however, was Whewell's fear that political radicalism would undermine the social order – a fear he shared with a great many of the gentlemen of science. It should be remembered that the first decades of the nineteenth century were a period of serious social uproar, for which the English were quick to blame the French. It is therefore no surprise that the gentlemen of science attempted to keep away from political radicalism and its plea for free trade, its attack on landed nobility, and its preoccupation with the corn laws.

After its initial tour, the meetings of the BAAS moved into the heartland of the industrial revolution that was plagued by social unrest, and these meetings served not only to show the advancements of science, but also to display a mode of gentlemenlike conduct that went with it and that should happily accommodate with the existing social order. Samuel Smiles's much later written biographies of workmen–scientists can be seen as serving this very same goal (Secord 2003). Coming from his humble background and rising to the fore at Cambridge, Whewell fits like no other to the ideal of the gentleman of science. It is therefore more than just that Whewell, on Coleridge's challenges, coined the very term "scientist".

RICHARD JONES ON RICARDIAN THEORY

We have seen how vested social institutions mattered to Whewell and how he considered them in conformity with the purpose of science – to objectively reveal the providential order in nature. It is therefore no surprise that Whewell seriously rejected any revision of the obligation to subscribe to the thirty-nine articles of belief of the Anglican Church when entering the Oxbridge system. It is well-known that Jeremy Bentham and James Mill were heavily involved in the founding of University College, London, the first institute where dissenters could receive higher education in England (and where Bentham's body still surveys the scene).[11] This contrast is exemplary for their respective attitudes towards science and the role of science in society. The differences between Whewell and the Ricardians are most acute in their wildly differing views on the scientificity of political economy.

It is impossible to discuss Whewell's views on political economy without invoking his lifelong engagement with his friend Richard Jones (1790–1855). There is hardly anyone else with whom Whewell corresponded so regularly. Whewell's views on the method and substance of political economy are really framed in his extensive correspondence with Jones, on whose authority on the subject he greatly relied. Jones entered Caius College, Cambridge, in 1812 and, somewhat older than his fellow students, easily moved in the same circles as Babbage, Herschell, and Whewell. After his studies, he served in the offices of the Church of England in Sussex. His affiliation with the Church cannot be separated from his political conservatism and his strong belief in the providential order in nature, a belief he shared with Whewell. It is interesting to note that Jones's first professorship in political economy was at King's College, London, expressedly established in 1833 as a countervailing institute to Benthamite University College.

Whewell was so convinced of the value of Jones's investigations in political economy that he almost literally bullied him to write his only book published, *An Essay on the Distribution of Wealth, and on the Principles of Taxation* (1831). In later years, Marx would be so impressed by Jones's work, especially his lectures on labour at King's College and, later, at Haileybury College, that he considered Jones's work a "fundamental advance over Ricardo". On 21 May 1822, Whewell asked Jones when "we are to see and hear" of his political economy (Add. Ms.c.51/11). After the publication of John McCulloch's *Political Economy* in 1824, Whewell pressed Jones that it was now time to combat these wrong-headed theorists in print. Whewell and Jones considered Ricardianism not only completely flawed and unscientific, but also a major threat to the stability of English society. They had two main

---

[11] University College, London was founded in 1826 as London University, and got its present name after the Whig government created the University of London in 1836.

complaints that are, in effect, closely linked. The first relates to the substance of the theory, the second to the method.

In relation to the first issue, Whewell and Jones challenged the indiscriminate use of Ricardian analysis and policy prescriptions to different social arrangements. Early in their correspondence, Richard Jones made it a point of high importance that the Ricardian rent scheme was only relevant to "one percentage" of the world. Whewell at some point even sent Jones a world map to "paint in the most brilliant colours by which rent can be represented" (Add.Ms.c.51/31). Jones made remarks on the alleged absurdity of the political economists to take the market and market exchange as their prime focus, while market arrangements were not even to be found in most parts of the world or in most epochs of history.

Jones's fundamental objection to the Ricardian theory of rent (the origin of which he attributed to Malthus, not mentioning Anderson) was that rent was universally explained from differences in fertility between the marginal and intramarginal soils. Jones took further issue with the political consequences the Ricardians drew from their theory – opposition of the landed interests with those of capital and labour in particular. Both of these generalisations were in Jones's view based on only scant observations, which subsequently were declared universally true. The Ricardians thus violated what Jones considered the true basis of all sound scientific inference: Bacon's inductivism. By taking recourse to historical and geographical data, Jones claimed to remedy this sorry state of affairs.

Both historical and contemporary data taught Jones that rent payments were crucially dependent upon the social organisation of production. This organisation was in most parts of the globe very different from that in England (and Holland), and Jones aimed to show that the rent schemes of these advanced countries were the exception rather than the general case. To ascribe the emergence of rent to different gradations of the soil was simply passing over the much more important influence of the social order, which in some cases simply amounted to the necessity of the farmer to pay rent to avoid starvation. In a phrase with which Marx proved much taken, Jones wrote that rent "has usually originated in the appropriation of the soil, at a time when the bulk of the people must cultivate it on such terms as they can obtain, or starve" (Jones [1831] 1964, 11). Most of Jones's book was devoted to a meticulous discussion of the different tenure systems, and only the last chapter was devoted to a discussion of so-called farmers' rents, the tenure system with which the English were almost uniquely acquainted. Because of his emphasis on the separate and important roles of social institutions, Jones is commonly seen as a precursor – if not founder – of the British historical school. But, if Jones was, Whewell was as well.

Jones emphasised that the English scheme of rent payments only came into existence once a "race of capitalists" had made its appearance and taken its place between landowners and peasants. This new class did not find its origin in argriculture but in manufacturing, where craftsmen in the course of time "arranged themselves" under its management. Once capitalists were there, they sought the most profitable use for capital in whatever business, including agriculture. It was only in such circumstances, where rent became basically identical to "surplus profit", that the fertility of the soil became important. Thus, what the Ricardians presented as the natural state of affairs was fundamentally dependent upon social and historical circumstances.

Jones's firm belief in the providential order of nature and his conservative attachment to the old institutes of Britain were of importance in his denial of any conflict of interests between the landed interests and the other classes in society (labour and capital). This made him an early critic of McCulloch's wages fund theory. In contrast, Jones emphasised the fundamentally disruptive consequences for the social order of the emergence of this new class in society – the capitalists: "The ties which formerly bound the community together are worn out and fall to pieces; other bonds, other principles of cohesion, connect its different classes; new economical relations spring into being. . . . Not only is the great body of non-agriculturists almost wholly in the pay of capitalists, but even the laboring cultivators of the soil . . . are their servants too" ([1859] 1964, 557–8).

It has been plausibly suggested by William Barber (1975) that the skirmish over the Ricardian scheme of rent cannot be separated from British politics in India. After publication of his seminal *History of British India*, James Mill became an officer of the East India Company and in favour of Ricardian rent politics applied to India. Malthus – professor of political economy at Haileybury College, the college of the East India Company established in 1806 – was Ricardo's most prominent opponent. Though an examination of this issue vastly surpasses the outline of this book, it was certainly not incidental that Richard Jones, with his extensive knowledge of Asiatic rent tenure systems, was considered by Malthus a worthy successor for the Haileybury Chair in political economy.

Whewell and Jones on the Method of Political Economy

From the preceding, it is clear that we should not underrate the substantive differences between Whewell and Jones on the one hand and the Ricardians on the other – differences with immediate relevance to an assessment of the existing social order and preferred politics in England. However, as becomes clear from the extensive correspondence between William Whewell and Richard Jones, their prime objections against Ricardian economics considered issues of method rather than of substance.

Whewell and Jones were seriously offended by the – in their view – frivolous way in which Ricardian economists misused the inductive method of enquiry in the sciences. Ricardians illegitimately made "inductive inference" to a universal theory of human nature as driven primarily by self-interest that was then indiscriminately applied in different social settings. This "theory" rested for Whewell and Jones on false inductions made from just a few casual observations. Ricardians, by contrast, claimed that the departure from this universal nature of man was the more or less natural starting point of the science, and particular to the field, and yet as scientific as the inductions made in the natural sciences. But they emphasised that their universal laws were valid in the abstract and not immediately present in the complex concrete. In response to McCulloch's claim that Ricardo did not use the term rent "in the ordinary and vulgar sense of the word", Whewell pointedly asked the reader "to decide for himself which subject of inquiry is better worth his notice, – the rents that are actually paid in *every* country, or the Ricardian rents, which are *not* those actually paid in *any* country" (Jones [1859] 1964, xii–xiii).

McCulloch's claim made Ricardian theory "metaphysical" as opposed to the "ethical school" of Malthus and Jones, Whewell wrote to Jones. In Whewell's emerging emphasis on the importance of "guiding principles" in scientific research, that found its full expression in his famous classification of the science in the *Philosophy of the Inductive Sciences* (1840), "there are no peculiar principles of observation or deduction employed in [political economy] – they may as well talk of the metaphysics of chemistry" (Whewell to Jones, 16 August 1822, in Todhunter 2:49).

The idea that political economy was founded on principles of observation particular to the science was not only to be found with the Ricardians, but it was also a general vice of the political economists. This vice was the most important methodological heritage of Dugald Stewart. In a furious

letter to Whewell, Jones chastised Nassau Senior's claim that "the foundations of political economy" were "a few general propositions – deduced
from observations or from consciousness & generally admitted as soon as
stated", from which Senior concluded that "it might have been expected that
there would be as little difference of *opinion among Political Economists as
among Mathematicians*". Infuriated, Jones referred to Senior as the objec-
tionable "anticipator" of Bacon's *Novum Organon* to end in the Baconian
crescendo that Senior was a "father of errors & destroyer of the sciences"
(TCC Add.Ms.c52/20, letter of 24 February 1831 from Jones to Whewell).[12]

What Jones stated here of Senior held for the Ricardians as well. Both Jones
and Whewell took issue with the alleged inductive premises from which
the political economists started their deductive reasoning. In accordance
with their own endeavours to "Baconise" political economy, they argued
that inductions never should be based on introspection, but could only
legitimately follow from "observations and experiments". For this reason,
Jones insisted that when Whewell decided to publish his mathematisation of
the Ricardian theory of rent to show the errors in their deductive reasoning,
he should make it clear from the outset that he did not subscribe to the false
injunctions of the Ricardians. Whewell assured him in turn that the "axioms"
from which he started were not his, but theirs. Only in much later years
did Whewell acquiesce that there were, after all, not that many differences
between his views on political economy and those of the Ricardians. But,
that was really only after John Stuart Mill published his *Principles of Political
Economy* (1848) which struck a compromise between the Ricardians and
Jones. Around 1830, we were clearly not there yet.

"This Poor Word Metaphysics"

We have seen that Whewell and Jones differed from the Ricardians with
regard to the proper method of inductive enquiry. Whewell and Jones seriously objected to the idea that there was a universal selfish "nature" of man,
separate from the society in which he lived. Just this idea motivated many
of the proposals for social reform of the political radicals, which Whewell
and Jones found so threatening to the existing moral order in society. With
regard to political economy, Whewell relied, as said, to a great extent on

---

[12] Jones read these passages in Whately's *Logic*. As far as Whately's own text was concerned, Whewell responded to Jones, there was not "so much *we* should object to" (TCC
Add.Ms.c52/20, letter of 24 February 1831).

the work and ideas of Richard Jones. But, when it came to induction more generally, Whewell was far too "metaphysical" in his approach and a much less dogmatic adherent of Bacon than was acceptable to Jones.

Shortly after Jones had finished his book on political economy, he encouraged Whewell in a somewhat euphoric letter to write "a good thing to the public" on inductive reasoning. Jones considered that such a text should cover the moral as well as the natural sciences; it "must not be with a reference to natural philosophy exclusively". But, he added a warning on Whewell's metaphysical inclinations: "But mind if you insist on german phraseology or anything like it I wash my hands of the job". Jones made it clear that he did not want to have anything to do with "neological friends who speak high dutch & think smoke" (TCC Add.Ms.c52/20, letter of 24 February 1831).[13]

To have written so directly to Whewell in 1831 must have been cathartic for Jones after so many years of having been flagellated by Whewell to write his book. Speculations aside, Whewell had shown over the years much more sympathy indeed for "this poor word metaphysics" – and even worse "necessary truth" – than Jones,[14] despite his expressed willingness to exchange it for something better. Even though they saw eye-to-eye on political economy for most of the 1820s and 1830s, a corresponding agreement of their views on induction never existed. Whewell moved in the 1830s from a more or less naïve Baconian position to what Menachem Fisch (1991, 75), for lack of a better term, labelled a "post-Kantian" one that found its expression in the *Philosophy of the Inductive Sciences* (1840) and for which Charles Sander Peirce invented the notion of "abduction". Not surprisingly, traces of this method existed before 1830, and they are now and then to be gathered from frictions on the subject of induction as they arise from the correspondence between Whewell and Jones.[15]

---

[13] Whewell was a master of casting neologisms. The movie *Jurassic Park* could not have been made without Whewell's labelling of the different geological strata. Many of his phrasings in Tidology (itself a word of Whewell's invention) are still in use, and, most well-known, he coined the words "anode" and "cathode".

[14] On Whewell's use of the phrasing "necessary truth" in his *Elementary Treatise on Mechanics*, Jones responded, in his first preserved letter (of 1 October 1819) in the archives, "will you fight?" (TCC Add.Ms.c.52/1). Whewell referred to metaphysics as this "poor word" in a letter of 16 August 1822 to Jones, from which I quoted previously (Whewell to Jones, 16 August 1822, in Todhunter 2:49).

[15] As Menachem Fisch has argued, Whewell only "hit upon" his theory of induction in 1834. See Fisch (1991, 99–100). For a critical account of Fisch's interpretation, see Becher (1992).

When Whewell published his *Philosophy of the Inductive Sciences*, the differences between them became manifest. Jones wrote disappointedly to John Herschel that they were the only true Baconians left. In his review of Herschel's book on the inductive method in the early 1830s, Whewell had carefully managed to evade all conflict with the opinions expressed therein, but it was apparent even then that Whewell did not think there was any law in the sciences to be obtained from mere fact-gathering only – a view much closer to Herschel and embraced by Jones. Taxonomies or classifications, important though they were, became more and more only a step to the discovery of causal dependency relations, rather than a goal in themselves as they were for Jones. Concepts, when properly presented, became guiding principles in the discovery of laws.

Thus, the famous example of the *vis viva* controversy, which had been degraded by d'Alembert as "un disput de mots", was for Whewell much more than that. Force served for Whewell as an organising principle of mechanics, and, hence, of invaluable help in the discovery of the laws of nature; and the *vis viva* controversy served to sort out the meaning of this crucial concept for the discipline. The same could be said of Kepler, for whom the concept of an ellipsis served as an organising principle of the data. Whewell would use the example of Kepler in later years to pinpoint the absurdity of John Stuart Mill's rendering of it as "only" performing "an act of description" (Whewell [1860] 1971, 247).[16]

Whewell's use of concepts as similar to Kantian categories, guiding research, made the differences with Richard Jones manifest. However, it also made him depart from his adherence in his days of study to the short-lived Analytical Society. Whewell initially supported the adoption of Lagrange's algebraic version of the calculus that defined subsequent derivatives of a function as successive coefficients of a Taylor series expansion. The greatest immediate gain of this shift was notational; Newton's tedious fluxional system of dots was replaced with the d's of Leibnizian differentials. As Babbage famously put it, the proposed title for the (first and only) *Memoir* of the Analytical Society should have been: "The Principle of pure D-ism in opposition to the Dot-age of the University" (quoted from Smith and Wise 1989, 154). Whewell became increasingly worried with the detachment of the algebraic version of the calculus from its physical interpretations, which

---

[16] See especially Hanson (1965) for an extensive analysis of the Mill–Whewell debate on Kepler.

fitted poorly with his adherence to an inductivist view of the natural sciences. He perceived Lagrangean algebra more and more as a storage system, a "pigeon-hole system of formal labels or tabs" (Fisch 1994, 272), only fit to make flawless deductions.[17] Because of their value as signs only, without any reference to a reality "out there", Whewell did not think Lagrangean algebra fit as an engine of discovery, as it was perceived by someone like Babbage, for example (Wise 1989b, 414).

In the 1830s, Whewell effectively abandoned algebra altogether and replaced it with the geometrically inclined mode of teaching mathematics that had been dominant in the Cambridge curriculum before the Analytical Society seriously shook up mathematics teaching. This withdrawal to earlier forms of mathematics is evidenced by his extensive inclusion of diagrams of pulleys and levers in his teaching books on mechanics. According to Whewell, discovery did not result from the mechanical application of a system of notation; it involved the genius and intuition of the scientist, which could only be developed by educating students in close connection to concrete physical problems.[18] Although Augustus De Morgan (who was himself trained as a mathematician by George Peacock at Cambridge) embodied Whewell's spirit in teaching mathematics at University College, London (Richards 1987; Pycior 1983), in terms of its content, his course in mathematics was based on French analysis and well ahead of the Cambridge Tripos (Rice 1996b). This issue will prove to be of importance when we turn to Jevons's engagements with symbolic algebra.

SAVING THE PHENOMENA

During the early 1830s, Whewell was taking extensive notes that would eventually lead to his three-volume *History of the Inductive Sciences* (1837), and to the "moral" of that seminal work, the *Philosophy of the Inductive Sciences* (1840), which would take another two volumes. In these notes, Whewell

---

[17] There is burgeoning literature on the reception of French mathematics in Britain that cannot be done sufficient justice here. On the "varieties" of French mathematics around 1800, see especially Grattan-Guinness (1990b) and for a stunning amount of scholarly detail Grattan-Guinness (1990a). For further references, see Chapter 1, footnote 13. From this secondary literature, it is clear that a detailed study of the developments of British algebra provides a potentially highly revealing background for the marginalist revolution in Britain, and this is not only with regard to Stanley Jevons.

[18] For more extensive accounts, see Becher (1981) and Fisch (1994).

3-1. William Whewell's types of progress of the sciences of 22 July 1831. From his notes taken in the early 1830 on induction (TCC R.18.17/15:40). Courtesy of the Master and Fellows of Trinity College, Cambridge.

considered various schemes of classifying the sciences that in time would yield his famous classification of the sciences in the *Philosophy*. These early schemes are highly revealing for how Whewell's thoughts on induction developed over the years, but, more importantly, they shed light on the problematic status of political economy as an inductive science. His notebooks described a scheme that distinguished between two different types of sciences: the sciences of observation and the sciences of experiments. Whewell's schematic outline of the inductive method for both types (see Figure 3-1) is rendered in Table 3-1.[19]

Just before this "orthodox Baconian" scheme (Fisch 1991, 78), Whewell considered a distinction between the sciences of natural history and experimental physics, with the "queen of the sciences" (astronomy) not fitting either of them. Though Whewell objected to the term "natural history", the type of sciences belonging to this category was more or less clear: botany, zoology, comparative anatomy, and mineralogy. The experimental sciences were mechanics, optics, "thermotics", electrics, magnetics, and chemistry.

---

[19] This table is also reproduced in Fisch (1991, 77–8). Fisch's discussion concentrates on the second row, which is of the most immediate relevance for the physical sciences.

Table 3-1. *Type of the Progress of Sciences – July 22. 1831*

Sciences of observation	– of experiments
1. Common observation and Collection of instances (natural objects and regular occurrences).	1. Common observation and Collection of instances (occasional occurrences).
2. *Decomposition of Phenomena* by Perception of analogies.	2. Decomposition of Phenomena by perception of simple connexions.
3. Classification and *nomenclature*.	3. Insulation of facts and *Terminology*.
4. *Systematic observation* and technical description of the facts.	4. *Systematic experiment* and measure[ment] of insulated facts.
5. Induction 1 *Propositions concerning classes.*	5. Induction 1 *Laws of phenomena.*
6. Induction 2 *Causes of Laws.*	6. Induction 2 *Causes of Laws.*

These two extremes had observations of natural objects or occasional occurrences of relations between objects as their respective subject. Astronomy did not fall in either category, since it dealt with regular occurrences, as did the sciences of meteorology and tidology, amongst others. A third scheme showed this three-way division explicitly (see Table 3-2).

We do not find any of what Whewell called the "subjective" sciences listed – sciences that dealt with mental phenomena like motives, passions, and the like. It was clear that Whewell had great difficulty in fitting these sciences into his inductive schemes. Indeed, as we have seen, one of Whewell's biggest disagreements with political economists was their claim to a separate entrance to the phenomena of the mind. There was no such entrance, as Whewell pointed out to Jones in correspondence. Whewell could not think of any particular method of enquiry of political economy, if not the

Table 3-2. *Classification of the Sciences*

Sciences of observation		– of experiment
Observation of Natural Objects –	Regular Occurrences –	Occasional occurrences
Botany	Astronomy	Mechanics
Zoology	Meteorology	Optics
Comparative Anatomy	Physiology	Thermotics
Geology	Comparative Physiology	Electrics
Mineralogy		Magnetics
		Chemistry

ordinary route of induction followed by the other sciences, "for there are no peculiar principles of observation and deduction employed in that science" (Whewell to Jones, 16 August 1822, in Todhunter 2:49). Exactly what the route of observation was in the subjective sciences, including political economy, had yet to be clarified. Before we turn to Whewell's attempt to apply his scheme 1 to political economy, let us first have a look at this scheme itself (see Table 3-1).

The left-hand side of the scheme can best be thought of as comprising those sciences that were commonly listed under natural history. The purpose of these sciences was to provide classifications that would save the phenomena in their proper place. Their way of dealing with objects was by means of analogy. Analogies might help establish appropriate classes; they might also point at distinctive features of natural objects that might give reason to put them in one or the other class. The sciences of natural history did not look at relations between objects in the sense of a dependency relation; rather, the purpose was to establish the existence of a class or a classification. In the last instance, a cause might be found that produced the class or classification. Whewell's considerations on the inductive processes as applied to natural history thus clearly fit in with his endeavours in the *Bridgewater Treatise* to show the conformity of science and religion. By showing the order in nature, insight was gained into God's providential order.

Sciences like zoology and botany, exemplars of natural history, were clearly distinct from the experimental sciences in that they did not search for relations of dependency that might eventually be expressed in "laws of phenomena". The experimental sciences, including astronomy and meteorology, did so. The obvious problem of the scheme was that sciences dealing with regular occurrences, like astronomy, dealt with "connexions" – that is, with (causal) dependency relations – rather than with analogies leading to appropriate classifications, something that comes out clearly from scheme 3 (see Table 3-2). They proceeded therefore to laws of phenomena and causes of these laws, which in scheme 1 were part of the inductive process of the experimental sciences.

As Whewell explained, laws of phenomena stated the *form* of a dependency relation, but they did not give the cause for it. The relation of Kepler's laws to Newton's theory of gravity may again serve as an example. Kepler was able to describe the orbits of the planets as ellipses (law of phenomena), but did not state why these revolutions should be so. Newton's theory of universal gravity did, and Newton advanced from the laws of phenomena (stage 5 on the right-hand side of Table 3-1) to knowledge of the causes of these laws (stage 6).

In the experimental sciences, issues of quantification and measurement were involved that were not there in natural history. To determine the dependency relation of a variable on a variant, the scientist needed measurements that could be plotted in a grid (or tabulated) so that an inference could be drawn as to the form of the relationship. In the *Philosophy of the Inductive Sciences*, Whewell listed a range of instruments that the quantitative sciences had in their possession: "the *Methods of Curves*, the *Method of Means*, the *Method of Least Squares*, and the *Method of Residues*".

We can say, then, that both types of sciences, of observation and of experiment, or the sciences of natural history and the experimental sciences, including astronomy and meteorology, "saved the phenomena", but in different ways. Whereas natural history aimed at the classification of natural objects and thus gave them their natural place in the order of nature, the experimental sciences aimed at establishing the form and ultimately the cause of the relation between objects (whether naturally or artificially [experimentally] produced). We will see in more detail in later chapters how Whewell used his just-mentioned "instruments" for this purpose and how Jevons made similar use of them, especially the methods of means and graphs.

In relation to political economy, it makes a difference whether one perceives it as part of natural history or as part of the experimental sciences. In the first case, it may, like botany or zoology, strive at taxonomies, and this is clearly how Richard Jones perceived political economy. If it is an experimental science, it strives at dependency relations, or even causal explanations of these relations.

Now it is clear that political economists (not just Ricardians) aimed at the explanations of causal relations and not at taxonomies, but it was clear as well that its claimed route of induction via introspection was not the ordinary one as was followed in sciences like chemistry, electrics, or mechanics. Introspection, by all means, did not make use of the sort of instruments used in these sciences.

If introspection was rejected as a viable means of induction, and it was rejected by Whewell and Jones alike, political economy should have its place as a taxonomic science. Or, alternatively, it should be able to isolate "laws of phenomena" from statistical data, in ways similar to those of astronomy and

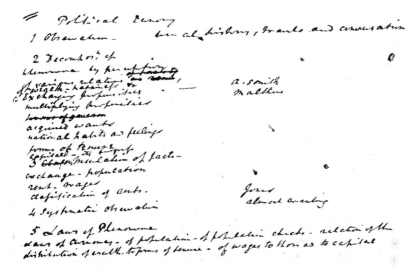

3-2. William Whewell's inductive scheme for political economy. From his notes taken in the early 1830s on induction (TCC R.18.17/15:41). Courtesy of the Master and Fellows of Trinity College, Cambridge.

meteorology. The question then is, and it haunted all debates on the method of political economy through the Victorian age, how to apply the quantitative methods discerned by Whewell – averages, graphs, least squares – to the phenomena of the mind.

POLITICAL ECONOMY AS AN INDUCTIVE SCIENCE

Let me now turn to the application Whewell made of Table 3-1 to political economy. It was clear to Whewell that political economy fell somewhere between the "subjective" and the "objective" sciences: "Many of its ... facts are external (statistical and commercial details). Some internal (motives, happiness & virtue, vice & misery)" (R.18.17/15: 46). This provoked an ambiguity as to the kinds of methods that could be used to make inductive inferences in political economy.

Whewell's inductive scheme for political economy (see Figure 3-2) is rendered in Table 3-3. As might be expected, especially in 1831, Whewell's attempt to fit political economy into his scheme of induction shows heavy traces of the influence of Richard Jones. Adam Smith and Thomas Malthus are only listed as "decomposers" of phenomena, while Jones reaches a higher

Table 3-3. *Induction in Political Economy*

Political economy	
1. Observation	... history, tracts and conversation
2. Decomposition of phenomena by perception of various relations of wealth – happiness Exchanging propensities multiplying propensities acquired wants national habits and feeling forms of tenure capital – its progress	– a. smith malthus
3. Insulation of facts – exchange – population rent – wages classification of rents	Jones
4. Systematic Observation	almost wanting
5. Laws of Phenomena Laws of currencies – of population – of population checks – relation of the distribution of wealth to forms of tenure – of wages to those as to capital	

stage of induction with his classification of rents. The various ways in which political economists made observations reflect the way Richard Jones had collected his own material, greatly helped by Whewell's search for pamphlets and tracts in political economy, as the scheme even reminds us of the casual conversations Whewell had with farmers on the rent scheme in Cambridgeshire. Although far from compelling from a modern point of view, it does show how little quantification was involved in Whewell's thoughts on political economy in the early 1830s. Like the sciences of natural history, political economy was considered to have its goals in the appropriate classification schemes of social orderings, and it was indeed in these terms that Whewell discussed the inductive method of political economy when Jones first presented part of the manuscript for his book to him.

Whewell pointed out to Jones how he could reorder the introduction so that his rendering of the inductive method could be clearly set against the false inductions and premature deductions of the Ricardians. While "the modern economists ... jump ... from one or two trivial facts to the conclusion that every man will get as much money as he can, an axioma generallissimum", Jones followed the appropriate method of "gradation of general principles" – a method that would eventually find its way in the *Philosophy of the Inductive Sciences*.

> The *primary facts* are the condition of such persons as are taken for specimens of particular classes in different countries – The *first generalization* is the characteristic description of the state of society and property in each country; and your original writers and authorities have very often made this step of induction for themselves and give you the facts as subordinated to it – the *next generalization* is *your* classification of the different kinds of rent, which step distinguishes you from the anticipators.
> (all quotes TCC Add.Ms.c51/93, letter of 7 December 1830)

The principal use of the method of gradation was to distinguish sharply between different classes. The sort of observations used here were of various sorts; some quantitative, most not. Whewell perceived the purpose and limits of Jones's work in political economy in that Jones produced a classification of clearly distinct economic orderings. He did not proceed to its causes, that is, the general moral order. Jones's classification scheme saved the phenomena, but did not explain them.

Yet, Whewell's scheme of induction combines elements from the observational sciences with those of experiment. The "insulation of facts" is listed, and this was an important step in the experimental sciences to determine what should be listed upon the axes of a grid so that a dependency relation – a "law of the phenomena" – might be found. We see Whewell enumerating various relations for which such laws of the phenomena might be derived, but we find no names of political economists who might have attempted to derive such relations in ways that were acceptable to Whewell. Indeed, for steps 4 and 5 of the inductive process, practical examples are "almost wanting" or absent.

Given the dominance of Ricardian economics, this hardly comes as a surprise. While Dugald Stewart had actively degraded the relevance of statistical data in the search for laws of political economy, Ricardians seemed to agree that statistical data, as "insulated facts", were unfit for the inference to laws just because they did not do justice to the complexity of concrete historical events. Statistical data might have been gathered for practical purposes – and they were – but not for the purpose of "systematic observation" in Whewell's sense, let alone for the inference to laws of phenomena. Hence, Ricardo's laws were only true in the abstract, not in the concrete.

It appears then that Whewell wavered between two modes of induction in political economy: the one striving towards a scheme of classification and the other deriving "laws of phenomena" from an avalanche of statistical data – that is, the form of a dependency relation between two variables. The first saved the phenomena by properly rubricating them, the other by heading them under an explanatory law. In the 1830s, Whewell moved to give this second mode of induction priority in all of the sciences. In his *Philosophy of the Inductive Sciences*, the ultimate aim of all sciences became to find the laws of phenomena and their explanatory causes.

Whewell was at a loss, however, as to how political economy might make the leap from systematic collection of data to the derivation of laws of phenomena. His attempts to frame the inductive steps for political economy only sparsely found their way into the *Philosophy of the Inductive Sciences*. Here, the mixed character of political economy, of being a "subjective" and to some extent an "objective" science, worked against it. Whewell was clear about the "modes of aiding the induction of laws of phenomena, when the connexions have been insulated". In those cases, the "*form*" of the law could be determined, and following on this its cause. Whewell listed "averages – tables – curves" as means in support so that "*numerical expressions*" of these relations could be derived, just those methods he treated more extensively in the *Philosophy of the Inductive Sciences* as those methods that were of special help in the quantitative sciences. At this stage, Whewell did not consider political economy as a quantitative science – that is, as a science whose objects could be measured. For the "subjective sciences as opposed to the objective", it was hardly possible "to discover a *law of phenomena* but by a perception of its cause" (R.18.17/15:41b–42). The difficulty was induced by the fact that the causes in the "subjective sciences" were "facts of consciousness", and there was no obvious way to objectively observe these facts in the same way as facts of "external objects" – indeed, the very concept seemed to exclude the possibility. Even though many of the facts of political economy were "external (statistical and commercial details)", its classificatory concepts, like "wealth, property, exchange, relations of social life", were "mixed" (R.18.17/15:46). Unequivocal observation, let alone quantification, therefore seemed impossible. This was needed to turn political economy into a genuine science of regularities.

Of course, political economists filled in this gap with their recourse to introspection as a viable means of induction. This recourse was condemned improper as jumping to conclusions from casual (internal) observations. It is therefore illuminating to see what was left out of the inductive scheme for political economy altogether; there was no inductive step from the "laws of phenomena" to the causes of these laws, as in fact the scheme practically stopped with Jones's work. The highest point of induction political economy was able to reach was classifying facts. Introspection, however, jumped to the last stage – the causes of laws – and then deductively worked backwards to the tendency laws of political economy. These tendency laws obviously did not cover all that we find listed in Whewell's scheme – indeed, most of the items listed were not considered relevant to political economy at all and slowly came to be considered part of another science, that is, the science of man in the social state – history – and following on Comte, sociology.

In his practical endeavours in political economy, Whewell proved much more flexible than is apparent from the view on induction depicted here. Indeed, he highlighted just those tools and methods (averages, tables, graphs) that were of so much use in the experimental sciences. An example of Whewell's liberal appraisal of methods was his favourable reference to a table on marriages and birthrates from his former student Lubbock. The table did not show isolated facts, but showed the "dependence of the increase of population upon the number of marriages and the number of births per marriage, and vice versa". As a consequence, it showed "how any alteration in one portion of these elements of the law of population would affect the others" and was therefore of much use in giving insight in the "mathematics of population", making "many of Malthus's statistical details" more obvious than they appeared now (TCC Add.Ms.c.51/67, letter of 28 January 1829 to Jones).

Another example was his interest in a table of corn prices and shortages of supply originating from Gregory King, commonly referred to today by historians of economics as the King Davenant table. Whewell played on several occasions with this table, which he took to establish at least roughly an inverse relationship between prices and demand. He used the table in his mathematical exposition of the Ricardian theory of rent. In his first mathematical paper in economics, Whewell considered that "it would be easy to find the law by which the increase in supply may depend on the defect and the square of the defect of supply, so as nearly to satisfy the above data" (1830, 201). But this and his later explorations in this search for functional form were ignored or criticized as of no use by political economists and statisticians alike, as will be seen.

As a final example, we note his approval of the use Sir Edward West made of a curve in which the price of corn was plotted against time, in an anti-Ricardian pamphlet on corn prices and wage rates. Perhaps referring to this curve, Whewell addressed the usefulness of curves in the establishment of dependency relations in political economy in his *Philosophy of the Inductive Sciences*.

All of these examples, some of which will be discussed in more detail later, show Whewell approving tools and methods of research in political economy that might be useful to derive "laws of phenomena" from quantitative data, and thus fill the most important missing link between the collection of data and the establishment of causal claims. Whewell did not pursue his examples, or only did so (as in the case of the King Davenant table) in the negative context of showing the absurdities and flaws of Ricardian economics. These attacks, cloaked in the language of mathematics, were generally ignored by Whewell's contemporaries.

It is clear that Jones was much less "sanguine" about the use of such tools in political economy than Whewell. Jones, who in his younger years had been "as mad about functions as Babbage", did not consider the tools and methods of the experimental sciences relevant to political economy. He was more than willing to restrict his pursuits in political economy to the development of appropriate schemes of classification. The divergence in their opinions will prove to be of importance when turning to the establishment of section F of the BAAS and the Statistical Society of London, respectively.

Section F of the BAAS and the Statistical Society of London

Whewell's political disagreement with Ricardian economics was an important impetus to organise countervailing forces. The BAAS was not just a neutral institution, but expressly designed to diffuse the message of science's neutrality, without affecting the order of society, and Whewell sought similar institutional support in the case of political economy. Whewell's efforts focussed of consequence on method, not on political content. His aim was to replace the deductive approach of the Ricardians by a science of political economy, based on induction (Henderson 1996, 29). The details of Whewell's endeavours have been extensively examined by Hilts (1978), Cannon (1978), Goldman (1983), and recently by Henderson (1996).

As one of the most important "spin doctors" of early Victorian university politics, Whewell knew how to use his central place in the scientific community to organise an institutional forum for his projected change. Whewell's prolific scientific and social activities at Cambridge University in general and Trinity College in particular made him the perfect man to convince his friend Adam Sedgwick – president of the BAAS in 1833 and like Whewell a fellow of Trinity College – that a statistical section should be added to the BAAS which would be "devoted to mathematics and facts, not social rabble-rousing" (Henderson 1996, 31, quoting Sedgwick).

Whewell had bullied Jones over the years to work harder and produce more pages of his book on political economy instead of tantalising himself on his shortcomings and leaving the subject to the "rotten, pseudo-political-economists" who had been "driving tandem with one jack-ass before the other" (Add.Ms.c.51/41, letter of 10 September 1827). When this "Euridice of Political Economy" finally appeared in 1831, Whewell actively organised reviews of it – some self-written – and sent the book to a broad audience, including Malthus and the Ricardian enemies as well. As might have been expected, it received a very negative review from McCulloch, one of the most devoted and ardent Ricardians, but it was greeted favourably by Whewell's close colleagues and friends in Cambridge, Sedgwick, Herschel, and Babbage. It was certainly instrumental in convincing Sedgwick that something scientific could be done in the inductive way of enquiry in the field of political economy.

Whewell's and Jones's chance came in 1833, when a group consisting of Whewell, Jones, Malthus, and Babbage invited Adolphe Quetelet to attend the meeting of the BAAS, to persuade the BAAS to install the so-called section F, devoted to political economy and statistics.[20] To allay the fears and objections of section A – the mathematics and physics section – that some sort of political party would be added to the BAAS, the new section was explicitly restricted in its research to the collection of facts that could be expressed in numbers and that eventually might indicate general laws.

---

[20] Accounts of the actual course of affairs are not all consistent, some giving more weight to the importance of Babbage's interventions, some more to those of Whewell and Jones. The first version is largely based on later written notices of Babbage on the subject. Since Babbage is not particularly known for his modesty, and since the correspondence between Whewell and Jones clearly shows they discussed the matter in advance, the last version is the more credible.

Indeed, statistical "objects, whether of pure or mixed nature" that were "capable of being reduced to measurement and calculation", were "legitimate objects of our enquiry", Sedgwick clarified the purposes and limitations of section F to the BAAS (Hilts 1978, 34, quoting Sedgwick). This restriction met with the full consent of Whewell, who was as fearful for the intrusion of opinion in the field of science as was the audience. As an offspring, the Statistical Society of London was founded in 1834.

Although roughly the same group of people was involved, Whewell's presence was felt much less and Richard Jones's much more in the second case than in the first. Jones designed the classification of subjects for the Statistical Society, that was then accepted in modified form, and the prospectus of the Society was signed by him, Babbage, Drinkwater, and Hallam (see Table 3-4).[21]

This prospectus reveals an important distinction in the plan of operations of the Statistical Society of London from that of section F: While the BAAS document made mention of the establishment of laws, this reference completely vanished in the prospectus of the Statistical Society. The Society, it read, should "exclude all Opinions from its transactions and publications [and] confine its attention rigorously to facts – and, as far as may be found possible, to facts which can be stated numerically and arranged in tables" (Newmarch 1869, 386). That was it. There followed an enumeration of the classes of facts to which the enquiries of the Society should be limited. The emphasis of the Statistical Society was from the very start on proper classification of facts rather than deriving laws – dependency relations – from them, as was the case for section F.

In his account of the history of the Statistical Society, Mouat (1885) emphasised that this strict limitation to the gathering of facts in tabulated form was motivated by Whewell's fear of the "daemon" of opinion and discord.[22] This certainly may have been the case. The limitation to fact-gathering only, rather than using these facts as building blocks in an inductive search for the laws of political economy, was contrary to Whewell's intentions. However, as Hilts (1978) points out, it was exactly this limitation which made the Statistical Society an acceptable forum for widely different audiences.

---

[21] For details on these statistics classifications, see Henderson (1996).
[22] Mouat wrongly considered Whewell to be the president of the BAAS in 1833, as his quotation from Whewell's speech is actually from Sedgwick.

Table 3-4. *The original classification systems proposed by Richard Jones, then adopted by the Statistical Society of London*

JONES'S PROPOSAL	ADOPTED BY THE STATISTICAL SOCIETY OF LONDON
	The whole subject [of subdivisions] was considered, by the Statistical Section of the British Association at Cambridge, as admitting a division into four great classes:
	1. ECONOMICAL STATISTICS 2. POLITICAL STATISTICS 3. MEDICAL STATISTICS 4. MORAL AND INTELLECTUAL STATISTICS
	If these four classes are taken as the basis of a further analysis, it will be found that the class of
Economical Statistics: 1. agriculture, 2. manufactures, 3. commerce & currency, 4. distribution of wealth, i.e. rent, wages, & profits	*Economical Statistics* comprehend, 1st, the statistics of natural productions and the agricultural nations; 2ndly, of manufactures; 3rdly, of commerce and currency; 4thly, of the distribution of wealth, or all facts relating to rent, wages, profits, &c.
Political Statistics: 1. statistics of elements of institutions, jurors-electors-&c., 2. legal statistics-number of national & local tribunals, nature of coureses tried &c. &c., 3. finance-taxes, expenditures, public establishments &c. &c.	*Political Statistics* furnish three subdivisions: 1st, the facts relating to the elements of political institutions, the number of electors, jurors, &c.; 2ndly, legal statistics; 3rdly, the statistics of finance and of national expenditure, and of civil and military establishments.
Medical Statistics: 1. general medical statistics, 2. population (the doctors say they shall want subdivisions).	*Medical Statistics*, strictly so called, will require at least two subdivisions; and the great subject of population, although it might be classed elsewhere, yet touches medical statistics on so many points, that it would be placed most conveniently, perhaps, in this division, and would constitute a third subdivision.
Moral & Intellectual statistics: 1. crime, 2. education & literature, 3. ecclesiastical statistics (Jones to Whewell in the Whewell Papers Collection, TCC Add. Mss. C. 52/60).	*Moral and Intellectual Statistics* comprehend, 1st, the statistics of literature; 2ndly, of education; 3rdly, of religious instruction and ecclesiastical institutions; 4thly, of crime. Although fourteen subdivisions have now been enumerated, it is probable that more will be required (*Report... British Association* 1833, 492-93)

Source: Table 2.1 James Henderson 1996, p. 36.

These audiences were all in attendance at the formal founding meeting in London. Some 250 people were present, among them members of the nobility, statesmen, businessmen, leading political economists, and men of science. Measured in these terms, it was an overwhelming success, forming quite a contrast with the "irregular" foundation of section F and the small group surrounding Jones and Whewell. All of these different audiences had different agendas, however, some not at all devoted to the purposes of science as perceived by Whewell. A strong impetus in the demand for statistics came from businessmen, (local) administrators, and statesmen who needed them for practical policy purposes. The very idea of using statistics for ready-made policy prescriptions was far off Whewell's intentions. The exclusion of "opinions" in the pursuits of the Society seemingly prevented this, but in fact encouraged an opportunistic handling of the data for political purposes.

Contrary to the intentions of both Jones and Whewell, the restriction to fact-gathering only made the Society more accessible and acceptable for political economists like Nassau Senior and John McCulloch – who Whewell and Jones had typified as the worst of what could happen to political economy. It would be wrong to think that Senior or McCulloch were uninterested in statistical data. Senior, for example, withdrew for the chair in political economy at King's College, London, to become a member of the better-paid Poor Law Committee. For this purpose, statistical data were clearly relevant, only these data did not relate to the "truths" of political economy. In correspondence with Quetelet, Nassau Senior even went so far as to claim that he did "not consider the truths of political economy" to depend on "statistical facts" (Cullen 1975). Similarly, in the early 1830s McCulloch was one of the leading statisticians, only his statistical pursuits did not at all affect his zealous defence of Ricardian economics. The first volume of the *Transactions* (the later *Journal*) of the Society expressed the division of labour between political economy and statistics explicitly:

> The Science of Statistics differs from Political Economy, because, although it has the same end in view, it does not discuss causes, nor reason upon probable facts; it seeks to collect, arrange, and compare, that class of facts which alone can form the basis of correct conclusions with respect to social and political government.
>
> (*JSSL* 1838, 1)

When Whewell published his *Philosophy of the Inductive Sciences*, his small remarks on the possible usefulness for political economy of methods used in the experimental sciences, including of course astronomy, went easily unnoticed in its 1,400-plus pages. The Statistical Society of London had settled down on gathering data in tabulated form as its sole and primary task, as it had been formulated in its prospectus. Nothing much came from the possibility that was left open in the constituency act of section F – that statistical data might be used to uncover the laws of society. The logo of the Statistical Society of London (that had been selected by Charles Babbage) – a loosely bound weathsheaf with the words *Aliis Exterendum* – precisely expressed the self-imposed restriction to the collection and classification of beautiful numbers, preferably stated in tabular form, and excluding all reference to opinions. There was no link to theory, which was left to Ricardian political economy.

In practice, and in contrast with the original intentions, papers presented at section F, as well as at the Statistical Society, all too easily jumped to preconceived policy prescriptions on the basis of data that did not bear scrutiny. Jones and Babbage soon lost interest in the Society, and Whewell became so annoyed with the sort of papers produced and the political upheaval they occasionally brought about that he seriously regretted the establishment of section F and considered possibilities for its abolishment when he was president of the BAAS in 1841. In his opening address as president of section F in 1860, Nassau Senior also expressed his disappointment and concern with the "unscientific character of many" of the papers produced (JSSL 1860, 357). Statistics was turned into the "rabble-rousing" Whewell had so feared.

Whewell's failure to establish a viable counterweight against Ricardian economics can be traced to the different purposes that were set for section F and the Statistical Society of London, respectively, as well as to his own wavering in the way political economy should proceed to inductively establish what he called the "laws of the phenomena". Whewell considered two different modes of induction that were not readily compatible, one in line with the classificatory approach of natural history and the other in line with searching for causal dependencies, as pursued in the experimental sciences – including astronomy and meteorology. Whewell was not able to bring either of these notions effectively into play against the Ricardians. When John

Stuart Mill self-confidently proclaimed the recourse to introspection as the only fully legitimate mode of inductive enquiry in the moral sciences, including political economy, Whewell had little rebuttal.

Coda

Let me return to the antagonism between the two most important philosophers on induction in Victorian England: Whewell and Mill, not so much to further discuss their respective views on the subject, as to see where Mill gained and Whewell lost. It was generally considered one of the great advantages of Mill's *Logic* (1843) that he devoted a separate book to the methods of the moral sciences, that is, including political economy. Whewell, we have seen, denied any separate method but was unable to show how the scientist might reach back from statistical data to this most enigmatic of causes: human motives. Mill triumphed by expressly and explicitly advocating introspection as a legitimate tool, indeed as legitimate as the "ordinary methods of observation and experiment" in the natural sciences. Even Whewell finally conceded: "In Mental and Social Science, we are much less likely than in Physical Science, to obtain new truths by any process which can be distinctively termed *Induction*; and that in those sciences, what may be called *Deductions* from principles of thought and action of which we are already conscious ... must have a large share; and I may add, that this observation of Mr. Mill appears to me to be important, and in its present connexion, new" (Whewell, [1860] 1971, 285).

To this staggering statement of Whewell, after all his disdain for the comedy of errors of political economists, we may add his reception of Mill's *Principles.* One of Mill's central tenets was that, if social circumstances were different, it might well be that the tendency laws of political economy were in need of qualification – this, however, without altering the substance of these laws themselves.[23] There was a universal nature of man (selfish) expressing itself differently in different social settings. Mill's allowances were sufficient to silence critics like Jones and Whewell, as they were necessary to fence off the tendency laws of economic theory from history's complexity. Indeed, with the publication of Mill's *Principles*, which Jones and Whewell

---

[23] In my view, none of the examples provided in Hollander and Peart (1999) convincingly show that Mill at any point seriously questioned the fundamental laws of political economy.

admitted they enjoyed reading and could not find much to be opposed to, Ricardianism attained a status that all but flattened debate on the subject and method of political economy for decades to come. The distinction between the science and the art of political economy made it all the more easy for economic theorists to consider statistics as not bearing on the "laws of political economy".

In the *Logic* and in the *Principles of Political Economy*, Mill could thus easily acknowledge Jones's criticism of Ricardian economics that its conclusions were only fit for the British case, and not for other countries where, for example, "the almost universal landlord is the state, as in India". But Mill relegated these peculiarities to the "empirical laws" of political economy, or even to his "science of ethology" that should take account of the characteristics of different people and nations. On Mill's account, statistical data could not alter the fundamental truth of the tendency laws of the political economists. For John Stuart Mill, Jones's book was merely a "copious repertory of valuable facts" – as Whewell noted, a most effective way to discredit an author's claim to be of theoretical value (quoted from Rashid 1979, 169). This "curious separation between abstract theory and empirical work" (Blaug 1976) found, we have seen, much support among political economists and statisticians. In the middle decades of the nineteenth century, Ricardian economics reigned supreme and was unaffected by the fact-gathering of the statisticians.

FOUR

◠

MIMETIC EXPERIMENTS

"A Fool, Mr. Edgeworth, is one who has never made an experiment".
Such are, I believe, the exact words of a remark which Erasmus
Darwin addressed to Richard Lovell Edgeworth. They deserve to be-
come proverbial.

William Stanley Jevons, *Experimental Legislation
and the Drink Traffic*

HUMBOLDTIAN SCIENCE

In a brilliant essay (1978), Susan Faye Cannon wrote that "if you find a 19th-
century scientist mapping or graphing his data, chances are good you have
found a Humboldtian". Cannon framed this notion of a Humboldtian to
indicate that many early-nineteenth-century scientists did not fit the image
of naïve Baconian data-gathering, despite their proclaimed adherence to
Bacon's inductivism. Rather, these scientists formed hypotheses in a loose
way from the data, making use of as wide a range of tools and instruments
as possible, with the aim to derive general conclusions – "laws".

The Humboldtian scientist, in Cannon's account, combines the use of
techniques like graphs and maps with a vivid interest in scientific instruments. He does not reserve all these methods and tools to the laboratory, but
applies them to the complex variety of real phenomena, whether they belong
to the physical, biological, or human world. Without insisting on the label Humboldtian scientist – though definitely more cosmopolitan in sound
than the British proxy of a Victorian polymath – it is of use in pinpointing
a type of scientist highly interested in precise and accurate measurements,
not for the sake of itself, but to derive general laws from them, preferably in
mathematical form.

As we will see, Jevons fits this image, as does Whewell to some extent. For Whewell, we may think of his investigations in geology, crystallography, or tidology. We may also think of Whewell's journey with George Biddell Airy, the later Astronomer Royal, to Cornwall for making experiments with a pendulum at Dalcoath Mine to measure the density of the Earth, experiments he considered unsuccessful "in consequence of a rascally piece of steel deviating 1/10,000th of an inch from a straight line" (Todhunter 2:93, letter of 9 September 1828, to Richard Jones). Finally, we may think of his early correspondence with Richard Jones, where he wrote about a trip he planned to the Lake District, to the mountains of Cumberland and Westmoreland. He had lived there in his younger years without ever setting a foot in them. But now this would be all different:

> You have no idea of the variety of different uses to which I shall turn a mountain – after perhaps sketching it from the bottom I shall climb to the top & measure its height by the barometer, knock off a piece of rock with a geological hammer to see what it is made of, and then evolve some quotation from Wordsworth into the still air above. He has got some passages where he has tumbled the names of those hills together till his verses sound like the warning of the sea or like a conjunction which would call the spirits of them from their dens.
> (Todhunter 2:43, letter of 4 August 1821, from Whewell to Jones)

A variety of different uses, indeed – displaying the breadth of Whewell's endeavours in the sciences and in the humanities – which in Whewell's case all seemed to be kept together by a firm confidence in the unity of nature and the spirit of God's creation. In the same letter, Whewell censured the vested "academical professors" for being "so slow in abandoning what is obsolete everywhere else" that they resemble "very obstinate artillery-men" who "stand by their guns even after they have been spiked" (Todhunter 2:44).

Jevons shared in the enquiring spirit that is expressed in these words, as he shared in their boldness. However, as we have seen, Whewell only loosely hinted at ways to apply the methods of the sciences to political economy that he considered more as a form of natural history applied to society than as an experimental science, or a science of "regular occurrences", like astronomy or meteorology. This was the move Jevons would make. At first sight, it may seem obvious that economics could learn from sciences like astronomy or meteorology. With both being sciences of regularities, searching for averages and means among the multitude of data – using graphical and mapping techniques to search for regularities – may provide an obvious connection.

The previous chapter served to undermine the self-evidence of this idea. As long as political economists used introspection to access their first principles, quantitative tools of enquiry did not come into view. And neither did they, in any consistent way, for Whewell, who thought of political economy as a taxonomical science rather than a science of regularities. Political economy turned into a natural science when this distinction between taxonomical sciences and sciences of regularities lost its relevance. Mechanical analogies played an important role in this process, as we will see in Jevons's work. Mechanical analogies were crucial to replace introspective evidence and enabled Jevons to think of political economy as a natural science (like meteorology) using the same tools and methods of enquiry. For those instances in which observations escape control, mechanical analogies mimic the mechanism that is assumed, but remains hidden to the eye. In political economy, mechanical analogies replaced the trust and reliance that was put in introspection.

This chapter will look at an instance of Jevons's early investigations in meteorology in which observations equally escape control: the formation of clouds. When Jevons turned his attention to political economy, in the second half of his stay in Australia, he took the tools and methods he had used in his meteorological pursuits with him, deciding to resurrect political economy on what he considered a firm scientific basis.

Naming the Clouds

Clouds had become something of a hot topic in the beginning of the nineteenth century, when an essay by Luke Howard, a Quaker dissenter, presented in 1802 to the Askesian Society and then published in *A Journal of Natural Philosophy, Chemistry, and the Arts* of 1803, transformed clouds from indefinable objects into objects that could be classified into a scheme of three basic forms or "modifications" and their combinations (on Howard, see especially Richard Hamblyn 2001). Even though Howard's Latin names initially met with resistance, they had a certain poetic appeal, which was enforced by the skilful water colourings that accompanied the text (Figure 4-1).

The ensuing debate on Howard's classification scheme was settled by the intervention of one of the towering poets and natural philosophers of

4-1. Luke Howard's clouds, showing (a) "different appearances of the cirrus", (b) a "regular cumulus" and (c) a "stratus occupying a valley at sunset". From Luke Howard, "On the Modification of Clouds and on the Principles of their Production, Suspension, and Destruction", *Journal of Natural Philosophy, Chemistry, and the Arts*, 1803, 17:3–32.

the era, no lesser than Goethe, who honoured Howard's naming of the clouds:

> But Howard gives us with his clearer mind
> The gain of lessons new to all mankind;
> That which no hand can reach, no hand can clasp,
> He first has gain'd, first held with mental grasp.
> Defin'd the doubtful, fix'd its limit-line,
> And named it fitly. – Be the honour thine!
> As clouds ascent, are folded, scattered, fall,
> Let the world think of thee who taught it all.

Howard's "modifications of the clouds" was considered a contribution to natural history in the first place. Howard not only gave a "natural history of clouds" (the title of one of his essays on the subject), but he also proposed an explanation of the manner in which clouds were formed, combined, transformed to another type, and disappeared.

Most of what Howard had to say on this transformation of clouds into other forms, or their combination, was descriptive rather than explanatory. He had some ideas about the initial process by which clouds were formed. It seemed obvious that clouds had something to do with condensation and therefore with temperature differences in the air. It was another thing entirely to explain from this exactly how the basic forms of clouds came to differ from one another. Howard considered differences in temperature and electricity the two principal factors involved in the formation of the clouds. The formation of a cloud followed the evaporation of water, combined with "caloric" as an invisible gas into the air. Howard referred to John Dalton's theory of heat in which "caloric" was considered as an elastic fluid surrounding atoms. In accordance with the "specific heat" of different types of atoms – that is, their capacity to bind heat – caloric would move from the one to the other atom. Dalton distinguished "specific heat" from the "specific gravity" of the atoms. He also distinguished between heat and temperature. Hence, to raise the temperature of different types of materials with the same amount required different amounts of heat, depending on their differences in "specific heat".

Using Dalton's ideas, Howard argued as follows: After the initial evaporation of water, the vapour subsequently "decomposed" into small particles of water due to the air's greater "affinity . . . to caloric". Depending on the temperature of the air, a dense cloud might be immediately formed or the water particles might form a cloud "by simple aggregation, or by electrical attraction". The specific form of a cloud had something to do with differences in temperature between different layers of air in the atmosphere. This was the case with a stratus, the horizontally layered cloud we also know as fog when it touches the ground (Figure 4-1, cloud c). Differences of temperature between different layers of air were also involved in the horizontal basis of a cumulus. When temperature inequalities disappeared, Howard argued in line with Dalton's theory, clouds disappeared as well.

With Howard's classification, interest in clouds increased rapidly in late Georgian and Victorian England. Artistic circles used his classification to study how to paint clouds most effectively, as witnessed from John Constable's use of Howard's essays. John Ruskin, in *Modern Painters*, would also pay reverence to his work (see Hamblyn 2001; Anderson 2003).

Once classified, clouds gained increasing attention from experimental scientists. The young Jevons was no exception. On his long voyage from England to Australia, we find many descriptions of beautiful clouds in his diary, and he occasionally made sketches of them. He took his notebook, barometer, and camera with him on his travels through the Australian wilderness, making numerous meteorological observations and sketches of cumuli and thunderclouds, of which the best example is found in his account of a two-week journey to the gold diggings at Sofala that was preceded with thirty pages of temperature and barometer readings.

However, the most intriguing thing he did was, in line with his training and great interest in experimental science, to "bring clouds to the laboratory", to use a phrase of Galison and Assmus (1989; see also Galison 1997).

MIMICKING NATURE

Whewell classified meteorology as occupying a middle ground between the observational and experimental sciences. It dealt with regularities, regular occurrences of events, yet it did not possess the means to isolate causal relationships in the same manner as the experimental sciences. Careful observation, using instruments like the barometer and the thermometer (for the difficulties surrounding their use and reliability, see on the thermometer especially Chang 2001), and searching for an appropriate nomenclature were all part and parcel of meteorology at the beginning of the nineteenth century, very much like Whewell himself had practised geology and then tidology, where we still make use of some of Whewell's ingenious neologisms. As tidology was obviously closely related to astronomy, meteorological investigations were equally driven to not only classify, but also to discover the laws governing the phenomena. Just as Whewell attempted to discover regularities in the multitude of observations, meteorologists turned to averages and ever more refined measuring devices to discover causal dependency relations. Howard's contribution to meteorology was, however, generally considered to be a contribution to "natural classification" and not an explanation of cloud formation.

The fact that Howard's classification of the clouds appealed equally to natural scientists and artistic circles can be attributed to one of the characteristics of natural history itself – namely that it should do justice to the complexity of nature; that is, the schemes and classifications the scientists invented should fit nature perfectly. Whewell considered Howard's naming of the clouds as a scheme of natural classification, because it fitted nature well. Constable and Ruskin were also enthusiastic, basically for the same reason.

In a fascinating article on Charles Wilson's cloud chamber, Galison and Assmus (1989; and more extensively Galison 1997) show how the distinction between the sciences of natural history and the experimental sciences gradually changed during the nineteenth century. Although they use a different terminology, their distinction between abstract scientists and morphological scientists covers rather well the nineteenth-century distinction between experimental sciences and the sciences of natural history.

Following their terminology, "abstract" scientists aimed to extract universal laws in mathematical form from isolated observations, while morphological scientists, more like Linnaeus, aimed at systematically cataloguing the concrete phenomena of nature, investigating the morphological particulars of each separate class. We have seen this divide in Whewell's classification of the sciences in the previous chapter. These different attitudes explain the different ways in which both strands of scientists appreciated experiments. Abstract scientists aimed to isolate a specific causal relation under laboratory conditions in order to estimate the quantitative relation between cause and effect. Morphologists aimed to do justice to the "dramatics of nature" – nature's complexity. Galison and Assmus show how these different approaches to the investigation of nature met one another during the course of the nineteenth century in an approach to experiments that aimed to reproduce the "dramatics of nature" under laboratory conditions. The goal became – to use another of their apt phrasings – to "mimic" nature's complexity.

Thus, we follow Charles Wilson from his field observations on clouds at the top of the Ben Nevis in Scotland to his reproduction of clouds at the Cavendish Laboratory at Cambridge, where he constructed what we now know in elementary particle physics as the cloud chamber, for which he was awarded the Nobel Prize in 1927. As Galison and Assmus show, Wilson's research followed and extended upon earlier experiments on the formation of clouds made around 1880 by the Scottish engineer John Aitken, who investigated the influence of dust in cloud formation. Galison and Assmus call these experiments mimetic because they aim to reproduce nature's complexity under laboratory conditions. They were experiments in that they aimed to isolate just one causal relation, but Aitken and Wilson wanted the result of the experiment to "look like" nature.

This marks a break with earlier ideas of experimental scientists. When striving to general laws isolating a causal relationship, there was no need to have outcomes that in any way resembled nature. The purpose of the experiment design was to derive a functional relation between the variant and the variable; scientists were unconcerned with the resemblance of the experimentally produced phenomena to events in the outer world. In mimetic experiments, however, the resemblance of the experimental result with natural observations – and thus with nature itself – was an index of its truth.

Galison and Assmus do not address an experiment on cloud formation that was "mimetic" in an even stronger sense and that was made by Jevons in the 1850s and reproduced by Lord Raleigh at the Cavendish around 1880, with the purpose of investigating diffusion in a fluid of varying density. Jevons's original experiments of the 1850s not only intended to reproduce the drama of nature – taking the visual experimental outcome as an index of their truth – but they did so by changing to another medium: not air, but fluid. The behaviour of fluid was taken to mimic the behaviour of air.

Jevons's (and Lord Raleigh's) experiments proved to be dead ends. There was no follow-up on them, and, when rediscovered in the twentieth century, they turned out to be about something quite different: salt-fingers in the ocean (Schmitt 1995), the result of double diffusion – not single diffusion, as Jevons and Raleigh both thought. My discussion of Jevons's experiments on clouds, therefore, is not intended to "dust off" some forgotten pearl in the history of the experimental sciences, but rather it is meant to show how Jevons used mechanical analogies to move meteorology from a classificatory science to an experimental science, able to derive laws of phenomena like the other experimental sciences. Jevons thus bridged the gap between two distinct modes of induction, which as we have seen were still kept separate by Whewell in his early thoughts on the subject. It will be seen how Jevons's experiments may serve as a model for Jevons's approach to the sciences: the natural and the social. In his experiments, Jevons moved the target of explanation from particular natural instances to the stable experimentally produced clouds. Jevons's similar search for stability in the unstable statistical data of society would revolutionise the methods of investigation in political economy. To get there, not only did the gap between natural history and the experimental sciences have to be bridged, but also the categorical abyss between the sciences of mind and matter.

JEVONS'S EXPERIMENTS ON THE FORMATION OF CLOUDS

Jevons conducted his experiments on clouds during his five-year stay in Australia (1854–1859), where he was appointed as assayer at the new Mint of Sydney. The work at the Mint soon gave him ample opportunity to pursue his scientific interests, which were primarily devoted to meteorology. Jevons published three articles on his experiments on clouds.[1] He assured his cousin Harry Roscoe that he was convinced of the truth of his experimental findings, although he did not expect to be credited for it in the future: "I am quite reconciled to the expectation that everything which I have said will be attributed to some previous writer or adopted by some subsequent one, so that I shall be quite shorn of all credit" (PC 2:354, letter of 9 October 1858).[2]

Jevons's aim was to show that the various "modifications", or forms, of the clouds could be attributed to simple mechanical causes only. While Howard argued that electricity and differences in temperature were involved

---

[1] "On the Cirrous Form of Cloud" and "On the Forms of Clouds" appeared in the London, Edinburgh and Dublin Philosophical Magazine and Journal of Science (1857, 1858a). The first article was communicated to the journal by his former teacher of chemistry, Thomas Graham. "On Clouds; Their Various Forms, and Producing Causes", a more comprehensive and detailed version, appeared in the Sydney Magazine of Science and Art in 1858 (1858b). At this time, Jevons regularly chose the Philosophical Magazine to communicate his findings.
[2] How right he was! – as demonstrated in Galison and Assmus (1989) and Galison (1997, Chapter 2). These detailed accounts of Victorian scientists' involvement in cloud experiments fail to mention Jevons's experiments or those of Lord Raleigh in the early 1880s, the only person who paid proper tribute to Jevons's experiments (see especially Schmitt 1995).

in cloud formation, Jevons jumped on suggestions in Howard's articles that it was not so much temperature itself, as its effect on the density of the air that accounted for the various forms of the clouds. In his "natural history of clouds", Howard suggested that "the cumulus acts, as well by electrical attraction, as by that of gravity, on the surrounding materials" (1812, 55). In the vocabulary of Dalton's theory of heat, Jevons's aim was to show that it was not so much differences in the "specific heat" of air and water, as differences in the "specific gravity" in the air, that caused the formation of clouds. His second aim was to show that electricity was of no importance in the formation of clouds itself. It was a derived, or secondary, phenomenon that was the result rather than the cause of condensation of vapour into water (and, eventually, rain).

To prove his claims, Jevons designed an experiment in which he reproduced clouds on a miniature scale in another medium: liquid rather than air. Jevons thus not only mimicked the formation of clouds (as in Aitken's and Wilson's experiments later in that century), but he also mimicked the medium of their production – that is, what made them genuinely mimetic. Jevons was convinced that in cloud formation, air (or gas in general) and liquid could be considered as analogical media, so that conclusions for water equally held for air. Jevons performed his first series of experiments in a round vessel to produce two of the three basic forms of clouds of Howard's classification: a stratus and a cirrus (Figure 4-2).

Before Jevons entered into the details of his experiments, he gave some preliminary considerations that motivated their setup. The starting point was Howard's felicitous definition of a cirrus, that unfortunately combined with an infelicitous explanation of this type of cloud. Howard "merely attempts to explain its formation by comparing it with the well-known experiment of the electrified lock of hair", but this emphasis on electricity and the analogy with hair were, in Jevons's view, delusive. A far more "simple and natural explanation" of "cirrous fibres" was to be found when considering the cirrus as "minute streamlets of air forcing their way through a stratum of air of different temperature and moisture". On the only supposition of "two neighbouring masses of air, completely or nearly saturated with aqueous vapour and moisture" and of different temperatures, these two masses would "*filter* into each other in minute streamlets" and water would precipitate in the form of a cloud. This precipitate would then arrange itself in the form of a "cirrous cloud".

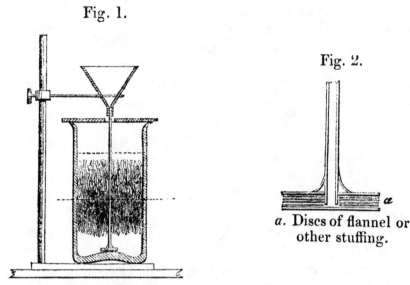

4-2. Experimental setup of Jevons's first experiments on the formation of clouds (1857, 24). Jevons emphasised that a double glass beaker should be used to shield for temperature disturbances. The image shows "cirrus clouds" – in fact, as Schmitt (1995) pointed out, precipitates formed by the same process of double diffusion as salt fingers in the ocean. On the right-hand side is an enlarged drawing of the tube used to inject a second layer of fluid into the beaker. Courtesy of Teylers Museum, Haarlem.

The difficulty of testing this explanation was, of course, the "extremely lofty position in the atmosphere at which these clouds nearly always occur". Goethe might have considered it sufficient to name "that which no hand can reach, no hand can clasp", but this was for Jevons distinctly insufficient to "ascertain... the conditions of the air surrounding" the cirrus. This problem motivated Jevons to "produce miniature representations of clouds, under conditions in which the cause of formation could be certainly known" (all quotes Jevons 1857).

Jevons then addressed the considerations that led to his experiment design. He chose water rather than air, in part as a matter of convenience: Its higher density and "sluggishness" not only made it more "observable in its motions", but also "prevented accidental disturbances by temperature, &c". In later articles in the *Sydney Magazine of Science and Arts* (1858a) and in the *Philosophical Magazine* (1858b), he gave more extensive arguments why water was a feasible substitute for air for the purpose of his experiments. Jevons emphasised that his experimental results could be obtained in a variety of ways. The experiment he used produced "the most complete and striking representation of a *cirrous* cloud" (1857, 24). The experiment itself consisted of a gradual mixing of two layers of fluid that differed slightly in specific gravity. To show how this was reached, it is most convenient to quote extensively from Jevons's 1857 article:

> *Exp.* 1. To about 800 grms. of pure water add 2 or 3 drops of hydrochloric acid, and 1 grms. measure of a strong solution of white sugar (spec. grav. of solution 1.15). Warm this to rather above 100°F., and pour the greater portion into an ordinary glass beaker about 5 inches in diameter and 9 or 10 in height (fig. 1) [i.e., Figure 4-2 here]. This beaker should be surrounded by a second larger one to prevent disturbance of temperature; and a tube-funnel, allowing only a very slow stream to pass, must be placed in it reaching to the bottom, and with a termination like in fig. 2 [i.e., the right-hand side of Figure 4-2 here]; or with such similar contrivance as shall prevent all violent currents.

After having poured in the "remainder of the hot solution of sugar" and some pure cold water to clean the funnel, 800 milligrams of distilled water at ordinary temperature was poured in (to which had been added 0.2 of a "gramme of crystallized nitrate of silver"), all without disruption and preventing "accidental and irregular mixture from taking place".

Due to a slow exchange of heat, the upper layer containing sugar would cool and therefore rise in density, and because of that slowly sink through the distilled water of ordinary temperature. This would cause the silver nitrate and hydrochloride to react and to form a white precipitate, "thus representing closely the precipitation of watery particles by the mixture of portions of moist air of different temperature", as in the formation of a cirrus (1857, 25).[3] Jevons then altered the experiment by adding the sugar solution to the distilled water of ordinary temperature instead of the heated water. In this case, no mixture of fluids arose and the silver nitrate and hydrochloride reacted only where the layers made contact, giving rise to a horizontal precipitate that Jevons identified as a "stratus".

The difference between experiments being only the layer of water to which sugar was added, Jevons concluded that the different effects arose from

---

[3] Schmitt (1995) notes that, for an active photographer and assayer at the mint, Jevons's choice of silver nitrate goes without saying : Silver nitrate was used to check for gold purity and to fix photographs.

"slight differences of specific gravity alone" and not from heat exchange – a conclusion he had reached by wrongly assuming it was obvious that "the difference of temperature of the strata in this experiment is not a material point, being simply a means employed to enable us to lay one stratum upon another of a slightly greater density when of the same temperature, so that we may afterwards observe the mixing process and change of place in the most gradual manner possible" (1857, 26).[4]

In other experiments, Jevons enlarged the range of miniature clouds produced to all their basic forms – that is, the cirrus, stratus, and cumulus – as well as their composite forms – of which the most important was the combination of all three different basic forms – also known as the nimbus, raincloud, or thundercloud. Since Jevons's theory of cloud formation depended in his view only on the way in which layers of moist air and varying specific gravity mixed with one another, the nimbus or thundercloud provided a test of alternative theories in which electricity was considered a causal factor in cloud formation.

His 1858 article in the *Philosophical Magazine* was accompanied by a drawing of the experimental apparatus and engravings from photographs of the original experiment showing a cumulus, two cumulostrata, and a nimbus or thundercloud (Figure 4-3). The less detailed engravings in the *Sydney Magazine* contained a drawing from the round vessel, in which Jevons produced a cirrus and a stratus.

The experimental apparatus consisted of two glass plates held in a wooden frame at a distance of about one-third inch. Jevons called it a "section-glass . . . because it contains a thin section of liquid", which was supposed to represent a "section of the atmosphere" (1858a, 243; 1858b, 163). Jevons (1858b, 167–8) used a *stratus* as a benchmark which resembled Howard's image and should convince the reader of the validity of his explanation (Figure 4-1, Howard's image c). The experiment design was in fact similar to his earlier experiments, but with this difference: On some occasions, he now made use of several layers of water of different specific gravity, to which an additional one was added to be able to form the combination of basic forms of clouds that constituted in their ensemble the nimbus or thundercloud. Water was injected from the lower side of the instrument to mimic the formation of

---

[4] This assumption led Jevons astray over the true meaning of his experiment, which was in fact about double diffusion (see Schmitt 1995).

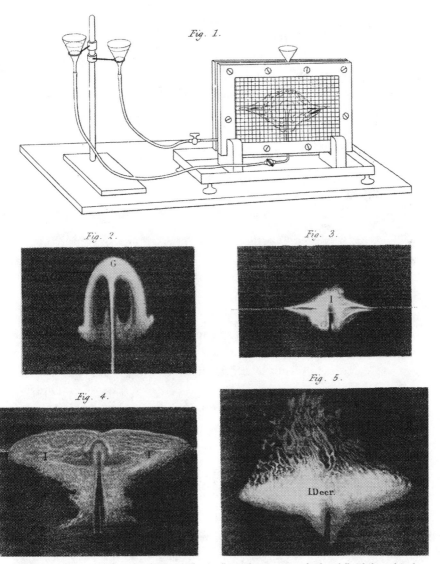

4-3. Engravings of Jevons's photographs in "On the Forms of Clouds", *Philosophical Magazine*, 1858. Courtesy of Teylers Museum, Haarlem.

the cumulus, which Jevons considered the result of a jet of vapour of higher temperature – and therefore of lower density – that crossed through the lowest layer of air to then fall back on this first layer when cooled by the higher layer of air (and thus increasing again in density). Jevons clearly alluded here to Howard's own explanation of the horizontal basis of the cumulus, but again did not attribute this to differences in temperature but to differences in the density of the air.

As previously described, the purpose of the extended experiments was to not only reproduce Howard's taxonomy of clouds, but also to show the uniform mechanism involved in their formation. According to Jevons (1858a, 244; also 1858b, 164), "a little reflection" showed that "the whole variety of the phenomena" was the result of "only two *essentially variable* conditions":

- 1st – Original impressed *momentum*,
- 2nd – *Gravity*, which is called into play whenever we use two liquids differing, however slightly, in specific gravity, but which does not *in the least affect the internal motions of a perfectly homogeneous fluid*.

To mimic the formation of the cumulostratus, a combination of a cumulus and a stratus, Jevons projected a jet of water containing a trace of silver nitrate and 1 part per 1,000 of sugar from the lower side of the section glass through two layers of water that he had made differ in specific gravity. The specific gravity of the injected jet lay in between those of the two layers of water in the section glass. The injected stream would ascend through the lower stratum to a certain height in the second. But there, "its superior gravity will overcome its momentum" and it would fall back into the lower stratum, where it again would be "checked" by the lower fluid's greater specific gravity, thus securing its horizontal basis. During its journey through both layers of water, the silver nitrate in the injected stream would react with the ordinary salt contained in them, producing "a cloud of chloride of silver . . . shown in figs. 3 and 4" [in my Figure 4-3 here] (1858a, 247–8, 255).

In a similar way, an experimental setup was made in which an injected stream containing silver chloride and 1 part per 5,000 of its weight in sugar was added to only one layer of liquid containing a slight trace of salt. This showed the "general form and internal motions of the cumulus" (1858a, 246). Jevons assumed that the slight traces of salt and silver nitrate, which were added to the separate parts of the liquids, did not affect the specific gravity of the water. Mistakenly, he again assured the reader that the experimental setup excluded "the action of all other chemical or physical forces" (1858b, 164).

Jevons thought he had transcended Howard's classification scheme of the clouds in an important way. By mimicking cloud formation under conditions in which the causal factors were known, he believed he had proven that there was a uniform mechanism at work in the formation of all clouds, producing different forms under different circumstances. His conclusion was that the "*miniature representation*" of clouds "under conditions in which the immediate causes can be certainly known" gave reason to "assume with complete confidence that similar motions and differences of specific gravity have operated in the production of the atmospheric clouds in question" (1858a, 241).

The harvest of all this was that Jevons with full confidence dismissed all hypotheses that attributed any role to electricity in the formation of clouds. This hypothesis could reckon on great popularity among meteorologists after first having been proposed by Luke Howard. Because the experiment excluded electricity from its setup, Jevons rejected such theories as "*utter nonsense*" (1858b, 175):

> Possessing, as I assume, a clear idea of the motions and changes which constitute a cumulus, and therefore the thunder-cloud, which is essentially a cumulus with a derivative and, as it were, organised system of cirrus and stratus, I see no difficulty in offering an explanation which is at least plausible (1858a, 253).

Jevons gave the following alternative explanation for the obvious important presence of electricity in a thundercloud: The "faint charge of electricity" which is always present in the atmosphere became collected in the "watery particles" which, as in all rain or storm clouds, became separated from the air. The air, deprived of its electrical charge and of its "moisture", left the cloud at its summit (due to its smaller specific gravity). As long as newly moisturised air was fed from below, the electrical charge of the cloud became greater and greater until it reached "such a pitch" that a discharge would occur between the cloud and its electrical counterpart, the Earth. Hence, Jevons concluded, electricity was not a "cause" in the formation of thunderclouds, but a secondary, derived phenomenon.

Jevons admitted that his experiment did not give evidence that this reasoning was correct, but he could refer to none other than John Herschel, "the highest philosophical authority", who had expressed "the opinion that [the agency of electricity] as a meteorological cause is exceedingly limited, indeed that it may be altogether left out of the account as productive of any meteorological effect of importance on the great scale" (1858b, 175, quoting Herschel's *Essays*, 245. See also 1858a, 253).

A basic assumption of Jevons's experiment was that the behaviour of the water in the instrument was similar to the behaviour of gases in the atmosphere. Jevons was aware that such a claim required supportive arguments. In the *Sydney Magazine*, Jevons paid great attention as to "how to *translate*" the conditions in the section glass, "so to speak, into the language of the atmosphere" (1858b, 164, original emphasis). In this process of translation, he gave some plausibility to the claim that the only relevant forces at work in real, atmospheric cloud formation were the same as those working in the section glass. According to Jevons, "gases are subject to the same laws of equilibrium and pressure as liquids, excepting only as far as they are modified by the property of elasticity" (1857, 26); gases can be more compressed or expanded than liquids. He argued that this property was irrelevant for the formation of clouds, since elasticity in itself could not "be *directly* productive of force or motion". The consequence of the argument was that "free air will resemble in its motions a very rare liquid, and any part of the atmosphere will be subject to the same hydrodynamical laws as the interior of a body of liquid" (1858a, 242)[5] – hence the conclusion that cloud formation was governed by momentum and differences in the specific gravity of gases.

ARTIFICIAL CLOUDS, REAL CLOUDS, AND CLOUDS "ON AN AVERAGE"

The obvious thing about Jevons's engravings is that they only faintly resemble real clouds. Jevons's thick precipitates lost at least one of the characteristics of clouds that John Ruskin emphasised in the context of art: their airiness. According to Ruskin (1995, 34), many landscapists painted clouds as a "comparatively small, round, puffed-up white body", thus "depriving" them of their buoyancy and transparency – their perpetual motion and change. To what extent, then, could Jevons's precipitates be regarded to mimic nature?

John Herschel, one of the outstanding scientists of his day, was receptive to the analogy. After his return to London from Australia, Jevons read Herschel's entry on meteorology in the *Encyclopaedia Britannica* (1861) and sent him copies of his two articles in the *Philosophical Magazine*. In the accompanying letter, Jevons remarked that his experiments produced explanations of

---

[5] Jevons examined the relation between the "elastic force" of a vapour and temperature in his entry on the hygrometer for Watts's *Dictionary of Chemistry and the Allied Branches of the Sciences* (1868 2:205–12).

atmospheric phenomena "in substantial accordance" with those of Herschel, but which, apparently, "had not fallen under [his] notice" (*PC* 2:432–3). Acknowledging the articles, Herschel wrote that he had not come across them and would have "assuredly" referred to them had he known of them. Herschel added that "being ... somewhat of a dabbler in chemistry", he had "often noticed and been struck with the resemblance of finely derived precipitations formed by gradual mixture without agitation of mutually decomposing fluids to the forms of Cirrous and other Clouds" (*PC* 2:433–4).

Even though Herschel considered the analogy convincing, Jevons did not think it would be obvious for less learned readers that his engravings of clouds produced in the section glass resembled true atmospheric clouds. It was an informed and not a naïve mind which established this resemblance:

> The mind having once received a clear and salient idea as to a probable cause of the cumulostratus, will apply it to every instance of that cloud which meets the eye in nature. This comparison is the test of the theory, and must be the main ground on which my readers may judge of the truth of my conclusions.
>
> (1858a, 248)

The apparent test of the theory by a comparison to daily clouds was not its true test, however. To see the similarity between the miniature cloud and a "real" cloud, the mind had to have a "clear and salient idea" of its "probable cause" – that is, it had to have knowledge of the mechanism Jevons claimed to be at work in the section glass. Jevons adapted the interpretation of his precipitates accordingly. He assured the reader that the precipitates produced were not direct reproductions of daily observed clouds, but contained their "essential characteristics"; they were "typical" clouds or clouds "on an average". Jevons thus exchanged his experimentally produced clouds for clouds of daily observation and even for the clouds as depicted in Howard's taxonomy.

Jevons paid great attention to the translation of ordinary observations into the language of his theory. With respect to thunderclouds, he warned the reader that "it will very probably be impossible ... to recognize in the peculiar result of the last experiment any resemblance whatever to the ordinary conception of a thundercloud" (1858a, 250). In his 1857 article on the cirrous form of clouds, Jevons included a drawing of an "imaginary" section of a thundercloud which resembled the engraving of its experimental counterpart with

Imaginary Section of a Thunder-cloud near Sydney.
Fig. 3.

D (dotted line) shows junction of two currents of air, the directions of these being indicated by arrows (A A).
B B, arrows showing upward and backward current of moist air.
L, lightning striking from thunder-cloud to earth.
C C, cirrous crest moving with upper current.
S, scud moving in lower moist current.
E, the appearance of *dropping portions of cloud* at foot or back of storm.

4-4. Jevons's drawing of an "imaginary Thundercloud" in "On the Cirrous Form of Cloud", *Philosophical Magazine*, 1857, p. 30. Courtesy of Teylers Museum, Haarlem.

regard to the "cirrous crest moving with upper current"(1857, 30) – that is, the fragment labelled CC in the sketch of the "imaginary" thundercloud (Figure 4-4). Also in his diary, though not unambiguously, he referred to the "curled curious edges" as the elements which made thunderclouds "known" (*PC* 1:218).

In his 1858a article in the *Philosophical Magazine*, Jevons emphasised that the main difficulty of recognising a thundercloud in the experimental result was that, "under varying circumstances", thunderclouds might be produced which "to the superficial observer" differed completely "in form and nature". But "closer examination" would reveal that all these clouds contained "in greater or less degree" the "essential characteristics of the perfect or typical thundercloud" (1858a, 250). Comparing the "imaginary section" of the thundercloud drawn in the 1857 article with the 1858 photograph (see in Figure 4-3; Jevons's Figure 4), it seems that the only "essential characteristics" of the thundercloud were the cirrous threads at the top of the precipitate.

To the untrained eye, the recognition of the "general form" of the cumulus in Figure 4-3 (i.e., Jevons's Figure 1 in this figure) will cause even greater difficulties. For example, compare this engraving, which shows a "regular and extremely graceful fountain-like form", with Jevons's drawing of a cumulus in his diary, "which for magnificence & beauty" he had not seen "surpassed" (*PC* 1:218) (Figure 4-5). Just like Howard's cumulus (Figure 4-1, Howard's

4-5. Jevons's drawing of a cumulus, made during his journey to the Gold Diggings at Sofala, 9–23 March 1856. *Papers and Correspondence* 1:218. Courtesy of Palgrave/ Macmillan Press.

image b), the drawing shows a much greater similarity to a "real" cumulus than the engraving made after the experiment. Both made by Jevons, we may ask which of the two included the "essential characteristics" of the cumulus or, in other words, what the criteria were that he proposed to assess these characteristics.

Jevons assured the reader that in order to see the similarity between the experimental result and atmospheric clouds, the mind had to go through a process of "*abstraction*" to detect the "essential particulars" of the various forms of clouds (1858a, 250; also 1858b, 175). Thus, he was able to *isolate* the causal structure that gave rise to the formation of various types of clouds *in general*. The plate of drawings attached to the *Sydney Magazine* version of Jevons's article, of which Figure 4-6 gives the relevant part, offers us more information on the factors at work in the process of visually abstracting an experimental from a real cloud. Jevons's Figure IV in Figure 4-6 is a description of the elements involved in the "*Natural Form of Cumulus*". When we compare this figure in the *Sydney Magazine* with the drawing of the cumulus in his diary, we see that it not only registers the form of the cumulus, but also *adds* theoretical elements to it. The drawing illustrated "the general form and the internal motions of the cumulus" (1858b, 170).

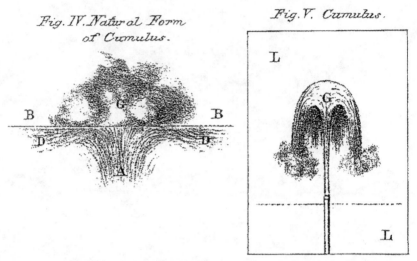

4-6. Fragment of Jevons's drawing of a cumulus after the experimental results in "On Clouds; Their Various Forms, and Producing Causes". *Sydney Magazine of Science and Arts*, 1858.

Capital letters A, B, C, and D serve to structure our observation. Jevons (1858b, 178) explained the letters as follows:

A: Ascending current of warm moist air
B: Plane of precipitation of cloud
C: Cumulose cloud
D: Streams of air descending from the cloud and spreading out beneath the plane of precipitation

The "general form" of the cumulus was illustrated "with some approach to accuracy" by the experiment, from which figure V was drawn (see in Figure 4-6).

When we consider the sequence of Jevons's images of a cumulus, we gain an idea of how Jevons identified and isolated the causal factors of cloud production and convinced the reader that the experimental result visualised these causal factors as the essential features of our common observations. The temporal sequence of these images, from the 1856 drawing of the cumulus in his diary to the drawings and photographs in his articles, suggests some sort of inductive process by which he identified the simple causal factors explaining the form of complex "real" clouds. The object of study shifts from the study of *particulars*, of observations or data, to the *essential characteristics* of these particulars. In the *Sydney Magazine* version, Jevons interestingly referred to these characteristics as indicative of how various types of clouds behaved "*on an average*" under the influence of the sole causal determinants, momentum and specific gravity (1858b, 174, original emphasis). The essential characteristics of clouds were captured better by an average or mean value rather than by any particular real object. By shifting from daily observations to theoretically informed phenomena, Jevons constructed the proof for his own theory.

Having reached this point, it is important to realise that Howard's water colourings were idealised renderings of clouds. Like Jevons's experimental images, they did not refer to individual observations but to something like an average or ideal. But there was a difference between Howard and Jevons. While Howard's clouds represented the characteristics of their respective definitions, Jevons's clouds embodied their mechanism of production. Under the assumption of a known causal factor (differences in specific gravity), a mathematical rendering of the problem, embodying a causal mechanism, came into view. Jevons hinted at this possibility in his 1858 articles on the subject. Rather than visual resemblance of his experimental miniatures with daily observations, a mathematical rendering provided the ultimate explanation of cloud formation. Since Jevons mimicked clouds by means of fluids, he considered that this mathematics had to come from the dynamics of fluids. Apart from a general allusion to this possibility, we find in none of the articles any attempt to genuinely pursue such an enquiry. Given the state of hydrodynamics in the mid-1850s and the obvious lack of access to current research elsewhere that Jevons experienced in Australia,[6] it is perhaps unsurprising that Jevons did not make any strides in this direction.

---

[6] A note of the editor of the *Philosophical Magazine* to another of Jevons's contributions ("On a Sun-gauge", November 1857) reads that Jevons was "evidently not acquainted with the interesting researches of Pouillet [from 1838] on the amount of solar radiant heat falling on our globe" (Jevons 1857, 356, note of the editor). Generally speaking, Jevons was very careful in his coverage of the existing literature on a subject. Jevons hints at his difficulties in getting access to current and past sources in one of his letters to Sir John Herschel. Despite the flourishing of periodical culture in Victorian England, communication failures were not uncommon, as witnessed from Herschel's reply to Jevons as well. From his detailed entries on various measuring instruments – such as the barometer, hydrometer, and hygrometer – he contributed to Watt's *Dictionary* (see note 5) in the early 1860s, we can infer that Jevons was well-informed about the contemporary state of knowledge in hydrodynamics. He also contributed the entry on clouds to this *Dictionary*, which gives some indication of how Jevons's work on clouds was valued at the time.

Raynold Schmitt recently (1995) uncovered how Lord Raleigh, who received the Nobel Prize in 1904 for the discovery of argon, repeated Jevons's cirrus experiments in the early 1880s at the Cavendish Laboratory and referred to Jevons's original experiments in his 1883 paper on the mathematical formula governing a fluid of variable densities. Raleigh wrote that his "calculations were written out in 1880, in order to illustrate the theory of cirrous clouds propounded by the late Prof. Jevons" in 1857. Notes on these experiments, taken by Eleanor Balfour, the later Mrs Sidgwick who served as his research assistant, show that they reproduced the experiment design of Jevons's 1857 article and that they observed similar results. There was no reference to these experiments in Raleigh's published article, and it is mere guesswork as to why this was so. It may be, as Schmitt suggests, that "he decided that Jevons's description was sufficiently complete and accurate", it may also be just the opposite: that Raleigh was not sure about its merits. Regardless, Raleigh derived on purely theoretical grounds the propagation law of slight disturbances in density through time, taking Jevons's two-layer case of heavy fluids over light fluids as one of his examples.

Because Jevons only considered differences in the density of layers of air (and not differences in their temperatures) as the relevant causal factor in the formation of clouds, it did not occur to him that his experiments were in fact about double diffusion. Like Jevons – and as Schmitt (1995) suggests, perhaps because of him – Raleigh similarly missed this fact. Raleigh's result was independently rediscovered in 1950 by Sir Geoffrey Taylor and is now known as the Raleigh–Taylor instability: "an important process in plasma dynamics, super-novae explosions, and heavy-nuclei collisions" (Schmitt 1995, 14). For Jevons, Raleigh's mathematical results came too late. He drowned before the article appeared.

Jevons's Uniform Approach to the Sciences

There is a clear message to be drawn from Jevons's experimental approach to cloud formation. Jevons designed his experiments on strong mechanical assumptions. He did not satisfy himself with an experimental reproduction of Howard's taxonomy, but aimed to uncover the general laws governing the formation of clouds. He was well-aware that his experimentally produced clouds did not resemble any particular real cloud. Rather, his experimentally produced clouds should be taken as average values that captured the essential characteristics of their unstable natural counterparts. The index of truth for these experiments was twofold. First, the experimental results should "mimic" nature's complexity – but this was only so for the informed eye that understood the causal mechanism embodied in the experimental results. Second, the ultimate criterion of truth was a mathematical rendering of the experimental results – that is, a mathematical function makes the mechanism explicit of the production of the experimental observations.

In subsequent chapters, we will see how Jevons approached political economy in this same spirit. As a preliminary observation, we can see from these experiments that it is virtually impossible to separate theory and data – rather, theory and data are inherently intertwined. In the case of political economy, there is no clear separation between "pure theory" and "statistical data", which might confirm or disconfirm the theory. Averaging plays a major role in this regard. By focussing on average values rather than on particular data, the mechanism could be uncovered that governed social and natural phenomena. Mathematics, when properly targetted, spelled out this mechanism. This approach to political economy could surface once Jevons broke out of the methodological limits that had been erected by John Stuart Mill and that were institutionalised in the Victorian split between economic theory and statistics. Before we investigate Jevons's struggles with Mill more closely, we need to first ask why Jevons was so satisfied with mechanical explanations in the first place. To investigate this, we need to look more closely into the mechanical worldview that fused his scientific investigations.

FIVE

~

ENGINES OF DISCOVERY

It is well-known that Jevons was one of the first in Britain to catch on to the importance of the newly developed formal logical systems of George Boole (1815–1864) and Augustus De Morgan (1806–1871). In the opening lecture of the academic year he held at Queen's College, Liverpool, in October 1865, Jevons singled out Boole's *Investigations of the Laws of Thought* (1854) as being of pivotal importance for his own logical work. In the same breath, Jevons invoked Charles Babbage's calculating engines:

> Having given much attention to this most remarkable work of Professor Boole, I have been led by it to perceive that if we had a number of objects with mechanical devices for arranging them in any desired classes or ranks, we might argue concerning them by machinery, and bring out a conclusion by the motion of wheels or levers, somewhat as Pascal worked an arithmetical equation, or Mr. Babbage solves an equation, or calculates a page of logarithms by turning the handle of the calculating machine. I am confident of being able to show this when I come to the proper point in my logical studies, by a very simple mechanical device, which shall not only solve Aristotle's dilemma's, but shall exhibit to the eyes the working of Boole's logic, the most general and perfect system of logic yet proposed.[1]

The mechanical device which takes a prominent place in this quote, exhibiting "to the eye" Boole's "general and perfect system of logic", was Jevons's so-called Logical Machine, a mechanised version of his Logical Abacus – a manual contrivance that was of help in making logical deductions

---

[1] Jevons's opening address at Queen's College, in 1865, was in substance devoted to the "great reform in logical science", the discovery of formal logic. Supplement to *The Liverpool Daily Post*, Tuesday, 3 October 1865. I will return to this lecture in Chapter 8.

from a given (and limited) set of propositions. Mechanising this last contrivance was the driving force of his logical work throughout the 1860s and
proved of fundamental importance for his *Principles of Science* (1874). However, Jevons's machine was widely neglected by the scientific community
of his day, as was sadly noted in 1883 in an address of a certain Professor
Sonnenschein to the Birmingham Philosophical Society.[2] Indeed, Jevons's
work on logic left no permanent impression, even though his *Elementary
Lessons in Logic: Deductive and Inductive* (1870) was an outstanding success
if measured in reprints (49!).

John Stuart Mill proved as negative about Jevons's formal logic as he
was about the *Theory*. When he wrote to Cairnes about the limited merits
of the last book, he reproached Jevons in particular for having "a mania
for encumbering questions with useless complications, and with a notation
implying the existence of greater precision in the data than the questions
admit of. His speculations on Logic, like those of Boole and De Morgan,

---

[2] Sonnenschein (1883, 72). There may be good reasons for this neglect, Jevons being obviously
a less original logician than Boole or De Morgan. In his accompanying remarks to the
exchange of letters between Boole and Jevons, Grattan-Guinness (1991, 22–3) suggests that
the editors of Jevons's *Papers and Correspondence* apparently attempted to present "Jevons
the economist, uncontaminated by Jevons the Logician".

At first blush, there appears to be some justice in Grattan-Guinness's remark, for it is
true that the image one gets from the *Papers and Correspondence* is biased to Jevons's
economics, neglecting his work and correspondence on logic. A nice example of this bias
seems a fragment of a letter from Stanley Jevons to his brother Herbert. It reads (*PC* 3:62).
". . . logic & critique upon his, as he declined to see it until he had finished a mathematical
book he was engaged upon. I have received from a German Professor an elaborate essay
on Prices in Hamburg, containing also a great deal of criticism of my pamphlet". The
German professor referred to was Laspeyres, who criticised Jevons's use of the geometric
mean in his pamphlet on the fall in the value of gold (originally published in April 1863).
One might wrongly infer that the editors thought Jevons's mentioning of Laspeyres the
only important part of this letter, ignoring Jevons's reference to his work on Boole's logic,
which also appeared in 1863. Jevons's reference to this work is hardly to be inferred from
the reproduced fragment. The reproduced fragment is, however, all that remains of it.

The neglect of Jevons's logical work in the *Papers and Correspondence* may be partially
due to a division of tasks between the logician Professor Mays, who did much to promote
interest in Jevons's work on logic in the 1950s, and the economist Professor Black, who was
the co-editor of Jevons's *Papers and Correspondence*. This division proved to be unfortunate.
In an article on Jevons's scientific method, Mays wrote that he was "now hoping to edit some
of Jevons's correspondence together with relevant pieces of his logical and philosophical
writings. . . . This would form a natural complement to the extensive work Professor Black
is carrying out on Jevons's economic studies" (Mays [1962] 1988, 223) The promised volume
never came to pass. Apart from classical studies of Mays and Henry ([1953] 1988) and Mays
([[1962] 1988), recent corrections to this neglect are Schabas (1990), Grattan-Guinness
(1991), Mosselmans (1998), and Maas (1999).

and some of those of Hamilton, are infected in an extraordinary degree with this vice".[3]

My purpose in this and the following chapter is to show how Jevons's work on the Logical Machine is embedded in an emerging discourse on mechanical reasoning taken in a variety of senses: (1) as straightforwardly relating to reasoning by machines; (2) as relating to a mode of understanding the human mind by comparing it with a mechanical contrivance; and (3) as understanding reasoning machines (like those of Babbage and Jevons) as engines of discovery, as instruments to overcome the notorious problem of induction, and by their help to uncover the mechanical laws governing the universe. None of these senses entails the other in a straightforward sense, but they are all, as will be seen, closely related. The first two senses relate to the inner processes of these machines in relationship to the work of the mind; the last relates to their outcomes. They all form instantiations of Lord Kelvin's dictum (Thomson [1884] 1987, 111, also 206) that we can only understand something if we can make a mechanical model of it. Babbage's Difference Engines and the new formal logic developed by Boole, De Morgan, and Jevons were driving forces in the development of mechanical reasoning in all these senses. The Logical Machine was designed to draw infallible logical deductions and demonstrate to the eye the power of Bode's logic. It also helped Jevons to conceive of the human mind as similar to a machine, obeying the same mechanical principles. Finally, it served as an engine to discover the mechanical laws governing the universe. Thus, Jevons's work on the Logical Machine crucially sheds light on his approach to political economy and the sciences in general.

Babbage and his Calculating Engines

The background for Jevons's work on his reasoning machine is to be found in Boole's logic and Babbage's calculating engines. The story of Babbage's machines has nowadays spread so widely that it hardly needs to be told again. Babbage's calculating engines project emerged out of a growing need for precise and accurate tables by the quickly industrialising British economy. These tables were necessary, among other things, for navigation and

---

[3] In his already quoted letter to Cairnes: *Mill* 17:1862–3, Letter 1698: 5 December 1871 to Cairnes. Mill's judgement is still widely shared, as witnessed from Mirowski's (2002, 42) summary judgement on Jevons's logic, and his Logical Machine, as "utterly useless".

for insurance companies that were rapidly growing in importance. John Herschel, Babbage's lifelong friend and fellow student, once compared a fault in a table with a rock just under the surface of the sea. There were so many faults that could be made in the production of numerical tables, in the computations of the "avalanche of numbers" comprised in them, in the copying of the outcomes, and in the various stages of the printing process that Herschel and Babbage spent many hours checking these tables themselves for their own scientific purposes. On one such occasion, as the story goes, Babbage exclaimed in exasperation that he wished these computations had been made by "steam" (see, for example, Swade 2000, 15).

Babbage was clearly aware of the growing need for precise and accurate tables. These factors were equally stressed by Dionysius Lardner in his description of the working of the Difference Engine I, published in *The Edinburgh Review* of 1834, which he wrote under the "detailed direction" of Babbage.[4] Also, the necessity of speeding up the process of calculation was an important factor in all of Babbage's endeavours to "compute by steam".[5] Indeed, in many ways as will be seen, the mastery of time was one of the driving motives and major problems in Babbage's engines project.

One only needs to have one look at the enormous octavo volumes filled with numbers up to many decimals to get an impression of the amount of mental effort that was needed to calculate tables and the sheer impossibility to decide on their trustworthiness.[6] Good calculators, in many cases autodidacts extraordinarily gifted with calculating capabilities, were valuable and hard to find. Augustus De Morgan, having himself been employed at an insurance company for some years, relates the story of one such mathematical autodidact, a certain Barrett, who had developed a method of calculating life annuities that proved as good as that of a German university professor.[7]

---

[4] See Anthony Hyman (1989, 51).

[5] Babbage emphasised the increased speed of calculation of his Analytical Engine, on which he worked from 1833 to 1847, as one of the great advantages over the Difference Engine I. The importance of increased speed of calculation can also be found in Andrew Warwick (1995, 331, 343) especially with reference to the Colmar arithmometer. The saving of "tedious mental labour" was stressed by Jevons in an address to the Royal Statistical Society of 1878 on the Colmar arithmometer.

[6] See, for example, Georg von Vega's *Thesaurus Logarithmorum Completus* (1794). See Swade (2000, images 4 and 5).

[7] Augustus De Morgan tells the story with almost visible pleasure. See De Morgan (1854). Attached to his account are some letters De Morgan received from Babbage in Spring 1862. These can be found in the University of London Library (ULL) call mark [DeM] L.4.

His employer clearly had no idea of the complex demands of his work. This Barrett was fired by his employer, apparently because it took him too much time to come up with his tables. In desperation, Barrett wrote:

> Whatever may have been your motives, it must be conceded, that thirty thousand different computations, are not so soon performed, as some may imagine... My nephew and myself might probably, by a constant application, finish the work in two years, or in two years and a half; but I am positive it cannot be done sooner.
>
> (letter attached to De Morgan 1854)

Precision, accuracy, and time were the important factors posing severe constraints on the construction of the requested tables. It is well-known how Gaspard de Prony's calculating project, commissioned by the French Revolutionary regime to facilitate the conversion to the decimal system, gave Babbage the clue in how to solve these problems jointly by the use of machinery.[8] The new revolutionary regime had ordered the mathematician Prony, an important member of the renowned *Ecole des Ponts et Chaussées*, to calculate new mathematical tables to facilitate the use of the newly introduced decimal system. Political economy provided the means to solve this seemingly impossible task. Accidentally reading Adam Smith's *Wealth of Nations*, Prony immediately realised the importance of Smith's principle of the division of labour and split up the work into three different task levels. In the first, "five or six" eminent mathematicians (including Lagrange and Prony himself) were asked to simplify the mathematical formulae to polynomials. In the second, a similar group of persons "of considerable acquaintance with mathematics" adapted these formulae by the method of differences so that one could calculate outcomes by simply adding and subtracting numbers. This final task was executed by a large number of unemployed hairdressers. The work of this last group of computers or calculators, as they were commonly referred to, can be rightly seen as a *reductio ad absurdum* of manual computation (Grattan-Guinness 1992, 40; see also Grattan-Guinness 1990c).

Prony's approach showed Babbage that it was possible to mechanise not only physical, but also mental, labour. His interest in the French project fits into his wider perception of algorithmic procedures in "mathematics,

---

[8] See Babbage's own account ([1835] 1963, 191–6). The most detailed description is found in Swade (2000). See also Daston (1994), Schaffer (1994a), and Warwick (1995).

science, and other walks of life" (Grattan-Guinness 1992, 34). Babbage emphasised in *Machinery and Manufactures* ([1835] 1963), still one of the most fascinating studies on the emerging mechanisation of the economy, that the lowest task of Prony's project was "almost" a form of mechanised mental labour. Babbage designed his so-called Difference Engine to mechanise this lowest stage of computing. Its method of computation ingeniously incorporated the method of differences in its wheels and gears, hence its name. Babbage's Difference Engine promised to fulfil all requirements Herschel and Babbage had been lamenting about: It saved calculation time and produced accurate and precise numbers. The computations would be more accurate than when done by a human individual – for machines, as opposed to humans, were thought not to make unpredictable mistakes. An attached printer would prevent errors in transcribing the outcomes. By thus excluding human interference from the whole process of computing and printing, all sources of faults – human faults – would be prevented, and the numbers would be precise, accurate, reliable, and reproducible.[9] All this, of course, was based on the assumption that the machine itself operated flawlessly, a matter of great concern to Babbage. For all his calculating engines, he designed automatic checks and stops to secure its proper working.

Prony's approach affected the traditional view of the hierarchy of mental and physical labour. Before Prony started his table project, computations were, for the most part, made by mathematicians themselves for their own purposes (Warwick 1995, 317–8). The routinisation and then mechanisation of computing downgraded calculation to the lowest of mental activities, thus equating it with the routine labour executed in the emerging factories.[10] Babbage exploited the comparison of calculation with routine factory labour in straightforwardly paralleling Prony's division of tasks with the division of tasks necessary for the construction of a "cotton or silk-mill". The "multitude of other persons" (the calculators or their mechanical equivalent) used in their employment the "lower degree of skill" (Hyman 1989, 143).

On the advice of the Royal Society, wherein the interference of his friend John Herschel on his behalf had done much to convince its members of the usefulness of the Difference Engine, the British Government commissioned Babbage in 1823 to do the construction of a calculating engine. The positive

[9] See Warwick (1995, 313–17 and passim).
[10] See Daston (1994).

advice of the Royal Society was far from unanimous, however. Important members, like Sir George Biddell Airy, thought there were too many "private friends" of Babbage who were "blinded by the ingenuity of their friend's invention" (quoted from Swade 2000, 37). Thomas Young judged that the machine would be "useless". The financial arrangements were only vaguely agreed on, and during the project Babbage had considerable difficulties getting additional funding. When the government stopped its funding in 1834, it had furnished a total sum of £17,470 – an astronomical amount of money when compared with the costs of a first-class steam locomotive such as the *John Bull*, which only cost £784 7s.[11]

Babbage's temper, as well as publications like *Decline of Science in England* (1830) in which he blamed the Royal Society in general – and some of its members in particular – for the deplorable state and status of science in England, did not help to keep the government and scientists he needed support from interested in his costly endeavours. Also, Babbage's endless quibbles with his toolmakers made the government increasingly sceptical of his chances of success.[12] More importantly, however, the early scepticism about the usefulness of Babbage's engine rose to principled resistance (especially by Airy) to prolongation of the project. In 1826, Airy and Babbage had both solicited for the Lucasian Chair in mathematics at Cambridge University, but Airy easily won. Upon his resignation to become Plumean professor in 1828 (and Astronomer Royal afterwards), Babbage was elected, and he kept the post until 1839 when he resigned to devote all of his time to the all-absorbing Analytical Engine project. Asked for advice on funding of this last project, in 1842, Airy stated "without the least hesitation that I believe the machine to be useless, and that the sooner it is abandoned, the better it will be for all parties" (quoted from Swade 2000, 142).

Airy's prime reason for this harsh judgement was that "the difficult parts" of the computations in any case had to be done by humans. As Swade (2000,

---

[11] See Swade (1991, 18). The failure of the project has been attributed to a variety of reasons, of which one can be eliminated. It was not due to technical limitations that the construction of the Difference Engine did not succeed, the construction of the Difference Engine II at the Science Museum in London on the occasion of Babbage's bicentennial birthday makes this sufficiently clear. See Swade (1991, 24–8) and more detailed Swade (2000).

[12] On Babbage's quarrels with Joseph Clement on the removal of the construction of the Difference Engine from Clement's workplace in Lambeth to Babbage's backyard in wealthy Marylbone and its broader implications for the growing control on labour in the factory system, see Schaffer (1994a).

148–54) notes, Airy has been judged by history the "dim bureacrate" who did not understand the great merits of Babbage's calculating engine project, just as he missed the discovery of Neptunus. But his objections were not all off the mark. The enormous weight of the engine forced it to stay in one place. Then, there was the time-consuming process of production, given the precision forgery demanded for crucial parts of the machine, like the gears. Further, if the engine would crash, not unlikely because of the last demands, it had to start anew. This made precision forgery for Babbage an "incessant anxiety" and for Airy a good reason not to start on the project in the first place.

It is therefore more than a mere curiosity that the Science Museum in London, with the financial support of five computer companies, constructed the Difference Engine II on the occasion of the bicentennial of Babbage's birthday in 1991. This engine was a simplified and much more efficient version of the Difference Engine I, the design of which greatly benefited from Babbage's work on his most ambitious Analytical Engine. The Difference Engine II was built by making use of Babbage's very detailed drawings. The machine, of course, is a marvel of ingenuity. Yet, a demonstration of its working convinced me that Airy's objections were not far off the mark. The machine was in the process of computing large numbers of a polynomial equation of the seventh degree. Babbage considered the automatisation of printing the outcomes an important step in guaranteeing the accuracy and reliability of the machine, since it would exclude any errors between reading off the results of the computations and the printing process. The greater the numbers processed in the machine, the greater the chances the engine will crash. This is especially so with regard to its most vulnerable part: the printer, which indeed crashed almost immediately once the engine started to throw up its numbers.[13]

For practical purposes, a much simpler contrivance, the so-called arithmometer invented around 1820 by the French army officer Colmar, was of much more use. In a lecture to the Statistical Society of London (1878), Jevons showed himself a great enthusiast of this simple contrivance for statistical enquiry. The Colmar arithmometer was an instrument rather than a machine,

---

[13] While I was writing the main part of this chapter, the museum was in the process of building the printer to the Difference Engine II (see *The Economist*, 5 December 1998), work now completed. On my visit in Autumn 2002 to the museum, Doron Swade kindly showed me its working.

and in fact no more than an improved version of Blaise Pascal's calculating device. This arithmometer, rather than Babbage's engines, became part of the standard inventory of the first mathematics laboratory of Whittaker in Edinburgh at the end of the century, where their careful routinised use by scientists served the purposes Babbage dreamed of with his calculating engines.[14] The bureaucratic Airy got it right in the end; Babbage's purpose should not have been to incorporate the factory system in his machine, but to factorise scientific enquiry itself, as done in Whittaker's mathematics laboratory (see Warwick 1995).[15]

The Difference Engine II at the Science Museum fulfils the very same role as its famous predecessor at Babbage's *soirées*; it is a demonstration device, a monument of ingenuity, fit to tease and please the audience and to nourish its imagination. But it does not serve any practical purpose. Those who see the machine on the third floor of the museum look at an anachronism: a relict of the steam era that never was, but that looks as well-oiled and polished as the steam engines in the basement conducting their mechanised manual work. This museal arrangement symbolises a perfect division of

---

[14] On the influence of the Colmar arithmometer on Victorian scientific practice, see Warwick (1995) and Johnston (1997).

[15] As a side remark, let me add the following: Emphasis on mechanical processing of outcomes fits the image of mechanical objectivity as pictured by Daston and Galison (1992) and Galison (1998). However, Warwick (1995) rightly points out that the reliability of results obtained mechanically is as hazy as when human judgement is involved. From his discussion, it becomes clear that objectivity crucially depends on the procedures to assess the results. The same image comes to the fore from Porter's (1995) discussion of mechanical objectivity. Porter explicitly uses the term to refer to the public transparency of the routines and procedures used to establish the result. There is a close correspondence, of course, between mechanical objectivity as used to refer to a strict regime of rules, and mechanical objectivity as used to refer to rules embodied in machines (i.e., Daston and Galison's use of the term). In my view, Warwick's and Porter's notion generally fits far better with Victorian scientific practice than the one used by Daston and Galison. Failure of Babbage's project may well be attributed to the fact that the routinisation and control of the labour process, as practised in Whittaker's mathematical laboratory (and explained by Warwick), fitted much better to the age than Babbage's attempts to mechanise routinised labour itself (see also Chapter 8). The subject of mechanical objectivity will be touched upon, though not explicitly discussed, in Chapter 10, when discussing Jevons's entry on the balance in the *Dictionary of Chemistry and the Allied Branches of the Other Sciences*. It merits, of course, a more elaborate discussion, especially since it ironically became of pivotal interest to the United States' presidential election that was or was not won by George W. Bush. The embarrassing skirmish over the outcome of the 2000 election pinpoints the political meaning of mechanical objectivity: Is it about the transparency of rules to assess a result (that is where Porter locates it) or about mechanically counting votes (that is where Galison and Daston see it)? The choice of one or the other meaning may well imply a different president.

head and manual labour, of industry and mind, in which are nonetheless embodied the very same principles of the lever.

God Is a Programmer

It was as if Babbage foresaw the collapse of his life's work. Just before the government definitely stopped financing the Difference Engine I, in 1834, Babbage asked his toolmaker Joseph Clement to construct a fragment to have a physical proof of its enormous calculating powers. This little fragment, which is rightly seen as the icon of the computer era, could be admired in Babbage's salon in wealthy Marylbone. Ironically, the Difference Engine was admired more as an edifice of reason and engineering than for its practical usefulness. Schaffer and Swade both relate how this little fragment showed its "devil's tricks" during Babbage's popular *soirées*, though his guests were even more enchanted by a mechanical danseuse he had once bought from the remnants of James Cox's famous museum.[16] Time and again, the spectators fell silent in amazement as the apparatus, after having counted a series of 2, 4, 6, 8, etc., for a hundred times, all at once made a jump in the series of numbers, returning to the original series immediately or continuing the new one. It moved Lady Byron, the mother of Ada Lovelace, to describe the Difference Engine as a "thinking machine".[17]

Babbage was well-aware of the speculative vistas opened up by his machine. He never tired of telling his visitors that what seemed so miraculous and amazing to them had been programmed by him beforehand. The machine was set in advance to add 2 for a hundred times and then to add a different number, for example, 23. Thus, what seemed a miracle to the audience was not a miracle after all. It was, as Swade imagined Babbage saying to his staggered audience (Swade 2000, 79), the "manifestation of a higher law known to me, but not to you". Babbage was so content with this that he developed this idea more generally to refute Hume's argument against miracles. The regular–irregular output of the machine did not fit into Hume's idea of causation as a regular sequence of events – the punchline of Hume's argument – and yet this output was produced by the actions embodied in the

[16] See Swade (1996, 42–6) and Schaffer (1996, 62–3). On James Cox's museum, see also Marcia Pointon (1999).

[17] Swade (1996, 42) and Schaffer (1996, 62).

mechanics of the calculating engine. Could it not be, so Babbage wondered, that all apparent irregular sequences in nature were governed by mechanical laws? God, Babbage argued in his unsolicited *Ninth Bridgewater Treatise*, was the programmer of nature, who imposed mechanical laws on it, even if we, as limited human beings, were not always able to decipher them.[18]

But Babbage did not just provide an argument against Hume; he also ran into a collision course with William Whewell's much-acclaimed *Bridgewater Treatise*, an eloquent defence of natural theology in which Whewell "with the greatest propriety, den[ied] to the mechanical philosophers and mathematicians of recent times any authority with regard to their views of the administration of the universe; we have no reason whatever to expect from their speculations any help, when we ascend to the first cause and supreme ruler of the universe" (Whewell 1833).

Acutely to the point as always, Babbage chose these words as the motto for his own *Bridgewater Treatise*. Whewell, as seen previously, retreated from French rational mechanics because he considered its mathematics too deductive, too much a storage system of knowledge that was not in contact with physical reality and, hence, not fit as an inductive instrument of enquiry. But his firm belief in the providential order of nature was an important factor as well. Induction could, and should, unveil the laws of nature and thus show the providential order. This was what taxonomies – like those of Linnaeus, but also his own geological taxonomies – produced; the ultimate cause revealed in such taxonomies was the superior providential order in nature.

The axioms and definitions of rational mechanics were in Whewell's views random starting points for deductive reasoning, and Laplace's remark to Napoleon that his system of the world did not need the "assumption" of a Creator only served to bring out its inherent agnosticism (just as the assumptions of Ricardian economics were for Whewell random starting points for deductions that had no connection to the providential order in society). Insight into the moral value of the universe was derived from "a higher region than that of mathematical proof and physical consequence". Whewell defended a sharp divide between this moral and providential order of the universe that we access intuitively, and the order of nature that could

---

[18] Though originally directed against Hume, Babbage thus undermined all earlier arguments against the old *natura non facit saltus*. Babbage's argument was also mentioned by Dionysius Lardner. See Hyman (1989, 96n). See also Sophia De Morgan (1882, 90).

be revealed inductively. For Whewell, French mathematics did not serve as an instrument to discover this godly order. In an open letter to Babbage, published in the *Athenaeum* for 30 May 1837, Whewell wrote that if "the mathematician" thinks that "his mathematical knowledge alone must bring him into a nearer proximity to his Maker and Master, he will, I fear, find that the road is interrupted by a wide chasm, and he may, perhaps, turn back frustrated and hopeless". It was "only by rising above his mathematics and his physics; – by recognizing the utter dissimilarity of moral and religious grounds of belief, from mathematical and physical reasonings upon established laws of nature" that the mathematician could "make his way to the conviction of a moral constitution and providential government of the world" (Whewell 1837, 4–5).

Babbage found it "difficult to interpret" Whewell's thoughts on the limits of mechanical enquiry and used his engine to give full force to the new French mathematics of Lagrange and Laplace, as the "theory of invention" he had been looking for from the days of the short-lived Analytical Society: Mathematical analysis, in the *Bridgewater Treatise* exemplified by Laplace, showed that miracles, probability, and free will all could be approached as the same issue. That this was the case was visualised in his Difference Engine. In the chapter on freedom of the will, he made a Turing experiment *avant la lettre* of which the message was that the voluntary and deliberate turning of a wheel of the machine by someone and the unexpected, but programmed jump in a string of numbers were indiscernible by an outside observer. Hence, there was no contradiction between the consideration of the universe as governed by mechanical laws and these other so-called higher issues.

Babbage's arguments against Whewell spilled over into the inner province of the mind. What reason was there to suppose that the human mind functioned in a *different* way from a calculating machine? Consciousness and freedom of the will, to name the two great puzzles of the mind, could be mere spectres in the machinery of the mind. What the individual perceived as an act of free will could basically be governed by the same laws that produced the miraculous jump in a string of numbers. Equally, consciousness could be the by-product of the invariable mechanical laws of nature. Babbage's work on his calculating engines thus "governed", as Schaffer rightly claims, his "stories about machine intelligence" (Schaffer 1996, 62).

Thus, advanced mathematics and a recourse to the Difference Engine worked jointly for a defence of the mechanical constitution of the universe.

The order in the universe, the natural and the moral, might well obey mechanical laws. Babbage went even further to argue that it would be presumptuous to postulate any knowledge over and above what our mathematics and our machines showed to us to argue for any nonmechanical insights. In line with these arguments, Babbage's invitees were quite amazed, if not shocked, when Babbage remarked that he himself was often left in wonder about the actions of his machine, even though he was acquainted with its intricacies and had "programmed" the machine himself.

The Difference Engine thus genuinely functioned as an engine of discovery. It fulfilled the best of Simon Stevin's dictum "wonder en is gheen wonder" (that is, "wonder but not incomprehensible") and extended this to the external world. The jump in the string of numbers conveyed the message that all laws of nature, in the end, might be as mechanical as the laws governing the engine itself. To search for these laws was to search for an algorithm producing the plethora of concrete events. Such an algorithm is a machine.[19]

Babbage's severe blow to traditional categories of natural theology and moral philosophy was only convincing, however, on the assumption that the caprices of his calculating engines served as analogies to the world at large, the natural and the moral, which is more or less a definition of mechanical reasoning: to understand the world by means of machines. This was plainly denied by Whewell. To safeguard natural theology and moral philosophy from mechanics, Whewell, in Kantian fashion, restricted the domain of discourse of mechanics to problems of mechanics and no others. For insight into the higher, providential order in nature and morals, he took recourse to "intuitions". The calculating engine and French rational mechanics proved Babbage to the eye that nature and mind were no more than complex computational machines. There was no place for Whewellian "intuitions" here.

An Intelligent Machine

With Babbage's Difference Engine, thoughts on machine intelligence were really only speculations, for it was obvious that the calculating capacities of the machine still involved a considerable amount of separate mental activity

---

[19] It is somewhat ironic that Pierre Duhem, at the turn of the century, labelled Babbage's sort of approach typically English, as it distinctly had its roots in French rational mechanics as well.

that was not captured in mechanical terms. Not all analytical functions could be reduced to fixed differences; and, for these functions, it had to be decided by the human mind at what intervals to make corrections to reduce computational errors. The machine could not do so. The development of an even more ambitious machine, the Analytical Engine, seemed to overcome these limitations. The new contrivance derived its name from its ability to perform all ordinary analysis. Babbage seems not to have been very active in raising funds for its realisation. Neither was the British government. After the failure of the first project, the government had its fill of Babbage's inventions, and Prime Minister Peel only asked himself how "to get rid of Mr Babbage and his calculating machine".[20]

In her *Memoir of Augustus De Morgan*, Sophia De Morgan relates that Lady Lovelace, Byron's daughter, clearly understood the "working and beauty of the *Difference Engine*, while other visitors gazed at the working of this beautiful instrument" (1882, 89). Lady Lovelace, it is well-known, became fully absorbed by Babbage's new project. She translated a tract on the Analytical Engine, written by a certain Menebrea, an Italian army officer, on the occasion of a lecture held by Babbage in Turin. Encouraged by Babbage, she added to Menebrea's already superb exposition notes that surpassed the article twice in length. In contrast to the Difference Engine, the Analytical Engine could be really programmed. In fact, as is well-known, the design showed great similarity with von Neumann's computer design a century later (see Swade 2000; Mirowski 2002). The comparison Babbage made with a silk mill, in *The Economy of Machinery and Manufactures*, should be taken literally; the Analytical Engine incorporates in its design the architecture of a factory. The Analytical Engine combined the calculation of various functions without the interference of human mind and hand. This was attained by the

---

[20] Swade (1991, 26). See also Swade (2000). Grattan-Guinness emphasises Babbage's poor planning abilities as one of the reasons for the failing of the Difference Engine project. Another reason he offers relates its failure to Babbage's underestimation of the relevance of probability and statistics for production engineering: "A lack of understanding of production processes led him to waste time and money on the excessively precise manufacture of some of [the engine's] parts" (Grattan-Guinness 1992, 41). However, Babbage was highly annoyed by the excessive, precise (and therefore overly expensive and time-consuming) manufacturing of nonessential parts of the machine by Joseph Clement and unsuccessfully attempted to increase his control on the work. The construction of Difference Engine II has shown that the statistical measures of precision of our present-day mass manufacturing did not meet the requirements of Babbage's machine. See especially Doron Swade (2000).

use of punched cards, an idea that Babbage got when he was working on *The Economy of Machinery and Manufactures*. The idea originated from the famous Jacquard loom. In this loom, a complex mechanism of levers regulated the lifting of the warp in accordance with the desired pattern. This was done by triggering the right set of levers by a role of punched cards. These cards activated a system of levers to lift the intended column of gears. Lovelace famously wrote that "the Analytical Engine *weaves algebraical patterns*, just as the Jacquard-loom weaves flowers and leaves" (Hyman 1989, 273).

Even more forcefully than its predecessor, the Analytical Engine provoked discussions as to whether this machine was itself able to think. Algebra clearly was an advanced product of the human intellect. Menebrea was very explicit that however beautiful a contrivance this machine was, it was nevertheless an automaton. He argued that the Analytical Engine could follow only prescribed rules. It could not come to any correct results by "trial and guess-work", but only by fully written-out procedures. "It is necessarily thus; for the machine is not a thinking being, but simply an automaton which acts according to the laws imposed on it" (Hyman 1989, 252). Only the "mechanical section" of the intellect could be built into the machine, "because it was subjected to precise and invariable laws". The higher part of the intellect, "demanding the intervention of reasoning", belonged to the sphere of the imagination and understanding and did not lend itself to mechanisation (Hyman 1989, 246). Menebrea thus pinpointed the frontiers of the engine's capacities. The machine would be able to calculate, but the mechanisation of our "reasoning faculties" was beyond its reach, unless, Menebrea implicitly qualified, the rules of reasoning themselves could be algebraised. Apparently, Menebrea took it for granted that this was impossible because he concluded that though the machine could perform the conceptions of the intellect, it was unable to reflect on them (Hyman 1989, 265). In other words, the machine lacked consciousness.

Tempering her mother's enthusiasm for the intellectual capacities of the Difference Engine, Ada Lovelace stressed that the Analytical Engine should be seen as a *substitute* for the human mind as far as concerned its ability to compute, and at the most as an *extension* of it – its high speed enabling it to undertake problems that until then were beyond the computing capacities of the individual. The Analytical Engine, Lovelace emphasised, was not itself able to develop original thoughts; it could not think. Nevertheless, Lovelace suggested more than once that the design of the new machine established an "intimate and effective connection" between "the mental and the material" (Hyman 1989, 273). She qualified Menebrea's assertion that the Analytical Engine would only be able to execute mechanically prescribed rules by pointing out that its ingenious mechanism of anticipation gave the machine the possibility "of feeling about to discover which of two or more possible contingencies has occurred, and of then shaping its future course accordingly" (Hyman 1989, 252n).[21] She was convinced that mathematics "constitutes the language through which alone we can adequately express the great facts of the natural world" (Hyman 1989, 272). No coincidence then that she made a straightforward parallel between the activities of the brain and the workings of the machine:

> It were much to be desired, that when mathematical processes pass through the human brain instead of through the medium of inanimate mechanism, it were equally a necessity of things that the reasonings connected with *operations* should hold the same just place as a clear and well-defined branch of the subject of analysis.
>
> (Hyman 1989, 269)

Reasoning along these lines clearly implied that the reasoning processes of minds and machines were organised by means of the very same science of operations that first came into existence with Babbage's Analytical Engine. Though the "hardware" of minds and machines was of course very different, there was no principled distinction between their modes of operation. Man and machines alike could "feel" what was to happen and act accordingly.

Is the Mind a Reasoning Machine?

Babbage dedicated his (never published) essays on the philosophy of mathematics to Dugald Stewart, and this was, as shown by Helena Pycior (1984), not by accident. In his *Elements of the Philosophy of the Human Mind* (1792), Stewart emphasised the importance of developing a "system of logic" that would lay down "the rules of investigation" for the different sciences. With regard to mathematics, Stewart distinguished between two different forms of reasoning: the "geometrical" and the "algebraical". Geometrical reasoning

---

[21] This aspect of the Analytical Engine was jumped upon by Alfred Marshall in his curious tract on the analogy between man and machine, *Ye Machine*. For a discussion, see Raffaelli (1994, 2003).

was about an individual of a class as representative of all individuals; algebraic reasoning used a "generic word" that bore no resemblance to the individuals of a class. The algebraist reasoned on arbitrary symbols. In a stunning preview of what was to come, Stewart wrote:

> All the rules of logic, with respect to the syllogism, might be demonstrated, without having recourse to any thing but the letters of the alphabet; in the same manner, (and I may add, on the very same principles), on which the algebraist demonstrates, by means of these letters, the various rules for transposing the terms of an equation.
>
> (quoted from Pycior 1984, 437)

Babbage had incorporated the "rules" for "transposing the terms of an equation" in his calculating engines. Hence, at the fundamental level, there was a relation between logic, algebra, the operations of the mind, and machines. The crucial difference with Whewell's logic of induction was that, on the model of algebra, the mind was not guided by, nor guided to, fundamental ideas; the mind proceeded on its formal rules of operation. The logic of investigation became intimately connected with the logic of machines.

The question of whether the mind could be conceived as a reasoning machine was placed most strongly on the agenda with the appearance of George Boole's *Laws of Thought* (1854). The title of Boole's work suggested that logic was not merely an abstract, formal discipline, but described laws inherent in our mental organisation. Boole's introductory words (Boole [1854] 1958, 1) leave little doubt on this:

> The design of the following treatise is to investigate the fundamental laws of those operations of the mind by which reasoning is performed; to give expression to them in the symbolical language of a Calculus ... and, finally, to collect from the various elements of truth brought to view in the course of these inquiries some probable intimations concerning the nature and constitution of the human mind.

Boole's psychologistic claims that logic was a science of the operations of the mind met with considerable reservations. One of the sceptics was James Martineau, a Unitarian minister teaching mental philosophy and political economy at Manchester New College, the principal institute of higher education for Unitarians (with whom Jevons took classes on mental philosophy for a while). Though originally educated in the association psychology of David Hartley, Joseph Priestley, and James Mill, Martineau had gradually

shifted towards a position which stood at odds with their "maxims of mechanical causality". His study under the great German Aristotle scholar Trendelenburg was decisive for this shift towards a Kantian and "even" Hegelian
position (Martineau [1885] 1901, ix, xiv) that showed important influences
of the eighteenth-century so-called faculty-psychology, as witnessed by his
attention for the faculties of apprehension, imagination, and so on.[22] In a
letter of January 1865 (JA 6/2/270) to Jevons, Martineau therefore unsurpris-
ingly wrote that Boole's system "seems . . . not to stand quite straight with
psychology".

Another sceptic was John Stuart Mill, who by then was one of the great
propagators of the association psychology and whose *Logic* had considerable if not overwhelming authority. Though wildly different from Kantian
epistemology, the association psychology aimed at a substantial theory of
the formation of knowledge. This theory was captured under the heading of
logic. From this perspective, Mill (JA 6/2/271) characterised Boole's logical
system in a letter of 15 May 1865 to Jevons as follows:

> I look upon it as I do upon Mr. De Morgan's elaborate system of numeri-
> cally definite propositions and syllogisms: as a remarkable fact of mental
> gymnastics, capable of being very useful in the way of a scholastic exercise,
> but of no considerable utility for any other purpose.

From very different sides, reservations were made as to the relevance of
Boole's logic as a science of mental operations. The issue was really: What
was the proper field of logical inquiry?[23]

It has recently been argued by Nicla Vassallo (1997, 2000) that Boole has
been unjustly chastised for his psychologism. To adstrue this thesis, Vassallo
quotes Boole as resisting a theory which conceives the mind as having different "faculties or powers . . . as Attention, Simple Apprehension, Conception
or Imagination, Abstraction &c" (Boole [1854] 1958, 41). True as this may

---

[22] Trendelenburg was a student of Hegel. It should be noted, however, that when Trendelenburg turned to Aristotle, he became a severe opponent of Hegel's philosophy.

[23] No attempt will be made here to give a full account of the intricacies and reception of
Boole's logic, which as Grattan-Guinness (1991, 21n9) observed, "needs considerably more
research". Relevant in the context of this essay are Vassallo (1997, 2000) and Forster (1997).
For a general account of Boole's logic, MacHale (1985) is the place to start. See also Bachir
Diagne (1989) and Kneale and Kneale (1971). An anthology of important essays on Boole
is Gasser (2000). A concise introduction to Boole's logic, as well as a collection of Boole's
own writing, is Grattan-Guinness and Bornet 1997.

be, it only proves that Boole resisted a *specific* and important contamination of logic and psychology that had been the dominant approach, especially in Scotland and Germany. All these faculties, according to Boole, could be "merged...under one generic name of *Operations* of the human mind", of which he would "seek to express their ultimate laws" (Boole [1854] 1958, 41). Martineau's reservations related exactly to the dismissal of the established faculty-psychology that was entailed in Boole's enterprise.

As Babbage's machines had put into question the traditional conceptions of the "intimate connection between mind and matter", the same was true for Boole's logic. Boole did not accept traditional mental categories, but reduced them to one: The mind's reasoning could be described by operations that could be treated algebraically. Boole's logic proved to be the "ultimate engine of reason" (Wise and Smith 1989b, 439). Boole was, however, reluctant to "subject" man's reason "to the rigour of technical forms" (Grattan-Guinness 1992, 44, quoting Boole) and showed little interest in Babbage's Difference Engine. Though he visited him to see it working, he "at no stage seems to have contemplated its use as a primitive computer" (MacHale 1985, 235). Grattan-Guinness and Bornet (1997, xliv) consider that for Boole the mind was capable of "grasping general laws from particular cases...and so he would not have welcomed the association of his logic with the *repetitive* actions of computing". But Boole's program was to algebraise logic, and algebra could perfectly well be executed by the routines of Babbage's machines.

In a very interesting review of Boole's *Mathematical Analysis of Logic; Being an Essay towards a Calculus of Deductive Reasoning* (1847) in *The Athenaeum*, De Morgan emphasised Boole's disinterest in mechanising logical inference and his own interest in it:

> "Mr Boole and Mr De Morgan have two different objects. The former desires to bring ordinary reflection on the proposition and the syllogism into a form which will be aided by symbolical notation: the latter attempts to dispense with such reflection, except in the establishment of processes, and then to use these processes as mechanical aid to the development of results".

Even though Boole did not "advocate the substitution of mechanical work for mental inference", De Morgan continued, "[h]is tract is the assertion that it can be done, and the demonstration of a mode of doing it" (all quotes from Sánchez Valencia 2001, 77). Hence the question: Was Boole's logical system a *representation* of the laws of thought, was it the *blueprint of a machine*, or was it an *abstract formal system* only?[24]

Mill's reference to De Morgan in his letter to Jevons makes clear that the question of the relation between logic, mechanics, and psychology was not limited to Boole's algebraic logic, but extended to all attempts to formalise logic. In line with the dominant attitude towards syllogistic, Aristotelian logic, Mill only valued the new formal logical systems as a form of "mental gymnastics". The true problems of logic were thought to belong to quite a different field, which if not identical with the association psychology was at least closely related to it. The study of logic, in this sense, should reveal the laws of mental reasoning and should not focus on the formal operations of our mind. For so divergent writers as Martineau and Mill, Boole's formal logic was thought to be of no direct interest.

De Morgan, founding professor of mathematics at University College, London, and extremely popular with his students (see Rice 1996b, 1999), was with Boole one of the great propagators of formal logic. In his *Syllabus of Logic*, he argued that Mill rightly refused the use of "learned logic" in daily life, but for reasons "entirely wrong" (De Morgan 1860, 116).[25] Taking issue with Immanuel Kant, De Morgan argued that the reason the "educated world" commonly thought "lightly" of the ordinary syllogism was that it had "arrived at some use of those higher developments of thought which that same common logic has never taken into its compass" (1860, 96n).

De Morgan called this ordinary, or Aristotelian, logic the "*logician's* abacus". "Educated man" had no more reason "to have recourse to the logical abacus for his reasoning, than to the chequer-board, or arithmetical abacus, for adding up his bills". With the "higher developments of thought", De Morgan was referring to his own extended system of logic. Whereas the "logician's abacus" – ordinary logic – was a "fit and desirable occupation for childhood", such was not the case for his own system, which embodied a true revolution in logic (1860, 116n).

The "true revolution" De Morgan referred to was the so-called quantification of the predicate. The claim to the discovery of this innovation in logic

---

[24] Grattan-Guinness (1992, 44) notes that, though Babbage read and acknowledged Boole's work in logic as that of a "real *thinker*", he "did not make use of Boole's ideas developing his engines". See also Bromley 1987. When Boole's first work on logic appeared (1847), Babbage's main work on the Analytical Engine was done.

[25] Reference is made to section numbers.

provoked an exchange of reciprocal accusations, charges, and reproaches between Sir William Hamilton, Professor of Logic and Metaphysics in Edinburgh, and Augustus De Morgan.[26] This exchange makes a most "melancoly" impression upon the modern reader – to use one of Hamilton's favourite expressions. The crux of the contested discovery was that whereas in Aristotelian logic the syllogism was comprised of genus–species relationships, these propositions could be equally well reversed. Thus, "all humans are mortal", where the class of humans is a subclass of the class of mortal beings, could be rendered as "some mortals are humans". There was no reason to exclude propositions such as "all humans are some mortals" from consideration, in which the extension of the predicate was limited. It consequently became possible to use nonuniversal quantifiers, even to limit quantifiers to a specific number as De Morgan did. In fact, by these "numerically definite propositions", as De Morgan called them, logic and probability theory became connected.[27]

The importance of this discovery lay, amongst others, in the fact that the proposition of the classical syllogism could be *reversed*. As a consequence, De Morgan extended the classical notion of the copula "is" to mean all sorts of relation terms with this property. Thus, for example, in "John is a fellow of James", "is a fellow of" is transitive and convertible and serves the same function as the traditional copula "is". According to Boole, the reversibility of the copula implied that it differed in nothing from the mathematical sign of equation "=". A proposition could thus be expressed as an algebraic equation. But Boole's innovation in logic was more concerned with the further and thorough algebraisation of logical operations than with the quantification of the predicate. His important innovation was to interpret

[26] Augustus De Morgan carefully compiled the complete exchange of letters between them, of which Sophia De Morgan's *Memoir* gives an excellent impression. This exchange of letters can also be found at University Library London (ULL) MS 775/354. Though Hamilton's allegation of De Morgan of plagiarism is highly overstated, the sequence of events do in my opinion justify some of it. De Morgan's explicit requests on the history of logic and Hamilton's willingness to send him his own rough draft of a new system of logic reached De Morgan before De Morgan's own proposal for a new system of logic was published. De Morgan defended himself against Hamilton's charge with the argument that by the time he got Hamilton's proposal, his own formal logical system was in the hands of Whewell being considered for publication. This, I think, should have settled the issue, but it did not. The quarrel went on for years, mainly in the *Athenaeum*, and involved in the end all those interested in the new developments in logic.

[27] Not incidentally Boole, De Morgan, and Jevons discuss logic and probability theory jointly in their publications.

logical processes in terms of algebraic operations. His logic, as is well-known, reduced to a branch of mathematics and is now commonly referred to as "Boolean Algebra".[28]

If the sphere of reasoning itself were to be algebraised, *and* if it were possible to embody algebra in a machine, as in Babbage's Analytical Engine, what independent or separate quality remained for the mind itself? According to De Morgan, who was much intrigued by Boole's logic, the right answer seems to have been: none. In *The Application of the Theory of Probabilities to Some Questions of Evidence* (1850), De Morgan remarked that "I should wonder at no one who suspected that the manifestation of the secrets of the brain would exhibit something more like a calculating machine" (De Morgan 1850, 42). Both machines and minds obeyed the algebra of operations. In the sequel to this quote and referring to Kant, De Morgan easily passed over the very different conception of the human mind which formed the leading thread of Kant's philosophy. Even if Kant somewhere makes the comparison between the human mind and a machine, the general tendency of his work obviously points in the opposite direction. Kant's investigation into the limits and necessary forms of our knowledge, though explicitly not an empirical but formal analysis of the human mind, was premised upon the psychological theory that our mental organisation contains separate faculties. For Kant, logic was essentially embedded in an analysis of the judgements of the human mind, and this analysis could not be separated from his conception of consciousness.

We have seen how Boole distanced himself from such an approach.[29] The same can be said of De Morgan. In the second volume of *Formal Logic* (1847), De Morgan only *mentions* the use made in old systems of logic of the division of mental acts into "*apprehension, judgement*, and *discourse*, taking cognizance of notions, propositions, and arguments" (ULL MS 776/1, 227).[30] In vain one searches in this book for a further discussion of these terms. What

---

[28] Boole's original system underwent so many changes under the influence, amongst others, of Jevons's criticism that "Boole's algebra isn't Boolean algebra" (Hailperin 1981).

[29] For a discussion of the relation of Boole to Kant, see Forster (1997) who takes their approaches to be quite close to one another. A radically different view is hinted at in the introduction to Bachir Diagne (1989, 10). Though Vassallo (1997) does not discuss Boole in relation to Kant, her judgement on Boole's conception of logic in relation to Kant's reinforces Bachir Diagne's position.

[30] Use is made of Augustus De Morgan's annotated and interleaved copy. University Library London ULL MS 776/1.

should be understood under the marker "logic" had become a different thing for scientists like Boole and De Morgan, who thought of themselves more as mathematicians than as philosophers like Hamilton and Martineau, both of whom were heavily indebted to Kant; perhaps this explains the extraordinary and grossly exaggerated vehemence of Hamilton's reaction to De Morgan when he felt he had been misused on the issue of the quantification of the predicate, on which he claimed primacy.[31]

In *The Edinburgh Review* of April 1833, Hamilton evaluated ten recent books on logic, among them Richard Whately's influential *Elements of Logic* and George Bentham's *Outline of a New System of Logic, with a Critical Examination of Dr Whately's "Elements of Logic"*. For historical reasons, as Durand-Richard (2000) rightly remarks, it is interesting that Hamilton devotes most of the space in this review to Whately, saying very little about George Bentham's book, which indubitably contains the idea of quantifying the predicate.[32] Hamilton, discussing Whately's system of logic, argued that his definition of logic as analysing "the *process of mind in reasoning*" or the "*process (operation) of reasoning*", is "delusive". Logic, according to Hamilton, has "nothing to do with the *process* or *operation* [of reason], but is conversant only with its *laws*". Whately's definition, he complained, would "identify logic and psychology and metaphysic" (Hamilton 1833, 207).

Hamilton clearly interpreted the process, or operation, of reason as an empirical process, while logic should be occupied with the form of the processes of reasoning only. In his review, Hamilton somewhat differently, but relatedly, distinguished two meanings of the Greek word "logos", of

---

[31] A more prosaic "explanation" of the strength of Hamilton's reaction can be found in a review in the *Athenaeum*, No. 1724, 10 November 1860, 623, of the posthumous edition of Sir William Hamilton's *Lectures on Metaphysics and Logic*, edited by perhaps the one most devoted to his philosophy – the Rev. Henry L. Mansel – and John Veith. In this review, we read that, in 1843, Hamilton was attacked by a paralysis of the right side of his face from which he never fully recovered. It is suggested that this might have enforced in this, as in other cases, "the acuteness of his polemics". See also "The Gorilla War", a notebook of De Morgan containing correspondence and newspaper cuttings relating to his dispute with Hamilton, ULL MS 775/366.

[32] In a letter of 21 December 1850 in *The Athenaeum*, it is made clear that Hamilton had read his *Outline* before proposing his own quantified system, as is of course obvious from Hamilton's review of it. De Morgan immediately examined George Bentham's book in the British Museum and personally confirmed Bentham's right on primacy (small leaflet dated 26 December 1850 and call mark of Bentham's book inserted at the beginning of his own exemplar of *Formal Logic*). In his reexamination of the issue of primacy in the *Contemporary Review*, May 1873, Jevons confirms this claim. I could not retrace a suggestion made by Jevons that George Bentham's discovery was inspired by his uncle Jeremy's tract on logic which was first published in the 1830s.

which might be derived two different conceptions of the science of logic. Either logic addresses "reason, or our intellectual faculties in general", or its subject matter is speech or language. These two definitions were, according to Hamilton, entirely conflated by Whately. On the one hand, he made "*the analysis* of the *operation of reasoning the appropriate office of logic*" (the first, material option), but on the other hand he made "*logic entirely conversant about language*" (the second, formal option). This, according to Hamilton, was "expressly contradicted by Aristotle", for "it involves a psychological hypothesis in regard to the absolute dependence of the mental faculties upon language, once and again refuted, which we are confident that Dr Whately never could sanction" (208).

Whately's definition of logic as a science of operations conceived of logic as a material science, not as a formal one. Logic, according to Hamilton, treated neither the operations or acts of thought (a matter of psychology) nor language in relation to these acts (involving an undefendable position on the relation of our mental faculties to language). The "proximate end" of logic, according to Hamilton, was to analyse the canons of thought (their laws), and "its remote, to apply these to the intellectual acts" (209).

In *Formal Logic*, De Morgan distinguished only *one* meaning of the Greek word "logos": the "communication of thought, usually by speech. It is that name which is generally given to that branch of inquiry... in which the act of mind in reasoning is considered, particularly with reference to the connection of thought and language" (ULL MS 776/1, 26). We can be very sure that Hamilton never saw this definition of the science of logic, for the copy De Morgan sent to him was sent back by return mail. In his own copy, De Morgan noted that "the returned work was uncut except a little at the beginning and all the appendix"[33]. We see in De Morgan's definition the contamination of both different definitions of logic that Hamilton criticized in Whately. The same mix can be found in Boole who analysed the "operations of thought", while De Morgan made the "act of the mind" in relation to language the proper subject of logic. In both cases this meant, for Hamilton, conflating logic, metaphysics, and psychology.

De Morgan was, however, quite adamant that logic, metaphysics, and psychology should be forcefully distinguished. In his much-later *Syllabus of Logic* (1860), used for his courses in logic at University College, De Morgan derived the distinction between logic, metaphysics, and psychology

---

[33] ULL MS 776/1, interleaved page 4.

differently than Hamilton. Whereas Hamilton's "canons of thought" referred to the formal laws of thought, logic, according to De Morgan, was concerned with its *results*. Any reference to the acts of the mind was, in fact, squeezed out of logic by a definitional trick. A proposition (a relation between terms) and a judgement (according to De Morgan, a *decision* of the mind upon a proposition) were *joined*, and interchangeably denoted by one name or the other. The constituents of a proposition, words, were taken as pure "labels" or "markers", thus furnishing the "key to the *mechanical*, or *instrumental*, treatment of the ordinary proposition and the ordinary syllogism" (De Morgan 1860, 5). Substitute judgement for proposition as an interchangeable term, and it turns out that the *decision* of the mind upon a proposition can be mechanised. We need no consciousness or separate capacity for judgement.

We can hardly expect Hamilton (or Martineau)[34] to have agreed with equating a proposition (a concatenation of terms) to a judgement (a decision of the mind upon a proposition). It is informative that Hamilton time and again stressed that judgement was not a matter of mechanics. This was brought out by Hamilton in a review of the 1829 French edition of the work of the Common Sense philosopher Thomas Reid, the teacher of Dugald Stewart and in his day the greatest proponent of the distinction between the realms of mind and matter. Hamilton complained about the mechanical consequences of French materialist philosophy:

> From the mechanical relation of sense with its objects, it was attempted to explain the mysteries of intelligence.... The moral nature of man was at last identified with his physical; mind was a reflex of matter, – thought a secretion of the brain. A philosophy so melancoly in its consequences, and founded on principles thus partial and exaggerated, could not be permanent: a reaction was inevitable.
>
> (Hamilton 1829, 194–5)[35]

---

[34] See, for example, Martineau ([1885] 1901, 2:566–7).

[35] Daston (1994, 185) claims that "eighteenth-century philosophers conceived of intelligence and even moral sentiment to be in their essence forms of calculation". This claim undoubtedly holds for French materialist philosophers. However, in my view, the Scottish and German Enlightenment philosophers – with the exception of Francis Hutcheson, whom Daston refers to on page 192 – know too many exceptions to substantiate such a general claim. See Maas (2003). Only when Hartley's *Observations on Man* was popularised by Priestley, and Bentham referred to Priestley and Hartley in support of his felicific calculus, did Daston's summary statement rise to the fore in Britain. In the next chapter, however, we will see even a proclaimed utilitarian like John Stuart Mill was well into the nineteenth century not committed to the view Daston expresses.

It may have been that Hamilton sensed in De Morgan's views on logic a similar tendency as in French eighteenth-century materialism to mechanise thought. If Hamilton had only cut the pages of *Formal Logic* and read them, he would have seen that this tendency indeed was prominently there, but that De Morgan nevertheless was very careful and much less definitive in his claims than in his 1850 essay on probabilities:

> With respect to the mind, considered as a complicated apparatus which is to be studied, we are not even so well off as those would be who had to examine and decide upon the mechanism of a watch, merely by observation of the functions of the hands, without being allowed to see the inside.
>
> (ULL MS 776/1, 26)

In the case of a watch, a mechanician can infer its internal structure by analogy with other machines, "but in the case of the mind, we have manifestations only, without the smallest power of reference to similar things, or the least knowledge of structure or process. It is the problem of the watch to those who have never seen any mechanism at all" (26). In the case of the mind, the only possibility at hand to get an idea, however imperfect, of its operation, is to compare the "manifestations of thought with those of things in corporeal existence". But, continues De Morgan, in the case of the comparison of the mind with "an apparatus, or piece of mechanism", we cannot know "where the resemblance begins to be imperfect" (27). De Morgan added that there always had to be made "an assumption of the uniformity of process in all minds", but that different analogies might be used:

> One might use the pendulum and the weight, another the springs and the balance: one might discover the combination of toothed wheels, another a more complicated action of lever upon lever. Are we *sure* that there are no differences in our minds... if so, *how* are we sure?
>
> (27n, all quotes ULL MS 776/1)

De Morgan indulges in mechanical reasoning: taking mechanical contrivances, like the pendulum, the balance, or the lever to explain the working, not of material bodies (to which purpose such simple instruments were used in mechanics), but to explain the working of the mind itself. Even though De Morgan was very careful not to make any definite claims, it is obvious that the distance to Hamilton's strand of thinking had become an insurmountable gap. As with Babbage's Difference Engines, the universe of discourse had clearly shifted towards the attempt to understand the realm of the mind by means of machines. Like Babbage, De Morgan largely preferred this me-chanical discourse over the ultimate recourse to Divine Providence that Hamilton, with all differences, shared with William Whewell.

Ironically, it was a dispute about an explicit advocate of Divine Provi-dence – the Unitarian reverend James Martineau, filling the chair in mental philosophy and logic at University College – which caused De Morgan to resign. Though there was no doubt in the college about Martineau's excel-lent fitness for this chair, his election had been suspended for the reason that there were objections by others to Martineau's "*psychology* as well as his *religion*" (in the words of De Morgan's letter of resignation, 10 November 1866). To this De Morgan added, with characteristic acerbity, that "the first is too far removed from atheism to please the philosopher, the second too far removed from orthodoxy to please the priest" (De Morgan 1882, 341–2). For De Morgan the resistance in the college evidenced a return to the old principles of exclusion practised at Oxbridge, to which the dissenters at the end of the eighteenth century had raised their voices, and which had been the principal reason for the foundation of University College, London, in the 1820s with the help of those very same philosophical radicals who now blocked Martineau's appointment.[36]

The chair was given to Croom Robertson, a faithful pupil of Alexander Bain, who succeeded Bain as the editor of *Mind*. Martineau's dissenter's views in matters of logic and mind did not get a hearing at University Col-lege. Association psychologists like Bain and Robertson and the new formal logic of Boole and De Morgan did away with references to consciousness as a sensible mental category. Any reference to the mind as embodying "con-sciousness" was dismissed by Bain, who preferred to take consciousness as "mere feeling" (Bain 1868, 604). With Boole's and De Morgan's new logi-cal program, the idea crept in that the judgements of the mind could be reproduced mechanically.

---

[36] For a description of this episode, see Bellot (1929, 342).

SIX

~

THE MACHINERY OF THE MIND

A law of thought, a necessary part of the machinery of our minds, of
no practical use! Whose fault is that?

Augustus De Morgan, *Syllabus of Logic*, 1860

We have seen that De Morgan made some qualifications with regard to the
comparison of the mind with a *specific* machine. The universe of discourse,
however, was clearly delineated: It was some kind of machine. What was
needed was a mechanician who could give a "guess as to its structure" (De
Morgan ULL MS 776/1, 26). This was done by De Morgan's faithful pupil
William Stanley Jevons in his work on the Logical Machine. Jevons did not
attribute much practical value to his contrivance, its "chief importance"
being "of a purely theoretical kind" (*PL* 170). Yet, this did not make the
machine useless, but made it by contrast of value for those "interested in the
speculative or theoretical views of the subject" (*PL* 144).

Jevons used his contrivance similarly as Babbage: to speculate on the
mechanical character of the mind and the universe at large. In its first
quality, it served to bridge the distinction between mind and matter that
was so overwhelmingly present in Victorian intellectual and scientific discourse, though there were other sources that Jevons drew upon in this regard (as will be seen in the next chapter). In its second quality, Jevons used
it to overcome one of the serious conundrums of all contemporary discussions on scientific discovery: how to think about induction. Both issues
combined show an inherent tension in all mechanical notions of human
reasoning; mechanisms display fixed rules – that is, what makes them a
mechanism. However, induction is about discovering novelty, which does

not fall straight by following fixed rules. Where Babbage's and Jevons's machines served in Victorian discourse to capture reasoning in mechanical terms thinking – the use of the imagination escaped these terms and therefore raised questions about any belief in the mechanical constitution of the universe and about mechanical notions of judgement and thinking as well.

The Logical Abacus

Jevons clearly saw that the newly developed systems of formal logic lent themselves to De Morgan's suggestion for mechanisation. Taking Boole's logic as the point of departure, Jevons constructed in the 1860s a machine that he termed the Logical Abacus, drawing the same parallel as De Morgan with the arithmetical abacus. While De Morgan used the expression to refer somewhat dismissively to Aristotelian logic, Jevons upgraded the term to refer to the higher calculus of reasoning developed by himself, Boole, and De Morgan. Jevons's first mention that he had a "rough model to work excellently" of "a reasoning machine or logical abacus" was found in a letter of 25 May 1865 to his brother Herbert. This "machine" had to be handled manually and with considerable knowledge of logic to make accurate logical deductions (Figure 6-1).

Jevons referred to his Logical Abacus again in letters to his sister Lucy of 4 November 1865 and to Herbert in a letter of 18 November 1865. Early in October, he gave his opening address at Queen's College, Liverpool, in which he mentioned the Logical Abacus in the same breath as Boole, De Morgan, and Babbage. In later years at Queen's College and at Owen's College, Manchester, Jevons used this Logical Abacus for classroom instruction purposes to help the students become acquainted with the new systems of formal logic and to visualise the different steps that are made in logical inferences.

Jevons presented the Logical Abacus at the Literary and Philosophical Society of Liverpool on 19 March 1866, and at the same Society in Manchester three weeks later. In May, he travelled to University College, London, where he presented it to "old students & others", including Professor Thomas Hirst (who succeeded De Morgan in 1867 as professor of pure and applied mathematics). Jevons described the design of the Logical Abacus minutely in his *Substitution of Similars*, which appeared in June 1869, and he also referred to it in his *Principles of Science*, including a sketch of the apparatus. It

THE LOGICAL ABACUS.

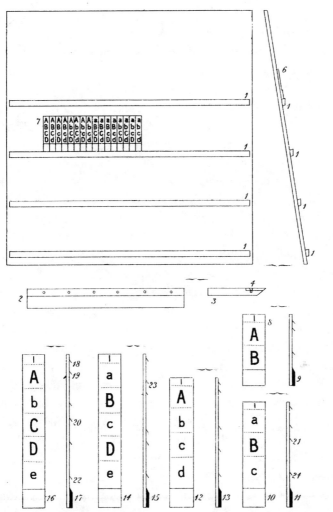

6-1. Jevons's drawing of the Logical Abacus. *Pure Logic and Other Minor Works*, 1890, opposite to p. 8. Courtesy of Palgrave/Macmillan Press.

functioned similarly to an arithmetical abacus (hence its name) and involved considerable manual and intellectual dexterity to obtain faultless results.

In the same diary entry in which Jevons makes note of his visit to University College, he also mentioned his visit to Gladstone, following on the success of his *The Coal Question* (1865) and understandably the most "striking event" of his London journey. He also mentioned a visit to his old mathematics teacher, Augustus De Morgan, to whom he showed his Logical Abacus.

In early correspondence in 1863 (JA 6/2/114), De Morgan was highly cautious about the merits of Jevons's own logical system and on his criticism of Boole, especially Boole's treatment of disjunctions. Apparently, Jevons had sent the manuscript of his tract to Boole, and from De Morgan's letter to Jevons it can be gathered that Jevons sent De Morgan a copy of the manuscript and Boole's reaction as well. Emphasising the "ingenuity" of Jevons's views and the "truth of the bulk of them", De Morgan urged Jevons to ponder the wisest strategy to follow. The letter reads like advice in publishing strategy, to first publish only a very short tract in which he would explain his queries with Boole's system and would give a short exposition of his alternative. Otherwise, so De Morgan feared, there was a fair chance Jevons's views would go largely unheard, as all larger works of Boole and himself had hardly received any attention.

Jevons did not quite follow De Morgan's advice. Although his first work in logic was rather slim, it consisted predominantly of an elaborate exposition of his own logical system that defended the inclusive interpretation of dysjunctions and insisted on the distinction between quality and quantity, where logic treated quality and mathematics dealt with quantity. In an appendix, Jevons briefly and critically examined Boole's logic. The peculiarities of Jevons's system have been examined recently in Mosselmans (1998). De Morgan correctly feared for the fate of Jevons's book. In a letter to his brother Herbert, Jevons complained it made "no noise"(PC 3:52, letter of 18 February 1864), thus, adding to the series of disappointments Jevons had experienced since his return to England.

It was clear though that De Morgan's concerns with Jevons's manuscript were not just strategic. De Morgan substantially diverged from Jevons in his views on formal logic. In his review of Jevons's book in The Athenaeum for 30 January 1864, De Morgan praised Jevons's "remarkable book" as "a work of much talent, and abounding of acute remarks". In line with his earlier letter to Jevons, De Morgan not only hailed the opportunity that Jevons's book gave to enhance discussions about the use of the calculus in logic, but also made clear that he liked the book "much better when taken apart, than when considered in contrast to Mr Boole's system" (quoted from Sánchez Valencia 2001, 78).

Jevons's insistence on the difference between quality and quantity – of so much importance for his subsumption of mathematics to logic (Mossel- mans 1998) – was the least of De Morgan's concerns. Of more importance was Jevons's opposition to and abandoning of "much of the *calculus*" of Boole's logic that was prompted by his adherence to the inclusive, rather than the exclusive, interpretation of the sum operation. In line with his strong inter- ests in algebra, De Morgan made it no secret that he sided with Boole. De Morgan gave an elaborate example to show the merits of Boole's algebraic approach over Jevons's alternative system, and concluded from this that it might well be granted to Jevons that there were propositions that could be handled by Jevons's "subtle deductions", but that "there were others which are not so" (Sánchez Valencia 2001, 78–9).

De Morgan's criticism made it, of course, a matter of some importance for Jevons to show his former teacher that his logical checkerboard was as perfectly able to produce unequivocal results as Boole's more complex system. De Morgan was not someone easily convinced, and it must have been with some satisfaction that Jevons noted in his diary that De Mor- gan "allowed that it [the logical abacus] achieved very well the exclusion of contradictories" (*PC* 1:206).[1] Their different appraisals of Boole's algebraic logic reveal, however, a much deeper difference between De Morgan and Jevons. Although De Morgan was interested in mechanising logic, his pri- mary interest was in mathematics. This was exactly the reverse for Jevons. Although interested in mathematics, his interest was in mechanising logic. Jevons was a natural scientist who trusted instruments to disclose the laws of the universe, the natural and the moral. To one of Francis Galton's questions on the power of visualising for Galton's *English Men of Science* (1874), Jevons answered: "I have no doubt that *mathematical power* depends upon some mental conformation quite different from mine" (letter of 7 December 1879 to Galton).[2]

Still involving the interference of the human mind and hands, Jevons was not content with the Logical Abacus in its current state. In a letter of 18 November 1865 to his brother Herbert, he wrote that he was engaged in

---

[1] I have found no evidence for Mirowski's claim (2002, 40) that "Boole and De Morgan were also less than enthusiastic" about "this simple combinatorial device". In the case of Boole, Mirowski's claim is particularly hard to substantiate, because Boole died in 1864–that is, before either the Logical Abacus or the Logical Machine had been constructed.

[2] I owe this reference to Judy Klein.

"getting my reasoning machine into a true machine form, it having previously been an abacus or counting board, not a machine" (*PC* 1:198n2 and 3). We can infer from the *Papers and Correspondence* that Jevons worked on this mechanised version in later years. In September 1867, he wrote to Herbert that he had found a young clockmaker in Salford, Manchester's workmen's twin city, for its construction. Although the design and construction of this machine fell far below the difficulties of Babbage's highly complex machines, Jevons still feared that "it will be necessary for me to go there almost every day to see that he is getting on right" (*PC* 3:157). Jevons referred to this version of the abacus as the Logical Machine. Although not in particularly good shape, the Logical Machine is presently in the collection of the Oxford History of Science Museum (Figure 6-2). A report of the committee of the museum shows it was still in working order in 1953.[3]

According to Jevons, the great advantage of this machine over the earlier counting board form was that it would be "free from the possibility of error" (*PS* 107). The Logical Machine was not only able to draw the ordinary inferences of Aristotelian logic, but also incorporated – so Jevons claimed – the whole force of Boole's newly developed system of logic. Thus, whereas Aristotle had promised an *organon*, finally here was a real instrument that at the same time was "physical proof" of the incompleteness of ordinary logic (*PL* 120).[4]

THE LOGICAL MACHINE

It is not quite clear how Jevons arrived at the design of his Logical Machine. A general inspiration from Babbage's calculating engines explains little, especially because Jevons did not perceive of his machine as a *calculating* but as a *reasoning* machine – an issue that lays at the root of his distinction of logic and mathematics. There almost certainly is no influence on Jevons from Stanhope's Logic Demonstrators – invented at the end of the eighteenth

---

[3] Tom Freshwater, conservator at the Oxford Science Museum, informed me that the Logical Machine was restored to working order shortly after my visit in the Autumn of 2002.

[4] Dodd (1988, 1) claims that Jevons's Logical Machine comprises the traditional Aristotelian interpretation of the copula. The copula would have been the equation relation if one had to press: A copula AB stop. But it is only necessary to press: A copula B stop. From Dodd's comment, one might falsely conclude that Jevons's Logical Machine is no more than a mechanical rendering of Aristotelian logic. As I argue in the body of the text, the design of the levers incorporates Jevons's views on the inclusive "or".

6-2. Jevons's Logical Machine. Courtesy of Museum of the History of Science, Oxford, inventory no. 18,230.

century. The third Earl of Stanhope was close to the circles of Bentham and the "Lunar Men" and was an active supporter of Joseph Priestley (Wess 1997; Uglow 2002). Stanhope was so successful in his deliberate endeavours to keep his logical instruments – which were not really machines – secret from the public that they fell into complete oblivion rather than bringing him the fame he had hoped for (Wess 1997).

It may have been that there was a less direct influence on Jevons from, again, Babbage and De Morgan. We have already seen that De Morgan took great interest in Babbage's calculating engines and a more general interest in the mechanisation of reasoning processes. In 1840, Thomas Fowler (1777–1843), a Devonshire book printer of humble background, presented a calculating machine of his own invention to Charles Babbage and others, possibly Sir John Lubbock (Vass 1999).[5] Babbage responded enthusiastically to the machine that was based on a design clearly different from his. In the same year, Samuel Baily corresponded an account of this machine by Augustus De Morgan to the Royal Society. Sir George Biddell Airy gave a roughly similar account at the British Association for the Advancement of Science (BAAS) meeting in 1840 in Glasgow, of which a report can be found in the *Athenaeum* for 31 October 1840. All these gentlemen of science were positive about the machine's capabilities. Instead of using the decimal system, Fowler used the ternary system, which made it necessary to convert the decimal input and reconvert the result – something that had to be done by hand and was, as De Morgan noted, a possible and serious source of errors. Made of wood, the machine itself was "large and difficult to move", but "easily used". It consisted of separate systems of rods for each algebraic operation, that were moved by a carrying apparatus. The end result was mechanically reduced to its simplest form.

From De Morgan's description, there is little more to be gathered of the actual design of the machine, and Fowler was more than reluctant to reveal any details in writing, having been robbed of an earlier invention of a printing machine. Airy was irritated by Fowler's reluctance to furnish any drawings, and nothing came of any further investigation of the prospects of his machine. Thus, for the same reason, Fowler's invention – like Stanhope's – went into oblivion, although his simple contrivance looked "vastly more promising than Babbage's" (Swade 2000, 312).[6] Given De Morgan and Jevons's mutual interest in calculating engines and in mechanising logic, it

[5] I would like to thank Doron Swade for drawing my attention to Pamela Vass's work, and Pamela Vass for sending me her article and providing further information on Thomas Fowler and his calculating project.

[6] Pamela Vass (1999) reproduces the only known image of Fowler's machine, a stained-glass window in St. Michael's Church, Great Torrington. However, this artist's impression gives little clue as to the functioning of the machine.

is perfectly likely that Fowler's use of moving rods gave Jevons the idea for the mechanism of his Logical Machine.

Jevons gave a full description of this Logical Machine in his essay *On the Mechanical Performance of Logical Inference* written in 1869 and read to the Royal Society in 1870 (Figure 6-2). Jevons paid full tribute to Babbage. Babbage's machines were proof to Jevons that the "mind [was] able to impress some of its highest attributes upon matter, and to create its own rival in the wheels and the levers of an insensible machine".[7] Where Babbage's had relegated mental computation to a mechanical contrivance that was able to compute faster and faultless, Jevons claimed to have made a similar machine with regard to logical inference. His Logical Machine was able to reason upon propositions and to do so faster than the human mind. This did not mean, as suggested by Mirowski (2002, 40), that Jevons "really did believe ... that mind was directly reducible to matter". Jevons considered his machine to *mimic* the operations of the mind, and this is not identical to Mirowski's claim. In *Principles of Science* (*PS* 110), Jevons stated: "When any proposition is worked upon by the keys, the machine analyses and digests the meaning of it and becomes charged with the knowledge embodied in that proposition". In *On the Mechanical Performance of Logical Inference* (*PL* 144), Jevons similarly explained that once the machine was "charged, as it were, with a certain amount of information", it was "able to perform a complete analysis of any logical problem impressed upon it". Thus, logical deduction became "a matter of routine" (*PL* 151).

As in Boole's logic, the copula "is" was taken as the mathematical sign of an equation. For Jevons, this was the fundamental step. It was the *conditio sine qua non* of what he termed the *substitution of similars* or *substitution of equals*. It was what "common" – that is, actual – "reasoning" essentially was about. Common reasoning was by analogies. The condition for making an analogy between different subjects depends on there being sufficient aspects of similarity to draw an equal sign between them. Jevons maintained that reasoning by equations was "the fundamental principle of all the sciences" (*PL* 50).

---

[7] Michael White recently informed me about a visit of Jevons to Babbage in 1866. In relation to this visit, Jevons's brother Thomas wrote to him: "I was much interested in the account of your visit to Babbage" (letter from Thomas Jevons, 1 May 1866, Box 14, Seton-Jevons Collection, Seton Hall University). Unfortunately, there is no other information left. There can be little doubt, however, that the context of this visit is to be sought in their application of machinery to mental operations. See White (2001, 25).

But, Jevons diverged importantly from Boole's algebra. According to Jevons, the main reason why "learned man", like Kant and Mill, took so low a view of the ordinary syllogism was because the Aristotelian syllogism did not fit in with actual reasoning. In this, he echoed De Morgan. However, where De Morgan shared Boole's views to fully "algebraise" logic, Jevons was convinced that logical reasoning and algebraic reasoning were not equivalent: Logical reasoning encompassed mathematical reasoning, and not the other way around.[8]

Jevons's main complaint with Boole's algebraic system was that its "obscure" rules of inference meant that Boole's algebra did not represent the way men "as superior beings" normally reasoned (*PL* 143). The advantage of his own logical system and of his Logical Machine, Jevons claimed, was that it reflected "the laws and conditions of thought in reality" (*PL* 67). This did not mean that Jevons considered the mind to consist of "spindles and levers"; it meant that Jevons believed that his mechanical contrivance mimicked the *process* of logical inference of ordinary individuals. Interestingly, Babbage made a similar argument in relation to his calculating engine: "When we attempt to perform . . . additions by machinery we might follow exactly the usual process of the human mind" (*Babbage* 11:59). Both Babbage and Jevons considered their machines to materially mimic the operations of the mind.

On various occasions, most elaborately in his *On the Mechanical Performance*, Jevons described how his machine made logical deductions. In the Logical Machine, the principles of the lever were as important, if not more so, than in the Jacquard loom and Babbage's engines. An appendix to *On the Mechanical Performance* made this abundantly clear. Without repeating the example Jevons gave, we can get an impression of how it worked from Jevons's drawings (see Figures 6-3 and 6-4).

In my Figure 6-3, Figure 3 shows part of the inner machine, Figure 4 the keyboard, and Figure 5, the so-called Abecedarium or display. The inside of the machine consists of a system of levers that are connected to the keys of the keyboard by slender pieces of rope. The levers are moved backwards by the springs attached to them. On the inner front- and backside of the machine, mutually connected rods hang over two pulleys, on which

---

[8] See Mosselmans (1998) for a detailed analysis of Jevons's "unusual and particular" (Mosselmans in Inoue 2002 1:67) position in the history of logic.

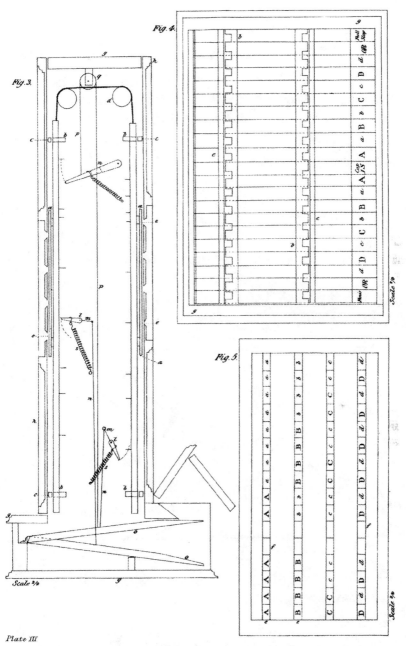

6-3. Jevons's drawing of the inside of the Logical Machine. *Pure Logic and Other Minor Works*, 1890, after p. 156. For reasons of clarity, Jevons left out most of the levers from the inside. Courtesy of Palgrave/Macmillan Press.

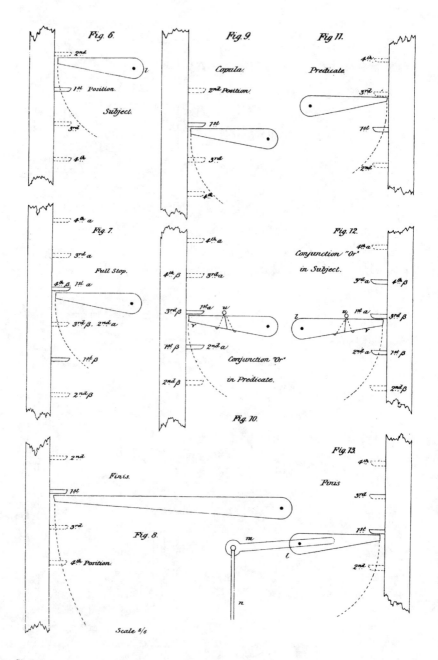

6-4. Jevons's drawing of the inside of the Logical Machine. *Pure Logic and Other Minor Works*, 1890, after p. 156. Courtesy of Palgrave/Macmillan Press.

the letters are printed that (may) appear in the display. The left-hand side of the keyboard represents the letters in subject position and the right-hand side, those in predicate position. By pressing the keys, the levers, indicated for example in Figure 3 (see my Figure 6-3), with the letters n and l, move the rods by a system of pins upwards and downwards. In my Figure 6-4, Figures 6 to 13 show the other levers of the apparatus, all of which represent different logical functions and operations, such as subject (Figure 6), copula (Figure 9), predicate (Figure 13), and conjunction (Figures 10 and 12). The rods could be moved to four different positions with the help of all these keys. Depending on their position, letters could be included, provisionally excluded, or definitively excluded from a logic problem impressed on the machine. The conjunction keys need some extra attention since they show Jevons's divergence from Boole's views on the sum operation that materialises. When pressed, the key makes the lever raise a pin upwards; however, the key slips back if it touches a pin in returning; thus, the key materially embodies Jevons's views on the sum operation. By pressing the "full stop" key, lever 7 moves the Abecedarium to its end position, showing all possible conclusions that can be drawn from given premises. The "finis" key removes all input from the machine so that a new logical problem can be fed into it. In that blank state, the machine "represents a mind endowed with powers of thought, but wholly devoid of knowledge" (PS 110).

Jevons described the machine as if it mimicked part of the reasoning process of the human mind. If a logical problem is fed into the machine, the machine "analyses and digests the meaning of it" by moving the rods and levers up and down, "and becomes charged with the knowledge embodied in that proposition" (PS 110). Thus, the Logical Machine "really accomplishes in a purely mechanical manner... the true process of logical inference". Though not able to interpret its propositions, it was able to faultlessly reason upon them. The Logical Machine thus represented "the proper condition of a mind exempt from mistake" (PS 111).

Despite the limited capacity of Jevons's machine, Jevons was the first to show the possibility of mechanising Boole's logic. However, we have seen that his machine materially incorporated his own logical system, rather than Boole's algebraic logic. He corresponded on his machine with Allan Marquand, who constructed a much more efficient logical machine than Jevons's. Marquand was also the first to suggest the use of electronic relays

6-5. Jevons Exhibition, organised on the initiative of Professor Wolfe Mays, Christie Library, Manchester, 1952. From the *Manchester Guardian*, Wednesday 15 October 1952, p. 7. Courtesy of *Manchester Guardian*.

for the construction of logical machines (McCallum and Smith 1951; Mays and Henry [1953] 1988). It would take until 1938 before C. E. Shannon demonstrated that electronic circuits could be described by Boolean algebras. In 1949, the Ferranti Company (the builders of the Manchester Mark I computer and the first commercial producers of computers) constructed, to the design of Professor Mays, an electronic equal of Jevons's machine. Both the electronic version and the wooden nineteenth-century original could be admired at an exposition devoted to the work of Stanley Jevons at Christie Library, Manchester University, in 1952. There is a photograph in the *Manchester Guardian* for Wednesday, 15 October 1952, p. 7, showing the Logical Machine and the Ferranti Logical Computer side-by-side (Figure 6-5).

Herbert Stanley Jevons is standing in front of them, with the bust of his father surveying the whole.[9]

THE MACHINE MIND

How was Jevons's Logical Machine to be taken? Was it a material representation of the *laws of thought*, was it a material representation of an *abstract formal logical system*, or was it an *engine of discovery*? As Wicksteed (1905, 433), one of the first economists who wholeheartedly embraced Jevons's mathematical approach to economics, rightly remarked, the confusion in effect emerged from the name of the machine: "he called his logic machine a 'logical' machine, as though the machine itself were logical and could reason".

We have seen that both Boole and De Morgan reacted reservedly to Jevons's logical system. Jevons's harsh words on the "obscurity" of Boole's system were ill-spent on both. However, Boole's letter of response to Jevons's original 1863 manuscript makes it clear that Boole was as concerned as Jevons with mimicking the "real" operations of human reasoning. Even if Jevons were right in assuming that ordinary men would find it difficult to recognise themselves in his algebraic logical system, Boole argued, it did not follow that it was wrong. In his reply to Jevons, Boole expressed his belief that his "fundamental laws" were no "arbitrary assumptions", but that they were "really grounded" in the constitution of our thought (JA 6/2/53). In other words: Even if there were men who did not understand a syllabus of algebra, it could not be excluded that these men were thinking algebraically on a fundamental level.

Jevons's analysis of Boole, and Boole's reaction, make it clear that Boole and Jevons did not limit their analysis to the *results* of thought, as De Morgan would have it, but attempted to formalise the "processes [that] pass through the human brain instead of through the medium of inanimate mechanism".

---

[9] I owe this information to Stephen Johnston, conservator of the Oxford Science Museum. Let me add the following observation. If we compare both machines just on their outward appearances, I would think – but one might easily disagree – that the more fancy appearance of the Ferranti computer gives a greater impression of a "thinking machine" than the outdated Victorian appearance of Jevons's contrivance. Both are, however, equally powerful. See also Gardner (1958), Akl (1980), and Dodd (1988).

Rather than considering the "palpable *physical* laws of motion of the machine" equivalent to the "laws of thought" of ordinary man, as Mirowski (2002, 41) suggests, Jevons considered the physical *organisation* of his machine to mimic these laws. The formal rules and routines of reasoning that were embodied in the mechanism of Jevons's Logical Machine fitted to the structure of man's nervous organisation. That is what Jevons meant with his statement that he and Babbage had created in the "wheels and levers of an insensible machine" a "rival" of the reasoning processes that "pass through the human brain".[10]

There was no longer any *categorical* distinction to be made between mind and machines. Both functioned according to the very same organisational principles that were embodied in the Jacquard loom. The differences between mind and machines were reduced to a difference in *complexity*. Although Babbage's algebraic machine itself was far more complex than Jevons's, both Babbage and Jevons dallied with the idea that a machine could think by a simple press on a key or a turn of a crank. In both cases, "labour" that originally belonged to the sphere of the mind became represented by the routine processes of a machine. A "simple manual worker" could, with the right instructions, come to faultless results.

As a result of Babbage's and Jevons's machines, there was then no longer a distinction to be made between the routine labour of a manual worker and the routines of reasoning. This was made explicit by Boole's widow in some extraordinary statements. In *The Message of Psychic Science* of 1868, she wrote:

> If I were asked to point out the two greatest benefactors to humanity that this century has produced, I think I should be inclined to mention Mr. Babbage, who made a machine for working out series, and Mr. Jevons, who made a machine for stringing together syllogisms. Between them they have conclusively proved, by unanswerable logic of facts, that calculation and reasoning, like weaving and ploughing, are work, not for human souls, but for clever combinations of iron and wood.

---

[10] The whole construction of their machines facilitated the rhetoric of the machine being a simile of the human mind. It was no coincidence that both Babbage and Jevons referred to the zero states of their machines as the *tabula rasa*. Was not this exactly the way Locke had conceived of the human mind? See also *PL* 120: "Not only are the syllogisms and other old forms of argument capable of being worked upon by the machine, but an indefinite number of other forms of reasoning can be represented by the regular action of levers and spindles".

Much later, in her *Symbolical Methods of Study* of 1884, we read:

> The reasoning-machines of Babbage and Jevons...seem to me to have brought to a *reductio ad absurdum* the worship of intellectual power and artistic genius.[11]

Jevons's correspondence with one of the most prolific Victorian writers in mental philosophy, G. H. Lewes, shows how Jevons speculated on the implications of his simple machine for more complex ones.[12] Jevons made clear that his Logical Machine had only limited capacities in several respects. A first limit is, of course, the limited number of premises it could deal with. But it was also limited in a wider sense. It was not, as a human being, able to make wrong inferences from these premises. The Logical Machine was, in fact, the mind's superior and might serve as an important aid to prevent false deductions. Framed otherwise, the Logical Machine embodied the formal operations of reasoning in a more perfect way than the human mind. Jevons was explicit that the machine itself, in contrast with human beings, is "*devoid of knowledge*. Thus it is utterly incapable of judging whether a proposition submitted to it is absurd or not". In *On the Mechanical Performance*, Jevons emphasised equally the limited capabilities of his machine, yet his phrasing reveals that there was no principled hindrance to the construction of more complex machines. Thus, we read that "a certain mental process of interpreting and reducing to simple terms" was required, "for which no mechanical provision is made in the machine *as at present constructed*" (*PS* 169, emphasis mine).

In his letters to Lewes, this did not prevent Jevons from playing with the idea of a more complex "imaginary machine" that would be able to accumulate "knowledge & experience". He compared this imaginary machine with "Mr Babbage's imaginary mechanical chess-player, except that the latter had the still more difficult task of learning by induction instead of deduction". This imaginary machine thus resembled the "mind of a pupil who was incapable of forgetting anything delivered to him or of reasoning wrongly from what he knew".

---

[11] Both quotes from MacHale (1985, 235–6).

[12] I would like to thank Philippe Bazard for having drawn my attention to this correspondence and having sent me Jevons's letters to Lewes. I have not been able until now to trace Lewes's letters to Jevons. The dates of Jevons's letters to Lewes are listed in an appendix to the 1995 edition of Lewes's letters (1995, 2:251).

We might consider the mind of such a pupil as a mere logical possibility, only serving to illustrate in an anthropomorphic way how one might conceive of an automaton, tooled up with memory and the laws of reasoning. Jevons's depiction of the way this pupil acquired his knowledge came extremely close to the cramming of students he so much favoured in his 1877 article on Cram. In effect, in an illuminating reference to Babbage's chess player in an article on how to regulate and bring into control the drink traffic, Jevons (1883, 253–4) explicitly stated that such a pupil was not just a mere thought-play, but was exemplary of the way the human mind really acquired knowledge. Such a complex machine mimicked the inductive process of the human mind:

> Our mental framework . . . is marvellously contrived, so as to go on ceaselessly registering on the tablets of the memory the favourable or unfavourable results of every kind of action. Charles Babbage proposed to make an automaton chess-player which should register mechanically the numbers of games lost and gained in consequence of every possible kind of move. Thus, the longer the automaton went on playing games, the more experienced it would become by the accumulation of experimental results. Such a machine precisely represents the acquirement of experience by our nervous organisation.

Babbage's chess player was not merely imaginary. Babbage certainly had seen the "automatic Turk", an allegedly mechanical chess player built at the end of the 1860s by a Slovak engineer, Wolfgang von Kempelen. After his death in 1804, Johann Maelzel, a Viennese musical engineer, bought it for his shows throughout Europe. The very design of the chess player was to make people guess where the magic was hidden, and many guesses were made about a dwarf hidden inside the chess table and manipulating the arms of the Turk, while he saw the moves of the pieces through the eyes of the puppet via an ingenious system of mirrors. The truth was different; hidden in the machine were the top chess players of Europe and America who knew about the secret, but used the "machine" for another type of guessing: whom they were playing against when playing against the puppet.[13]

In Maelzel's show at Spring Gardens in 1818, it could be admired together with an automatic dancing lady that was displayed earlier in James Cox's

---

[13] Elaborate versions of this story are found in Standage (2002) and in Gaby Wood's very imaginative 2002 book. See also Schaffer (1997).

famous museum.[14] In the 1830s, Babbage bought this dancing lady and placed it in his dining room alongside the fragment of the Difference Engine I.[15] As Schaffer (1997, 80) puts it, similar trickeries are at work in all stories of automated intelligence: "if such machines look intelligent because we do not concentrate on where their work is done, then we need to think harder about the work which produces values and who performs it".

In this context, two undated letters (JA 6/2/99 & 100),[16] apparently written after 1878, from Henry Cunynghame to Jevons are of interest. Of distinguished descent, Cunynghame was a favourite student of Alfred Marshall in the 1870s, and he invented a machine for drawing a grid of rectangular hyperbolae for him (*New Palgrave*, 1998, entry on Cunynghame). In two letters to Jevons, Cunynghame makes mention of a logical machine he had invented and sent to Jevons for inspection. In one of these letters, Cunynghame expressed his fear that his machine did not make any logical deductions after all: "has the *machine* done the work or have *I*. Is this not merely a mechanical *register* of results otherwise arrived at. I fear it is" (JA 6/2/100).

Schaffer's acute remark, and Cunynghame's confusion about who (or what) did what, pinpoint a difficulty in all attempts to understand the world, the mental or the natural, by means of machines. How do we know a reasoning machine mimics the operations of a mind? How do we know in the case of the external world, as in Jevons's cloud experiments? If we have only the output of machines, that is, observational evidence, to answer these questions, we cannot know – we can decide to use machines as modes of understanding or categorically reject this idea. Jevons, it will be clear, chose the first option. In his *Principles of Science*, he made his Logical Machine the cornerstone of his theory of induction.

"INDUCTION – THE INVERSE OF DEDUCTION"

Not incidentally, an image of the Logical Machine served as a frontispiece of Jevons's *Principles of Science* (1874). In a letter to his brother Herbert, Jevons

---

[14] On Cox's museum at the turn of the eighteenth century, shortly referred to as "the museum", see Pointon (1999) .

[15] See Schaffer (1997) for a persuasive interpretation of the meaning of these automata in relation to Babbage's Difference Engine project.

[16] I would like to thank Michael White for drawing my attention to these letters and Peter McNiven, of the John Rylands Library, Manchester, for sending them to me.

once described the book as a work on logic in disguise. As his contemporaries were well-aware, Jevons used his Logical Machine to not only speculate on the mechanical nature of the universe, but also to throw light on (rather than solve) the problem of induction. "Doubtless", Jevons wrote, "there is in nature some invariably acting mechanism, such that from certain fixed conditions an invariable result always emerges". Unfortunately, the position of the scientist, "with his finite mind and short experience", was rather different. "We are in the position of spectators who witness the productions of a complicated machine, but are not allowed to examine its intimate structure" (*PS* 222).

We are reminded of De Morgan's comparison of the mind with a complicated apparatus. "A Mechanician, to whom the watch was presented for the first time, would be able to give a good guess as to its structure, from his knowledge of other pieces of contrivance". In *Formal Logic*, De Morgan wrote that, "with respect to the mind, considered as a complicated apparatus", we can only study its manifestations, "without being allowed to see the inside . . . it is the problem of the watch to those who have never seen any mechanism at all" (ULL MS 776/1, 26). This problem was not just there with respect to the mind; it was a general problem in our efforts to gain knowledge from nature. The "infinite depth of mystery" that in the end haunted the scientist in his strive for knowledge was overcome, so Jevons argued in heavy reliance on his Logical Machine, by making assumptions on the mechanical laws that might plausibly govern the relevant part of the universe under study.[17] With these considerations, Jevons followed Babbage's *Ninth Bridgewater Treatise*, "this most profound and eloquent work" (*PS* 743), and it is of interest that he considered writing a *Bridgewater Treatise* himself. Jevons referred especially to Babbage's examples to argue that mechanical laws governing the universe need not be in discord with the idea of a deity – this source of "infinite depth and mystery".

Jevons used his Logical Machine in particular, however, to thresh out its consequences for the tools and methods of discovery in the sciences. It was

[17] The "infinite depth and mystery" Jevons speaks of were for De Morgan a living reality. His experiences with clairvoyance, "table-turning, spirit-rapping, and so on" secured for him "the reality of the phenomenon", without him being able to explain them. See Sophia De Morgan (1882), letter to Rev. W. Heald, 221–2. As he covertly admitted in *A Budget of Paradoxes*, De Morgan wrote the preface to his wife's *From Matter to Spirit*. How De Morgan's vivid interest in spirits links up with his scientific work deserves, in my view, a separate study (that to my knowledge does not exist to date).

clear to Jevons that no distinction was to be made between the natural and the social sciences. If there was any difference between them, it consisted solely of the "enormous perplexity" of the latter subject (*PS* 759). All attempts to construct a separate method for the moral sciences – including history – only produced "parodies of science" and should be passed over as quickly as possible (761).

Using his Logical Machine, Jevons showed how the assumption of simple "laws" might guide the investigator in getting a grip on the complex plethora of data with which he was confronted. Jevons relied on the distinction between direct and indirect deduction to show how induction was connected to the latter. Induction, the inference to a uniform law from a complex set of data, proved to be the "inverse process" of indirect deductive inference.

The following example of Jevons is as good as any to illustrate indirect deduction (*PS* 125):

$$A = AB \tag{1}$$
$$B = BC \tag{2}$$

(which he interpreted as: iron (A) is a metal (AB), and a metal (B) is a good conductor of electricity (BC)). The full list of possible combinations of terms was given by the so-called Logical Alphabet: a list growing exponentially with the number of terms involved. Jevons denoted negations of terms with a small letter; the three terms A, B, and C, then yield the following eight combinations of terms (listed in the Logical Alphabet): $ABC(\alpha)$, $ABc(\beta)$, $AbC(\gamma)$, $Abc(\delta)$, $aBC(\epsilon)$, $aBc(\zeta)$, $abC(\eta)$, and $abc(\theta)$.

Making indirect deductive inferences was, according to Jevons, essentially similar to the method of negative proof in mathematics: proving that the opposite leads to contradiction. Of all the possible combinations of terms, those inconsistent with the assumptions were eliminated: γ and δ are inconsistent with (1), and β and ζ with (2). Hence, only ABC, abC, aBC, and abc remained. The mechanism of the Logical Machine embodied this process of striking out contradictions, retaining only those inferences that were consistent with the initial propositions.

It thus appeared to Jevons that, from a limited set of simple premises, an avalanche of conclusions could be drawn. These conclusions were shown on the Abecedarium, the display on the Logical Machine. At the time, it was considered to be a disadvantage that his machine gave *all* possible inferences, instead of selecting the interesting ones and summing them up efficiently. Jevons turned what was considered a vice into a virtue: It gave him the clue to one of the great philosophical puzzles – inductive inference.

The great difficulty of induction, according to Jevons, consisted of reasoning from concrete events to their unifying laws. This problem was similar to reasoning from the complex set of conclusions back to the original simple set of premises. In this sense, induction was the "reverse process" of deduction. Reasoning backwards from the four combinations ABC, abC, aBC, and abc to the original premises, the reader would, according to Jevons, "probably remember at once that they belong to the premises $A = AB, B = BC$". Should the reader not remember this, he "would need a few trials" (125).

The complexity of inductive inference grew explosively with the number of terms involved. This made it highly improbable a straightforward inference could be made from an avalanche of data to their underlying "laws". This made induction "imperfect". The premises became hypotheses on the laws of nature, and the problem of induction was how reasoned guesses to these laws could be made. To tackle this problem, Jevons emphasised the importance of reasoning by analogy and invoked all methods William Whewell discussed in relation to the quantitative sciences, especially the method of means and the method of graphs.

According to Jevons, reasoning by analogies in science and the importance of formulating hypotheses were flip sides of the same coin. Though he agreed with Bacon, and all empiricists since – that science started from observations – Bacon was at fault when he claimed that lawlike knowledge could be derived by just collecting data. The scientist had to use analogies and formulate hypotheses: He had to have recourse to analogies to arrive at the simple laws producing the empirical complexity (Mays [1962] 1988, 228).

Reasoning by analogies is a major theme in *The Principles of Science*; it runs through the whole book and receives special focus in Chapter 28. Jevons made it clear that discovery in science was most often "accomplished by following up the hints received from analogy". Analogy functioned as a "Guide in Discovery" (*PS* 629), as a heuristic tool to discover the simple unifying laws of nature. Jevons highlighted Faraday's use of analogical reasoning in particular. The difference between the search for generalisation and analogies was "only a matter of degree" (627). Analogical reasoning was sometimes even described as equivalent to science itself, as "the detection of identity and the recognition of uniformity existing in many objects" (644). It was what Jevons's "principle" of the "substitution of similars" was all about.

If the object of study was quantitative in nature, as Jevons (with reference to John Herschel) assumed them to be in all of the sciences, the ultimate goal was to find the mathematical formula that expressed the law governing the phenomena. Just as the wide variety of permutations of terms was governed by simple laws, a seemingly unconnected array of numbers could equally be governed by a simple formula. Jevons took Babbage's example of Bernoulli numbers from his *Ninth Bridgewater Treatise*. These numbers, which "seem to set all regularity and method at defiance", were nevertheless "derived from the most regular and symmetrical laws of relation" (124). As Babbage concluded from his examples, so Jevons concluded from his Logical Machine that the task of the scientist was to search for the unifying law governing the phenomena: "It is the same throughout nature; the laws may be simple, but their combined effects are not so simple, and we have no clue to guide us through their intricacies" (126). For Jevons, the Logical Machine showed the centrality of hypotheses and analogies in scientific research.

The hypothetical character of the formulae arrived at made science essentially probabilistic. This did not mean that nature itself was probabilistic – quite the contrary. Jevons's framing of the problem of induction by means of his machine only made sense with the assumption that the universe was governed by deterministic laws – a deity could have programmed the world as a Babbage machine (766). Referring to Laplace as his authority, Jevons considered it due to our ignorance – to the principled impossibility to predict the outcome when not knowing all causes – that we need to reason probabilistically: "*Probability belongs wholly to the mind*". Limited knowledge and limited data made probability arguments unavoidable in arguing for the existence of laws and regularities in nature. Jevons presented many such arguments in a rather offhand way to illustrate how regularity in observations gave reason to assume the existence of a causal mechanism, even though the possibility of "fortuitous coincidences" could never be excluded.

Interestingly, Jevons's use of his Logical Machine to elucidate the process of induction quite unexpectedly revealed that it made no sense to strive to certainty in the sciences. Using analogies and hypotheses was central to science itself, and Jevons has rightly been depicted as an important forerunner of the hypothetical–deductive method in the sciences (Schabas 1990).

Paradoxically, Jevons's use of his machine also pinpointed its limits: Wherever analogies or hypotheses came from, they were not handed out by his Logical Machine. The machine reframed the problem of induction, and it showed where the actual work of induction was done – in the mind of the scientist, not in the machine.

"To Decide What Things *Are* Similar"

At a very young age, Jevons devoted a few lines in his diary to the concept of genius:

> I have often thought much about what is called cleverness & genius. The oftener an action is repeated, the more easy it is to perform it again, & the more perfectly it will be performed. It is by long repetition that workmen or jugglers acquire such perfection . . . but I think that it is exactly the same case with students, for if they have been accustomed for a long time to study diligently . . . they get *practised or clever* in acquiring knowledge while those who have been lazy or have studied in a careless manner cannot expect to become expert in it.
>
> (*PC* 1:58)

The model of thinking that emerges from this quote is hard, repetitive work, just the model that fits his Logical Machine. In later years, the idea that genius really was a matter of endured repetitive training made him favour the common practice of cramming in teaching. There was no difference between the work of the hands and the work of the mind. In his 1877 article on Cram, Jevons referred to his much-beloved teacher De Morgan, who always gave "an abundance of exercises" (Jevons 1883, 92). Jevons by then had apparently forgotten De Morgan's opposition to the system of cramming, to which De Morgan even devoted his introductory lecture at the opening of all classes at University College in 1848. In reaction to this speech, John Herschel wrote to De Morgan: "I was greatly delighted with your protest against the cramming system in your opening lecture"[18].

---

[18] Quoted from Sophia De Morgan (1882, 169). See also Taylor's account of De Morgan's "sovereign contempt" of all cram. Taylor remembers De Morgan saying, just some days before the exam: "I noticed that many of you have left off working my examples this week. I know perfectly well what you are doing; YOU ARE CRAMMING FOR THE EXAMINATION. But I will set you such a paper as shall make ALL YOUR CRAM of no use" (Sophia De Morgan 1882, 100).

Indeed, whereas logical deduction for De Morgan perhaps could be compared with the working of machines, thinking was in the end something of a different order. As Joan Richards (1987, 8) points out, De Morgan was "passionately concerned with mathematical rigor and wrote explicitly and extensively about mathematical foundations". But De Morgan "did not believe that mathematics was essentially logical". For De Morgan, the "vagaries of mathematical history", rather than its rigorous reconstruction, showed where the work of the mathematician was done. History showed that the search for clear and distinct axioms for mathematical systems was driven by mathematical ideas. In this regard, De Morgan shared Whewell's conviction that scientific history saw the unfolding of fundamental ideas and concepts that were only gradually groped at. Mathematical investigations never were "blind symbolic manipulations" (Richards 1987, 23; see also Rice 1996b). Consistent with this, De Morgan severely criticised all competitive examinations that examined the student against other competitors and not against the subject, and rejected the worthless practice of cramming. Mathematics teaching should help the students think for themselves (Rice 1996a, 387).

By contrast, for Jevons there seemed to be no essential difference between the routine labour of a workman, the cramming of a student, and the working of a machine. The calculator, degraded as a consequence of Prony's project to a routine labourer, was taken as the example of intellectual labour as such.[19] In *The Substitution of Similars or the True Principle of Reasoning*, which appeared just one year before *On the Mechanical Performance of Logical Inference*, Jevons explicitly equated reasoning with the routine acts in common life.

> I need hardly point out that not only in our reasonings, but in our acts in common life, we observe the principle of similarity. Any new kind of work is performed with doubt and difficulty, because we have no knowledge derived from a similar case to guide us. But no sooner has the work been performed once or twice with success than much of the difficulty vanishes, because we have acquired all the knowledge which will guide us in similar cases.
>
> (*PS* 127)

---

[19] See Daston (1994) and Schaffer (1994a) for an extensive discussion of this point. Both take the routinisation of calculating as degrading the calculator. From Jevons's point of view, we cannot distinguish the one form of mental activity from the other, all being based on a form of routinisation.

Downplayed was the original act of the intellect to *decide if*, in a certain case, a certain object was so similar to another as to admit substitution. This original act is incompatible with following rules and routines (Daston 1994, 290–3, especially 291). For an extreme variety of authors, from Mill to Martineau and from Herschel to even Bain, this original act of the mind presented the really interesting question. In a letter to Jevons, John Herschel formulated this most explicitly:

> And then, after all, the difficulty of reasoning correctly lies not in the mechanical application of logical formulae to which your abacus is fully competent – but in the application of reason and observation to decide what things *are* similar: *so* similar as to admit of substitution for each other in the argument in hand; which is not a province of formal or Aristotelian logic, however largely supplemented by Dr Boole, Dr Thomson or yourself.
> (8 July 1869, JA 6/2/196, original emphasis)[20]

"To decide what things *are* similar": Herschel's criticism went to the heart of Jevons's logical system. Not incidentally, Herschel laid emphasis on the copula. For Mill, Herschel, and many others, the copula could *not* be reduced to a simple sign of equation. Its use involved a separate act of the intellect. The analysis of this act was the real and ultimate subject of logic. It was this act of the intellect that, according to philosophers like Martineau and Hamilton, was the real and distinct province of the mind. It escaped rules and routines, and in this sense showed the open nerve of the factory system that played such an important role in the transformation of Victorian Britain. This act was the main focus of analysis (and of controversy) of all continental philosophy after Kant. In the Anglo-Saxon world, it is what the theory of induction is all about.

---

[20] This letter is wrongly dated in the hand list to the Jevons archives as 8 July 1863. In the letter, Herschel explicitly thanks Jevons for sending him a "little treatise on logic under the title of "The Substitution of Similars", which was published in June 1869. The Herschel–Jevons correspondence at the Royal Society is, however, equally misleading. A copy of the letter, archived as item no. 24.203, apparently constructed from Herschel's original is dated quite clearly as 1867. It is possible that the year was transcribed inaccurately. In the typewritten index to the Herschel Collection in the Library of the Royal Society, someone has circled the date 8 July 1867 next to item no. 24.203 and written in pencil "9?". The date must be 1869, given that in his letter to Herschel (Dover, 9 July 1869, item no. 10327 at the Royal Society – an original item, the date of which there can be no disputing), Jevons talks of receiving that morning his remarks on "my little logical work". I owe this information to Paul Byrne, researcher at the Royal Society.

Reviews of the *Principles* equally emphasised the central role of Jevons's method of indirect deduction in his approach to induction. A Millian like Croom Robertson, for example, argued in *Mind* for 2 April 1876 that this "crowning" method should be judged by its ability to do better than the old Aristotelian logic. If it did, it would give its "true mark of its superiority" (Robertson in Peart 2003, 4:23). Without bothering to genuinely examine the issue, Robertson concluded from Olympian heights that "Well then! I affirm that the most complex problems" could be more easily solved with the old "theoretically sound" system than with the new "theoretically unsound" one. Robertson's main charge was against the formalisation of logic as such. If Boole's use of + is so much against common practice, as Jevons argued, why not "tell with equal force against the use of the symbol =, the true fount and origin of the evil". According to Robertson, Jevons did not distinguish sufficiently "between mere verbal expression and real thought" (Peart 2003, 23).

Jevons was concerned with "real thought" in his sketch of the characters of the best minds science had brought about. According to Jevons (and despite Newton's claims to the contrary, in his famous *regulae philosophandi*), scientists like Newton, Huijgens, and Faraday possessed the capacity of "hypothetical anticipation" – so vehemently condemned by Francis Bacon – and the skills to draw inferences deductively from their hypotheses that they experimentally put to the test. As their genius was "essentially creative, and consists in divergence from the ordinary grooves of thought and action, it must necessarily be a phenomenon beyond the domain of the laws of nature" (*PS* 576). No wonder Jevons concluded their minds combined "contradictory attributes" (592). Where Jevons throughout much of the *Principles* maintained that induction essentially was the "reverse process" of deduction, the formation of hypotheses asked for gifts of nature that were themselves unnatural. As an anonymous review of the *Principles* in *The Criterion* brought home the point, "the art of discovery is not the science of logic, and the intuitive insight of genius is not to be interpreted as the universal type of mental processes" (quoted from Inoue 2002, 2:19). In Jevons's view, this original act of genius, the ability to perceive similarity between two objects, became a dark and inexplicable gift which was in stark contrast with the routinised deductions of his logical machine. The relation between both resembled the organisation of modern science. "So-called original research is now regarded as a profession, adopted by hundreds of men, and communicated by a system of training". But there was no guarantee at all the "inexplicable germ" of genius would arise from this. Perhaps even "military science" and genius were more in need of one another in these days than in former ones, because of the increased possibilities to communicate new ideas (*PS* 574–5).

However, with the emergence of formal logic in England, the importance of the ability to judge similarity came to be more and more marginalised as a feature of the intellect. Babbage's incisive insights into the consequences of the division of labour for the labour of the mind paradoxically gave rise to the idea that there was not that much difference, after all, between mental deliberation and purely physical work, obeying mechanical principles. A Millian like Alexander Bain reduced consciousness to "mere feeling". To facilitate the mechanisation of reasoning, De Morgan dropped the distinction between proposition and judgement. In doing so, what had been the proper province of reason in eighteenth-century thought – judgement – could now only be conceived of as "intuition". Reason, in Victorian England, became fully mechanised. Consciousness, or the capacity of judgement, turned into an unexplainable gift – it was the spectre in the machine.

SEVEN

~

THE PRIVATE LABORATORY OF THE MIND

What will our physicists say to a *strictly physical science*, which can be experimented on in the private laboratory of the philosopher's mind? What a convenient science! What a saving of expense in regard of apparatus, and materials, and specimens.

William Stanley Jevons, *John Stuart Mill's Philosophy Tested*

In the late 1870s, Jevons set out to refute Mill's philosophy as thoroughly and definitely as he could.[1] "Nobody questions, or at least ought to question", Jevons wrote, "the force of Mill's style, the persuasive power of his words, the candour of his discussions, and the perfect goodness of his motives". Unfortunately, these virtues were, in his view, more than offset by Mill's "essentially illogical" mind; "in one way or another Mill's intellect was wrecked" (*PL* 201). One may guess some hurt feelings behind these harsh words on Mill. We have seen Mill's sceptical reaction to the *Theory* in his famous letter to Cairnes in which he complained that Jevons's "mania for encumbering questions" with delusive formal notation was as useless in economics as it was in logic, but this was in private correspondence only. Public reviews and responses to his *Theory* by influential Millians like John Elliot Cairnes and Henry Sidgwick were equally reserved and challenged the novelty of his ideas or the fruitfulness of his mathematics.

These responses were no doubt motivated in part by the harsh tone Jevons employed in the *Theory* against the "noxious influence of authority", which he saw embodied in the "wrong-headed" doctrines of Mill and Ricardo. An

[1] In a series of four articles in the *Contemporary Review*, published from December 1877 to November 1879.

anonymous commentary in *The Examiner* for 28 November 1874 complained about Jevons's tone in a lecture he delivered to the Manchester Statistical Society on the progress of mathematical economics. "A more melancholy specimen of a disappointed man envying the success to which he cannot attain, we never saw" (quoted from Inoue 2002, 2:67). Sidgwick even devoted an appendix to the introduction of his own *Principles of Political Economy* (1883) to discuss the exaggerated and violent tone of Jevons against Mill as utterly unproductive.

More was at stake for Jevons than a personal *vendetta* against Mill, however. So convinced was he of the "immense injury" done "to the cause of philosophy and good intellectual training in England" by Mill's authority, that he, for his part, was no longer willing "to live silently under the incubus of bad logic and bad philosophy which Mill's Works have laid upon us" (*PL* 201–2). In the late 1870s when Henry Sidgwick, for whom Mill was the "Locke and Bacon" of their day, privately called Jevons to order for his "attack on Mill's *logicalness*", he unreluctantly insisted that he would once "prove [his] assertions" that "in Mill, contradiction is of the essence of his method".[2]

With his articles Jevons clearly had something similar in mind, in content and effect, to Mill's own demolishing criticism of Sir William Hamilton's philosophy (1865).[3] Jevons promised to go to the heart of Mill's philosophical views. Many had only been "skirmishing round the outworks of the Associationist Philosophy, firing in here and there a well-aimed shot. But their shots have sunk harmlessly into the sand of his foundations". By contrast, Jevons would, as a real "engineer", explode "the citadel of his logical reputation" (*PL* 202).

The question that will concern us in this chapter is why Jevons took so much offence at Mill's philosophical views, especially in relation to political economy. In particular, why did the association psychology figure prominently in Jevons's attacks on Mill? The answers to these questions will be sought in Jevons's engagement with psychophysiology to introduce the ordinary tools and methods of the sciences into political economy, rather than

---

[2] To be inferred from Jevons's letter to Sidgwick of 28 February 1879, TCC Add.Ms.c.94.59, from which these quotes are taken.

[3] The comparison is made by Croom Robertson, who (as might be expected from his Millian predilections) was highly critical of Jevons's first article against Mill. See Peart 2003 4:35–8 for Robertson's reaction and the same volume for other critical responses to Jevons's attacks on Mill. See also Inoue 2002 2:125–36.

relying on the introspective method favoured by association psychologists to gather insights into the laws of political economy. More specifically, as will be seen in greater detail in the next chapter, psychophysiology enabled Jevons to think about economic behaviour not just in terms of quantities, but in terms of functional form. From this perspective, Mill's insistence on a separate route to truth in political economy was without ground and a hindrance to its progression as a science.

JEVONS BETWEEN JONES AND MILL

Jevons made clear that his essays on Mill's philosophy were the result of his lifelong engagement with Mill's work, dating back to the 1850s. [4] John Stuart Mill's *Principles of Political Economy* (1848) was the dominant account of the science, and his methodological views as put forward in his famous 1836 essay and his *Logic* (1843) were clearly framed within the idea of economics as an abstract, deductive science, while simultaneously biased against the use of numerical data in support of theory. Those favouring the collection of data, like Richard Jones in earlier days and the statistical societies in mid-century Britain, showed allergic reactions when it came to theory. Jevons clearly aimed to bridge this divide that prevented political economy from becoming, in his view, truly scientific. In the introduction to the *Theory* (*TPE1* 24), Jevons contrasted Mill's "Concrete Deductive Method" with Richard Jones's classificatory approach to induction, favouring Mill's side:

> I think that Mr. Mill is right in considering [political economy] an in-
> stance of the Concrete Deductive Method... which Mr. Mill has so ad-
> mirably described. Political Economy is, undoubtedly, grounded upon
> observed facts, and is, so far, an inductive science; but it does not pro-
> ceed by an elaborate collection of facts and their gradual classification, as
> Mr. Richard Jones would have us believe.

---

[4] Croom Robertson ridiculed the fact that it apparently took Jevons "about twenty years" to discover that Mill's philosophy was "essentially illogical". "It is all very curious: curious that it should have taken ten years to discover Mill's defects; curious that in ten years more it should not have been discovered that all of them that are real have been well-known to philosophical inquirers for a long time past. ... Is it not the fact that those who think most highly of Mill are some of those who differ most gravely from him? They think of him as one who gave an unsurpassed expression... to the philosophy of individual experience, but they left this behind" (Inoue 2002 2:128). Robertson's reference to Mill's philosophy as being about "individual experience" is revealing and provides, as will be seen later, a major difference from Jevons's emphasis on averages.

Implied in Jevons's words was that Mill considered political economy to follow the concrete deductive method. But this was not quite so. For Mill, typical examples of sciences following this method were astronomy and, in recent days, physiology – two of those sciences that in Whewell's classification of the sciences occupied a middle ground between natural history and the experimental sciences. As we have seen, Mill argued that political economy followed the somewhat narrower a priori method. The concrete deductive method took all causes into consideration in the explanation of a social or natural fact. Due to the complexity of society, this was simply way beyond the possibilities of the social sciences, including political economy. Political economy found its experimental secure basis in the introspectively established laws of mind, based on the association psychology.

Jevons's innovation was to move the basis of political economy from the laws of mind to those of physiology. As Michael White (1994a) has shown, one of Jevons's main sources of inspiration in this was Richard Jennings's *Natural Elements of Political Economy* (1855), which contained many suggestive allusions to the new physiological theories of William Carpenter, Henry Maudsley, and Thomas Laycock. Culminating in Thomas Huxley's provocative 1874 essay in the *Fortnightly Review*, "On the Hypothesis that Animals are Automata", physiology promised a treatment of the phenomena of the mind by the ordinary tools and methods of the experimental sciences.

In shifting the "basis" of political economy from the association psychology to physiology, Jevons knocked down the long-standing categorical distinction between the "sciences of mind and matter". The reduction of man's mind to physiological states promised to make mental phenomena as measurable and objectively accessible as any other object of the sciences. Taking recourse to physiology enabled Jevons to reframe the "laws of human wants" in terms of mechanics and hence to introduce the ordinary methods of the physical sciences, – like mathematics, material (not introspective) experiments, and statistics – in their study, so that numerical expressions of dependency relations could be derived. The shift to physiology and the mathematisation of the subject, in short, were two sides of the same coin. This was the program Jevons captured in the famous phrase that his *Theory* might be "described as the mechanics of human interest" (*TPE1* 24).[5]

---

[5] A vast body of literature exists on the science of mind in the nineteenth century. For succinct histories of psychology, see Danziger (1990, 1997). An extremely useful collection

The reverse side of this was that the image of man as an automaton, implied in the new physiology, was difficult to reconcile with the notorious issue of free will that proved to be the recurring fishhook in mind–matter debates throughout the Victorian Age.[6] It was one of the attractions of the association psychology that it could claim scientificity and yet account for man's freedom of will. Jevons never systematically confronted this tension between psychophysiology and the association psychology, though it is clear from his scattered remarks on the free will issue that it was a matter of serious concern to him. Rather than confronting the free will issue on the level of individual experiences, as Mill had done, he moved to aggregates. Jevons took recourse in statistical averaging procedures to search for social laws; for this reason, Quetelet – and not Mill or Comte – was the "true founder of the social sciences".[7] Jevons thought about laws in terms of aggregates or mean values, while maintaining freedom of will on the level of observations on individuals.

The Association Psychology and Freedom of Will

John Stuart Mill's account of the method of political economy and the moral sciences more generally appealed to a large audience for several reasons. Apart from his dextrous handling of introspection as a scientifically acceptable method of enquiry, Mill managed to make this method consistent with one of the classical problems in mental and moral philosophy: how to account for man's freedom of will. By the early 1830s, Mill (and many of

of essays on the emergence of psychology as a science is Woodward and Ash (1982). A good history of association psychology which is still relevant today is Warren ([1921] 1967). For the history of experimental psychology, Boring (1950) is still the standard reference. For the reception of Gall's phrenology in the nineteenth century, in England as well as on the Continent, in particular see Young (1970); also Parssinen (1974). On the background of psychophysiology in the natural sciences, see Smith (1973). Rick Rylance's *Victorian Psychology and British Culture, 1850–1880* (Rylance, 2000) came too late to my attention to fully benefit from its content, especially from its discussion of Alexander Bain. On Victorian reactions to psychophysiology, see also Daston (1982), and Jacyna (1983). A history of German psychophysics is provided in Murray (1993). As already indicated, within the history of economics, White (1994a) opened up the debate on the influence of psychophysiology on the work of Victorian political economists.

[6] The literature on the Victorian free will debate is vast. See, for example, Danziger (1982), Daston (1978, 1982), and Jacyna (1981, 1983).

[7] On the differences between Mill and Jevons concerning the meaning and use of averages, see especially Peart (1995a).

his contemporaries) had been grappling with this issue for a long while. He
finished a first draft of the chapter on liberty and necessity in *Logic* (1843)
between 1830 and 1832, just after first considering to write this monumental
book. From *Autobiography* (1873), it is clear how much Mill's concern with
the free will issue was interwoven with his reading in – and personal experience with – his father's association psychology, especially the educational
message James Mill and Jeremy Bentham drew from it.

The very period of his so-called mental dejection coincides with the ma-
turing of his father's *Analysis*, which he extensively commented upon (as he
did much of his father's writing and that of Bentham). In this same period,
he read Joseph Priestley's 1775 abridged edition of David Hartley's *Observations on Man, his Frame, his Duties, and his Expectations* (originally published 1749) in his debating club. According to his father, Hartley's book still
was the best reading on psychology available. Priestley's rendition of Hartley emphasised its physiological reductionism and monistic determinism.
Priestley's support for this position was the redundancy of the mind: Once
we know how the complicated human body is composed, the appropriate
stimuli will automatically produce the accompanying mental phenomena.
There is no need to assume an additional and distinct mental substance.
According to Priestley, "my mind is no more *in my body*, than it is in the
moon" and therefore, the "business of the philosophers" was "abundantly
satisfied" once they had knowledge of "the probable affection of the brain"
that corresponds to our perceptions and ideas (1775, xx). An explanation of
human conduct need not search for mental motives, only the physiological
mechanism of its production.

The identification of James Mill's psychological doctrine with these mech
anistic and necessitarian views was and is widespread. The prolific early
nineteenth-century publicist and populariser of (Ricardian) political economy, Harriet Martineau, considered James Mill's *Analysis* as a defence of
Priestley's necessitarianism and a denial of the doctrine of the freedom
of the will – a judgement that was shared but not embraced by her brother
James, who was himself an important Unitarian minister and philosopher of
the mind. John Stuart Mill's *Autobiography* (1873) contributed considerably
to the mechanistic image of the association psychology. Mill described his
own behaviour during the period of his mental distress as if his actions were
merely "mechanical", acting on his father's associationist doctrines without
"truly" incorporating them. In his 1881 account of the relation of James Mill
to David Hartley, Bower considered that "there can be little doubt... that

[James Mill] would have adopted what Hartley calls the theory of the Mechanism of the Human Mind, as opposed to that of Free Will" (1881, 174). In his history of the association psychology, Howard Warren ([1921] 1967, 88) argued that James Mill's association psychology may "properly be termed mechanistic", because he "practically makes the physical–mechanical type his sole pattern for the laws of mental coexistence and succession". The "widespread notion" that the association psychology is "essentially physico-mechanical" (88n2) is echoed by Philip Mirowski (1989, 171) when he writes that it is "one of the tenets of Philosophical Radicalism . . . to pattern human psychology upon the physical sciences".[8]

Although in general terms one can agree with such an assessment, it is simply not specific enough to capture the very different methodological views of the sciences in general and the moral and physical sciences in particular that were current at the time. While John Mills and his supporters contented themselves with identifying the method of the physical sciences by its alleged deductive–nomological structure (to put it anachronistically), for someone like Jevons, such a characterisation fell short of capturing what the sciences – and hence physical science – were about. Even with regard to the immediate issue at stake here – man's freedom of will – it is interesting to note that James Mill, in his younger years, argued against necessitarians such as Joseph Priestley and Thomas Belsham precisely because of just such a denial of free will implicit in their ideas. In his review of Belsham's *Elements of the Philosophy of the Mind* (1801), written for the *Anti-Jacobin Review and Magazine*, he defended the method of enquiry of Common Sense philosophers like Thomas Reid and Dugald Stewart as the true mode of enquiry for the realm of mind. They were "chemical philosophers" who regarded the phenomena of mind as "simple substances" unless proven otherwise, and this method of analysis was according to James Mill "approved by all just reasoners" (1802a, 7). In the *Analysis*, he contrasted this method of analysis with the "synthetic method" of Newton, which he considered unfit for the study of psychology. James Mill clearly changed grounds from Reid's Common Sense school to the position held by Priestley and Belsham, but he did not accept their

---

[8] Interestingly, Alfred Marshall patterned his speculations on a machine that mimicked the human brain in detail on the principles of the association psychology. However, as Mirowski correctly remarks (2002, 42), Marshall's speculations on a machine mind "would not be recognized by contemporary engineers". This only strengthens how far off the association psychology itself was from the image of physics, let alone engineering mechanics. For an extensive discussion of Marshall's speculations, see Raffaelli (1991, 2003).

necessitarianism nor their physiological reductionism. Rather, he reversed the arrow of causation, emphasising that physiological actions might be caused by mental phenomena and not the other way around, consistent with "what is called the Freedom of the Will" as defended by Thomas Reid and Dugald Stewart (James Mill [1869] 1982, 2:348).

James Mill's defence of free will did not carry off the generally shared impression his actual stance was just the opposite. It would be one of his son's main concerns to reconcile the scientificity of the association psychology with the doctrine of free will. Scientific method was about the proper way to make inferences to causal relations. This was his starting point in the chapter on freedom and necessity in the *Logic* where he jumped upon the notion of causation to argue his stance. Like Hume, Mill argued against those who considered the notion of a causal relation to entail more than a regular sequence of events. Like Hume, he denied that such a "mysterious spell" existed. The "more intimate connexion . . . or mysterious constraint" that a great many thinkers assumed to exist between the "antecendent" and the "consequent" was absent (*Mill* 8:838). However, while Hume had modified the concept of necessity to make it consistent with his regularity view of causation, Mill disentangled the two concepts, necessity and causation. The error of attributing "irresistibleness" to the concept of causation, Mill wrote, "would be prevented, by forbearing to employ, for the expression of the simple fact of causation, so extremely inappropriate a term as Necessity" (8:839).

This preliminary consideration in the famous Book VI of the *Logic* proved crucial for a proper scientific understanding of the phenomena of the mind. According to John Mill, the necessitarianism that was implied in physiological reductionism was neutralised once mental phenomena were considered to have an explanatory power of their own. In line with this, the conviction that man had the "power of resisting a motive" was in Mill's view "the really inspiriting and ennobling in the doctrine of freewill" (*Mill* 1:177). Introspection salvaged man's freedom of the will (*Mill* 8:838):

> We are certain that, in the case of our volitions, there is not this mysterious constraint. We know that we are not compelled, as by a magical spell, to obey any particular motive. We feel, that if we wished to prove that we have the power of resisting the motive, we could do so . . . and it would be humiliating to our pride, and (what is of more importance) paralysing to our desire of excellence, if we thought otherwise.

The individual experience of free will matched with the proper method to make scientific inferences about the phenomena of the mind: by means of introspection. The reconciliation of the association psychology with the notion of free will came to John Stuart Mill as a true relief: "From that time I drew in my own mind, a clear distinction between the doctrine of circumstances, and Fatalism; discarding altogether the misleading word Necessity... I no longer suffered under the burden... of thinking one doctrine true, and the contrary doctrine morally beneficial" (*Mill* 1:177). The harness of mechanical obedience to the laws of association vanished: "I was no longer hopeless: I was not a stock or stone" (145).

It was therefore no coincidence that John Mill approved of the limitation of his father's *Analysis* to the phenomena of the mind only, excluding the study of man's physiology as having no bearing on the subject. In particular, he considered that his father had rightly dismissed David Hartley's "premature hypothesis respecting the physical mechanism of sensation and thought" (James Mill [1869] 1982, xi).[9] However, by breaking the "magical spell" of necessitarianism in a different way than Hume, Mill introduced another one by stipulating that freedom of the will was a capacity of human nature of which introspection gave immediate evidence. Mill could maintain both sides, freedom and causation, because of his reliance on introspection as an infallible judge on both issues.

"A Vexed Question in Psychology"

Mill's conclusion that freedom of will is compatible with the notion of universal causation paved the way for a science of the mind. His digression from Hume made him not just argue against the notion of necessity, but also against that of a mechanistic image of the mind as such. John Stuart Mill considered the dispute of "whether our thoughts, emotions, and volitions are generated through the intervention of material mechanism" as "one of the *vexatae quaestiones* in the science of human nature" (*Mill* 8:850). But it was for him beyond dispute that "the successions... which obtain among mental phenomena, do not admit of being deduced from the physiological

---

[9] Hartley himself had underlined the independence of the associationist doctrine from his theory of vibrations. See, for example, Hartley's *Conjecturae* (1746), reprinted (1967). This point is emphasised in Halévy ([1901] 1995, 1:16, 192n17).

laws of our mental organization". With the necessary and mechanical junction of man's physiology and his mental states denied, "it remains incon-
testable that there exist uniformities in succession among states of mind"
and that, therefore, "there is a distinct and separate Science of Mind" (8:851).
Mill thus established a categorical difference between the lawlike character
in the sequence of cause and effect among natural objects, and the lawlike
character of associations between mental states that was heavily dependent
on introspection as the proper method of enquiry in the moral realm.

Nancy Cartwright (1989: 173) has remarked how "peculiar" Mill's separation of mechanics and geometry is "from the standpoint of a modern
empiricist". However, this separation is central to an understanding of Mill's
views on mental philosophy as a science. It was motivated by his distinction between the laws of mind and matter. His separation of geometry from
physics was premised on his strongly felt need to reconcile the conflicting
notions of freedom and necessity. It enabled him to relegate any allusion to
necessity from mechanics to geometry (which he perceived as the Euclidian
science of pure reasoning); necessity became virtually identical with logical
consistency, and mechanics was about causal regularities.

The consequences of Mill's solution can be illustrated by his notion of the
"annihilation of forces". If we take a look at a material balance, we can see
that counteracting forces of equal magnitude "annihilate" and that therefore
the balance is in equilibrium. Mill would consider this situation in terms of
adding and subtracting forces. However, there is a notion of necessity at work
in the balance that has to do with its "material mechanism" and is brought
out by its geometry, not by arithmetically adding or subtracting forces. This
becomes evident when one of the pans on the arm of the balance is moved.
For a balance to be in equilibrium, not forces, but moments, should add up to
zero. The arm, or the beam of the balance, of necessity ties the different forces
at work together – that is what makes the balance a mechanism. The implied
notion of necessity provided the Common Sense philosopher Thomas Reid
(1967 1:238) with his most important reason to reject the comparison of
human deliberation with a mechanical balancing process, even though he
considered this analogy "one of the strongest that can be found between
mind and matter". According to Reid, the necessity implied in the mechanical
balance moved judgement out of moral deliberation. The same can be said
of Mill. Hence, for Mill it was of importance to argue that even if causal
regularities were mechanical, they were not necessary. In the realm of the

mind, there was for Mill no material mechanism leading automatically to the annihilation of conflicting motives, as equal moments annihilate in a mechanical balance. Some sort of conscious deliberation process that could be analysed in its own terms was always needed to effectuate this. Mill's views on physics, geometry, and mental philosophy were, in short, linked. The categorical distinction between mind and matter enabled Mill to account for causal regularities in the mental realm without violating the possibility of freedom of will. States of mind were conscious, regular, and free.

We have seen how Mill's antipode on issues of scientific method, William Whewell, was at a loss as to how to apply the methods of the experimental sciences to the phenomena of the mind. For Whewell, the notion of free agency was as central as it was for Mill, as is witnessed from his *Bridgewater Treatise*: "There can be no wider interval in philosophy than the separation which must exist between the laws of mechanical force and motion, and the laws of free moral action" (*Whewell* 9:374). However, Whewell had no problem at all with the very close relationship between geometrical and mechanical reasoning, and he persistently (and to Richard Jones's annoyance) kept the word "necessity" in his inductive vocabulary. Geometry, mechanics, and necessity being linked, it was unclear how to apply geometry to the phenomena of the mind. As unwilling as Mill to give up the notion of free agency, Whewell withdrew to a position much closer than Mill to Common Sense philosophers like Reid and Stewart. For Whewell, "intuitions" granted moral agency, and moral philosophy itself became sharply separated from the sciences.

We have seen that, in his criticism of Mill's views on induction, Whewell moved considerably in Mill's direction by hinting at a scientific role for introspection in the realm of the mind. Thus, the two men were seemingly united on the limits set to mechanical philosophy with regard to the realm of the mind and on the role introspection had to play there. This union was only apparent because for Mill introspection was the method of the association psychology and not the recourse to the "intuitions" of Whewell and philosophers like Hamilton and Martineau. In his *Examination of Sir William Hamilton's Philosophy*, Mill carefully distinguished between his own "psychological" method of enquiring about the phenomena of the mind and the "introspective", read "intuitive", method. In his 1872 essay "The Place of Mind in Nature and Intuition in Man" in the *Contemporary Review*, Martineau asked how to distinguish between the phenomena of the mind,

as given to consciousness, and their allegedly more simple constituents –
an issue most pressing when turning to Mill's own consciously observed
fact of free will. At the end of the nineteenth century, such criticisms of the
association psychology found eloquent expression in the work of William
James and Henri Bergson, who both, in their very different ways, argued
that the "demand for atoms of feeling, which shall be real units", was "a
sheer vagary, an illegitimate metaphor" (James 1884, 11), leading to "the
most inflexible determinism" (Bergson 1959, 117).

"THOUGHT – A SECRETION OF THE BRAIN"

Mill's introspective claim for man's freedom of will remained a key recourse
throughout the nineteenth century. It centred on the central role of the
experiences of the individual in support of the scientificity of psychology
and the existence of freedom of will. In his *Methods of Ethics* ([1874] 1962,
65), Henry Sidgwick argued in a similar vein against the "formidable array
of cumulative evidence" for determinism, which in his view was more than
offset by the "immediate affirmation of consciousness in the moment of
deliberate action". In the same year that Sidgwick's seminal book appeared,
Thomas Huxley published his provocative and highly influential "On the
Hypothesis that Animals are Automata" in the *Fortnightly Review*.

Huxley's article can be seen as the culmination of heated debates in mid-
century Britain on the relation of the phenomena of the mind to man's
physiological constitution and its consequences for the issue of free will
(Daston 1978, 1982; Smith 1997). Huxley's article was a review article in disguise on nineteenth-century developments in psychophysiology, especially
in the theory of reflex action and its consequences for the mind–matter
distinction. Taking Descartes as the foil against which to view these recent
developments, Huxley gave an uncompromising materialist, reductionist
and necessitarian account of man, and did not conceal his sympathy for
the "shibboleth of materialists that 'thought is a secretion of the brain'".
According to Huxley, the developments of nineteenth-century physiology
made consciousness into "something manufactured by the mechanism of
the body". In his influential presidential address to the 1874 Belfast meeting of
the British Association for the Advancement of Science (BAAS), John Tyndall
similarly paralleled mind states and brain states: "We can trace the development of a nervous system, and correlate with it the parallel phenomena of

sensation and thought. We see with undoubting certainty that they go hand in hand. But we try to soar in a vacuum the moment we seek to comprehend the connexion between them. An Archimedean fulcrum is here required which the human mind cannot command" (1874, 59).[10]

Though one may dispute Huxley's rendition of Descartes, there is no doubt that Descartes's notorious distinction between *res cogitans* and *res extensa* was at the root of the debates on the limits and methods of mental philosophy in comparison with the natural sciences. But also, and perhaps even more importantly, Locke, with his famous suggestion that matter can think, and precursors of reflex theory – like Haller in Germany, Robert Whytt in Scotland, and David Hartley and Joseph Priestley in England – from very different and sometimes conflicting angles downplayed the separate and distinct roles of consciousness for human agency.[11] The writings of French Materialists like Holbach, Helvétius, and LaMettrie (especially, of course, his *L'Homme-Machine*) and so-called rational recreations like Vaucanson's famous flute player and other products of mechanical ingenuity conveyed as the message to their eighteenth-century audiences that man, after all, was no more than a machine.[12] Anson Rabinbach (1992, 52) quotes Voltaire as probing Vaucanson's ultimate goal: "to create an automatic figure whose motions will be an imitation of all animal operations, such as the circulation of the blood, respiration, digestion, the movement of muscles, tendons, nerves and so forth".

The developments in physiology over the nineteenth century made to Huxley the assumption "perfectly justifiable" that man was "in the condition

---

[10] Huxley and Tyndall's addresses touched on many of the same issues and were equally provocative to those attempting to defend free will in light of recent developments in physics and physiology. The influence of Tyndall's address on the Scottish natural scientists' debates on free will – invoking William and James Thomson, Fleeming Jenkin, Clerk Maxwell, and others – is most carefully examined in Smith and Wise (1989, Chapter 18).

[11] The literature on these eighteenth-century debates is too vast to be covered here. Some cursory references must suffice. The standard account of mechanism and materialism in the eighteenth century is Robert Schofield (1970). On the "thinking matter" debate in Britain, see Yolton (1984). On Scottish physiology and its relation to moral and political philosophy, see Underwood (1977), Lawrence (1979), Barfoot (1983), Jacyna (1994), Wright (1990, 2000), Maas (2003), and Wood (1990, 1995). Especially Wood (1995) is worthwhile for its comprehensive referencing to relevant secondary literature. On the relation of physiology to politics in the eighteenth-and early-nineteenth-century English context, see especially Jacyna (1981, 1983). On the differences between Priestley and Bentham in relation to physiology and politics, see Schaffer (1990).

[12] On Vaucanson's automata, see especially Gaby Wood's wonderful 2002 book.

of one of Vaucanson's automata – a mechanism worked by molecular changes in his nervous system" (1874, 570). Huxley quoted the eighteenth-century French natural philosopher Charles Bonnet: "Give the automaton a soul which contemplates its movements, which believes itself to be the author of them, which has different volitions on the occasion of the different movements, and you will on this hypothesis construct a man" (1874, 579). At the dawn of the nineteenth century, the Edinburgh physiologist and political radical John Allen wrote in similar terms as Bonnet that man was nothing but an "Automaton ... endowed with Sensation" in which "the effect of new impressions shall be modified by preceding ones" in accordance with the structure of his nervous organisation (Jacyna 1994, 63–4, quoting Allen). Such materialist positions perceived man as some sort of machine which infallibly acted in accordance with the laws of his physiological constitution. Echoing such authors, Francis Ysidro Edgeworth (1877, 24), Jevons's immediate follower in mathematical economics, questioned Sidgwick's argument of the indubitable conscious fact of free will most acutely: "If both motive and action are not cause and effect, but *co-effects* of the same physical cause", what separate role and need was there then for a sphere of mind distinct from matter? The implied answer was, of course: None.

CARPENTER'S "CORRELATION OF FORCES"

The physiological approach to psychology that was highlighted by Huxley became known in Victorian Britain as psychophysiology. It made its breakthrough with Marshall Hall's theory of reflex action in the 1830s and was then further developed by such diverging physiologists as William Carpenter (1813–1885), Henry Maudsley (1835–1918), and Thomas Laycock (1812–1876). Also, the extremely popular phrenological movement, stemming from the German physiologists Franz Joseph Gall (1758–1828) and Johann Gaspar Spurzheim (1776–1832), played an important role (Winter, 1998). From the publication of the *Origins of Species* onwards, these debates would crystallise around the challenges set by Darwin's evolutionary theory (Smith 1997).

Hall's theory was that so-called sensory motor acts were performed independently of man's consciousness. Examples were the sucking reflex of newborn children, sneezing, and so forth. These acts were mediated by the spinal marrow and arose from an irritation of the sensory nerves. Hall limited the domain of reflex actions and excluded the higher functions of the nervous system (the brain) that were, according to him, governed by the soul. Hall's theory made great strides initially in medicine and thereafter among psychologists. Most notably, Thomas Laycock extended the scope of Hall's theory in his 1845 article in the *British and Foreign Medical Journal* to also include the higher functions of the brain, including man's alleged volitional activities. Drawing on the discourse of phrenology, Laycock even went so far as to declare that man's consciousness was effectively just a "coincident phenomenon", the body being put in motion by our neural organisation only (Jacyna 1981, 116, quoting Laycock). Laycock echoed eighteenth-century comparisons of the "animal machine" with a balance where the brain and the spinal chord served as the fulcrum passively transmitting the sensations that put the muscles into "voluntary motion", reducing human agency to a mechanical balancing act (Maas 2003).

The physiologist William Carpenter (1813–1885) obviously did not want to go so far. His *Principles of Human Physiology* (first edition 1842), fulfilled a similar function in the medical discipline as Mill's *Principles of Political Economy* did for political economy. Carpenter persistently took issue with those scientists who, like Laycock, ignored "those facts of consciousness which John Stuart Mill has truly characterized as the only realities of which, philosophically speaking, we have any evidence" (Carpenter 1875, 398).

Carpenter essentially accepted Mill's recourse to introspection as a legitimate defence of free will, but his solution to the questions raised by the theory of reflex action pointed in the opposite direction. In a review article of 1852, *On the Relation of Mind and Matter*, Carpenter argued in Millian terms against an exchange of letters between Harriet Martineau and the physician and mesmerist Henry George Atkinson on "the laws of man's nature and development".[13] Published in 1851, the letters emphatically argued that man's mental life was mechanically and deterministically the offspring of man's physiology. Carpenter quoted Harriet Martineau, who set the tone in one of the first letters: "I am what I am; a creature of necessity; I claim neither merit nor demerit.... I feel that I am as completely the result of my nature, and impelled to do what I do, as the needle to point to the north, or the puppet to move according as the string is pulled". Carpenter commented that in thus "reducing the Thinking Man" to a puppet, psychophysiology placed itself in "complete opposition" to the "undoubting conviction" that

---

[13] On mesmerism and Victorian culture, see Winter (1998).

everyone was possessed of a "*self-determining power*" that could "mould external circumstances to its own requirements, instead of being completely subjected to them" (Carpenter 1852, 510).

Carpenter's implicit recourse to Mill is illuminating, for Carpenter was at the time one of the most important propagators of the theory of reflex action in Britain. Rather than doing away with the distinction between mind and matter, he suggested replacing it by fixing "our attention exclusively on the relation between *Mind* and *Force*" (1852, 513). To effectuate this shift, the psychologist had to distance himself from "the older methods of research, in which Mind has been studied apart from its material instruments, and Matter has been weighed and measured, tested and analysed, as if its properties were self-derived and self-dependent" (508). Carpenter stipulated that there was "evidence" for the existence of "certain forms of Vital Force" that made it possible for the mind to act upon the body, just as physical forces existed which acted upon matter. This brought him to the notion of a correlation of forces, a notion reminiscent of Sir William Grove's seminal 1846 article, "On the Correlation of Physical Forces":[14]

> We are led to perceive, that, as the power of Will can develope Nervous activity, and as Nerve-force can develope Mental activity, there must be a *Correlation* between these two modes of dynamical agency, which is not less intimate and complete than that which exists between Nerve-force on the one hand, and Electricity or heat on the other.
>
> (1855, 799)

Carpenter explicitly used his notion of a correlation of forces to indicate that the spheres of mind and matter were independent, though related, thus enabling him to defend freedom of will on its basis. The very purpose of Carpenter's notion of a correlation of forces was to counteract the idea that

---

[14] Sir William Grove is known as the father of the fuel cell. His 1846 article predates Helmholtz's "On the Conservation of Force" by one year. Carpenter's notion of the "correlation of forces" should, however, be distinguished from those of the "conservation of force" or the "conservation of energy" that were vigorously debated in mid-century Britain. The possible influences on and relations between Carpenter's work and debates over the conservation of energy have been examined in Hall (1979). In relation to Jevons, White (2004b) provides the most extensive discussions to date. We find a similar notion of a "correlation" of mind states and brain states in Laycock's *Mind and Brain* (1860), and in the already quoted 1874 address of John Tyndall to the BAAS.

the human body functioned like a self-sufficient system, akin to a steam engine, and not in need of any other input than fuel.

Carpenter's suggestion of a "correlation of forces" is important for its moving away from introspection as the primary method to study the phenomena of the mind. Rather, bodily states could be used as *indices* for mental states, just as the thermometer was used to indicate temperature. As Alfred Barratt, the author of *Physical Ethics* ([1869] 1991), described it, there was no more circularity in the last measurement procedure than in the measurement of pleasures and pains by the actions of an individual agent (quoted in Edgeworth 1877, 6). Bodily states served to measure mental states, or, alternatively, outcomes of actions served as measures for motives.

In Britain, the association psychologist Alexander Bain suggested this measurement procedure explicitly. Independent of the German psychophysics of Helmholtz, Fechner, and Wundt that developed around the same time, Bain stipulated a strict parallelism between mental and bodily states:

> Mind is indeed, as a phenomenon, widely different from physical forces, but, nevertheless, rises and falls in strict numerical concomitance with these: so that it still enters, if not directly, at least indirectly, into the circle of the correlated forces.
>
> (1867, 378)

In this article and elsewhere, Bain used notions like "correlation of forces" and "conservation of energy" interchangeably. Peter Guthrie Tait heavily criticised Bain for this use as being a complete misunderstanding of his and Thomson's theory of the "conservation of energy". However, perhaps because of his annoyance with Bain, Tait missed the suggestion to measure mental states by states of the body. Changing vocabulary from "force" to "energy", this suggestion was picked up by another commentator on Bain's work: "What Mr. Bain aims at, so far as the doctrine of energy is concerned, is to show that mental states and changes can be numerically estimated by reference to the changes of physical energy which take place through the nervous machinery" (Heath 1868, 73).

Such proposals for measurement of mental states robbed introspection of its privileged position in psychological research and suggested other methods more consistent with measuring procedures used in the other sciences.

Leaving the exact causal relationship between mental and bodily states un-determined – just assuming them to be "correlated" – left the issue of free will undetermined as well, although the inherent conclusion was that physical phenomena were the cause of mental states, rather than vice versa.

In further discussions of Bain's theory, reference was made to similar discussions in Germany. The physician Bastian (1869b, 439), for example, referred to experiments made by Ernst Weber, and the second edition of Bain's *The Senses and the Intellect* (1868) included many references to the German and French contexts. It may have been that, in these years, Bain be-came conversant with Ernst Weber's numerical experiments on the relation between reaction time and pain stimulus (heat).

In Germany, Weber's experiments were further pursued by Helmholtz, Fechner, and Wundt. Their programme of psychophysics reached its well-known accomplishment in Fechner's work, providing a mathematical ex-pression between the intensity of stimuli in relation to the intensity of mental sensations (Heidelberger 1993). Though Nicolas Chaigneau (1997, 314n3; see also 2002) has correctly observed that psychophysics proper was not known in England prior to 1872 (i.e., after James Sully's review article on German psychophysics in the *Westminster Review*), there were clearly ideas about us-ing bodily states to make numerical estimates on states of mind in England before that time. Helmholtz presented his physiological work to the Royal Institution in April 1861 – a presentation in which he "supported a reduc-tionist and deterministic view of physiology" (Smith and Wise 1989, 617), and his ideas immediately became the subject of extensive, heated debates.

Regardless, Bain did not make any progress in the direction of German psychophysics, and it is more than likely that fundamental differences about the perceived target and ensuing method of psychological research were important for this (Danziger 1982). Despite having suggested measuring mental states through bodily states, such measurement strategies remained an anathema for Bain. For Bain as for Mill, psychology ultimately dealt exclu-sively with individual states of consciousness, with "ideas and conceptions", and introspection was in their view the only secure way of gathering evidence on them. According to Mill, it was evident that "if the word mind means anything, it means that which feels" (*Mill* 8:849).[15] Instead of exploring the

---

[15] In his *Examination of Sir William Hamilton's Philosophy*, Mill mentions an experiment aiming to account for the fact that, particularly when events follow one another with

consequences of his own suggestion, Bain defended, as late as 1893, the introspective method in opposition to Fechner's experimental method as the "alpha and the omega of psychological inquiry; it is alone supreme, everything else is subsidiary. Its compass is ten times all the other methods put together, and fifty times the utmost range of Psycho-physics alone" (1893, 42).

THE PHYSICAL GROUNDWORK OF ECONOMICS

In the preceding, we have seen that by the time Thomas Huxley published his thought-provoking essay in 1874, association psychology had lost its privileged claim as the one and only true theory of the mind, with its concomitant introspective method as the favoured method to establish laws of mind. From what can be gathered from his diary and letters, it is clear that when Jevons returned to University College, London, in the early 1860s, he took a warm interest in these debates on the relation of physiology to the moral sciences and their possible meaning and implications for political economy.

Jevons was very disappointed when he was only ranked fourth at his political economy examination taken in June 1860 – and this "after having read some fifteen of the best works in the subject", as Jevons wrote to his brother Herbert. John Elliot Cairnes' series of lectures, published as *The Character and Logical Method of Political Economy* (1857), certainly was on this list, and it proved an important source of inspiration for Jevons when it came to the possible role and importance of psychophysiology for political economy. Cairnes, Mill's spokesman in matters of theory and method, eloquently defended Mill's views. Cairnes argued that the "circuitous" route of induction propounded by William Whewell was perfectly fit for the natural sciences, but not for political economy, where it was "superseded by proof of a more direct, and therefore unequivocal character" (1857, 52, 184). Rather than starting with the tedious process of "observation and classification",

extreme rapidity, parts of the chain of association disappear. This was especially important since one of the suggested hypotheses was that the lost part of the chain passed the mind "without consciousness". This solution was unacceptable for Mill, because associations between mental states were associations of feelings, and it was, on these terms, impossible to associate feelings that were not felt. The experiments Mill discussed were all attempts to deal with reaction time, as in the case of the production of the visual illusion of white, when rapidly turning the prismatic colours on a wheel. The measurement of reaction time would become one of main occupations for experimental psychology, especially building on the work of Fechner and Wundt.

the political economist could assess the truth of the "axioms" of the science directly, since these were found "in our own consciousness" (1857, 52). Hence, anyone would find that self-interest guided his economic actions.

The advantage of immediate evidence and truth of such basic principles was counterbalanced by the disadvantage of the inexactness of the subject. More explicitly than Mill, Cairnes declared that human motives "from their nature" did not "admit of being weighed and measured like the elements and forces of the natural world" and that they therefore were not "susceptible of arithmetical or mathematical expression". For this reason, "Political Economy seems... necessarily excluded from the domain of exact science".

Cairnes contrasted this situation with the "more advanced physical sciences" whose laws "assume the form of precise quantitative statement" (1857, 79–80). Even if motives of action could be expressed in numbers (which they could not), insuperable problems remained. In a footnote immediately following this passage, Cairnes criticised attempts by Henry Dunning Macleod and Richard Jennings to turn political economy into an exact science. Cairnes questioned the availability of the appropriate sort of data. As he illustrated with a variety of examples – among them the King Davenant table of changes in prices and quantities of grain and the influence of the gold discoveries in California and Australia on the price of gold – even when such data were available, the problem was not just one of numbers, but the more fundamental one of the meaning of these numbers. In the case of the price of grain, for example, the various causes contributing to a change in supply and demand would make an exact computation of "what the price ought in consequence to be an insoluble problem" (1857, 82n).

In an appendix to his lectures, Cairnes returned to Richard Jennings's attempts to ground political economy in physiology. He wrote with manifest disgust about Jennings's attempts to trace the phenomenon of consumption back to the "instrumentality of the afferent trunks of nerve-fibre" (1857, 230). As far as Cairnes was concerned, there was no doubt that "if political economy is treated in this way, it is evident that it will soon become a wholly different study from that which the world has hitherto known it" (231).

By founding political economy in man's physiology, Jennings violated "the limits of economic inquiry" as "laid down by Mr. J. S. Mill". To substantiate this, Cairnes pointed to Mill's distinction between laws of mind and matter and emphasised Senior's fundamental agreement with Mill that only "the laws of the human mind, and no others, belong to Political Economy" (1857, 179, Cairnes quoting Mill). Cairnes observed in conclusion that "as a rule, every economist, so soon as an economic fact has been traced to a mental principle, considers the question solved, so far as the science of wealth is concerned". Having their general principles ready at hand (in man's consciousness), political economists "are entirely independent of those refined inductive processes by which the ultimate truths of physical science are established" (1857, 55).

Jevons read Cairnes's lectures intensely, but he did not approve of their conclusions. Indeed, much of Jevons's work in the 1860s can be interpreted as a direct response to Cairnes. In contrast with Cairnes, Jevons greeted Jennings's attempts to ground the laws of political economy in man's physiology with approval. In the *Theory*, Jevons wrote that Jennings "most clearly appreciated the nature and importance of the laws of utility" by treating the "physical groundwork of Economy, showing its dependence on physiological laws. It appears to me to display a great insight into the real basis of Economy" (*TPE1* 65). While Cairnes dismissed Jennings's suggestion to "exhibit" the "results of the principles of human nature ... by the different methods of Algebra and of Fluxions" as alien to the subject (1857, 121n), Jevons considered the very same passage "a clear statement of the views which I have also adopted" (*TPE1* 18).

In the early 1860s, Jevons was working on his new theory of value, based on utility, as he was reading in physiology as well. In February of that year, Jevons wrote in his diary that he had arrived "at a true comprehension of Value regarding which I have lately very much blundered" (*PC* 7:120). Immediately preceding this remark, we find Jevons "reading up to the *Nervous System*", a reference Michael White (1994a) plausibly suggests to Marshall Hall's *Memoirs of the Nervous System* (1837). His strong interest in the relation of physiology to psychology in this period is witnessed by his attendance of James Martineau's mental philosophy class at Manchester New College, of which he did not think highly: "when he does become comprehensible he generally goes palpably wrong" (White 1994a:223, quoting Jevons). It is more than likely that William Carpenter's and Alexander Bain's works were on his reading list as well.[16]

---

[16] A newspaper cutting from the *Manchester Guardian* in the Jevons Archives (JA 6/36/85) reveals Jevons's continued interest in the new developments in physiology. The undated newspaper cutting gives a detailed account of Huxley's 1874 article in the *Fortnightly Review*.

Previously, I quoted from Jevons's letter to his brother Herbert from 1 June 1860 in which he clearly indicated many of the decisive elements of his new theory of utility, especially "the most important axiom" of the declining degree of what he then called the "*ratio of utility*", and the assumption that, "on an average", this ratio of utility "is some continuous mathematical function of the quantity of commodity"; a "law" that, according to Jevons, had been assumed by political economists "under the more complex form and name of the Law of Supply and Demand" (*LJ* 151). Hence, Jevons's new theory of utility and his reading into the new physiology were at least intimately connected in time.

But there was a more substantial connection between the two. The decisive contribution of physiology to Jevons's new theory was the idea of how to consider motives for action in terms of functional form. This was Jennings's most important suggestion, which Jevons wholeheartedly embraced. Jevons extensively quoted Jennings's account of the "law according to which the sensations . . . vary in degree with changes in the quantity", and this for consumption as well as for labour.

Reading the introduction to the *Theory*, one receives the impression that Jevons treated pleasure and pain in quantitative terms. In the *Theory*, Jevons expressed this with the famous phrase that "wherever the things treated are capable of being *more or less* in magnitude, there the laws and relations must be mathematical in nature" (*TPE1* 4). This statement is commonly taken as identifying the quantitative nature of the subject matter of political economy with its mathematical character. It is in these terms that Jevons in the *Theory* took recourse to "dry old Jeremy" Bentham or William Paley, who "fully recognized the quantitative character of the subject" and of consequence the "thoroughly mathematical character . . . of the method" of political economy.

It goes without saying that Bentham's theory of pleasures and pains was an important source of inspiration for Jevons's new theory of utility, as recently argued by Sigot (2002). But it would be merely a shortcut to consider Jevons's mathematical treatment of the fundamental motive forces of human action, pleasure and pain, or of the principle of utility to follow from Jevons's own strong emphasis on their quantitative nature. Jevons attributed the mathematical character of political economy not just to *quantities*, but to a *relation* between quantities. His discussion of the dimensions of pleasure, pain, and the derived notion of (dis-)utility shows that these quantities themselves embody functional form.

In *Economic Theory in Retrospect*, Blaug rightly points to the similarity in functional form of Jevons's utility curves and the so-called Weber–Fechner's law in psychophysics. It is almost certain that Jevons's graph of the utility function was not influenced by the German psychophysical context, although there is a similarity in substance. Jevons's main reference was Jennings. Following Jennings, Jevons perceived the possibility of laying out a mathematical relation between stimuli and satisfaction, the form of which determines how satisfaction reacts to stimuli. "All our appetites are capable of *satisfaction* or *satiety* sooner or later, both these words meaning, etymologically, that we have had *enough*" (*TPE1* 62–3). Even though this principle, according to Jevons, had been perceived by a great many economists, including Senior and Banfield, it had been expressed most clearly by Richard Jennings, "showing its dependency on physiological laws" (65).

For Jevons, economics was not just about quantities; it was about functional relations, a point recently emphasised by Ivor Grattan-Guinness (2002). To obtain these functions, Jevons did not just take recourse to Bentham's hedonic calculus, but was motivated by the role notions of pleasure and pain played within the context of contemporary research in physiology. It was another question whether such functions could be given numerical values (i.e., could be made exact). In subsequent chapters, we will see in greater detail how Jevons made efforts to do so.

FREE WILL IS SIMPLY CHANCE

We have seen that the association psychology was at the heart of Mill's philosophy. It paved the way for the introspective method of the moral sciences, including political economy. For Mill, introspection made political economy equally scientific as the natural sciences and salvaged man's freedom of will. All these virtues of Mill's philosophy were vices for Jevons, and we need to see why to understand the methodological rift between Mill and Jevons.

It is well-known that Mill had only secondary knowledge of the constraints set by real experiments. In *Autobiography*, we read: "One of my greatest amusements was experimental science; in the theoretical, not the practical sense of the word; not trying experiments – a kind of discipline which I have often regretted not having had – nor ever seeing, but merely reading about them" (*Mill* 1:21). One of the major criticisms raised already by Whewell against Mill's four "canons of experimental inquiry" in *Logic* was that these hardly matched the way nature presented itself to the experimental scientist.[17]

Jevons came from a very different background than Mill. Having won gold medals in experimental science and chemistry during his first years of study at University College, London, versed in the intricacies of precision measurement as a gold assayer and grounded in meteorology during his stay in Australia, his ideas of what constituted evidence for theories and how to think about the relationship between both were fundamentally different from those of Mill.

Mill's deductive economics, which took introspective experiences as its indubitable source of evidence, was able to make causal claims and to uphold freedom of the will – all without being forced to add numerical precision to its claims. For Mill and Millians, like Cairnes and Sidgwick, numerical precision belonged to astronomy and mechanics and not to the regularities that could be found in society, however lawlike. But, as Jevons pointed out in his *Principles*, in all of the sciences, experimental or not, the investigator had to deal with errors in observation and was for this reason forced to take recourse in averaging procedures to attempt to wash these errors out. "Even at the present day", Jevons wrote, "discrepancies exist between the observed dimensions of the planetary orbits and their theoretical magnitudes, after making allowance for all disturbing causes" (*PS* 457). The privileged access to exactness attributed to the natural sciences simply did not exist:

> When we operate with sufficient care we cannot perform so simple an experiment as weighing an object in a good balance without getting discrepant numbers.... We may look upon the existence of error in all measurement as the normal state of things. It is absolutely impossible to eliminate separately the multitude of small disturbing influences, except by balancing them off against each other.
>
> (*PS* 357)

---

[17] Mill addressed Whewell's criticism in later editions of the *Logic* (*Mill* 7:429–33). The deductive method effectively side-stepped Whewell's objections to the applicability of Mill's four methods of experimental inquiry: "To ascertain, then, the laws of each separate cause which takes a share in producing the effect, is the first desideratum of the Deductive Method. To know what the causes are, which must be subjected to this process of study, may or may not be difficult". In the case of "human actions", the "first desideratum" was of "easy fulfilment" (7:455).

Rejecting Mill's views on induction and referring to his own logic of the "substitution of similars", Jevons argued that any understanding of science that focussed on particulars as its source of evidence was essentially flawed: "No one who holds the doctrine that reasoning may be from particulars to particulars [as Mill did], can be supposed to have the most rudimentary notion of what constitutes reasoning and science" (PS 495).

Jevons's emphasis on the "ordinary procedures" of averaging in the other sciences gave him a way out of the free will conundrum. Laws were always about average or mean values; individual observations were inevitably loaded with errors in measurement. Translated to the social domain, this meant treating observations on individuals as containing random errors that cancelled out on average. In a short, undated notice, Jevons drew an explicit parallel between errors in measurement in the natural sciences and the free will issue in the social sciences (JA 6/36/78):

> What I ask to point out with regard to this question is that even the existence of free will would not[18] prevent the formation of t[he] social sciences.... As regards science free will is simply chance; it represents a cause acting sometimes one way & sometimes another but concerning which we have no information. For our purposes it is no more a difficulty than the coalescence of innumerable small causes of error which affect every observation of an astr[onomer] and eve[ry] cupel of a chemist.[19]

In line with this thinking, Jevons paid tribute to Quetelet for being the "true founder of the social sciences" in a short review of Harriet Martineau's condensed version of Comte's philosophy, published in *Nature* for 7 October 1875. Quetelet, Jevons argued, was the first to see that by taking averages, rather than observations on individuals, as the "target of explanation", laws could be discovered in the social domain. Averaging practices had not been uncommon among Quetelet's contemporary statisticians and political economists. John McCulloch, for example, argued that the moral sciences had "to deal with man in the aggregate ... and not ... the conduct of a solitary individual" (quoted from Wise and Smith 1989a, 285). In an extensive review of Quetelet's *Physique Sociale* in the *Foreign Quarterly Review*,

---

[18] Jevons changed his mind and replaced "just" with "not".
[19] Brackets indicate material either suppressed in the original (as with "astronomer") or partially illegible. A cupel is a vessel for assaying precious metals. It also means the act of assaying itself. Jevons clearly used it in this second sense here.

the Irish journalist William Cooke Taylor argued at length that "human actions would, if registered, present as vast a variety as the caprices of the will...yet, when we pass from individuals to masses, we find even in those actions which seem most fortuitous, a regularity of production, an order of succession, that can only arise from fixity of cause" (Cooke Taylor 1835, 212).

From the viewpoint of science, free will amounted to nothing more than errors in measurement that "balanced" in the aggregate or mean value.[20] Jevons considered the problem of free will to be solved by considering the target of scientific explanation, like all natural scientists, average values and not singular observations. If the target of explanation was average, rather than individual behaviour, there was no need to be so obsessed with the issue of free will as Mill, who invariably explained away necessity "so ingeniously, that he unintentionally converts it into Free Will" ([1890] 1971, 203).

In the *Theory* Jevons consistently argued that even though his theory of utility was true of individuals, it was simply impossible to obtain evidence on this level: "Motives and conditions are so numerous and complicated that the resulting actions [of individuals] have the appearance of caprice". When turning to "great masses and wide averages", however, it was possible to determine "a more or less regular law.... The use of an average, or, what is the same an aggregate result, depends upon the high probability that accidental and disturbing causes will operate, in the long run, as often in one direction as the other, so as to neutralize each other" (*TPE2* 86). From a statistical point of view, the free actions of individuals were for Jevons nothing more than "caprice", "balancing", or cancelling out in an average (*TPE1* 22). As Jevons described it in the *Theory*: the "movements of trade and industry depend on averages and aggregates, not on the whims of the individuals" (*TPE2* 136; see especially Peart 1995a on Jevons's use of "wide averages").

THE PRIVATE LABORATORY OF THE MIND

Let me at this point return to Jevons's harsh verdict on Mill. Why did he consider Mill's mind "essentially wrecked"? Jevons's enthusiasm for the new

[20] Wise (1989a: 287) argues that Quetelet was a late user of the balancing metaphor, which over the nineteenth century gave way to the dynamic metaphor of the steam engine. In later chapters, especially Chapter 10, I will examine in detail Jevons's use of the metaphor of the balance in his theoretical and empirical works.

developments in psychophysiology gave him every reason to reject the hazy procedures of introspection as a method of collecting evidence and to turn to the consideration of statistical observations in its stead. For Jevons, something such as the private laboratory of the mind in which scientists could make private experiments on mental phenomena simply did not exist. All scientists were in "the position of spectators who witness the productions of a complicated machine, but are not allowed to examine its intimate structure. We learn what does happen and what does appear, but if we ask for the reason, the answer would involve an infinite depth of mystery" (*PS* 222).

One of Jevons's main problems with John Stuart Mill was that Mill, on the one hand, claimed methodological monism for all of the sciences, whereas on the other, he claimed that the social and natural sciences dealt with categorically different phenomena. Mill argued that the moral and physical sciences made use of the same methods of "observation and experiment" and could not have done otherwise, but also argued for the privileged route to truth for the moral sciences by means of introspection. As a consequence, political economists falsely considered they did not need to make use of statistical data to assess their theories, having the causal relations implied in them ready in their own minds. According to Jevons, this prevented political economy from becoming truly scientific. In his lecture to the Manchester Statistical Society in 1874 (*PC* 7:77), Jevons fully blamed Mill for this state of affairs:

> I cannot help reitering here my feeling that in England the progress of true economical science is being immensely retarded by the excessive popular reputation attaching to the writings of the late Mr. Mill. So peculiar was the power excited over his friends and readers by Mr. Mill's zeal, his fearless independence of opinion, his high moral character, and his lucid, persuasive, and apparently logical style of composition, that his works have acted upon English readers like a spell, which it may take many years to break.

Mill's attempts to evade the mechanistic and necessitarian tendencies of scientific monism came most prominently to the fore in his 1836 essay on the definition and method of political economy. Most anthologies on economic methodology include only part of the essay, starting with Mill's famous or notorious definition of economic man. In doing so, the manifest oddity in the construction of this essay is missed.

In the first part of the essay, Mill made a clear distinction between the "laws of mind" and "laws of matter". According to Mill, "laws of the mind and laws of matter are so dissimilar in their nature, that it would be contrary of all principles of rational arrangement to mix them up as part of the same study" (*Mill* 4:317). He did maintain that only "laws of the human mind, *and no others*, belong to Political Economy", to which he added that political economy "sums up the result" of the combination of the laws of mind and matter. Just a few lines earlier, Mill had stated that "it would be a strange classification which included [the properties of the lever] among the truths of Political Economy" (*Mill* 4:315). If a scientist should not "mix up" the laws of mind and matter, it is completely unclear what a "summing up" of the results of both laws would look like. Mill's position *was* completely incomprehensible to Jevons, and rightly so, for did not research in psychophysiology support the idea that mental phenomena could in the end be traced to the "physical groundwork" of our bodily constitution?

According to Jevons, the difference between the sciences of the mind and the sciences of nature was not to be found in a *categorical distinction* between mind and matter, but in the completely different issue of *complexity*. This problem motivated Mill to his definition of economic man as solely striving for wealth, to which he added: "No economist ever was so absurd as to suppose that Mankind really were so constituted. But this is the mode science necessarily has to proceed" (*Mill* 4:322).

In Jevons's view, Mill attempted to have it both ways: to separate the laws of mind and matter to salvage freedom of the will *and* to conform to the procedures of science. For Jevons, this move turned him into someone who was "essentially illogical". In exasperation, Jevons wrote that "many people seem to think that the physical sciences form the proper sphere of mathematical method and that the moral sciences demand some other method – I know not what" (*TPE2* 78). The distinction between mind and matter being blurred, it was for Jevons an obvious consequence that the sciences of the mind and the natural sciences should be addressed in a similar vein:

> The application of Scientific Method cannot be restricted to the sphere of lifeless objects. We must sooner or later have strict sciences of those mental and social phenomena, which, if comparison be possible, are of more interest to us than purely material phenomena.
>
> (*PS* xxvii)

In contrast with Mill, Jevons wholeheartedly embraced the mechanistic implications of his plea for a uniform method in the sciences. As a direct provocation to Mill, Jevons (*TPE2* 44) wrote in the preface to his *Theory*:

> The Theory of economy, thus treated, presents a close analogy to the science of statical mechanics, and the laws of exchange are found to resemble the laws of equilibrium of a lever as determined by the principle of virtual velocities.

Instead of relying on introspection to isolate the motives political economy (or any other social science) dealt with, it seemed far more appropriate to turn to the physical basis of man's conduct, on which psychophysiologists had made great strides. In particular, the psychophysiological theory of reflex action opened up the route to what Jevons considered on many occasions equivalent to "a strict scientific treatment": the rendition of human conduct in functional form. The letter of 2 October 1862 accompanying the version of the *Notice of a General Mathematical Theory of Political Economy* which Jevons submitted to the *Philosophical Magazine*, recently discovered by Grattan-Guinness in the archives of Taylor and Francis, leaves little doubt about this: "The subject is not exactly physical science but is treated in a strictly scientific & math[l] manner, so as not to be unsuitable for the Mag. as I should think" (quoted from Grattan-Guinness 2002, 704).

Even if Mill's negative commentary on Jevons's *Theory of Political Economy* was based only on Cairnes's account of it, Mill correctly sensed in Jevons's theory a tendency not only to mechanise the laws of exchange, but also the laws of the mind and thus – in Mill's view – to fall back into the sort of fatalism Mill had so ardently combatted in his writings. As if to prove this to Mill, Jevons alternately described his theory as a "calculus of pleasure and pain" and a "mechanics of utility and self-interest".

In sharp relief with the certitude expressed in these passages, Jevons seemed to bow his head for the introspective method of Mill and Cairnes in the second edition of the *Theory*. Published in the same years as his heavy attack on Mill's "private laboratory of the mind", Jevons wrote that we may know the "ultimate laws" of political economy "immediately by intuition, as it was pointed out "by J. S. Mill and Cairnes" (*TPE2* 88) and that "John Stuart Mill is substantially correct in considering . . . that we may start from some obvious psychological law". The seeming congruence between Jevons and Mill and Cairnes is only superficial. Mill and Cairnes practised – in

Henry Sidgwick's terms – the introspective method, Jevons the "hypothetical method". While the "obvious start" in the search for the ultimate laws of political economy in the first edition of the *Theory* had been "a few of the simplest principles or axioms concerning the nature of the human mind ..., just as the vast theories of mechanical science are founded upon a few simple laws of motion" (*TPE1* 24), the suppression of a reference to mechanics did not attribute any more certainty to the "intuitions" from which political economy started. Rather, these "intuitions" or "axioms" served as "hypotheses" that still needed to be "tested" for their empirical validity. Introspection conveyed absolute certainty to Mill and Cairnes's motivational laws, whereas the borrowed axioms from psychology served for Jevons as mere hypotheses that were still in need of "*a posteriori* observations" for "ratification". In this regard, there was no difference between the way Jevons described the "anticipation" of hypotheses by his men of genius (Newton, Huijgens, and Faraday) in science and the anticipation of "axioms" by political economists.

Schabas correctly wrote that for Jevons, economics had become a branch of psychology. Economic theory, in Jevons's words, had "to investigate the condition of a mind, and bases upon this investigation the whole of Political Economy" (*TPE2* 86). But where Mill took recourse to the association psychology for the fundamental motivational laws of political economy, Jevons looked instead to the promises of the new physiology to express these laws in functional form. In the *Principles* (*PS* 735–6), Jevons wrote:

> The time may come ... when the tender mechanism of the brain will be traced out, and every thought reduced to the expenditure of a determinate weight of nitrogen and phosphorus. No apparent limit exists to the success of scientific method in weighing and measuring, and reducing beneath the sway of law, the phenomena both of matter and mind.

⌒

EIGHT

The Laws of Human Enjoyment

14 June Monday, Buxton. On Monday we left Buxton for Manchester
in a tremendous shower of rain . . . Manchester is a most disagreeable
town & we thought it the more so as we had hardly an hour of fair
weather all the time we were there . . . It is so full of manufactorys
that you are enveloped in clouds of smoke & the place is so hot we
could scarcely breath & we were very glad to breath the fresh air of
the country again the next morning.

John Ruskin, *A Tour to the Lakes of Cumberland*

How a painter would have enjoyed the sight which broke upon my
waking eyes this morning! To my right is one of the tributaries to the
Irwell, winding through the depths of a richly wooded and precipitous
valley, or rather ravine. . . . Before me . . . is the Hall in the Wood,
memorable for having been the residence of Crompton, the inventor
of the spinning-jenny . . . Beyond is the hill on which a great part of the
busy town of Bolton is built. The intervening valley is studded with
factories and bleach-works. Thank God, smoke is rising from the lofty
chimneys of most of them! . . . it produces variations in the atmosphere
which, to me at least, have a pleasing and picturesque effect.

William Cooke Taylor, *Notes of a Tour in the Manufacturing
Districts of Lancashire*

In successive years in the mid 1860s, Ruskin, art critic, and Jevons, famous
economist, gave open lectures to audiences in the urban heartland of the
industrial revolution.[1] Jevons, responsible for the 1865 opening address at

---

[1] Jevons just had entered the limelight because of the appearance of his *Coal Question*,
predicting a decline in Britain's prosperity due to the exhaustion of cheaply extractable

Queen's College Liverpool,[2] had attended Ruskin's lecture a year earlier in Rusholme Town Hall, near Manchester.[3] He was impressed with Ruskin's abundant use of "imaginative names and figurative expressions", which were "either beautifully true, or suggestive of truth" (LDP 1865).[4] The title of his address was "Reading and Study", a title inspired by Ruskin's lecture, so Jevons assured his public.[5]

On the surface, many similarities can be found between Jevons's thoughts on education and those of Ruskin. Jevons assured his audience to be as adverse of the practice of "cramming" as Ruskin. Students should be "active", "reflective", and should not approach their studies passively, as if they were being "dragged through a fixed course of instruction" (LDP 1865). Given Ruskin's examples of free libraries, well-filled with valuable books, accessible art galleries, and so on, we can easily imagine that his lecture produced some resonance even in Jevons's later essays on social reform. Indeed, the cultural and moral elevation of the working class was a subject that occupied Jevons's thoughts until the end of his life.

But there was an even stronger tie linking the two men: their mutual criticism of Mill. By the 1860s, Ruskin had begun to criticise political economists for their misguided theories on the nature and causes of human wealth, and he blamed John Stuart Mill in particular. Mill's image of mankind as merely seeking the possession of wealth, and not its enjoyment, was for Ruskin the root of the decline of culture he perceived in Britain. In his 1836 essay, Mill

coal. On Jevon's *Coal Question,* see White (1991a), Peart (1996, 2001) and Chapter 2 of this book.

[2] Queen's College was a department of the Liverpool Mechanics' Institute set up in 1857 to give the working classes an opportunity of studying for the London Matriculation in evening classes. It was intended to become the nucleus of a new University. The project was, however, abandoned in 1881. See Stephens and Roderick Gordon (1972, 258). In 1865 Jevons had been appointed as a part-time Professor in Logic and Political Economy at the College, a chair he only held for half a year and abandoned when appointed to the Cobden Chair at Owen's College. As noted in Chapter 2, Jevons enjoyed two years of education at Liverpool Mechanics' Institute after his mother died in 1845. See Schabas (1990, 13), and Jevons (*PC* 1:13).

[3] At the time of Ruskin's lecture, Jevons was tutor at Owen's College, Manchester, a position he attained through the mediation of his cousin Harry Roscoe, then Professor of Chemistry at Owen's College.

[4] Jevons's inaugural lecture was printed in full in a supplement to the *Liverpool Daily Post* of 3 October 1865 (LDP 1865), page number unknown. Michael White kindly sent me a copy of this supplement.

[5] Ruskin's lecture was to become "Of Kings' Treasuries" in his best-selling book *Sesame and Lilies.*

had defined economic man as driven by three motives only, the desire for wealth, counteracted by the aversion to labour and the preference for present rather than future consumption. In the same essay, Mill (*Mill* 4:318n) had made it explicitly clear that man's desire for wealth had nothing to do with the "laws of human enjoyment":

> Political Economy has nothing to do with the consumption of wealth, further than as the consideration of it is inseparable from that of production, or from that of distribution. We know not of any *laws* of the *consumption* of wealth, as the subject of a distinct science: they can be no other than the laws of human enjoyment.

Jevons fully agreed with Ruskin's verdict of Mill. Jevons had stated plainly in his *Notice of a General Mathematical Theory of Political Economy*, read in 1862 to section F of the British Association for the Advancement of Science (BAAS), and would restate in the *Theory* (*TPE1* 47) that "it is surely obvious that Political Economy does rest upon the laws of human enjoyment; and that, if those laws are developed by no other science, they must be developed by economists". Jevons also agreed with Ruskin that working men in present day Britain no longer knew how to amuse themselves: "There is no difficulty in seeing that there is a tendency, in England at least, to the progressive degradation of popular amusements... the amusements of the masses, instead of being cultivated, and multiplied, and refined, have been frowned upon and condemned, and eventually suppressed, by a dominant aristocracy" (1883, 3, 6).

We might expect, then, far reaching agreement between Ruskin and Jevons on the role and significance of the laws of human enjoyment for political economy. But, as we will see in this chapter, such agreement did not exist. From Jevons's opening address, it became clear that he was also thinking along different lines which were not consistent with those of Ruskin. As will be explored in this chapter, these differences are closely linked with the typical Victorian discourse about man–machine analogies in relation to human work.

For Ruskin, the laws of human enjoyment were developed by an aesthetics of production; to produce art and to produce consumer goods was really the same thing. Ruskin cherished an all-comprising notion of work, in which no distinction was made between physical labour and the exertion of the higher mental and intellectual faculties of mankind. Work was identified with life, almost in its full complexity, of which Ruskin considered the Gothic an historical instance. Noting little interest in this concept of work-as-life by economists, he turned, in Patrick Geddes's words (1884, 30), from an art critic into a critic of political economy. With evangelical zeal, Ruskin proclaimed that the age of machinery reduced the workman to a "machine . . . an animated tool" (Ruskin, 1985, 84). This degradation of the labour of the workman to merely manually performed repetitive tasks was the bane of Victorian society. Ruskin blamed the conditions of production in England for this – the factory system, for the instalment of which he faulted the political economists, Mill in particular.

It was commonly held at the time that Ruskin placed his reputation in jeopardy with such criticism. *Unto this Last*, his first major attack on political economy that appeared 1862, was greeted as "one of the most melancholy spectacles" of the year. The *Saturday Review* wrote of "eruptions of windy hysterics", "absolute nonsense", "utter imbecility", and "intolerable twaddle", and characterised Ruskin himself as "a perfect paragon of blubbering". The general opinion was that "it was no pleasure to see genius mistaking its power, and rendering itself ridiculous" (*Ruskin* 17:xxvii–xxviii).

Ruskin's aesthetic notion of work-as-life was anathema to Jevons. Instead, he used a concept of work in which human labour and machine work were considered in similar terms. Jevons explored this analogy in experiments on the exertion of muscular force, published in *Nature* in 1870, in which he tentatively examined the "physiological groundwork" of political economy. He used these experiments in the *Theory of Political Economy* as an example of how his utility theory of labour could be substantiated empirically. Jevons moulded the concept of labour to fit into a new discourse of work and waste, of work and fatigue, that was gaining currency in mid-nineteenth century Britain. Having examined Jevons's theory of labour, we can estimate the extent to which Jevons shared Ruskin's views on the cultural and moral elevation of the working class.

The Factory System and the Division of Labour

The rapid spread of machinery and the emergence of the factory system were clearly an issue in Victorian Britain or, as Doron Swade (2000, 16) stated: "Machines were the obsession of the times, and the extent to which motive power and mechanism permeated life sometimes touched on the absurd".

Tremendous contemporary debates raged, theoretical as well as political, about the impact of machinery and of technical progress more generally on the economy, and on the condition of the working class. Swade's example of a rocking chair – moving by a system of pulleys, the cradle of a baby, thus enabling additional "useful and profitable labour" – shows how much machinery and the factory system and its emphasis on maximum useful output pervaded society. According to John Stuart Mill, the "celebrity of England" no longer rested upon its traditional institutes, but "upon her docks, her canals, her railroads". The English were now admired for "doing all things which are best done where man most resembles a machine, with the precision of a machine" (*Mill* 10:34–5). Machinery and manufactures, both to be found in the title of Babbage's 1832 masterpiece, altered the way the division of labour was conceptualized, just as they altered the concept of labour itself.

A common element in many contemporary accounts was that the factory system conditioned and controlled the workman more perfectly than any previous system of production. As is well-known, Jeremy Bentham initially designed his panopticon to control and regulate prisoners more effectively and then extended his panoptic gaze to other places of social control, such as madhouses, hospitals, workhouses, and schools. Many of the propagators of the factory system emphasised the need for more effective means to regulate and control the behaviour of the emerging working class. At the turn of the eighteenth century, Samuel Bentham, Jeremy's lesser-known brother who in fact invented and first practised the panoptic system, stressed that the skills and crafts of the workmen were a threat to the efficient and effective organisation of production. To control the workmen, their skills and crafts had to be broken down into visible routines. The factory system realized these purposes most perfectly.[6]

Babbage shared much of the spirit of such dissenting and utilitarian voices, even though he never became a utilitarian himself. He described his *Machinery and Manufactures* as one of the "consequences" of his work on his Difference Engines. Many of Babbage's insights in the book can be traced to his rule out error and to reach the highest level of precision attainable. Once he realised that the principle of the division of labour did not relate just to manual labour but extended to the skills of the workman as well, he opened

---

[6] On Samuel Bentham, see especially Ashworth (1998).

up new vistas in calculating the efficiency of production and suggested, in analogy with his calculating engines, means of mechanising labour where possible. By dividing skills into separate activities, mental labour could be routinised, could be paid according to its separate contribution to the produce, and could, in fact, be mechanised, as witnessed from his Difference Engines. Babbage's own description of the working of his calculating engine in *Machinery and Manufactures* reads like a Taylorised scheme of labour organisation (*Babbage* 8:140–2). The reduction of a mental skill into a precise order of wheels and gears fits precisely to the exact timing of different manual activities by means of a clock. In Philip Mirowski's happy phrasing, "the very architecture of the Analytical Engine . . . constituted a projection of a more perfect factory" (2002, 34).

In his *Philosophy of Manufactures* (1835), with Babbage's *On the Economy of Machinery and Manufactures* one of the most extensive contemporary analyses of the factory system, Andrew Ure concurred with the views expressed by Babbage and the Bentham brothers that the factory system dramatically altered the concept of the division of labour. The factory system, he argued, made Adam Smith's discussion of the division of labour in the first chapter of *The Wealth of Nations* outdated if not straightforwardly "misleading the public mind as to the right principle of manufacturing industry". According to Adam Smith, specialisation spectacularly enhanced productivity while at the same time improved and challenged the skills and ingenuity of the workman. Well-known are his examples of the street porter and the philosopher, for whom training and education (i.e., specialisation) were more important in explaining differences in skill and ingenuity than their respective natural talents. Although Smith's account of the lad who improved the machinery provides a rather mixed message, it obviously served in context to show that specialisation called upon his ingenuity.

In contrast with Smith and in line with the Bentham brothers, Ure argued that under the new factory system ultimately no appeal would be made to the talents and skills of the workmen: "skilled labour gets progressively superseded . . . in fact, the division, or rather adaptation of labour to the various talents of man, is little thought of in factory employment. *On the contrary!*" According to Ure, the end goal of the factory system was "to substitute mechanical science for hand skill". Ure emphasised that the new organisation of the production process and its extensive reliance on machinery would reduce rather than enhance the appeal on the workman's skills. Its result was the degradation of the workmen into "mere overlookers of machines" (Ure 1835, 19–20).

Other voices on the effects on the division of labour under factory conditions were more in line with Smith's initial analysis. The Irish journalist and secretary of the Anti-Corn Law League, William Cooke Taylor, depicted the factory system in the most rosy words he could muster in his *Notes of a Tour in the Manufacturing Districts of Lancashire* ([1841] 1968). He argued that even in Manchester, the negative consequences of the factory system should not be overestimated. Without underplaying the enormous misery to be encountered there (and which was famously stressed by Tocqueville and Engels around the same period), his message was obvious: If what was considered the most unhealthy place in England to live in was not, after all, that detrimental, how much better might life be in all the other manufacturing towns and villages? It was of course clear that Manchester was not a place of pleasure, but related only to the business part of man. The crowd on the streets passed the visitor with "the look of thought and the step of haste". The lack of amusements made its inhabitants look like "insects", who had assumed the colours and character of the place. But they were not all living a shadowy life. At the exchange of Manchester, one was able to judge how the spread of manufacture stimulated the use of the intellect: "The genius of the place is talent and intelligence; genius and stupidity appear to be equally absent; but if the average of intellect be not very high, it is evident that not a particle of it remains unemployed" (11).

Avoiding the great Manchester metropolis, in which the effects of the factory system could not be seen in their purest form, Cooke Taylor chose instead to travel the Lancashire countryside and visit the mills of the Ashworth brothers near Egerton, amongst others. There, the factory system could be studied apart from the many disturbing causes obfuscating its true and positive moral impact. "Thank God, smoke is rising from the lofty chimneys", Taylor wrote, for otherwise the mills would have lain idle, providing no work, and consequently no income to the workmen. The interior of the mill he equally described as "lofty", and he assured the reader that he would have "very well contended to have as large a portion of room and air in my own study as a cotton-spinner in any of the mills of Lancashire" (26). The implicit equation of work and study conveyed the message that far from being deadening or degrading, the factory enhanced the skills and ingenuity of the workman.

The factory system proved to be a system of perfect order. Invoking Smith's image of the impartial spectator, the steam engine was anthropomorphised as the "common assistant and friend of all" and the "most impartial of arbitrators". Its central place and regular working impressed "habits of order, cleanliness, and propriety" upon the operators. This made "the organization of the community complete, and the human agents work with all the exactness of machinery". The picturesque scenery at Ashworth's Turnton Mill showed the best of this revolutionary new system of production in straightforward Benthamite terms: "So strange a combination of perfect despotism with perfect freedom never before existed, and to have produced such a state is one of the noblest triumphs of morality and intelligence" (121–4). Even though the operator worked "with the exactness of machinery", this did not mean that the work itself was mechanical. In contrast with those who emphasised the degrading aspects of factory work, Cooke Taylor highlighted in the Smithian vein the "frequent opportunities" the work provided "for the exercise of skill, ingenuity, and contrivance" (115). It was rather those branches of industry that were dependent on manual labour and were not aided by machinery that turned man into a machine.

Not all contemporary accounts shared the enthusiasm of Taylor and others. From Carlyle, via Dickens's *Hard Times*, to Marx, the subjugation of the workmen under the repetitive moves of the steam engine was severely criticised. With all political differences, these voices judged the "Age of Machinery" to reduce the former artisans into a piece of machinery and to turn them into the slaves of progress. Earlier, Jeremy Bentham had shown no interest in this equation of men and machines: "Call them soldiers, call them monks, call them machines: so they were but happy ones, I should not care". As one proponent of the factory system described it: To be able to work with machines, the operatives had to "identify themselves with the unvarying regularity of the complex automaton" (Shapin and Barnes 1977, 68 n29, quoting Arkwright). In short, external circumstances forced the operatives to work in a machinelike way, but this did not entail any inherent similarity between men and machines.

In later years, this idea of the workman becoming machinelike by the constraints of the system of production was examined extensively by Thorstein Veblen in his *Theory of Business Enterprise* (1904). According to Veblen, the operative – at least to some extent – had to be knowledgeable about the principles underlying the workings of the machine. This knowledge ran in quantitative terms, in terms of cause and effect. Veblen stressed that "other intelligence on the part of the workman is useless; or it is even worse than useless, for a habit of thinking in other than quantitative terms blurs the workman's quantitative apprehension of the facts with which he has to do". To be suited for working at a machine, the "habits of life and thought of the workman" had to run along the lines of "regularity of sequence and mechanical precision". The effect was a "standardization of the workman's intellectual life in terms of mechanical process", and this not only accounted for his life at the factory, but also his tastes became standardised (Veblen [1904] 1975, 308–9). Thus, according to Veblen, the institutional conditions of work in the end altered the internal constitution of the workman into a routinely acting agent. It was this standardising process and its consequences for the workman's life that Ruskin opposed, arguing that it deprived him of the enjoyment of his life, which was to be found in variety rather than routine monotony.

RUSKIN'S AESTHETIC-DRIVEN CRITICISM OF THE FACTORY SYSTEM

Concern with the effects of the division of labour on the "habits and thoughts of the workman" had in fact already been voiced by Adam Smith in an extraordinary passage in Book V of the *Wealth of Nations*. In this oft-commented on extract,[7] Smith elaborated on the detrimental effects of the division of labour for the moral elevation and conduct of the great mass of the people. Smith observed that many workers were confined to the exertion of just one or two simple operations. As a consequence, they lost the habit of exerting their understanding "and generally [became] as stupid and ignorant as it is possible for a human creature to become" ([1776] 1976 2:782). This image starkly contrasted with the emphasis Smith placed in the first book of the *Wealth of Nations* on the way the division of labour enhanced the skills and ingenuity of individuals, but it was grist to the mill of someone like Ruskin.

Drawing on a highly idealised image of the Gothic, Ruskin argued that in this period in history a craftsman was encouraged to use his "thoughtful part", his genius and imagination, to embellish each and every product with

---

[7] This so-called splenetic passage was of course happily embraced by socialists and commented on by Marx. Recently, Edwin West (1996) reopened the debate on its meaning and significance.

uniqueness and with originality in design. In contrast with contemporary factory conditions of production, it made the work itself enjoyable, as well as its products.

Ruskin's notion of the "grotesque", which he sharply distinguished from aesthetic notions of the "sublime" and the "picturesque", served to accentuate his claims. Originally, the picturesque denoted a class of objects that was outside the scope of the notion of the sublime, as developed by Edmund Burke and then by Immanuel Kant to denote objects that filled the spectator with a sense of awe and terror, and so – paradoxically – strengthened man's superiority over nature (see Ashfield and de Bolla 1996; Lyotard 1991). Picturesque objects were simply too small to convey this sense of horror. Around 1800, the notion of the picturesque provided an aesthetically legitimised way of looking at scenery that, according to traditional classifications, could only be considered ugly. It suggested harmony and order. Ruins, litter, or a disorderly pile of rocks, as in mountain scenery, became acceptable objects of admiration, provided they gave rise to morally elevated thoughts. One could admire Roman ruins, for example, because they stood for the Augustan Age, the last "golden age" before the fifteenth century. One could contemplate a basket of litter and become aware of the transitory nature of man's existence. Or one could admire a smoking chimney, as Cooke Taylor did, and realise its implicated beneficial and moralising effects on the working poor. In the end, the picturesque turned out to be a verbal chameleon which came to denote whatever was beautiful in a picture (Heffernan 1984, 4) and served to pinpoint its tranquillising effect on man's state of mind.

In contrast with Cooke Taylor's invocation of the picturesque to positively connote the factory system with just this tranquillising effect, Ruskin's criticism emphasised that the factory system was far from a system of perfect order. A lecture on architecture Ruskin gave in Edinburgh illustrates his concerns. Ruskin contrasted sixty-six heads of lions, all "exactly the same", which he had seen on a recently constructed Grecian building with the way ornamentation was executed on Gothic buildings. The west window of Dumblane Abbey in Edinburgh, for example, was ornamented with leaves. But no leaf was exactly the same as another. All the leaves reinforced the form of the window, which was itself a leaf. This demanded what Ruskin called *invention*: Imagination, ingenuity, and judgement cooperated to produce this architectural arrangement. Ruskin inferred that the workman had thought about the design of the window and had not merely executed the thoughts and designs of others. There was no place for exact replication here, as was enforced under factory conditions. Since "men do not commonly think the same thought twice, . . . you are to expect another and a different thought of them, as soon as one thought has been well expressed", and this message was conveyed by the leaf window (Ruskin 1854, 105).

Consequently, invention fulfilled a double function, not only in the arts, but also in all production of goods. It gave them something unique and distinctive: design. If a workman was able to use his imagination and judgement, his work itself was raised above the level of simple repetitive labour, in the execution of which "brute animals would be preferable to man" (Ruskin 1985, 83). Not only the *production* of goods would be an enjoyment to the worker, but also the *consumption* of the produce. Diversity, not monotony, provided nourishment for the eye.[8]

Invention thus acquired a very different meaning from the one it had assumed with an inventor like Charles Babbage. This related to the uniformity of the products and their pricing. Where Babbage's *Difference Engines* crucially relied on an exact replication of its wheels and gears, he ([1835] 1963, 119) argued also that "the first object of every person who attempts to make any article of consumption, is, or ought to be, to produce it in a perfect form; but to secure to himself the greatest and most permanent profit, he must endeavour . . . . to render the new luxury or want . . . cheap to those who consume it". This entailed a thorough separation and sequencing of the skills and ingenuity of the workman into a machinelike succession of actions and events. Perfection in the produce and a degradation of the workman's activities into a precisely timed sequence of events went hand in hand to ensure an exact replication of the produce. For Babbage, every other notion of invention or design was an expression of ornamentation, of uselessness, of waste.[9]

---

[8] Steven Medema has suggested to me that Ruskin overlooked the fact that the emerging mass consumption industry provided a different form of diversity, namely an exploding variety of consumer goods. Ruskin argued, however, as in the case of the sixty-six lion heads which were exactly the same, that "exquisite invention", which was a marker of the use made of the imagination of the workman, could be found within a single exemplar. Ruskin consequently did not limit his discussion to all of the lion heads being equal, but pointed out how a single exemplar might lack "exquisite invention". The exploding diversity of consumer goods which resulted from mass production was for Ruskin only an explosion of monotony.

[9] It is well-known that Babbage ardently fought against street music that eventually was forbidden in the 1860s. He considered street organs in particular (which made use of punched charts to produce their melodies) to make utterly unproductive use of technology.

Ruskin by contrast criticised methods of production that strived at uniformity rather than diversity in the produce. Products thus only served as a store of wealth, not of enjoyment. It was on this very point that he took offence at John Stuart Mill's definition of economic man as "solely" striving for wealth, for this man was depriving both himself of the enjoyment of consumption and the workman of the enjoyment of production. True wealth was life itself, Ruskin argued, and life made appeal to all aspects of the workman's personality and capabilities in the performance of his tasks, and promised the full enjoyment of the results of the labour thus performed. Ruskin considered the workman's capability to digress from preset schemes rather than to conform to them as an indicator of the extent to which these large concepts of work and wealth as identical to life itself were fulfilled. When buying goods of "exquisite invention", one was also paying for the invention, not for the mere finish or execution (Ruskin 1985, 88). The consumer could acquire his uniform goods cheaply, but this cheapness was also an indication that they were "utterly unnecessary". In fact, Ruskin considered all consumer goods as works of art and their pricing in terms of their uniqueness and acquisitiveness, in contrast with the mass consumer goods market emerging in his day. They thus escaped the "laws of supply and demand" that political economists used to explain pricing behaviour.[10]

Invention – that is, design – was a precondition for enjoyable work *and* enjoyable consumption. It was closely linked to the perceptual bewilderment that took hold of a spectator viewing Gothic architecture or Turner's landscapes, Ruskin's two favourite examples. Ruskin used the notion of the grotesque to mark this sense of bewilderment. According to Ruskin, Turner made the optical complexity of our sensations explicit by suggesting all

---

[10] Ruskin's analysis fits in uneasily with contemporary analysis of pricing behaviour. Being unique, a work of art resists one of the fundamental principles of the market: There is no quid pro quo for it, and consequently no market price can be determined. In the nineteenth century, uniqueness was considered a feature of works of art, which, as White (1999) shows, definitely puzzled nineteenth-century economists. Not incidentally, many of those thinking about the value of art took, and still take, recourse to criteria *outside* the sphere of the market, like that of its contribution to the "national heritage", as in the case of Lionel Robbins. See Balisciano and Medema (1999). We may question today whether uniqueness can still be seen as a distinguishing feature of modern art. Indeed, Walter Benjamin's famous and influential essay on the consequences of the modern technical reproducibility of a work of art departs from exactly the opposite thesis, as do most of Marxist aesthetics. For an overview, see Paetzold 1974. On the pricing of art more generally, see Olav Velthuis (2002), and in relation to Adam Smith, De Marchi and Van Miegroet (1999).

details without wholly revealing them. Not being able to grasp with the eye the details and variety of nature, looking at Turner's paintings forced the observer to continually reexamine his visual impressions to form a coherent image. Thus, one could see "the spots on the trout" as painted by Turner, without being able to "count" them (Smith 1995, 57). This was for Ruskin an index of what he called "truth to nature". The same "truth to nature" could be found in Turner's paintings of clouds. Turner did not deprive "heaven of its space, clouds of their buoyancy, winds of their motion, and distance of its blue" (Ruskin 1995, 34). Ruskin contrasted Turner's treatment of clouds with "our modern cloud-worship" and with the old Dutch masters who painted as a "stable fact" what was "uncertain and unintelligible" (277). Jevons stabilised the unstable facts of clouds in his experimentally produced thick precipitates to understand the mechanism of their production. Turner canvassed their instability and thus, according to Ruskin, conveyed their true message.[11]

By not painting but suggesting details, Turner brought this perceptual bewilderment and a sense of wholeness to the observer: "Abundant beyond the power of the eye to embrace or follow, vast and various beyond the power of the mind to comprehend, there is yet not one atom in its whole extent and mass which does not suggest more than it represents" (15). Turner's percep-tiveness of the variety and wholeness of nature thus conferred nature's true message. Indeed, for Ruskin, "nothing can be natural which is monotonous; nothing true which only tells one story" (129).

The paradoxical effect of Turner's landscapes was that in their "truth to nature", they conveyed the message of man's humility and man's inadequacy to grasp the whole of nature. This effect of the "grotesque" as distinguished from the sublime, was at right angles with the subsuming and consequently violent attitude towards nature implied by this other term. In reference to Turner's paintings, the term grotesque expressed the greatness and variety of nature, but also showed the imperfections of man and the imperfection of the eye.

In Gothic architecture, the grotesque thus became the expression of the liberty of the workman; he was not subsumed to the master, but left free to use his imagination and genius. Imperfection was not deliberately attained,

---

[11] See especially Anderson (2003) for an analysis of the interrelations between meteorology and pictorial culture in Victorian Britain.

but was an inevitable consequence of this appeal to the inventive ingenuity of the workman. It was a marker of human life itself. Ruskin (1985, 84) once gave an example that highlighted the difference between man working as an animated tool and as a thinking being:

> You can teach a man to draw a straight line, and to cut one, ... and to copy and carve any number of given lines or forms, with admirable speed and perfect precision ... but if you ask him to think about any of these forms, to consider if he cannot find any better in his own head, he stops; his execution becomes hesitating; he thinks, and ten to one he thinks wrong; ten to one he makes a mistake in the first touch he gives to the work as a thinking being. But you have made a man of him for all that. He was only a machine before, an animated tool.

The invariability of the buildings in Edinburgh expressed this corrupted state of modern conditions of production (Ruskin 1854, 61–2):

> Walk round your Edinburgh buildings, and look at the height of your eye, what will you get from them. Nothing but square-cut stone ... so that your houses look like prisons, and truly are so.... These square stones are not prisons of the body, but graves of the soul; for the very men who could do sculpture ... for you are here! still here, in your despised workmen: the race has not degenerated, it is you who have bound them down, and buried them beneath your Greek stones.

For Ruskin, the degradation of the workman and the deterioration of the aesthetic conditions of society were twin developments. Their effects were routine work and monotonous mass production of consumer goods. As Hewison remarks, "Ruskin came to see that art was an *expression* of society, an index of its health, not a cure for its corruption" (Hewison 1976, 132).

MILL AND THE "GOSPEL OF WORK"

In Ruskin's concept of work, the "toil and the trouble" of the workman was not to be separated from his inventive or "thoughtful" part. Work did not reduce to mechanics. In Ruskin's view, Mill's definition of mankind as "solely" striving to "wealth" ignored the importance of the enjoyment of wealth – that is, what a product was made for – which according to Ruskin was intrinsically connected with its mode of production. Hence Ruskin's rage against the factories, these "Bastilles for Labour build by Capital" (Ruskin quoted in Geddes 1884, 30). They divided not labour, but the labourer, and turned the workman into a cripple.

But Mill was not at all blind to the connexion between working conditions, work, and consumption, only, as already noted, he did not consider human enjoyment fit for scientific analysis. In an acerbic commentary on Thomas Carlyle's infamous defence of slavery, Mill had acutely pointed out the connexion between work, leisure, and enjoyment.[12]

Carlyle's defence of slavery ended in Mill's eyes in the "gospel of work", that is, work for work's sake. To give this gospel any "rational meaning", Mill challenged Carlyle, "it must first be known what he means by work. Does work mean everything which people *do*? No; or he would not reproach people with doing no work. Does it mean laborious exertion? No; for many a day spent in killing game, includes more muscular fatigue than a day's ploughing. Does it mean *useful* exertion? But your contributor always scoffs at the idea of utility" (Mill 1850, 466). Mill made it clear that work was more than the "toil and trouble" that inevitably made part of it. Its usefulness could not be separated from the conditions under which it was performed and from the goal for which it was done. "There is nothing laudable in work for work's sake"; it was only laudable if work was done for a "laudable" or "worthy" object. Just what a worthy object was, depended for Mill, as for Ruskin, on the conditions or circumstances of its production. Hence, "only a vitiated taste" can consider luxuries, produced under conditions of slavery, as worthy objects, as they are in fact the "fopperies of so-called civilization" (467). According to Mill, conservatives like Carlyle, Dickens, and Ruskin blamed present-day factory conditions as the main source of all evil – equating them with conditions of slavery – but ignored the ferocities of working conditions in earlier and present days in other social arrangements, especially under slavery. Mill judged to the contrary. In further contrast with Ruskin, he considered the workman's leisure time fit for his moral and cultural elevation, thus restricting the *inevitable* ferocities of work to a limited domain. This can be seen from his assessment of Bentham.

Mill frankly admitted that Bentham limited his analysis to the "business part of man" (*Mill* 10:100). This limitation enforced the "cold, mechanical,

---

[12] Without implying them in the content of this section, David Levy and Sandra Peart's search for the "secret origins" of the "Dismal Science" shows the relevance of Mill's critique of Carlyle in the present context. See Levy and Peart (2001–2002).

and ungenial air which characterizes the popular idea of a Benthamite" (10:112). But there was more to mankind than this mechanical Benthamite idea, as Mill became aware from his struggles with Jeremy Bentham's "doctrine of circumstances" and with his own father's association psychology. In his early essays on Bentham, dating from just after this period, Mill took issue with Bentham's one-sided reduction of man to a "reasoning machine" (10:112; see also 1:111), and he complained that the power of the imagination – the "deamon" inspiring artists and poets – "never was awakened" in Bentham (10:92). Bentham's condemnation of poetry as "misrepresentation" (1:112), epitomised in his infamous "pushpin is as good as poetry", blinded him to the "culture of feelings" for which Mill was searching, "as if a person's tastes did not show him to be wise or a fool, cultivated or ignorant, gentle or rough" (10:113). Mill's solution to this was to make the "cultivation of feelings" he learned from reading Wordsworth and Coleridge "one of the cardinal points of [his] ethical and philosophical creed". Mill superadded the aesthetic feelings to the business part of man. He replaced Carlyle's "gospel of work" by the "gospel of leisure".

For Mill, work itself did not reduce to its physical substratum: physical laborious exertion. Circumstances, rather than structural similarities, made man akin to a machine. In contrast with conservatives like Carlyle and Ruskin, however, Mill considered the production of the "necessaries of life" an unavoidable curse which was in need of counterbalance during the workman's leisure time. Mill considered cultural elevation, rather than physical recovery, the purpose of the workman's leisure.

A more equitable distribution of the hardships of work would provide the workman with the leisure time that could lead to an appreciation of culture and the refinements of society, from which he was presently excluded. On these grounds, Mill defended a separation of work and leisure which Ruskin categorically rejected.

WORK AND FATIGUE

There is an important difference between a view in which work becomes mechanical because of the institutional organisation of production, as in the factory system, and a view in which the work of a workman and the work of a machine are considered structurally equivalent. But even this last phrase may mean different things. For Babbage, one may take this structural equivalence in terms of a sequence of actions that can be performed either by a man or by a machine, or one can argue that there is nothing more to the concept of work than the work that is performed from a mechanical point of view. Thus, the measure of human and machine work is really the same.

This was the point of view that rose to prominence in nineteenth-century Europe. From the end of the eighteenth century, physiologists, chemists, and physicists had attempted to find a measure for the work done by machines. In these attempts, the work of a simple manual worker – a "mechanic" – was taken as point of reference. These studies gained full momentum with the invention of the steam engine and then developed to maturity in the laws of thermodynamics through the work of the French engineer Sadi Carnot; Hermann von Helmholtz, the German physiologist; and William Thomson and Peter Guthrie Tait, the British physicists. As a result, the human body was seen as a kind of engine, obeying the laws of nature just as well as inanimate matter. Just as a workman converted food into muscular power, so a machine converted fuel into work (see especially Rabinbach 1992). In these comparisons, the issue of the conditions of work that had been of so much importance for critics and enthusiasts of the factory system alike disappeared into the background. The workman did not reduce to the similar of a machine because of the organisation of the work, but because their work could be measured in the same terms.

Paralleling of man and machines was clearly favoured by the machine-era discussions of the nature of the work undertaken by both. But it had important predecessors that showed great overlap with the historical discourse of physiology we touched upon in the previous chapter. Andrew Ure referred to Vaucanson's flute player in his *Philosophy of Manufactures*, as a predecessor of a world that was inhabited by "self-acting machines" (1835, 1–9). But he complained that "self-acting inventions" like Vaucanson's flute player did "nothing towards the supply of the physical necessities of society"; they were merely invented for idle amusement. For Cooke Taylor, the steam-engine came very close to the ideal of reproducing life itself. To him, it seemed "that the machines can do everything but speak" ([1841] 1968).

But, it was not merely idle amusement to think that mankind differed in no respect from a complex machine. From the days of Borelli and Boerhaave in the seventeenth century, mechanical philosophers used machines to understand human life as mechanical. The regularity, reliability, and faultlessness of machines, adding to their capacity to deliver continued work, made them perfect replacements for men in the "Age of Machinery". The equivocity between replacement and understanding has proven a constant in all man-machine analogies ever since.

In his popularising science lectures in the 1850s, Hermann von Helmholtz probed the more serious goal inventors like Vaucanson pursued, that was in fact hinted at in Ure's phrase of "self-acting inventions": to replace mankind by machines that would never fatigue. To have made such a machine would have been the discovery of the philosopher's stone: Value would have been created from nothing. But Carnot's investigations and his own research into the "conservation of force" made clear that no such machine was possible. Helmholtz argued that inventors, scientists, and engineers only made real progress in the construction of their machines when they shifted from building "machines which shall fulfil the thousand services required of *one* man" – that is, an all-purpose machine resembling and replacing man – to the construction of specialised, single-purpose machines that greatly enhanced the amount of work done when compared with men, but did not replace all of him. The difference between eighteenth-century mechanical contrivances like Vaucanson's flute player and nineteenth-century machines was that the latter were specialised machines, not aiming to mimic animal life in its full complexity. Insofar as work was considered from a mechanical point of view, men and machines obeyed the same laws, but this did not reduce man himself, Helmholtz emphasised, to a machine.

Helmholtz gave the example of a pulley and block to illustrate the notion of work done by simple machines. The block was raised by labour power, as is obvious even from the image where we see the hand doing the work. When the weight fell it exerted work, but only for the length of the winded rope, as daily witnessed in a clockwork. The human work that empowered the machine and the work of a weight were equivalent. Work was considered under the aspect of force, and the force exerted to lift the block was lost again when the rope unwound. Helmholtz's important extension of the argument was to show that there was no essential difference between the exertion of muscular force to lift the weight of a clockwork and the conversion of heat into mechanical power in the steam engine.

Although the notion of work done by machines was clearly taken from human labour, human labour entailed more than the simple exertion of muscular force. Helmholtz emphasised that even the notion of manual work was a complex concept. It involved not only the "force" expended in it, but also "skill", "talent", and "instruction" – just the aspects of work emphasised by Smith and so much feared to be lost under factory conditions by Ruskin. But these last three concepts made no sense in the domain of machines. "In speaking of the work of machines . . . we must, of course, . . . eliminate anything in which activity of intelligence comes into play" (1995, 98). Helmholtz concluded that, "in a mechanical sense, the idea of work has become identical with that of the expenditure of force" (1995, 20). Insofar as mechanical force was considered, animate and inanimate matter followed the same law of what Helmholtz called the conservation of force.

To let the clock or the steam engine work, it needed recuperation on a regular basis; no machine could exert work perpetually. Helmholtz described this process of machine recuperation in anthropomorphic terms, thus tacitly showing the very close connections existing between his investigations into the laws of inanimate nature and (human) physiology: "When fatigue sets in, recovery is needed, and this can only be affected by rest and nourishment" (1995, 99). It was no different for the workman; work and fatigue were intrinsically connected. Helmholtz pointed out that, due to disturbing causes like friction, some of the work done was wasted in the process. This was true for any machine: the clock, the steam engine, or human work. Helmholtz's ideas on the conservation of force quickly spread to Britain through John Tyndall's early translations (in the 1850s) of Helmholtz's work and through the intimate connections that existed between Helmholtz's investigations and the investigations of William Thomson and many others in Britain in thermodynamics.[13]

While Helmholtz had been explicit on the limitations of the mechanical concept of work, the conclusion lay at hand that there was in fact nothing more to work than its physical measure. As early as 1841, Whewell wrote in his *Mechanics of Engineering* that "labouring force is the labour that we pay for" (quoted from Wise 1989b, 41). Force could be converted into different forms, and therefore the efficiency of machines and the efficiency of human labour could be analysed in equal terms. To my knowledge, Whewell never considered the consequences of his quoted phrase for political economy – others did. The goal increasingly became, as Wise (1989a,b, 1990) shows

---

[13] The standard reference here is, of course, Smith and Wise (1989). See also the incisive series essays of Norton Wise (1989a,b, 1990).

in-depth, to produce the greatest amount of useful effect with the least amount of waste or fatigue. We can see this in Babbage's *On the Economy of Machinery and Manufactures*, but it became a major theme from the 1860s onwards. Something of this strive to maximisation even transpires from Cooke Taylor's early account of the Manchester exchange, where "not a particle of [intelligence] remains unemployed".

Jevons's Experiments on the Exertion of Muscular Force

The new discourse in physics – in which work done was associated with physical exhaustion, not with skills, ingenuity, and talents – merged with Jevons's interest and enthusiasm for Jennings's *Natural Elements of Political Economy* ([1855] 1969). Jennings, we have seen, claimed to have found the true basis of the principles of political economy in the new physiological discourse taking hold in Victorian Britain, especially Carpenter's version of it. In a letter to William Whewell, he promised to exchange the "terra incognita" of classical political economy for its "terra firma" (TCC add.ms.c.75/50).

Clearly inspired by one of Jennings's suggestions,[14] Jevons undertook a series of experiments on the relation between the exertion of muscular force and fatigue and published the results in *Nature* (1870). I will first discuss Jevons's experiments and then explore their broader implications for his theory of labour and his views on popular culture.

Jevons designed his experiments to "throw some light upon the chemical and physiological conditions of muscular force". But more importantly, these experiments "might also point out how we could make some commencement, however humble, of defining the mathematical relations upon which the science of economy is founded" (1870b, 158). Oddly enough, Jevons did not refer to Jennings's book but to Babbage's *Machinery and Manufactures* and to Coulomb's studies, of which he knew only secondhand.[15] He made no reference to other empirical or experimental work in physiology. A notable omission was the work of the Irish physicist Samuel Haughton,

---

[14] Jevons's third experiment (holding the weights on a fully stretched arm) was suggested by Jennings's *Elements*. See Jennings ([1855] 1969, 116). Also, see White (1994a, 206; 2004b).

[15] White (1994a) plausibly suggests that Jevons had only secondary knowledge of Coulomb's *Mémoire* – from Babbage's reference to it in his *Machinery and Manufactures*. His attempts "to add precision and certainty to the ideas put forth by Coulomb and Babbage" (Jevons 1870, 158) ignored the fact that Coulomb had minutely computed the optimal "quantity of action" for a porter on a normal workman's day. See especially Vatin (1993).

who had regularly published on the same subject in the *Transactions of the Royal Society* that would eventually lead to his *Principles of Animal Mechanics* (1873). Also, the experimental work done by Helmholtz, Weber, Fechner, Wundt, and others on the Continent was not referred to.[16] This lack of reference is even more astonishing because Jevons was well-acquainted with Helmholtz's work on non-Euclidean geometry, on which he wrote a small article in *Nature* for 19 October 1871.

Jevons's experiments elaborated on one of Babbage's "many happy suggestions" in *The Economy of Machinery and Manufactures* on "the relation between fatigue and the rapidity or degree of muscular exertion". Jevons conducted three different experiments: the first throwing weights, the second lifting weights with pulley and cord, and the third holding weights with a fully stretched arm. Jevons considered fatigue and the work done in strictly physiological terms. According to Jevons, due to the "natural constitution of the muscles", man was able to develop only a "limited amount of force in a given time" that would at some point be offset by the increase in fatigue caused by the intensity and rapidity of the exertion. Thus, a "maximum efficiency" would be reached somewhere "in every kind of work" (1870, 158).

The first experiment gave pronounced results. "A little consideration" of the experimental data showed agreement with a hyperbolic function relating distance and weight. Jevons derived a numerical expression for these data by (incorrectly) using the method of least squares (see Kim 1995). This expression corresponded so "embarrassingly close" to the experimental data that he attributed the result "partly to chance" (Jevons 1870, 159). Although Jevons was "convinced" this was the "true formula", he did "not quite see how to explain it on mechanical principles". Taking the product of weight and distance as the "useful effect" there did not arise any maxima, but Jevons argued there was a "practical maximum of efficiency", because it was "impossible to raise the larger weights without exerting additional force", which was not considered in the experiment. Optimistically, Jevons concluded that this experiment "completely confirmed" Babbage's and Coulomb's earlier

---

[16] Helmholtz's experimental studies in animal physiology set more limited and clearer defined aims than Jevons's experiments. In fact, they derive much of their still exemplary character from these well-set limitations, which Helmholtz combined with a refined use of experimental apparatus and graphical techniques to measure the time span that was needed for a stimulus to reach the muscle (Holmes and Olesko 1995).

suggestions that there was trade-off between work and waste, between useful effect and fatigue.

To get more of a grip on the "rate of exhaustion of muscular fibre", Jevons made two further experiments: one with pulley and block, and the other holding weights at a fully stretched arm. Again, from an "inspection of the data" of the fifty or so experiments with pulley and block, Jevons inferred that "the total greatest amount of work can be done with small rather than with large weights", but he was unable to derive "any regular law" from these data. In the last experiment, the numerical values pointed more clearly to "systematic laws governing the rate of fatigue", although here as well Jevons was unable to state this law in mathematical form. The data showed, however, a clear trade-off between the amount of weight lifted and physical exhaustion – that is, between useful effect and fatigue.

Jevons initially seems to have been playing with the idea to enter into genuine physiological explanations of this phenomenon of a trade-off between useful effect and fatigue, making "reasonable suppositions as to the conditions of exhaustion and restoration of muscular power", but his attempts in this direction quickly became too complex to handle, and he left the subject to those better acquainted with physiology (and mathematics). In contrast with his preliminary intent to dig into the "physiological groundwork of political economy", Jevons emphasised that it had not been his "object ... to intrude into the domain of physiology", only to show that the "principles and laws" of political economy might be given mathematical form and numerical exactness on a physiological basis. Referring back to his early "speculations" on a mathematical theory of economics of 1862, Jevons used his experiments to argue against the accepted view among political economists that the complexity of the subject made it "excessively difficult" to determine the "character of the functions involved". Instead, they showed that it was possible to find "exact numerical functions connecting the amount of work done with the intensity and duration of labour" (all quotes Jevons 1870).

In subsequent issues of *Nature* (18 August 1870 and 9 February 1871), the physicist and geologist Samuel Haughton came to Jevons's aid in determining the exact functions of his experiments. Like his better-known countryman John Tyndall, Haughton was an Irish physicist, but unlike Tyndall, Haughton ardently attacked Darwin's evolutionary theory. In these attacks, he ingeniously argued on the basis of the principle of least action that if all species were perfectly well-adapted to their environment (which he considered to be expressed by this principle), it was incomprehensible how deviations could prove to be an evolutionary advantage. Haughton's extensive measurements on skeletons and on the precise direction and form of muscles all served to show that animal physiology obeyed the principle of least action.

Because his 1862 essay on the subject treated the same experiment as Jevons's third one, it comes as no surprise that Haughton showed great interest in Jevons's short article. He (1870, 324) argued that the human arm "instinctively" behaved as if obeying the principle of least action; seeking to minimise waste or to maximise useful effect. Haughton sought the proper mechanical analogy for all three experiments, making use of two "laws" he had stated in his 1862 contribution to the *Proceedings of the Royal Society*, of which the most important was that muscles could only deliver a fixed amount of work in a fixed amount of time. For the first experiment, he considered the human arm as a "compound pendulum", whose weight was "concentrated at the centre of oscillation of the loaded arm" (324), a claim he corrected in his second article, in that he "should have stated that it is the work of a body of equal weight moving with the velocity of the centre of *gyration*". Making some further assumptions on the mechanical properties of the human arm, Haughton showed that Jevons's experiments were really problems of mechanical engineering.

Haughton illustrated his results with three graphs that showed the close correspondence between Jevons's experimental data and his own mechanical explanation (Figure 8-1). Where Jevons's own experiments had failed either on the explanatory side or on the mathematical side, Haughton showed that it was possible to derive a relation between a dependent and an independent variable from Jevons's data that could be explained by engineering mechanics. His explanation showed by what mechanism work was done. Where Jevons initially had been worried about the extremely close correspondence between his experimental findings and the only formula he found (Haughton's graph N^o *I* in Figure 8-1), Jevons was no longer embarrassed by the close correspondence between data and theory. Quite to the contrary, Haughton's explanation fulfilled in Jevons's eyes the ideal to which all scientific explanations should strive in the end – that is, a "rational explanation" of the data in mathematical form – and he referred to them accordingly in *The Principles of Science* as well as in the *Theory of Political Economy*.

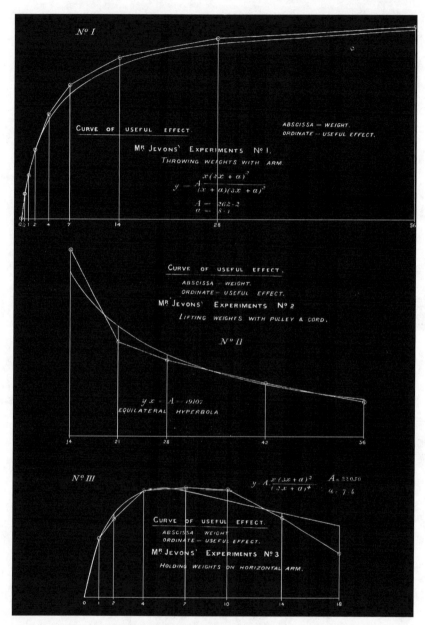

8-1. Haughton's graphs of Jevons's experiments on the exertion of muscular force. From Samuel Haughton. On the Natural Laws of Muscular Exertion II. *Nature* 1871, 3:289–93, 290. Each graph gives the "theoretical" curve of "useful effect" against the plotting of Jevons's experimental results. Courtesy of *Nature*.

MAXIMISING UTILITY WHILE MINIMISING PAINFUL EXERTION

Let us now turn to the *Theory of Political Economy* to see how Jevons's experiments on the exertion of muscular force fit with his more general theory of labour. Labour, as Jevons quoted Adam Smith upfront in his analysis of labour supply, was the "toil and trouble" of acquiring goods. It was the "first price . . . that was paid for all things". It was, so he summarised the history of economics thus far, "the beginning of the processes treated by economists, as consumption is the end and purpose" (*TPE1* 162). In earlier chapters of the *Theory*, Jevons had laid out his theory of utility, which drew upon Bentham's theory of pleasures and pains as the governing motives of our actions, but importantly quoted Jennings, Senior, and Banfield in support and to modify Bentham's original ideas. This theory of pleasures and pains intimately linked consumption, the "end and purpose" of the labour process that was in Jevons's view so infamously excluded by Mill from the domain of political economy, to the labour decision-making process of an individual workman. Labour was "the painful exertion" someone was willing to undertake "to ward off pains of greater amount, or to procure pleasures which leave a balance in our favour" (162). Pleasures and pains, not consumption and labour as such, were the relevant variables that should be taken account of in all explanations in political economy.

It was obvious to Jevons that labour could be considered as a quantity; but, rather than considering labour time only, the quantity political economists looked to, Jevons treated labour as a multidimensional magnitude of intensity and duration of pleasures and pains. By incorrectly concentrating on a homogeneous unit of labour time, political economists had overlooked the intimate relationship that existed between production and consumption via the intimate balancing process of pleasures and pains. This process ran in terms of intensity and duration. Intensity provided a quantitative measure for labour. Conceptually, it also closely linked the fruits of labour to its sacrifices. On the one hand, the intensity of labour could be seen in terms of "work done", that is, of the end product of the process of work, as its useful effect. On the other hand, it could be considered as the "painfulness of the effort" in making the product. Thus, three magnitudes should be considered to analyse the balancing act of a workman in determining his labour supply: the amount of painful exertion, the amount of produce and the pleasure or utility relating to the latter.

These three magnitudes were functionally related; the pleasure derived from the produce and the pain undergone in its production provided two functions. These were the laws of human enjoyment that formed the true basis of political economy, rather than Mill's and Ricardo's "wrong-headed" theories. They gave political economy its "terra firma". For the form of both functions, Jevons relied on Richard Jennings's *Natural Elements of Political Economy* (1855) – but not solely. Jevons described labour as a fund of energy, the use of which gave rise to "agreeable" or "painful" sensations. According to Jevons, "a few hours" of work each day might be considered agreeable. However, "so soon as the spontaneous energy of the body is drained off, it becomes irksome to remain at work. As complete exhaustion approaches, continued effort becomes more and more intolerable" (*TPE1* 166). A lengthy quote from Jennings's book served to show Jennings's clear understanding of this "law of the variation of utility". Jevons was convinced of its "general truth . . . although we may not have the data for assigning the exact law of the variation" (168). Like the steam engine used coal in providing work, the workman used up his initial fund of energy over the course of the day to end physically exhausted. Jevons analysed the sensations associated with this process in terms of pleasure and pain.

Jevons famously depicted his theory in the following diagram (Figure 8-2). The y-axis represents the pleasure and pain of labour (above and below the origin, respectively). The x-axis represents the amount of the produce. The curve p-q gives the "utility of the produce". The curve a-b-c-d represents the variational law of labour. With the exception of the interval b-c, in which pleasure is derived from the exertion of labour itself (relating to the "spontaneous energy" of the body), labour is considered as a pain. Only this arc of the curve was, Jevons made clear, relevant to the economist.

Thus, contrasting the "painfulness of labour" with the "utility of the produce", the workman's decision to supply labour was fixed at the point where their marginal increments equalised at a given "day's wages". The workman "balanced" the increment of pleasure of the produce with the increment of the "irksomeness" of the exertion of work. Jevons considered the workman as if he was automatically following a strategy of maximising pleasure, while minimising pain, just as expressed in the principle of least action. The equilibrium was given at "some point" m, that is, where the marginal increment of pleasure m-q equals the marginal increment of pain m-d (note that both curves depict increments of pleasure and pain, not totals).

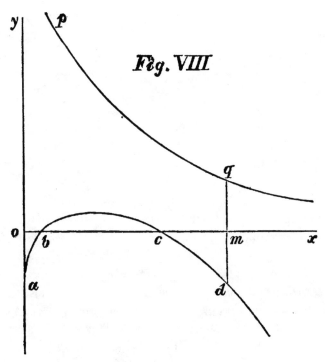

8-2. Jevons's graphical representation of his theory of labour. *Theory of Political Economy*, 1871, 168. Courtesy of Palgrave/Macmillan Press.

As we have seen, Jevons clearly distinguished between the mathematical and the exact character of political economy, especially in contrast with Cairnes. Mathematics dealt with functional relations that might be expressed in numerical form, but not necessarily so. Only in the last case did these relations gain exactness. The form of these functions was given by theory; they were empirically verified by making numerical estimates of their parameter values. Cairnes failed to distinguish between both aspects. For him, "strict mathematical expression" was falsely identified with "exact numerical" expression (Cairnes 1857, 79).

Though the general shape of the curves in his diagram was for Jevons beyond doubt, their exact shape and numerical values differed among individuals, professions, races, and even nations. From the effects of striving to reduce working hours in England, Jevons inferred that, in general, the workmen were inclined to prefer "greater ease to greater wealth", thus suggesting hypotheses on the shape of their respective functions of pleasure and pain, namely "that the degree of utility varies more rapidly than the degree of painfulness of labour" (*TPE1* 176). But, there were, as Jevons noted, exceptions to the rule, which were found "where the work is of a more interesting and exciting character", especially among the "learned professions". Jevons refrained from an analysis of the necessary skills and ingenuity for such professions other than in terms of physical exercise.

In general, natural disposition and training were the determining factors in a person's "energetic disposition" to feel labour as pain. For Jevons, it was "evident" that the "character of the race" was in its turn an important determining factor. "A man of lower race, a negro for instance, enjoys possession less, and loathes labour more; his exertions, therefore, soon stop" (177).[17] In the second edition of the *Theory*, Jevons emphasised that the linkages between someone's energetic disposition and his feelings of pleasure and pain could be modified by training, but could not be ignored. Even for the "the highest kinds of labour, such as those of the philosopher, scientific discoverer, artist, &c.", great success never came easily: "the mental powers must be kept in perfect training by constant exertion, just as a racehorse or an oarsman needs to be constantly exercised" (*TPE2* 197–8). The very comparison shows that, for Jevons, there was no difference between the use of the mental powers and those of the hands; both obeyed the same laws, which in the end reduced to laws of mechanics.

There was no difference in principle, then, between the work of the mind and the exertion of muscular force. Both could be analysed in similar terms of pleasure and pain, and these were, in their turn, related to the mechanical concept of work. Where Helmholtz had emphasised that even manual work did not reduce to the mechanical notion of work, intelligence had literally moved out of Jevons's diagram. The issue was posited as if the decision to work was a physical problem, requiring a physical solution.

Jevons motivated his experiments in the *Theory* (as in the original article in *Nature*) in that they could "throw light" upon the exact shape and numerical value of the lower function of his diagram, that is, to give exactness to political economy. Before embarking on his diagrammatic exposition, Jevons had noted that the economist "measures labour by the amount of pain which attaches to it" (*TPE1* 164). Pain was the relevant measure of the intensity

---

[17] On Jevons's implicit and overt racism, see White (1993, 1994c, 1994e) and Levy and Peart (2001–2002).

of labour. Jevons argued that "we may approximately measure the intensity of labour", that is, pain, "by the amount of physical force undergone in a certain time", even though it was "the pain attending to the exertion of force which is the all-important element in Economy" (192). Jevons shifted here from a discussion of pleasures and pains as mental motives of action to a discussion of pleasure and pain as physical forces.

Haughton's phrasing of the experiments and Jevons's approving words brought to the fore what conception of man lay behind it; man was conceived as a machine that converted *"all exertion of body or mind"* (*TPE1* 163) into useful effect. This conversion was checked by fatigue that set in after a certain amount of work was done with a certain intensity and duration. The shape of the curve relating pain and useful effect in the diagram, and the shape of the function relating the exertion of muscular force and useful effect in his experiments, should be similar, which was in fact only so for Jevons's third series of experiments. Jevons's experiments directly fitted into the general striving towards a unified framework from which to understand man and machines alike. There was no difference in principle between the work of the mind and the holding of a weight on a stretched arm, between the work of a philosopher and a street porter. This analysis formed the basis for Jevons's essays on social reform.

AMUSEMENTS OF THE PEOPLE

We have seen how positively authors like William Cooke Taylor evaluated the factory system and how much they stressed its benign effects on the cultural and moral elevation of the working class. Whatever the verity of such accounts, as witnessed by many contrary assessments, such positive sentiments were clearly not shared by Jevons. Although we get a vivid impression of Jevons's enthusiasm for the manufacturing districts of London from his diary and his letters to his family – he even writes that he prefers a walk in the dark alleyways of Spitalfields over a tour in the countryside (*PC* 1:90–1) – this enthusiasm did not entice him to propagandistic writing on the moral virtues of the factory system. Like many of his middle-class contemporaries, he considered the violent and riotous ways in which the working class behaved a general evil that had to be combatted.

This is the context in which we find his articles on social reform, such as the effects of women's labour, the drinking traffic, education, or popular culture. Like many of his contemporaries, he used the numerous weekly and monthly periodicals, such as the *Pall Mall Gazette* or the *Fortnightly Review*, as vehicles for his opinions. His more lengthy contributions were reprinted posthumously in *Methods of Social Reform* (1883). Of his articles, Jevons's essays and newspaper articles in the 1870s against women working in factories provoked the most heated controversy.[18] William Cooke Taylor, the Irish journalist, jumped on Jevons's suggestion that the factory system in this case was one of the causes of moral decline by successfully challenging Jevons's use of statistics. Using his own interest in and knowledge of statistics, he forced Jevons to admit that the "real proof" of his thesis was "not to be found in complicated statistical tables" (quoted in White 1994b, 64).

How to redress the low culture of the working class would occupy Jevons's thoughts until the end of his life. The trade-off between work and fatigue, which was driving his theory of labour, served several purposes at once. First, leisure well-spent would help to restore the original fund of labour power of the workmen. Second, leisure well-spent served the moral and cultural elevation of the working class. Third, by facilitating the proper spending of leisure time, the workmen's life could be better-controlled and disciplined. Surveillance of the workmen, their moral improvement, and the maximisation of useful effect thus went hand in hand.

Jevons's most relevant essay is "Amusement of the People", which originally appeared 1878 in the *Contemporary Review*. Jevons started with the observation that due to "riotous and vicious assemblages" of people, most popular festivals had been suppressed by the authorities.[19] England, according to Jevons, had become a "dull England". The suppression of festivals in fact left the public with nothing but the worst forms of leisure activity, such as drinking and violence. "The people seem actually to have forgotten how to amuse themselves, so that when they do escape . . . from their depressing

---

[18] Recently, many of the reactions and responses to Jevons's books, articles, and essays have been published in Inoue (2002) and Peart (2003). On Jevons's (mis-)use of statistics in relation to the question of women working in factories, see Peart (2001) and White (1993, 1994d).

[19] The authorities attempted to suppress these festivals partly as an off-spin of the French Revolution. The violent and riotous turn these festivals often took was regarded as a hotbed for revolt against the social order. Support for suppression also came from manufacturers who by then needed a well-regulated workforce. For an extensive discussion see Golby and Purdue (1984), especially 88–94. Their discussion makes it clear that, in the light of recent research, the then prevailing image of a decline in popular amusements is inaccurate.

alleys, there is no provision of music, no harmless games, nor other occupation for the vacant time". The effect of this was that the "English masses" were only able to amuse themselves in a "clumsy and vulgar way" (*MSR* 4–5). On his travels throughout Europe, it had struck Jevons as "extremely painful" that "the poor gentleman peasants of Scandinavia" were so much more well-behaved than "the rich, rowdy, drunken artisans of England" (*MSR* 5). Shortening a workman's day or raising salaries would only aggravate this, for Jevons feared most workmen would spend more earnings on drink. What was needed was an increase of culture, and this could be attained by the provision of suitable entertainment.[20] Jevons considered music to be the most suited for achieving this goal.

Jevons description of how listening to music could contribute to the elevation of the cultural level of the lower classes fits in with the physiological aesthetics that became increasingly popular in England with the work of Alexander Bain, Herbert Spencer, and Grant Allen. Allen in particular reformulated the idea of beauty itself in terms of work and waste, "as that which afforded the maximum of stimulation with the minimum of fatigue or waste" (quoted from Gagnier 2000, 136). But Jevons chose to see the value of music for the working class in a minimum of stimulation and a minimum of waste. Its value was not aesthetically driven, but driven by the demands of recovery from daily work.

Interestingly, listening to music was described by Jevons as having the properties of both the absence of mental and manual work. It was "merely passive abandonment of the mind to the train of ideas and emotions suggested by the strains [of music]" (*MSR* 9). In an unfinished manuscript on music, Jevons examined the mental and moral functions of music in greater detail. The appreciation of sounds, the building blocks of music, depended only "upon the nature of the *sense of hearing*" (JA 6/47/4). The function of music consisted of "a general removal of the mind from its ordinary course of duties ... causing it to forget ordinary affairs and thoughts". It caused a "feeling of Beauty or of Sublimity ... often excited, more or less, by every pleasant country walk, by sightseeing, by beautiful and extensive views or grand and striking scenery on sea or land, by magnificent architectural ... works or a

---

[20] Nowhere does Jevons make the inference that the factory system is to be blamed for poor workers' habits, though it is striking that poor Scandinavian *peasants* in his eyes behave better than the English working class.

fine piece of poetry" (JA 6/47/8–9). This feeling, Jevons suggested, "belongs to the *perceptions*, not . . . reason and is far below the level of a somewhat analogous but feebler feeling produced by the contemplation of wonderful and beautiful facts of science or knowledge in general". Music, in short, belonged to what Jevons termed the class of *"perceptive pleasure* meaning any emotion . . . produced by subjects of nature or Art through the medium of the sense or mind but without the necessary exercise of the higher faculties of reason" (JA 6/47/9, original emphasis). Listening to music kept the public in a state of mental and bodily rest. Of course, Jevons admitted, "there is some nervous waste even in the enjoyment of music, and it is greater as the attention is more excited", but music holds the mind "enchained just so long as there is energy of thought to spare; in the meantime the body remains in a perfect state of repose" (*MSR* 10).[21] In contrast with someone like Grant Allen or Walter Pater who thought the aesthetic condition was to give us "as many pulsations as possible into a given time" (quoted from Gagnier 2000, 139), Jevons considered the goal of popular music to bring the crowd into a state of physical and mental rest.

This state of repose, then, fulfilled two functions at once: It served to recover from daily work, and it served to elevate the moral condition of the working class. As there was always some "nervous waste" in listening to music, Jevons believed the music that minimised this waste was best fit to be played in parks or music halls. This music was highly conventional and consisted of "the better class of dance music, old English melodies, popular classical songs". The great mass of the public was not capable of listening to the "great musical structures" because these demanded "long musical training for their appreciation". But, a more important reason for Jevons's exclusion of the common man from the great musical compositions was that they would not induce a state of rest, but an excitation of the brain instead.

Jevons reserved the appreciation of complex music to those who were naturally gifted with imagination – in practice, the higher classes. If, in

---

[21] It is very hard at this point not to think of Ulysses and the Sirens. Enchained, Ulysses listened to the seductive hymns of the Sirens, while his deafened companions rowed past. In Ruskin's terms, this image might be taken as the ultimate and evil consequences of the division of labour, in which the manual workers are deprived of their senses and therewith of their power of imagination, the use of which comes to be reserved for the inventor. In Jevons's analysis, things are even worse, for there was no role to be played for the imagination at all. For an unsurpassed analysis of Ulysses, see Horkheimer and Adorno ([1947] 1986, 50–87).

other words, "low" art and not "high" art were provided to the public, the whole thing would be completely "harmless" and "devoid of coarseness or vulgarity" (*MSR* 16). Though the ordinary man was not able to understand what he heard or saw, he would be activated to emulate the conduct of the higher classes. In effect, the lower classes should be stimulated, in Jevons's words, to "aping [their] betters". They should thus be stimulated to spend their money on culture instead of on drink (*MSR* 7).[22]

By suppressing the use of man's brain, the only enjoyment to be had was simple relaxation. It served the recovery needed to be able to take part again in the work at the factory. Indeed, the feeling of "Beauty or Sublimity" suggested to the listener a superiority over nature that could only be attained by "forgetting . . . the ordinary course of duties . . . [the] ordinary affairs and thoughts". In Jevons's conception of the effects of the arts, there was no positive evaluation at all of the "perceptual bewilderment" which according to Ruskin, Allen, and Pater was the prime virtue of art. Far from putting the mind in a state of rest, for them art stimulated man's imagination. For Jevons, however, partaking in popular amusement involved a minimum of work of the mind, a minimum of waste of mental energy. Popular amusement consisted of the art of forgetting.

"OF KINGS' TREASURIES"

In his opening lecture at Queen's College, Liverpool, in 1865, Jevons expressed his great admiration for Ruskin's many "imaginative names and figurative expressions". How sympathetic *was* Jevons to Ruskin? "Of Kings' Treasuries" – the lecture to which Jevons referred – not only dealt with the question of how to read and how to address the great books of the past, but also analysed and commented on the adverse cultural climate towards reading. "We despised", Ruskin complained, all the great achievements of mankind: literature, science, the arts. Even worse, we despised "the deep and sacred sensations of scenery" – nature itself. In the course of his lamentations,

---

[22] Jevons used this expression provocatively. It foreshadows Veblen's theory of emulation. The importance of emulation in Jevons's epoch is also emphasised in Golby and Purdue (1984). At the end of his essay on popular amusements, he attributes the "degradation of English amusements" to the tendency of living up to the Joneses (*MSR* 24). It is unclear, however, what other criterion the public has in judging culture than aping their betters, not being incited to judge on the worth of culture for themselves.

Ruskin shifted from the use of "we" to "you", addressing the audience as those who were guilty of this despising. It is quite clear who this audience was: the middle and upper classes. They were not the workmen by "whose work, by whose strength, by whose life, by whose death, you live, and never thank them" (Ruskin 1985, 281). For Ruskin, these "common workmen" formed the "body and nervous force" of the nation, but they were excluded from participation in the amusements of the better-off classes, and this was because such amusements were not considered fit for their understanding. In one of his letters in a bottle to the "Workmen and Labourers of Great Britain", Ruskin explicitly questioned this assumption:

> I want to know why it is assumed so quietly that your brain must always be at a low level. Is it essential to the doing of the work by which England exists, that its workmen should not be able to understand scholar's English ... but only newspaper English? ... For my part, I cannot at all understand why well-educated people should still so habitually speak of you as beneath their level, and needing to be written down to ... as flatforeheaded creatures of another race, unredeemable by any Darwinism.
>
> (*Ruskin* 27:181–2)

For Ruskin, the word "dis-ease ... literally" expressed the decline of morals and culture in England that followed from this despising. It was a reflection of the conditions under which the majority of men was forced to work with the awful consequence that "we pour our whole masculine energy into the false business of money-making" (Ruskin 1985, 282). Ruskin obviously played with the life-giving connotations of this "masculine energy". With an ironic allusion to the Corn Laws, Ruskin urged the establishment of "corn laws" of a better sort: for the old Arabian grain, sesame, "which opens doors – doors not of robbers', but of Kings' Treasuries": the great achievements of mankind in literature, art, and science (282).

There was another and implicit play of words with energy and disease going on as well. The trade-off between work and fatigue that motivated Jevons's views on the use and usefulness of culture was unacceptable to Ruskin. For Ruskin, it was not so much labour per se that occasioned pain or fatigue, but the content of the work and the conditions under which the work was performed. Ruskin was convinced that the relation between work and fatigue depended on the moral conditions of production. If these were morally righteous, there was no need for recovery time, the function

Jevons attributed to culture. In one of his lectures as Slade Professor of Art at Oxford, Ruskin (1996, 120–1) expressed this as follows:

> Imagine that muscular firmness and subtlety, and the instantaneously se-
> lective and ordinant energy of the brain, sustained all day long, not only
> without fatigue, but with a visible joy in the exertion . . . consider, so far as
> you know anything of physiology, what sort of an ethical state of body and
> mind that means!

Whereas for Ruskin the demands of culture pointed to the abolition of the factory system altogether, a solution for which he was ridiculed in the press, Jevons adapted culture to the needs of industry. For Jevons, there was no essential difference between the enjoyment of art and the recuperation from the fatigue of factory work by means of cultural relaxation. Ruskin blamed, we have seen, the factory system for the moral and intellectual degradation of the workmen. It made the common workmen "to find their whole being sunk into an unrecognised abyss, to be counted off into a heap of mechanism numbered with its wheels, and weighed with its hammer strokes" (Ruskin 1985, 87). The gloomy observation of some of its proponents, like Cooke Taylor, that the factory system forced the operative to work with the minuteness of a machine and thus enhanced his moral qualities filled Ruskin with disgust. It meant to "unhumanize" man. "Men were not intended to work with the accuracy of tools, to be precise and perfect in all their actions" (Ruskin 1985, 84). Without imagination, Ruskin insisted, man's intellectual activities would be reduced to routine operations. Labour would only be mechanical, and consumption would be without taste.

The crucial point for Ruskin was that in no sphere of life should man *conform* to vested rules, but should himself deliberate and decide what path to follow. For Ruskin, art "must confess that we have not reached the perfection we can imagine, and cannot rest in the condition we have attained" (Ruskin 1985, 99). This "harmless" state of rest was exactly what Jevons had in mind. Jevons's proposals for social reform were directed at maximising productivity by pacifying the crowd. As he once stated: "As feelings [of pleasure and pain] are both the ends and instruments of the moralist and legislator, it especially behooves us to learn how to estimate these values aright" (*PL* 276).

Hence, Jevons's admiration for Ruskin's "beautiful and imaginative words" cannot conceal the differences between their stances on work and culture, which in the course of time only became more pronounced. When we read Jevons's essay on "Cram" in *Mind*, first published 1877, and compare this with Ruskin's scattered remarks on the same subject, we also see that on this issue their respective stances moved in opposite directions. Jevons had become of the opinion that a "well-ordered education is a severe system of well-sustained 'Cram'... the agony of the examination-room is an anticipation of the struggles of life. All life is a long series of competitive examinations". For Jevons, the "business" of the educator was to "impress indelibly upon the mind the useful knowledge which is to guide the pupil through life. This would be 'Cram' indeed" (*MSR* 99). Jevons's defence of "Cram" stemmed from the idea that it was possible to control "the plastic fibres of the youthful brain" (*MSR* 88). Ruskin severely opposed "the school of Cram" in education exactly because he thought it deadened the inventive part of man, man's genius, and defended "the school of Culture" in its place (see, for example, Geddes 1884, 40). According to Ruskin, the "best powers of the youth" could only be developed "without competition" (*Ruskin* 25:151–3). In *Fors Clavigera*, Ruskin related the story of an art student who had "the finest powers of mechanical execution I have ever met with, but was quite incapable of invention, or strong intellectual effort of any kind" (*Ruskin* 25:150). Ruskin fully blamed the educational system for the "mischief done to the best faculties of the brain", as its sole interest was "to keep order".

Ruskin's and Jevons's diverging attitude towards cram is paradigmatic for their different views on labour, the social order, and the role of culture in society. In the end, this divergence was perhaps motivated by the two different attitudes Cooke Taylor ([1841] 1968, 3) discerned with respect to the factory system. Either one could judge the factory system "by an inapplicable standard" and retreat to "previous reading and experience" or consider it as "an established innovation". Where Ruskin retreated into the Gothic past, Jevons embraced modernity.

︵﹀

NINE

Timing History

Tables, Graphs, and History

In the early 1860s, Jevons embarked on his most ambitious project, which he referred to as his "Statistical Atlas project".[1] There can be little doubt, as Keynes already suggested in 1936, that the name alluded to Playfair's magnificent charts from the turn of the eighteenth century. Jevons intended to produce about thirty diagrams, encompassing an extraordinarily wide range of topics. He designed his ambitious project for the use of businessmen, but more importantly to uncover the laws governing the dynamics of trade. In this vein, he wrote to his relative Richard Hutton that "my diagrams not only shew the minutest details given in the tables, but also supersede the taking of averages, since the eye or mind of itself notices the *general course* of a set of numbers" (*PC* 2:450, 1 September 1862).

By the time Jevons had finished a considerable number of his diagrams, he decided to show some of them to William Newmarch and to present him with an outline of the whole project, with the purpose of having it all published (Figure 9-1). But his visit to Newmarch turned out to be a grievous disappointment. Jevons wrote in his diary that Newmarch was an "ugly man, who looked at my diagrams *without interest* & almost without a word so that I soon left him" (*PC* 1:180–1). Jevons's letter to Hutton, which was written long after this visit, shows in retrospect a form of incomprehension: How was it possible for Newmarch to miss the obvious advantages of graphs over mere averages and tables of numbers, and why did he look "without interest"?

---

[1] The best analysis of Jevons's Statistical Atlas project is still Michael White's unpublished 1995 paper.

9-1. Page of Jevons's outline of his Statistical Atlas project. Courtesy of Royal Statistical Society.

Apparently, it was not at all obvious for someone like Newmarch to present a table of numbers in a graph. Newmarch was not just anybody. His contribution to volumes 5 and 6 of Thomas Tooke's monumental *History of Prices* was generally considered a marked improvement on both the content and scope of Tooke's work. In the early 1860s, he served as editor of the *Statistical Journal* of the Statistical Society of London and was honoured by being elected Fellow of the Royal Society for his achievements. Newmarch, a self-made Yorkshire businessman and one of the leading statisticians in Britain, did not recognize Jevons's graphs as relevant to the subject.

Much later, in 1879, Jevons somewhat grumblingly commented on a paper on "tabular analysis" by William Guy – like Jevons, by that time one of the older and respected members of the Statistical Society of London – that the "curvilinear or graphical method" was "the natural complement" of the tabular method. Guy should be complimented for his able exposition of the tabular method (as explained in a book by Dr. Todd). However, while they had "heared a good deal about Dr. Todd and his book . . . Englishmen had lost sight of the fact that William Playfair, who had never been heard of in this generation, produced statistical atlases and statistical curves that ought to be treated by some writer in the same way that Dr. Guy had treated the method of Dr. Todd" (Jevons 1879, 657).[2]

To understand why graphs were not considered to make a meaningful contribution to an economic argument, we need to revisit the attitudes of nineteenth-century British economists to the nature and methods of political economy and statistics. Central to the way political economists envisaged their explanatory strategies was, as we have seen, their attitude towards the relation of explanations in history and the natural sciences, and more particularly the consequences entailed in what counted as evidence for explanations in political economy. We have seen that, for most of the century, British political economists held statistics in disdain. This disdain was evident in their rejection of political arithmetic and statistical data for being able to modify their theoretical claims. In contrast, they had a stronger regard for the particularity of events and history. For this more limited purpose, statistical data were used and welcomed, as, for example, John Stuart Mill welcomed the inductive enquiries of an outsider like Richard Jones while at the same time marginalising their importance from a theoretical perspective.

For nineteenth-century political economists in the classical tradition, economic actions and behaviour, and so too their scientific explanation, were located in the motivations and propensities of individuals, understood by introspection and common sense reasoning followed by deduction. History was the canvas on which these actions were played out; it was the time and space in which the laws of economics might, perhaps, be evidenced. But these laws would rarely be observed directly because of the many other

---

[2] The book Jevons thought of finally, and recently, appeared as Judy Klein's (1997) *Statistical Visions in Time: A History of Time Series Analysis 1662–1938.*

contributing causes which melded together to produce particularity in each historical event. Statistical data on such events would thus reveal nothing but the particularities of history. Even if the laws were occasionally revealed, they would not give access to the motivations which underlay them.

We have seen that the outlines of this method were first formulated by Dugald Stewart at the turn of the century and then canonised by John Stuart Mill. That there had been precursors and contemporaries – like William Playfair and William Whewell, who played in a much more positive way with the relation of statistical data, graphs, and mathematics – was never picked up until Jevons made this a prime element of his approach to statistics as well as economic theory. Thus, the introduction of graphs, cannot be separated from debates on the "true" method of political economy in Victorian Britain.

One might say that the controversy between Mill and Whewell over the proper method of political economy led to the sharp distinction between economic theory and statistics that became institutionalised through the British Association for the Advancement of Science (BAAS) and the statistical societies. The important consequence of this institutional divide is to see that before graphs could reveal economic phenomena and feature in economic explanations, British economists had to rethink their position with regard to both political economy and statistics. To be more specific: Historical *events* had to be repackaged as *data*, something that I will refer to as the "timing of history". This change in understanding would have transgressed the traditional boundaries between the moral and natural sciences in the early part of the century, but became unproblematic by the end. These boundaries broke down during the century as economists like Jevons strove for a unified method of enquiry for the natural and the social sciences and as statisticians in Britain abandoned their self-imposed injunction merely to classify facts and moved to combining data in making causal explanations. In the process, multiple causes, which political economists and statisticians had understood as *contributing causes* in the construction of particular historical events, came to be seen as *disturbing causes* to be stripped away for explanatory purposes. This step was only taken from Jevons onwards.

TIMING HISTORY

To understand what I mean by the timing of history, first imagine a simple time-series graph picturing a century of data of corn prices. Nowadays, such a graph functions unproblematically both as a graphic representation of evidence and as material for economic explanation. But, just as the Law of (individual) Errors had to be reinterpreted as a pattern of natural variation and relabelled as the "normal distribution" for it to function in biometric explanations (see Porter 1986), political economists had to understand a set of data in time not as representing a series of individual or particular historical events, but as showing a pattern of comparable economic activity through time – a pattern which could form the basis for economic explanations.

This involved at least two things: the choice of a relevant time unit and the standardisation of events. Nowadays, this may seem so highly unproblematic that it may be useful to look at the first time history was charted on a horizontal axis: in Joseph Priestley's *Chart of Biography* (1765) (Figure 9-2). Priestley rendered the life of famous historical persons by a "longer or shorter" horizontal line parallel to the horizontal axis to indicate the length of someone's life in a spatial representation. The possibility of this may seem obvious, but it is important to note that Priestley needed four pages of written text to convince his readers of the possibility of depicting the length of someone's life by a horizontal line.[3] It is also important to note that Priestley's chart was a tremendous success; once time was spatialised, it was obvious it could be done.

In making such a chart, Priestley omitted all concerns about the accomplishments of the lives imaged, and the only elements that remain are their age in terms of years and the overlapping of their lives (a not inconsiderable aspect). When thinking about the historical importance of Mozart, or Schubert, for the development of music, we do not think about their age, but about their accomplishments. What does it serve our understanding of their greatness to picture their lives in the way Priestley suggests? The reason they are historically important cannot be figured from the graph, only from other sources.

---

[3] In his *Analysis of the Phenomena of the Human Mind* (1829), James Mill equally made a lengthy argument to convince the reader that time could be represented by a straight line, an argument that was extensively criticised much later by the French philosopher Henri Bergson ([1889] 1956), who distinguished between time as perceived in our memory (historical time) and natural, or physical, time. In this connexion, it may be useful to remark that Proust's *A la Recherche du Temps Perdu* (that was importantly influenced by the philosophy of Proust's relative Bergson) not incidentally leaves the precise age of Marcel throughout the book completely undetermined; there are no axes meaningfully fixing Marcel's memories in time and space.

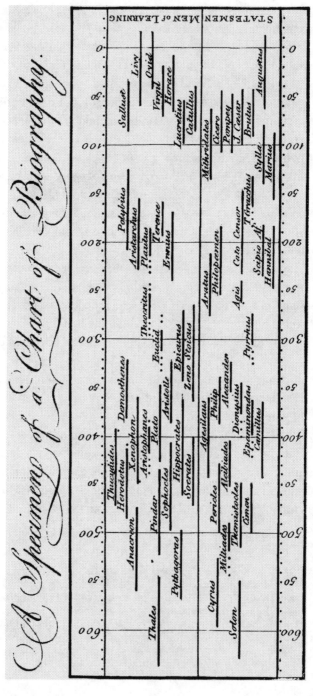

9-2. A fragment of Priestley's *Chart of Biography* (1765) running from roughly 2000 BC to 1700 AD. The chart shows the lives of "men of learning" (top half) and "statesmen" (bottom half). The length of the lives are represented by horizontal lines. Courtesy of University Library Groningen.

Priestley drew on a longer tradition of demarcation of historical time, in which B.C. time had been separated from A.D. time, and in which historical periods and centuries had been recognised. His chart was the first attempt to match historical time with equal chunks on the horizontal axis,[4] but it lacks the second critical element we associate with time-series graphs, namely a meaningful vertical axis upon which we can place our events and compare them in terms of relative magnitude and judge their relative importance. Thus, history is not imaged in the graph, only time. Priestley's chart took time for history. Our time-series graphs of the present day assume that life is already evaluated in standardised terms and numbered so that such a graph entails that we can rank a Livy over a Catullus or a Cicero over a Brutus (on the right-hand side of Priestley's chart).

If we change our view of what is historically relevant, we might be able to turn Priestley's chart into a tool for historical research. We may consider, for example, the impact of schools or groups on historical events, and if we could agree on a set of criteria on which to calibrate the existence of a school or group, we might use Priestley's chart as a measuring rod to identify such schools and groups in history, a rather modest goal it seems. That is, if we are able to agree on a standard of measurement, we convert Priestley's chart into a measuring instrument for doing historical research.

To make graphs relevant to history, then, history has to be standardised, not only along the horizontal axis, but also along the vertical axis. In the case of a time-series graph, we have to make information on events similar enough for valid comparison so that they can be plotted in a Cartesian grid – rather than understood as a series of *particular* events, always different and so incomparable; we have to turn them into entities to which numbers can be attributed. Paraphrasing Porter (1994), the introduction of graphs in social research is inextricably connected with the process of its quantification.

Graphs are also inextricably linked with changing ideas about strategies of explanation in social research. As long as political economy was seen as a subbranch of history, it was not obvious that graphs like those of Priestley could be relevant for explanatory purposes. Historical explanations were

---

[4] A successful one. Priestley's chart went through several reprints. The accompanying introductory text, explaining the possibility of depicting the length of someone's life by a horizontal line, disappeared after the first edition. The convention of a horizontal axis for time was not so well-established, even by the Jubilee volume of the *JSSL* of 1885, that Marshall could not argue, quite seriously, for a vertical time axis.

concerned with events like the Napoleonic Wars (1800–1815), that is, events that are complex and heterogeneous. There is nothing that indicates that such events in history have just the right format so that they can be divided into equal bits on the horizontal time axis, as well as comparable bits on the vertical axis, which – to be sure – assumes they are homogeneous in some respect.

The distinction between data and events, then, is related to the distinction between time and history in explanatory work. Time seems not the relevant factor when thinking about Napoleon's place in history. History is the narrative linking events like wars, their causes, outcomes, and how these involved and affected the motives for action of those involved. Each particular event is considered complex and explained by striving for a complete rendering of all contributing causes that account for its internal complexity. At least this is how history was long construed, and it brought Dugald Stewart, we have seen, to the distinction between facts of history and facts of nature.[5] For Stewart, time factored in when examining how distance, force, and velocity relate to one another, not when examining historical events: that is, for the interplay of institutions, people, and their motives and actions.

Mapping History in Graphs

The previous section showed that a transformation is needed in how to think about historical events before graphical means of representation can be brought to bear upon the subject. Instead of investigating all contributing causes to an observed complex event or to a sequence of separate events, historical explanation should be considered as dealing with comparable and recurring events in time.

It was in these terms that William Playfair (1759–1823), a contemporary of Stewart, explained his innovative use of graphs to display economic data.

[5] It is still an important methodological strand in the philosophy and methodology of history. Apart from Hayden White's influential (1975) book, see, for example, Ankersmit (1988, 2001), Carr (1986), Hartman (1970), and Mink (1970) for critical evaluations. The relation between (historical) narrative, economic theory, and evidence has been challenged after World War II from the side of cliometrics. Fogel and Engerman's *Time on the Cross* (1974) may serve as a hotly debated example. Over the past decades, Deirdre McCloskey, Arjo Klamer, and, recently, Mary Morgan have investigated the relation between narrative and economic theory most persistently. See Klamer (1990), McCloskey (2001), and Morgan (2001).

Playfair designed an elaborate book of plates which he called the *Commercial and Political Atlas*. First published in 1786, the work went through three extended and revised editions. Most of the plates concerned time-series graphs of the prices of corn, weekly wages, and export surpluses or deficits. It is important at this point to keep in mind that, at the turn of the eighteenth century, statistics was the collection of facts about the nation-state, but this by no means implied that such facts were numerically expressed and thus available for graphical display. Remember Whewell's enumeration of the "data" of political economy (texts, conversations, numbers), which sounds like quite a heterogeneous and odd collection from a modern point of view. Graphs represent things already numbered, already measured, already in the form of what we now understand as statistical data, whereas for most events in history (as for most aspects of political economy), such events were not already numbered. One of Playfair's key innovations was to decide on the quantities in which to measure these facts.

Playfair arrived at his graphs from various sources. He credits extensively his much-older brother John Playfair, the Edinburgh professor of mathematics who after the untimely death of their father assumed his role in the family. According to William Playfair, his brother taught him that "whatever can be expressed in numbers, may be represented in lines" (Costigan-Eaves, 1990, quoting Playfair). Between 1778 and 1781, he worked as a draughtsman for James Watt. During this period, Watt used graphic devices to check the variation of water pressure in the steam engine (Costigan-Eaves 1990, 324). Given the close contacts between "lunar men" like Watt and Priestley (Uglow 2002), he would certainly have been familiar with Priestley's historical schema and he may well have meant Priestley's successful chart when he wrote that geometry "had long before been applied to chronology with great success", while he himself "was actually the first who applied [geometry] to matters of finance" (Playfair 1796, iv). Playfair thus took insights from the humanities, mathematics, and engineering in constructing his charts and also credited geography.

In explaining the advantages of his charts, Playfair wrote persuasively about their role in comprehension, expression, and memory:

> As the eye is the best judge of proportion, being more accurate and quicker than any other of our organs, it follows, that where-ever *relative quantities*, a gradual increase or decrease of any revenue, receipt or expenditure of money, or other value, are to be stated, this mode of representing is peculiarly applicable, as it gives a simple, accurate, and permanent idea;

it produces form and shape to a number of separate ideas, which are otherwise abstract and unconnected; for in a numerical table there are as many distinct ideas given, and to be remembered, as there are sums. The order and progression, therefore, of those sums, are also to be recollected by another effort of memory, while this [the chart] unites proportion, progression, and amount, all under one simple impression of vision, and consequently one act of memory.

(1796, v–vi)

Memory does not serve here as a storage of heterogeneous events. Instead, it acts as an instrument of recognition, of insight in the "production" of a *new* event: the movement of a homogeneous entity, money, through time that is presented to the eye in the "form and shape" of the graph.

In the matter of the axes, Playfair's graphs made a critical innovation over that of Priestley by calibrating the vertical axis. Here, we may be struck by the simplicity of his explanation, but we might be equally struck by the fact that Playfair had to give it at all: "This method has struck several persons as being fallacious, because geometrical measurement has not any relation to money or to time; yet here it is made to represent both". Imagine, Playfair argued, that each night a man makes a pile of the guineas he has made from trade that day, so that in one operation "time, proportion, and amount, would all be physically combined". But still, this has to be shown, and here he looked to geography, which he took to be the obvious source for ideas on how to represent the wealth or trade of a nation-state in spatial terms by the use of scales: "Lineal arithmetic then, it may be averred, is nothing more than those piles of guineas represented on paper, and on a small scale, in which an inch, perhaps, represents the thickness of five millions of guineas, as in geography it does the breadth of a river, or any other extent of country" (all quotes, Playfair 1796, vi–vii). Money, a homogeneous quantity, is taken as the obvious token for wealth, which is not obviously as homogeneous and quantitative. Money formed Playfair's vertical calibrations and allowed him to show relative amounts. Playfair's lineal arithmetic of graphs scaled economic life in monetary terms and in time units.[6]

But these decisions about scales were not straightforward. Perhaps Playfair's most famous graph, showing a rise in the price of wheat against

---

[6] To take money as a token for wealth was not obvious. His contemporary, August Crome, for example, took population as the relevant scale for his "maps" measuring the "strength of states"(see Nikolow 2001).

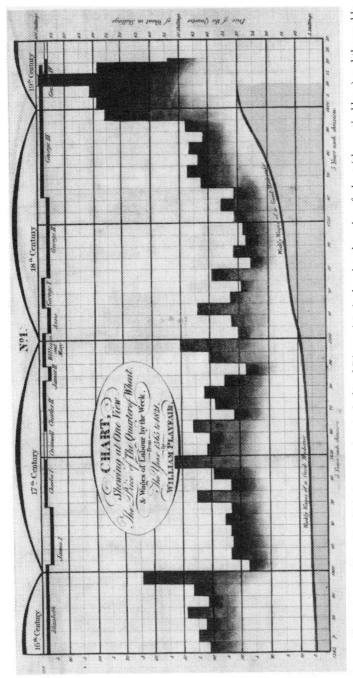

9-3. Diagram from William Playfair's *Letter on Our Agricultural Distress* (1821), showing the price of wheat (the vertical bars) and the weekly wage of a "good mechanic" (in the line beneath).

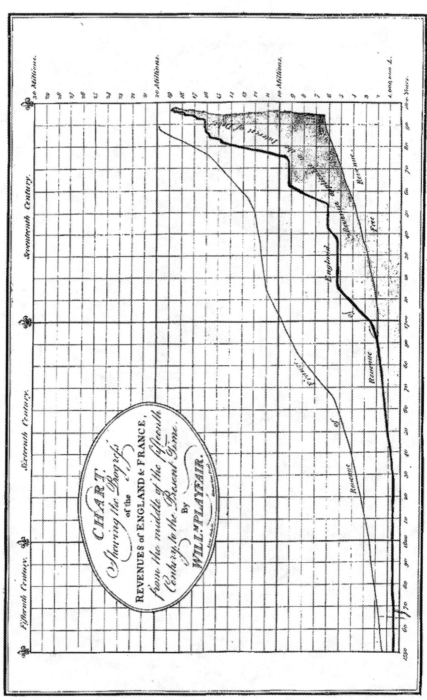

CHART,
Shewing the Progress
of the
REVENUES of ENGLAND & FRANCE,
from the middle of the fifteenth
Century to the Present Time.
By
WILL. PLAYFAIR.

Fifteenth Century.   Sixteenth Century.   Seventeenth Century.

30 Millions.

20 Millions.

10 Millions.

4,000,000 L.

20 Years.

Plate 1.

228

a rise in the wage of a "good mechanic", was misleading in that it suggested the prices of wheat to have risen much faster than the weekly wage, while the argument Playfair made was just the opposite (Figure 9-3). Work had still to be done therefore to establish a meaningful comparison of different curves in the Cartesian grid. That is, the different time series had to be made comparable to arrive at a meaningful result. The scaling of the vertical axis, as well as the manner of plotting the data, were matters of careful consideration rather than something that flowed from the nature of the subject or had been established by conventions elsewhere.

Recent accounts of Playfair's graphs have emphasised their convenience from rhetorical and cognitive points of view. As will be clear from the above, these elements are also to be found in Playfair's original texts. He praised the usefulness of his graphs, and he wrote that his graphs made statistics less "dry" and more "alluring" to the general public. Judy Klein (1995, 118) notes Playfair's "complete mastery of the graph as an instrument of persua-sion". Nevertheless, it was clear to Playfair that to grasp the meaning of his graphs was easier for those already acquainted with the spatial depiction of information. Thus, mathematicians and geographers would be far better able to read his graphs than those not educated in these subjects. Neither the rhetoric of graphs nor their cognitive power was historically obvious or conventional in the late eighteenth and early nineteenth centuries.

Facility in reading graphs thus spills over to another, even more important subject: how they function as tools of discovery. As Klein (2001, 112) notes, "Playfair asserted that his 'mode of painting' could isolate and capture the essence of permanent causes". Playfair made an explicit statement in this direction with respect to the following graph depicting the revenue of France and England, and England's surplus revenue (Figure 9-4), where he wrote that "another observation to be made on the French revenue is, that its increase and that of England going so nearly alike, proves that some *common* cause operates on both" (1796, 12). Playfair did not specify how to think of this common cause, nor why it would be a cause in the first place. He pointed to where a cause might be operating, but not what such a cause might be.

9-4. Diagram from William Playfair's *A Real Statement of the Finances and Resources of Great Britain* (1796) showing the progress of the revenues of England and France from 1550 to 1795. Reading from the top, the diagram shows the revenue of France, the revenue of England and the free revenue of England. The shaded area gives that part of England's revenue necessary for the payment of foreign debt.

Yet, his remark makes clear that Playfair designed his graphs to do more than make statistics fashionable to the public. His graphs did not merely give a convenient representation of data facilitating understanding. They go from graphical representation to graphical investigation, but usually of a limited kind. Playfair's charts were designed to reveal how history led through time to a particular historical event, rather than to reveal the general laws of history.

Images of Laws of the Phenomena

Stewart's classification of the sciences was far more important for the development of thinking on the method of political economy in Britain than Playfair's transgression of philosophical boundaries with his spectacular *Atlas*. We have seen how Mill ingeniously resolved Stewart's difficulty in dealing with complex historical events by reducing the number of causes involved in the case of political economy. For history, however, Mill refused to disentangle complex historical events into more simple data, thus safeguarding their essentially complex nature. While Mill considered all other causes as *disturbing* causes in the case of political economy, these were considered *contributing* causes when turning to historical events. By distinguishing between the *science* and the *art* of political economy, Mill relegated to the wise judgement of the statesman the task of translating the tendency laws of political economy into their concrete historical appearances. As a consequence, statistical data could give support to the truth of tendency laws, but they could never refute them.

We have seen how William Whewell took issue with Mill's stance. Even though Whewell had gone a long way in Mill's direction over the course of time – granting the somewhat different status of political economy vis-à-vis the other sciences – he persistently maintained that political economy could not evade the tedious path followed by the natural sciences to become truly scientific: "many of the principles which regulate the material wealth of states, are obtained, if not exclusively, at least most clearly and securely, by induction from large surveys of facts" ([1860] 1971, 282).

Over the years, Whewell gave several examples in his correspondence with Richard Jones of how such "principles" might be obtained, in most cases without going into any detail. He favourably mentioned a graph of corn prices against time, perhaps referring to the graph used by Sir Edward West in his 1826 tract on corn prices and wages.[7] Very early in his correspondence, Whewell plays with the so-called King Davenant table of prices and quantities of corn that became a recurrent subject in his engagements with political economy. From mentioning the possibility of deriving a functional relation between prices and demand from this table, Whewell proceeded to compute the exact fit by the method of differences. He mentioned Lubbock's table of birthrates that might be most useful for "the mathematics of population". His suggestion to Jones, that such representations might make his "general reasoning ... much more persuasive", was ill-spent on the latter. But Whewell held on to them.

In his *Philosophy of the Inductive Sciences*, Whewell addressed the usefulness of curves in the quantitative sciences in the establishment of dependency relations and mentioned a curve picturing corn prices against time (possibly West's curve) in the same breath as his theory of the tides. Statistical data might equally enable inductive inference to regularities in the natural and social realm, a transgression of domains that was neglected in all of the statistical societies at the time (who were more interested in drawing direct policy inferences from their tables) and ignored by political economists (who read Mill's *Logic* rather than Whewell's *Philosophy* to be illuminated about the methods of inductive enquiry in economics). For both tides and corn prices, Whewell discussed their relationship with time. In such cases, the graphic method was more helpful than tables of numbers, for "order and regularity are more readily and clearly recognised, when thus exhibited to the eye in a picture, than they are when represented to the mind in any other manner" ([1847] 1967, 396). The graphic method enabled the scientist to detect simple laws by seeing the patterns relating quantities and their changes:

> If, for example, we thus arrange as ordinates [along the vertical axis] the prices of corn in each year for a series of years, we shall see the order, rapidity, and amount of the increase and decrease of price, far more clearly than in any other manner. And if there were any recurrence of increase and decrease at stated intervals of years, we should in this manner perceive it . . . . And these resemblances and contrasts, when discovered, are the images of laws of phenomena; which are made manifest at once by this artifice, although the mind could not easily catch the indications of their

---

[7] West's anti-Ricardianism will certainly have contributed to Whewell's sympathies. On West, see Grampp 1970.

existence, if they were not thus reflected to her in the clear mirror of space.

Thus when we have a series of good observations, and know the argument upon which their change of magnitude depends, the Method of Curves enables us to ascertain, almost at a glance, the law of change; and by further attention, may be made to give us a formula with great accuracy.

(Whewell [1847] 1967, 397–8)

On the question of tides, Whewell was careful to point out that knowing the correct argument meant knowing the correct form of time unit. Tides vary not with solar time, but with lunar time, and only by using this correctly measured unit for the axis will the first law of tides – the time of high water – be fully revealed. Other aspects of tidal variation depend on other time-varying aspects of the moon's characteristics.[8] He did not discuss different time units for his corn price example beyond the use of calendar years, but we can immediately make the link from his tide–moon discussion to the standard time unit regularities of economics (long-term, cyclical, seasonal, and so forth) which later became commonplace in graphic methods of time series for economic data, and which were of so much importance in Jevons's attempts to get a grip on cyclical activity in the economy.

For the method of curves, data plotted in a Cartesian grid suggested, so Whewell explained, the general form of the relation between variables on the horizontal and the vertical axes. "Insulated facts" were joined together into "laws of the phenomena". Whewell's use of the word "variant" for the variable on the horizontal axis, and "variable" for the one on the vertical axis, occupied middle ground between a straightforward causal relation between two variables, and the loose suggestion of a dependency relation. For the tides, as in corn prices, time provides the measure upon which the variability depends, and – if the correct time unit is chosen, – reveals the pattern of variation and the law(s) of nature and society.

Whewell explained that to obtain the general form of the relation, one should not aim at drawing a graph through all separate spots, the insulated facts. Quoting John Herschel, Whewell argued that the individual

---

[8] For a history of tidology, see David Cartwright (1999). Whewell made pathbreaking contributions to the construction of cotidal maps. Many of Whewell's phrases in tidology are still in use, like "age of the tide" and "luni-tidal interval". Whewell read a paper on a mechanical graphical tide-recorder, constructed by T. G. Bunt, to the Royal Society in 1837. See Whewell (1838).

observations were loaded with "casual errours of observation", which one got rid of when drawing a curve "with a bold but careful hand". "By this method . . . we obtain data which are *more true than the* individual *facts themselves*" ([1860] 1967: 399). Whewell referred to William Herschel's *Investigation of the Orbits of Double Stars* (1804) as "one of the most admirable examples" of this "method of curves". There was no distinction here between mathematical dependency, scientific laws, and laws in the social realm.

DATA, PHENOMENA, AND THE GRAPHICAL METHOD

At the time Jevons embarked on his statistical studies in economics, in the early 1860s, statistics was still concerned with fact-gathering and, in political economy, Mill's distinction between the *science* and *art* of political economy reigned supreme. The overwhelming dominance of Mill's *Logic* over Whewell's *Philosophy of the Inductive Sciences* with regard to the method of political economy had made the search for causes, by mid-century, the monopoly of political economy and the search for facts, the monopoly of statistics. Convinced of its detrimental consequences for both sides, Jevons made it his lifelong task to combat this division of labour between political economy and statistics. Graphs were an important means to pull down this divide.

In his 1870 opening address as president of section F of the BAAS at Liverpool, Jevons strongly denied that statistics was solely the collection of numerical data in tabular form, and he went on to argue that, for a "scientific treatment", facts should be "analysed, arranged and explained by inductive or deductive processes" – just as was done "in other branches of science" (Jevons, 1870a, 309). In his comments on William Guy Jevons, he noted that once numerical variation was there, the "curvilinear method" was introduced.[9] This method was "the natural complement" to the tabular method. Jevons was clearly stretching the meaning of statistics to include "deductive processes" here. But, in stretching it in this direction, he also crossed the other divide, namely Mill's separation of the art and science of political economy, of history versus deduction.

---

[9] In a commentary on a paper by William Guy on tabular analysis (Jevons 1879, 657). I owe this reference to Judy Klein.

Examples abound of the use of the graphic method in Jevons's published and unpublished work. Jevons's decisive step was that he no longer considered the individual data as themselves historical events, but as representing, when taken together, a functional or dependency relation between two variables. Just as Whewell had explained in his *Philosophy of the Inductive Sciences*, the graphic method served not only to get at observations that were more true than the data themselves (by washing out errors of observation), but also to reveal the relations between variables by making a connexion between individual data.

The distinction between data and phenomena is essential to an understanding of Jevons's use of the graphical method in the *Principles*, as it is central to an understanding of the distinction he made there between "rational" and "empirical" laws or formulae. It relates to one of the major queries of historians of economics with regard to Jevons's work: the relation between his empirical and theoretical studies. In line with Jevons's own distinction between the "pure" and the "applied", theory and statistics seem to be worlds apart. In effect, Aldrich (1987, 248) pinpoints the issue at stake, when he, in reference to Jevons's *Principles of Science*, argues that the use of statistical methods was in Jevons's eyes only appropriate "once we are sure we have correctly ascertained the form of the function to be fitted". The true issue is how to ascertain the form of the function. This, as will be seen presently, involved for Jevons a complex interplay of theory and data.

Jevons's experimental practices are illuminating. Like many experimental scientists, Jevons was fully aware that empirical data do not speak for themselves: The experimental scientist is not a passive observer, perceiving reality and only then arriving at an explanation. Rather, he uses experimental practises to reveal the phenomena from the data, the actual observations being laden with error. One might think of these phenomena in terms of essential characteristics or mean values.[10] Phenomena could then be further

---

[10] The distinction between observations and phenomena is akin to Bogen and Woodward's (1988) distinction between data and phenomena. Bogen and Woodward introduce this distinction in order to distance themselves from "a widely shared view of science", in which scientific theories are supposed to "predict and explain facts about 'observables'" (303). They argue that this view is "fundamentally incorrect" (305). According to Bogen and Woodward, theories explain phenomena, or "facts about phenomena", and data (observations) give evidence for the existence of these phenomena (305). They provide a straightforward example to clarify the purpose of the distinction. To determine the melting point of lead, they say, "one must make a series of measurements". One typically "does *not* determine the

analysed to reveal the natural laws which they obeyed. For Jevons, these laws were stable functional relationships. The step from phenomena to laws depended critically upon the role of analogy, given the many possible relations consistent with the phenomena. In a nutshell, this procedure can be seen in Jevons's experiments on cloud formation, in his experiments on the exertion of muscular force, in his *Principles of Science*, and in his statistical studies.

From his experimental studies in particular, it is evident that his general approach to the sciences did not involve a split between pure theory and statistics, but rather was motivated by a unified framework in which analogical reasoning played a dominant role. Jevons based these analogies, we have seen, on very strong mechanical presuppositions. In fact, for Jevons, the mechanical character of the law governing the phenomena was never questioned. In many cases, such dogmatism proved extremely fruitful. It was a guiding principle in his theory of labour, as well as in his efforts to mechanise the laws of the mind. His strong convictions about the mechanical and deterministic character of social and natural laws gave him the liberty to introduce the tools and methods of the natural sciences into the social realm.

A "rational formula" gave an *explanation* of a relation between two variables; an "empirical formula" merely provided a *fit* of a formula to the individual data that could always be given "to a considerable degree of approximation" (*PS* 487). On page 493 of the *Principles*, Jevons offered as an example of the use of the graphical method (Figure 9-5) a minute description of how one might draw a continuous line "which will approximate the true law more nearly than the points themselves".[11] With modern eyes, we may be inclined to take Jevons's drawing as a very rudimentary fitting of a curve to the data. However, in Jevons's use of the graphical method, the

melting point of lead by observing the result of a single thermometer reading" (308). It is unlikely that all the different measurements will be exactly the same, nor does one *trust* just one single measurement, for how can one be sure that it has been measured correctly? If one can make "certain general assumptions" about the character of the "numerous other small causes or variation of 'error' – such as them being independent, roughly equal in magnitude, and averaging on the whole – then one will take "the mean of the distribution" to be "a good estimate of the true melting point" (308). Such assumptions are typical of those made in experimental research and play an important role in Jevons's discussion of his so-called Method of Means in the *Principles*.

[11] Jevons even gave the address of the merchant where the "engraved sheets" for drawing a curve might be obtained.

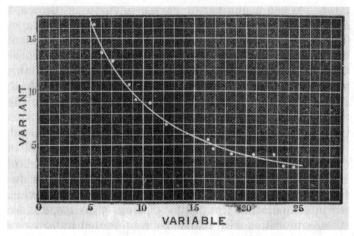

9-5. Jevons's illustration of the graphical method. *Principles of Science*, 1874, p. 493. Courtesy of Palgrave/Macmillan Press.

goal was not to *fit* the graph to the data, but to obtain an idea of the class of functions to which the "rational function" belonged – that is, to obtain an idea of the causal explanation of the phenomena behind the observed data.

Jevons's use of the graphical method was not a search for the best *fit* of the graph to the data; it was a first step to the best explanation. By using the graphical method, one might "ascertain with some probability" some of the properties of the function (are there any asymptotes, etc.). Jevons's distinction between the "rational" and the "empirical" formula – to indicate that it was always possible to fit a graph, or a polynomial, to an array of numbers – served to elucidate that not all curve-fitting had explanatory force. The "rational" formula *explained* the data by revealing the form of the causal connection between variable and variant.

Hence, one should only use this method in an informed way since "curves of almost any character can be made to approximate each other for a limited extent", which would require "a kind of *divination*" to ascertain what the actual function would look like. Jevons mentioned his experiments on the exertion of muscular force as an example where sheer luck had given the "true form" of the function, that is, a form matching with Haughton's mechanical explanation. Earlier research, analogies, and theoretical conjectures were necessary guides in all attempts to find the true form of the curve. Thus, the search for the rational formula would not be a blind guess, but would, on the contrary, use the "theoretical knowledge of the kind of function applicable to the case" (491).

Once we ascertained "what we believe to be the correct form of the function", the computation of the parameters became a matter of "mere mathematical computation to be performed according to fixed rules" for which the method of least squares might be used "to determine the most probable values as given by the whole of our experimental results" (491–2). But, in Jevons's view, the method of least squares only came into play *after* the "correct function" had been ascertained, as an optimising procedure for the value of the parameters:[12]

> Selecting some of our results widely apart and nearly equidistant, we form by means of them as many equations as there are constant quantities to be determined. The solution of these equations will then give us the constants required, and having now the actual function we can try whether it gives with sufficient accuracy the remainder of our experimental results (491).

JEVONS'S EXPRESSION FOR THE KING DAVENANT "LAW"

Jevons's mathematical rendition of the King Davenant Price Quantity table of corn is a good example to elucidate the differences in explanatory strategy between Jevons and those who considered individual statistical data to represent complex historical events. The origins of this table have been extensively examined in Creedy (1986, also 1992), and it is of no use to redo his exposition. Yet, a few remarks are in order here. Gregory King and Charles Davenant were political arithmeticians at the turn of the seventeenth century, and so held in low esteem by political economists of Jevons's day. It was therefore part of Jevons's rhetoric strategy to turn to these early statisticians to make the point that with regard to the relation of prices to demand "which reaches to the very foundations of Political Economy, we owe more to early than later writers" (*TPE1* 147).

Throughout the Victorian Age, the table had been ardently debated by political economists like John Elliot Cairnes, statisticians like Thomas Tooke, and men of science like William Whewell. Whewell made several suggestions

---

[12] For a description of these rules, Jevons referred to Jamin's *Cours de Physique de l'École Polytechnique*, vol. ii, 50, and he stated these in the sequel. Jevons's discussion of the graphical method in the *Principles* was not only influenced by Whewell (and Herschel), but also by Jamin's treatment of it in finding functional form.

Table 9-1. *Jevons's rendering of the King Davenant price quantity table of corn*

Changes in quantity of:	
Corn	Price
1.0	1.0
0.9	1.3
0.8	1.8
0.7	2.6
0.6	3.8
0.5	5.5

on the mathematical form that might be derived from the table in his early mathematical essay on Ricardian rent (1830), and then again in 1850 and 1862. The table played an important role in arguments at the time for and against the possibility of mathematising economics. Jevons jumped on it to use it in support of his new mathematical theory of utility. He used the table in the *Theory* to demonstrate how a mathematical function might be constructed between prices and utility from statistical data. The result was offered as positive evidence for the potential explanatory power and empirical relevance of his theory of utility. Jevons took the variations of prices of corn as the "only test we have of the utility of the commodity to the purchaser" (*TPE1* 140).[13]

Cairnes's views were the most outspoken against mathematising economics, and in his *Lectures* of 1857 he used the King Davenant table to illustrate his case. His strategy was to consider the data in the table as insulated complex historical events that should be analysed and explained individually. Comparing the reaction of the demand for luxuries and necessities to supply shortages, he argued that the only general conclusion that could be drawn was that prices would react differently in both cases, but one did not need the table to make this inference. Cairnes argued that those who attempted to "go beyond this general statement" and had attempted to derive an exact numerical relation between shortages of supply and price rises (like William Whewell) asked too much from their data "expressed in a tabulated form". The "causes" and the "circumstances" were too diverse

---

[13] For extensive discussions of the King Davenant table in relation to Jevons, see Aldrich (1987), Creedy (1986, 1992), Kim (1995), and White (1989, especially 431–43).

to place "reliance . . . on the accuracy of such calculations"; therefore, the "dispositions of people . . . can never, like the forces of physical nature, be brought within the limits of a formulated statement" (1857, 86–8).

The "circumstances" Cairnes referred to were all the other causes contributing to the observed changes in prices, and these obviated anything more than loose qualitative statements. According to Cairnes, an explanation in economics was reached once the "fact to be explained" had been traced back to the "ultimate axioms of Political Economy – that is to say, to the mental and physical principles from which its doctrines are derived" (1857, 91). Cairnes clearly did not consider that any meaningful explanation could be derived from the ensemble of numbers in the table.

Jevons, we have seen, was an intense reader of Cairnes, and Cairnes's objections to the use of mathematics went to the heart of his own program. In contrast with Cairnes, functional form and relations were central for Jevons. For Jevons, Cairnes focussed on the wrong target of explanation. Not the individual data, but the phenomena for which they gave evidence were to be explained. Even though Jevons did not draw a diagram relating the figures of the table in the *Theory*, it may well be that he made private use of the graphic method to obtain an idea of the function that would be the best *compromise* between the data of the table and the theoretical notions he wanted the function to incorporate, as can be witnessed from the many examples of such graphs in the Jevons archives (Figure 9-6). It may also be that Jevons borrowed the idea of its functional form from Whewell, whom he quoted in evidence that "the price varies inversely as the square of the supply" (*TPE2* 182). Jevons quoted here from Whewell's *Six Lectures on Political Economy* ([1862] 1967), and Creedy (1992, 12) takes this as unfortunate, since he thus "missed" the "hint" made in Whewell's 1850 article about the exact fit of these data to a cubic. It is important to dwell on this for a moment, because Creedy, not Jevons, missed the point of Jevons's numerical estimate.

In his second mathematical tract in political economy of 1850, Whewell showed by the method of differences that the figures in the table matched exactly to a cubic. By quoting from Whewell's 1862, rather than from the 1850, essay, Jevons missed this according to Creedy, and this despite Jevons's clear familiarity with the method of differences. In the *Principles*, Jevons demonstrated this familiarity, drawing an extensive parallel between the inverse deductive method, his logical alphabet, the arithmetical triangle,

9-6. Jevons's drawing of an alleged price law graph. Jevons Archives, Manchester, JA 6/48/89. The vertical and horizontal axes most likely state quantities and prices, respectively. Courtesy of the Director and University Librarian, John Rylands University Library, Manchester.

and the method of differences. Whatever the value of this parallel, this was all within the domain of a closed universe, where inductions could be "precise". But Jevons argued that as soon as one entered the real world, disturbing causes, errors in measurement, and imperfections in the measuring instruments were all present, making inductions always "imprecise". Indeed, as Jevons emphasised in the *Principles*, and reiterated on many occasions, for example, in his experiments on the exertion of muscular force, it would be a matter for worry and concern if our measurements fitted *exactly* to our data. This might mean we had measured an artefact rather than something in the real world.

Jevons clearly took the figures of the table as statistical data. It would therefore be a mistake to expect an exact fit between data and function. The data were not of the same sort as Bernoulli numbers that were found by arithmetically computing backwards, as was perfectly done by Babbage's Difference Engine. To use the method of differences in the case of statistical data to find an exact fit would make the application of mathematics to social phenomena a matter of arithmetic, rather than explanatory functional analysis. As Jevons stated in the introduction to the *Theory*, Whewell "regards questions in economy as little more difficult than sums in arithmetic" (*TPE1* 16). But Jevons persistently pursued functional analysis, not arithmetic, in his search for mathematical explanations of economic phenomena (see also Grattan-Guinness 2002). Graphs fulfilled an important role in the search for functional form. In a letter of 28 February 1879 to Sidgwick that related to Marshall's paper on international trade, Jevons pointed out the close relationship between graphs and mathematics, implicitly moving empirical statistics closer to mathematical theory:

> I notice … that you speak of the method of diagrams as being *opposed* to that of symbols, whereas I should not attribute this meaning to Marshall's remarks … I should prefer to say that if not ultimately the same methods they are parallel methods, the difference being one of convenience of apprehension.
>
> (TCC Add.Ms.c.94.59)

Jevons's estimate of the relation between price and quantity changes of corn was:

$$P = \frac{5}{6\left(x - \frac{1}{8}\right)^2}.$$

Steven Stigler (1994) succinctly solves the puzzle of how Jevons derived numerical values for his parameters by pointing out how Jevons used methods of calculation that were "commonplace in the handling of astronomical observations as far back as the seventeenth century" (1994, 188). These methods do resemble Jevons's account of how to calculate a function from a plotting of data, as discussed in the *Principles*. Stigler describes this procedure as an attempt to "fit" the equation to the data. This is to a certain extent justified, for once the form of the curve is chosen, the computation of the parameters is a matter of curve fitting. However, if it had been Jevons's sole aim to arrive at the best fit, his choice for the general form of the equation is far from logical. Following Creedy, Stigler notes that Whewell had already found "that the third difference of the relative price is constant and the 'data' can be exactly fit by a cubic" (1994, 185).[14] He continues that "an astute numerical scientist" (1994, 187) like Jevons, who was well-read in studies on the King Davenant table and equally well-read in the current research on the method of differences, would certainly have stumbled upon this equation. Apparently, Jevons rejected it, and the question is: Why? The answer, of course, is that it was *not* his purpose to just find the best fit. The form of the curve should give an *explanation* of the phenomena, not a reproduction of the data in the table.

Jevons's choice of the function for the King Davenant table was clearly theoretically informed by his theory of utility, even though his considerations were somewhat *ad hoc*.[15] Jevons assumed that a rise in price could be considered as an "approximation" or "test" of the "variation of the final degree of utility – the all-important element in Economy" (*TPE1* 140). Jevons proposed two further arguments that made the general form of the curve asymptotic to both axes. The first was that he did not think it plausible that "the price of corn should . . . sink to zero, as, if abundant, it could be used for feeding horses, poultry, and cattle, or for other purposes for which it is too costly at present" (151). Jevons referred to vague hearsay evidence that lent some credibility to this argument. The other argument was that the price would rise rapidly with exceedingly diminished supply, becoming infinite before the quantity was zero. This supplied him with an argument for including the constant *b* in the equation.

Even if his other considerations to "explain price movements of quantities which were much less or more than the normal production level" (White 1989, 441n45) would have been purely *ad hoc*, they nevertheless illustrate that it was not his purpose to find the best fit. The cubic function would have been one, but it did not provide a plausible explanation. The form chosen did: The explanation is, so to speak, *embodied* in the form of the curve. The theoretical considerations provide constraints on the form of the curve,

---

[14] For an exposition of the method of differences as applied to the King Davenant table, see Creedy (1986). The exact fit is: $y = 2562 \, 1/3 \, x + 55 \, x^2 16 \, 2/3 \, x^3$.

[15] This points, of course, to a recurring problem in utility theory since utility theory does not provide sufficient constraints on the form of the demand curves. It was, in effect, one of the reasons Jevons considered his numerical estimate of the King Davenant function only as an empirical formula.

which are at odds with the purpose of finding the best fit.[16] In his account of Jevons's treatment of the King Davenant table, White (1989) argues that, for Jevons, laws were statements of facts. To this we should add: Laws are facts about the phenomena, not about the data themselves.

Jevons made use of the table in support of his utility theory and his endeavour to mathematise economics, even granted the limitations in the availability and accuracy of data which economists faced in comparison with the other sciences. Thus, the utility of money was not a constant when income varied, and Jevons admitted that "great difficulty is thrown in the way of all such inquiries by the vast differences in the conditions of persons" (*TPE1* 142) – a point he reiterated in the *Principles* (759–61). Put whiggishly, his aim was to establish, in Kuhnian terms, a Gestalt switch. His curve did not fit the data as well as another, but it illustrated how one could take a new look at known data. By rendering the data of the King Davenant price quantity table into mathematical form and calculating a functional relation, Jevons argued, numerical insight could be gained into how changes in prices and variations in utility were linked. Even though Jevons was fully aware of the many problems, he did not consider them prohibitive. Rather, the important point was to treat the separate pairs of observations as comparable and equally contributory – standardised inputs – for specifying a functional relation between prices and utility on the basis of his new marginalist theory of utility.

JEVONS'S STANDARDISING AND TIMING OF EVENTS

In the previous paragraph, we have seen how Jevons used statistical data for explanatory purposes by linking them together, thus producing a new general event – a functional dependency between prices and utility, which

---

[16] See Cartwright (1983, Chapter 7). Also see White (1989, 441n45). Klein (1997, 12) gives a wonderful example of how, using the graphical method without being theoretically informed, it might lead someone astray as to the "true relation" between two variables. Creedy's discussion of Wicksteed's choice for the cubic function in fact offers a good example of i) the difference between fitting the data and explaining them and ii) the necessity of theoretical considerations when choosing a specific functional form. Wicksteed considered it a virtue of the cubic that it provided a "law connecting six points" exactly. In Jevons's case, however, the "law" was not connecting these six points at all. It was simply not Jevons's intention to do so. For Wicksteed, it was unproblematic to allow the "law" to fit the data exactly, since he had *moral* and *theoretical* reasons to reject the asymptotic form of the curve (Creedy 1986, 201–2). From these, he argued that the curve "will cut both axes" (202; Creedy quoting Wicksteed). A function cutting the axes makes the cubic a possibility, whereas it is excluded on theoretical grounds in Jevons's case.

was the object economists should consider but which they had ignored because of their adherence to the "wrong-headed" labour theory of value, and because of their resistance to linking theory and statistics. For Jevons, graphs served as important inductive tools in the discovery of social laws in functional form, and their numerical assessment. Already in the early 1860s, Jevons had advocated – without success – the use of time-series graphs for economic analysis; but, in some of his most innovative statistical studies of the 1860s, graphs were only introduced later in the reprinted and extended versions of these works.

An example is his successful study of the autumnal pressure in the money market, in which Jevons argued against explanations of the high withdrawals of coin from the Bank of England in October 1865 from a variety of accidentally contributing causes. By contrast, Jevons focussed on the "annual tide" in the money market, moving again from the explanation of individual data to the explanation of recurring *patterns* of events. Seasonal variations had been an important theme for the explanation of economic fluctuations in Thomas Tooke's *History of Prices*. There were clear and important reasons, Jevons argued, to distinguish a regular and recurring drain in the money market from an "irregular" drain and consequent fall in the reserves of the Bank of England. In the first case, the Bank could take appropriate measures admitting, for example, a lowering of reserves below normal, while the second case might be in need of another reaction. "It is a matter of skill and discretion to *allow for the normal changes. It is the abnormal changes which are alone threatening or worthy of very much attention*" ([1865] 1884, 181).

Thinking in terms of an annual tide enabled Jevons to consider yearly variations as a sufficiently comparable event that repeats itself over the years. In line with this, Jevons averaged out quarterly variations over the period under consideration (1845–1861) to derive the normal pattern of seasonal variation. Jevons's discussion clearly reminds us of Whewell's emphasis on the possibility of discovering "laws of phenomena" from the "recurrence of increase and decrease at stated intervals of the year" ([1847] 1967, 397) that we discussed earlier. Jevons concluded there was in fact nothing abnormal in the perceived extreme fall in money reserves in October 1865. Panic reactions to the phenomenon might be avoided by understanding its normal and regular occurrence and acting in accordance with this.

Jevons sought the explanation of the autumnal drain in "a concurrence of causes", of which he mainly considered the wage payments in coin of landworkers through August and September, which, with a lag, affected the Bank of England. This, combined with regular payment of dividends, created the drain of coin. But he explicitly refrained from a "complete explanation of all these variations, pointing out how much is due to each particular cause", an explanation that "could only be found on a wide basis of statistics, which do not exist" (1884, 172). Instead, Jevons contented himself with pointing out the "precise character and amount of the fluctuation in order that we may rightly appreciate the degree of disturbance they [these causes] will usually occasion in the money market" (1884, 172). The emphasis in Jevons's study then was on comparability and regularity of events, rather than the explanation of all contributing causes individually.

In the original study, Jevons stuck to the traditional way of presenting, namely in tabular form. It is only in the extended version printed in 1884 in *Investigations in Currency and Finance* that Jevons's graphs were added to "illustrate" the results of his tables and to suggest (rather than pursue) a further test of his original results by means of them (Figure 9-7).

Graphs were more important to Jevons's arguments in two of his better-known studies, the first his successful study on the fall of the value of gold, the second his highly unsuccessful studies into the relationship between sunspots and commercial fluctuations. Comments on the gold studies understandably have focussed on Jevons's innovative use of index numbers to flesh out a causal relation between the Australian and Californian gold discoveries and the depreciation of gold, a topic that will be dealt with in the next chapter. In the study itself, as in his correspondence with Cairnes on this issue, Jevons used his graph as evidence that a causal relationship between the discoveries and the value of gold could be found, thus arguing against those who considered that price changes had to be explained by doing justice to all contributing causes (1884, 48; see also letter of 3 June 1863 to Cairnes; *PC* 3:22–3).

In his sunspot studies,[17] Jevons used curves to single out a dependency relation between the solar period and trade cycles in the manner suggested by Whewell. Time was used as the ruler against which the two elements' relation would emerge. An example of his use of graphs to match the solar period with trade cycles can be found in his unpublished paper on the influence of

---

[17] The sunspot studies have been much analysed – see Mirowski ([1984] 1988), Morgan (1990), Peart (1996), and, negatively, Sheenan and Grieves ([1982] 1988).

COMMERCIAL FLUCTUATIONS.

Divergence of the Bank of England Accounts from their Average condition after Elimination of the Quarterly Variation.

the solar period on the economy, read to section F in 1875. Jevons began the paper with the observation that "it is a well-known principle of mechanics that the effects of a periodically varying cause are themselves periodic, and usually go through their phases in periods of time equal to those of the cause" (Jevons 1884, 194). It thus was a matter of prime importance to show that the time unit of the solar period and that of commercial fluctuations matched each other closely enough to infer a causal relationship between sunspots and commercial fluctuations.

These trade cycle graphs, constructed to illustrate their periodic nature, met with great suspicion compared with the good reception of his study of the autumnal pressure in the money market. In the latter case, a year presents itself as the natural unit to sort out seasonal variations, where seasons are to be found in the yearly cycle of the affairs of men and money. In the case of longer commercial fluctuations, Jevons sought to prove that the sunspot cycle was the natural unit for economic activity and thus to validate a certain periodicity in the trade cycle was to provide for a causal inference back to the sunspot cycle. In one example, Jevons reworked a graph from Milburn's *Oriental Commerce* by taking three-year moving averages and making a log chart to make the "strongly-marked decennial variation [thought to characterise the sunspot cycle], . . . more apparent" (1884, 218).[18] It is noteworthy that even a contemporary sympathiser in the analytical use of statistics, the Dutch lawyer Anthony Beaujon (1853–1890), remarked that this was an example of "manipulation".[19] In another example, published in 1882, shortly before his death, Jevons made even stronger causal claims.[20] He graphed the

---

[18] The date of publication of Milburn's treatise – 1813 – in the same period as Playfair's work may be noted.

[19] A margin marking on Jevons (1884, 212), University of Amsterdam, Central Library, call mark 539 B 21. On Beaujon, see Stamhuis (1989).

[20] In "The Solar–Commercial Cycle", published in *Nature*, 26:226–8, 6 July 1882. This short article is reprinted in *PC* 7:108–12.

9-7. Jevons's diagram (reduced) showing the divergence of the accounts of the Bank of England from their average values after elimination of quarterly variations. Reading from the top, the diagram shows notes in circulation, private securities, private deposits, bullion and coin, reserves and public deposits, respectively. From "On the Frequent Autumnal Pressure in the Money Market, and the Action of the Bank of England", reprinted in *Investigations in Currency and Finance* (1884, 192–3). Courtesy of Palgrave/Macmillan Press.

sunspot cycle (represented by Wolf's numbers)[21] against commercial crises (represented by the prices of corn in Delhi). From this graph (Figure 9-8), Jevons not only claimed support for the sunspot commercial cycle "relation between cause and effect which [he] had inferred to exist" (*PC* 7:108), but also went on to infer the existence of a missing sunspot maximum in the years between 1790 and 1804![22]

These examples show how the choice of the right time unit became of primary importance in making causal inferences and how graphs could figure in this. Whereas the seasonality in the money market graphs lent conviction to the argument, Jevons's ingenious reasoning about the sunspots did not convince his contemporaries, though here the problem did not seem to reside in the use of graphs so much as in the details of the particular causal chain being discussed. Jevons's claim that there was an "[almost perfect] coincidence of commercial crises in Western Europe with high corn prices in Dehli" (*PC* 7:108) was not considered a persuasive causal link, quite independently of whether sunspots influenced weather conditions in India or not. Consequently, the choice of time unit met with a suspicion that was absent in his study of the autumnal pressure in the money market.

Time-Series Graphs Take Hold in Economics

By 1885, the graphic method had apparently become sufficiently firmly established to be the subject of three major papers by Edgeworth, Marshall, and Levasseur, reported in the Jubilee issue of the *Journal of the Royal Statistical Society*.

In a complete reversal of the early-nineteenth-century views of political economists about history and statistics, Marshall argued that all the causes of historical events were best observed and revealed through the use of statistics shown in graphic form. Marshall's focus was on tracing the relevant historical causes operating through time. Marshall was confident that the

---

[21] Rudolf Wolf was a Swiss professor in astronomy who made a series of extensive historical studies that aimed at reconstructing the variation in the number of sunspots as far back in the past as possible, based on surviving notebooks and drawings of long-gone astronomers. By 1868, Wolf had a more or less reliable sunspot number reconstruction back to 1745. He pushed his reconstruction all the way back to 1610, although the paucity of data rendered these older determinations far less reliable.

[22] His inferences were supported by both a reestimation of the sunspot cycle and the finding of a small maximum in sunspots around 1797.

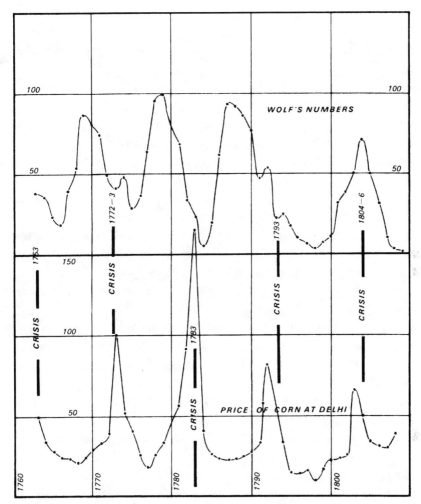

9-8. Jevons's diagram showing fluctuations in the sunspot activity (represented by Wolf's numbers) and fluctuations in commercial activity (represented by the prices of corn at Delhi). Time is depicted on the horizontal axis. Jevons did not provide a description of exactly what is stated on the vertical axis. From "The Solar-Commercial Cycle", 1882. Reproduced in *Papers and Correspondence* 7:112. Courtesy of Palgrave/Macmillan Press.

analysis of causes could be done by using many graphs together. He argued for a book, or many books, on each page of which were charted a group of curves. The sheaf of corn – the Royal Statistical Society's logo – was used by Marshall as an analogy to buttress his argument in an unusual rhetorical flourish: A sheaf with only a few stalks is not very stable; a sheaf with many stalks is soundly grounded. This implied not only lots of graphs for one country, but also an international comparative project, for the Jubilee meeting was in part called to consider the work of the International Statistical Institute.

Marshall's use of the Society's logo, however, differs markedly from its original intentions. While the Society had considered individual statistical facts as being loosely held together in a wheatsheaf, Marshall's reference to the individual stalks was no longer to isolated numerical facts, but to isolated graphs. In fact, the logo itself had changed over the years. The words *Aliis Exterendum* – to be threshed out by others – had been removed, the rope binding the stalks had become tighter, and the wheatsheaf itself made a much less disorderly impression. Even in its logo, the Society's distinction between theorising and data collection no longer held. Marshall understood his graphs to contain all the evidence for causal relations and historical explanations, and his suggestion to bind these all together expressed a hope to get at encompassing explanations of economic events through time.

We can also trace some of the earlier approaches to history in Marshall's remarks. Whewell had shown a clear awareness of the need to disentangle the different dependency relations from his graphs. Jevons had somewhat easily side-stepped this problem of interfering causes that had motivated John Stuart Mill to his deductive approach to economics. Marshall showed a clearer awareness of this problem, but approached it in Jevons's manner rather than Mill's. Marshall's use of the Society's logo entailed a return to the idea of economic explanations in terms of contributing causes. But these causes were no longer to be gathered by means of introspection; they were to be derived from comparisons of the graphs. Thus, the sort of historical events Marshall considered were constructed in the ways envisaged by Whewell and Jevons. Although for Marshall events remained in some sense individual, they were comparable events constructed from homogenised data connected through time; they were no longer heterogeneous independent events in history.

LOGICAL AND HISTORICAL TIME

It is well-known that Jevons was extremely careful in plotting the data, and his choice of grid enables one to read the original figures with fair precision from the graphs. For Newmarch, this virtue must have been a vice.[23] Why not state the data in their more precise numerical (tabular) form from the very start? Moreover, Jevons based his graphs on the very data collected by Newmarch and Tooke.

For Newmarch, Jevons's colourful plottings were only suggestive of more than could be attained with them and were therefore suspect. While statisticians like Newmarch focussed primarily on the explanation of the individual numbers in the tables, taking them as reporting heterogeneous historical events, Jevons by contrast took these data as homogeneous and comparable. By the use of the method of curves on these data, a regularity would emerge: A series of like events through time. Thus, a general phenomenon – the trade cycle, the variation in the final degree of utility – could be constructed and perhaps reveal its mathematical lawlike form.

Newmarch's lack of interest when Jevons entered the office with his enormous plates of statistics is consistent with the views of statisticians of mid-century. In order to change these views and introduce graphs into nineteenth-century British economics, historical time had to be reconfigured by the timing of history. Historical events had to be fundamentally reconceptualised before history could be graphed. This meant at least two things: the choice of historical events which are homogeneous and comparable (the vertical axis), and the choice of a relevant time unit, so that history can be imaged through time (the horizontal axis). To understand that there is a choice of time unit in economics requires an awareness of what the relevant time unit is that governs, or at least maps, economic activities of various kinds. To understand that there is a choice of comparable and homogeneous historical events requires rethinking both the nature of economic events and the treatment of their causes. Thus, the development from early-nineteenth-century political economy to late-nineteenth-century economics in Britain is marked by the change, for example, from historical descriptions outlining the complex and multiple causes of the wealth of the nation to the use of graphs of trade cycles to explain the monetary path of the economy through time. The usual problems and questions about such a graph – the problem

---

[23] Another aspect that might explain Newmarch's dismissive attitude is the comprehensive character of Jevons's undertaking. If Jevons showed Newmarch not only his plates, but also the general plan of the work, one can understand Newmarch's hesitations. Jevons planned encompassing graphs for all four branches that formed the basis of the Statistical Society. Imagine your own reaction to a student entering your office with similar plans in mind!

of an unchanging definition of wealth, of the correct index for measuring income, and so forth – were not discussed, because they follow the steps that are usually taken for granted, namely that there was an unbroken continuity in how historical events were conceptualised in economics.

It is precisely these steps that were problematised in this chapter. As we have seen, early-nineteenth-century political economics rejected statistics as being relevant to causal explanation and accepted history as being relevant for a discussion of causes, but only in terms of a full-scale, case study complexity.[24] Late-nineteenth-century economists used time-series graphs involving statistics as the realm of explanation for historical and scientific events conceived as comparable and time dated. But, at a certain point in the

---

[24] A very good example of such a full scale study in John Elliot Cairnes's *The Slave Power*. First published 1862 the book soon became an important instrument in questioning the widespread English support for the secession movement of the southern states of America. On a surface glance, neither the southern, nor the northern states addressed in any way the slavery issue to make their case. The southern states strongly argued for free trade, in contrast with the protectionism of the Union, and there was nothing much to be said against their expressed will to become independent. Moreover, the southern states were convinced that the wealth of nations was fundamentally dependent on the flourishing of the cotton industry. These reasons and circumstances provided wide support for the secession movement in England.

Encouraged by Mill, Cairnes made it his task to poke under this surface level and to show that the slavery issue was really the heart of the matter. Using some basic Ricardian notions, Cairnes argued that the economy of the southern states crucially depended on slavery, and then showed how this economic system of its own affected the whole of society, turning it into an aggressive and fundamentally degenerative force, that in the end threatened the progress of civilisation in other countries as well. Cairnes pictured the "slave power" as a system of production striving at complete control over the labour force. But this strive to control came at a cost. Agriculture based on slavery favoured large scale monoculture production and as a consequence only made use of unskilled (slave) labour. This was well to be contrasted with the emphasis in manufacture on skilled labour, and it was no coincidence manufacture was completely neglected in the southern states. To increase (or maintain) their profits, planters occupied the most fertile lands, and when the land was exhausted moved to new lands of higher fertility. Thus, what was sold under the labels of democracy and free trade was in fact nothing else than the most perverse social and economic system.

The Slave Power provides a fine example of how Cairnes made practical inferences from a priori principles. Looking back at his *Character and Logical Method of Political Economy* in the preface to the 1875 reedition, it is quite understandable that Cairnes did not see any reason to alter his views. Jevons's statistical and theoretical endeavours notwithstanding, Cairnes still did not believe that mathematics or statistics might contribute much to the advancement of political economy as a science. His own work followed a rather different format pointing in the opposite direction: towards the British historical school, rather than to the newly emerging mathematical economics. Thus standing at the cross-roads of British political economy of the second half of the nineteenth century, John Elliot Cairnes is rightly considered the "last of the classical economists".

mid-nineteenth century, represented so cleanly in Whewell's and Jevons's work, scientific and historical events were both depicted in the same way in graphic representations and were both interpreted in terms of functional dependencies. Neither in Whewell's work nor in Jevons's is there a clear distinction between the "mere" mapping of statistical data in graphs and the search for causal explanations. Out of this one kind of graph and dependency grew two different kinds of graphs: time-series graphs and causal dependency graphs. Time-series graphs take the time pattern to be important, whether the dependency is measured by the ordinary ruler of historical or calendar time or some other time unit ruler. Causal relation graphs abstract from time patterns, and consequently the dependency between the graphed elements cuts free of the timing of history. In effect, this chapter shows how Judy Klein's "logical" and "historical" times were at one time linked in the graphic mode and, by suggesting how they separated, provides an historical rationale to Klein's recently argued analytical distinction.[25]

Jevons's imaging of historical time in graphs and his approach to the King Davenant table mark a related change in British political economists' views towards history and statistics. His repackaging of historical events into data that serve functional explanations was premised on the assumption that there are lawlike regularities in society that can be inferred from the ensemble of statistical data. History, in being timed and standardised, had its explanatory range within economics tamed; statistics, when allowed to develop beyond tables of numbers, filled the explanatory void.

---

[25] See Klein (1995, 1997). Logical time, if I read her correctly, is unrelated to the "real" course of time. We can move backwards and forwards on a curve in logical time which violates the "irreversible paths of change in temporal processes". Hence, logical time is ultimately related to "static analysis" in economics and not to the plotting of actual or imaginary data changing over time. Historical time, by contrast, involves irreversible patterns of change, whether these relate to actual data or to mental abstractions "drawn to follow a path of a variable over time" (Klein 1995, 98–9).

TEN

~

BALANCING ACTS

23 May 1864

... But we noticed also the letters RJ1845. There can be no doubt
I think that they were carved upon the tree ... by my excellent but
unhappy brother.[1] ... I admired him & the things he made. I have
some few of them yet, for instance the little set of grain weights, which
he constructed for his chemical balance. The latter was ingeniously
made of wood with a common knife edge; the movement & pans
& weights were all complete, & he was able to make quantitative
experiments with considerable exactness.

Jevons, *Papers and Correspondence I*

In other branches of science, the invention of an instrument has usually marked, if it has not made, an epoch.

Jevons, *Principles of Science*

Jevons showed a keen interest in scientific instruments, as witnessed, for
example, from the eight entries he wrote for the *Dictionary of Chemistry and
Allied Branches of Other Sciences* (1863–1868), most of them on measuring
instruments: balance, barometer, hydrometer, hygrometer, thermometer,
and volumenometer. Jevons wrote these entries in the early 1860s, the period
in which his major statistical and logical studies saw the light and his outline
for a mathematical approach to economic theory was read to section F of

---

[1] Collison Black gives us the following information on Roscoe Jevons: Roscoe (1829–1869)
was Jevons's elder brother. He went insane at the age of about eighteen, shortly after their
mother died (*PC* 1:7).

the British Association for the Advancement of Science.[2] In his *Principles of Sciences*, he even devoted a separate section to measuring instruments to point out "the general purpose of such instruments, and the methods adopted to carry out that purpose with great precision" (284).

Measuring instruments were an indispensable part of Jevons's scientific practice. His daily use of these instruments shows, even more than the entries in the *Dictionary of Chemistry* or the attention paid to them in the *Principles*, the importance of using measuring instruments. For Jevons, measuring instruments provided access to the world. There is virtually no page in his diary in which Jevons did not record his measurements together with other impressions.[3] There was no walk in the country on which Jevons did not take his barometer with him to measure the height of the hills.

One instrument was predominant in these accounts: the balance. Lavoisier, Jevons's great predecessor in chemistry, had used the balance as the "most glorious weapon" in his battle against error,[4] and Jevons, I will argue, used it similarly. In the *Principles* (PS 272), he stressed the importance of scientific instruments for the formation of scientific disciplines, most notably for chemistry. Chemistry, he suggested, "has been created chiefly by the careful use of the balance", a claim widely supported by historians of science.

The balance was Jevons's weapon against those political economists, such as Mill and Cairnes, who considered political economy an inexact science in contrast to the exact natural sciences and hence not amenable to the use of numerical research tools. "In matters of this kind", Jevons wrote in the *Theory* (*TPE1* 9), "those who despair are almost invariably those who have never tried to succeed". Jevons's own empirical and theoretical investigations form, in contrast, benchmarks of accuracy and precision in economics.[5] My aim in this chapter is to show what role measuring instruments

---

[2] Another instance is Jevons's interest in the so-called arithmometer, which I mentioned briefly in Chapter 5.

[3] Jevons's diary of his journey to the gold diggings at Sofala, for example, is preceded by fourteen pages of meteorological observations.

[4] See Bensaude-Vincent (1992) and Levere (1990, 1994) on Lavoisier's revolutionary use of the balance; also Wise (1993) and Wise (1989a). Continuity with his predecessors comes to the fore in Holmes (2000). The use of the balance as an instrument commonly in use, especially in assaying, long before Lavoisier's chemical revolution is emphasised in Newman (2000). On Lavoisier's more general strategy of using precision instruments, see Golinski (1994).

[5] Though not all of them. In particular, his stubborn convictions on the issue of women working in factories were not supported by his statistics. See Chapter 8 and, for an extensive analysis, White (1994d, 1994e).

such as the balance played in this transformation of political economy. Its message is that not a real, but a virtual balance served to transform political economy into a natural science; the balance served as a mode to represent and measure the economy. Focussing on measuring instruments helps to reveal Jevons's essentially uniform approach to the sciences, including political economy.

In highlighting the importance of measuring instruments in economics, Jevons differed from his contemporary political economists, most notably Mill. The terms "measurement", "measuring instrument", and "instrument" are not to be found as entries in Mill's *Logic* (1843). This was not by accident, for the *Logic* was a book about proof, not about discovery, as Mill's friend and biographer Alexander Bain (1882) noted; and scientific instruments are primarily about discovery, not proof. Previously, we noted that Mill had no experience with concrete scientific practice and that all his knowledge was derived from secondary reading (*Mill* 1:21). It is noteworthy that Mill's most lucid spokesman, John Elliot Cairnes, had made the same remark as Jevons that "the use of the balance has brought chemistry into the category of those sciences the laws of which admit of quantitative statement" (1857, 79), but drew the opposite conclusion. Cairnes implied that no such instruments were available in the realm of the mind – there was no way, in Jevons's own words in the *Theory*, to "weigh, or gauge, or test the feelings of the mind" (*TPE1* 9).

Margaret Schabas (1990, 54) depicts Jevons's writing on philosophy of science as an "attempt to reconcile some of the disputes between Mill and Whewell on scientific methodology". Whewell was fully aware of the importance of measuring instruments in scientific discovery,[6] but did not know or want to apply them to political economy, and Mill, we have seen, ardently defended a deductive–philosophical approach to the subject.

Both Whewell and Mill approached the notion of measuring instruments too narrowly, however, due to their reluctance to extend mechanical philosophy to the realm of the mind. Babbage's thought experiments on his difference engine fulfilled for Jevons the very same function as Galileo's thought experiments in physics. Jevons's breakthrough in economics was not made

---

[6] A nice example I already referred to in Chapter 4 is his report to Richard Jones of his attempt to measure with Airy the density of the Earth by means of pendulum experiments. He complained that the whole enterprise was ruined by "a rascalling piece of steel deviating 1/10.000th of an inch from a straight line" (Whewell to Jones, letter of 9 September 1828, TCC Add.Ms.c.51/54).

with real instruments. Jevons used a virtual balance to revolutionise the field and this, we will see, was no less of an instrument. A virtual balance enabled him to actually measure the economy and to frame a mathematical representation of human choice behaviour in the market. Jevons's virtual balance was an analytical tool of investigation as well as a practical tool in giving numerical precision to the conclusions derived. Hence, it was certainly no coincidence when Jevons wrote that if physicists would have "waited until their data were perfectly precise before they brought in the aid of mathematics, we should have been in the age of science which terminated at the time of Galileo" (*TPE1* 7).

The remainder of this chapter is organised into five sections. Jevons's entry on the balance in the *Dictionary* demonstrates how the balance was both an analytical tool of investigation and a measuring instrument. These different functions will be addressed in the first two sections. The remaining three sections of the chapter investigate how Jevons's analysis of exchange, in analogy with the balance, changed political economy. The third section considers Jevons's use of the balance to arrive at a numerical causal inference about the fall in the value of gold. The fourth section explores how the balance was used as an analytical tool in the *Theory* in a way that restructured economists' thinking about the "laws of supply and demand" in social mechanics. In conclusion, I briefly recap the main argument of this chapter.

THE BALANCE AS A TOOL OF ANALYSIS

The balance played a pivotal role in Jevons's attempts to improve standards of precision and accuracy in economics. Jevons's educational background in the natural sciences cannot be emphasised enough, as has been noted in this book. His training at Liverpool Mechanics' Institute High School, and then – after a two-year interlude at a private grammar school – at the preparatory school for London University College and subsequently the college itself, was of importance. [7] But, as we have seen, his Unitarian, middle-class family background was significant as well.

---

[7] The importance of the educational structure for the development of political economy has been extensively discussed with regard to France. See, for example, Porter (1995). The obvious reference for the relation of French engineering to the development of neoclassical theory is Ekelund and Hébert (1999). In the British context, the influence of educational structure on the methodological and doctrinal developments in economics has, to my knowledge, never been systematically addressed.

After their initial foundation in the early nineteenth century, the Mechanics' Institutes spread rapidly throughout Britain.[8] The range of topics taught, in many cases by outstanding specialists in their fields, was extremely broad, ranging from the first principles of mechanical philosophy to lectures on Milton, German customs, or phrenology (see Stephens and Gordon 1972, 355; also Parssinen 1974). George Birkbeck, the founder of the London Mechanics' Institute, aimed at educating the craftsman, to "keep him abreast" of the technological changes that affected machines, tools, processes, and materials he worked with, rather than the education of the mere operative "doing a routine and mechanical job" (Stephens and Gordon 1972, 352). In some instances, schools for the education of youth were affiliated with these institutes designed for adult education, as was the case with Liverpool Mechanics' Institute.

Mechanical philosophy formed an important part of the curriculum. By close study of diagrams, the students learned to comprehend the mechanical principles obeyed by a number of mechanical contrivances, ranging from the balance to the steam engine. According to Henry Brougham, an early advocate of scientific education of the people, "enough will be accomplished, if they are made to perceive the nature of geometrical investigation, and learn the leading properties of figure" (Shapin and Barnes 1977, 49, quoting Brougham).

Whether or not the younger pupils gained practical experience in the use of measuring instruments, there is no doubt about it in Jevons's case. While he was still young, he conducted experiments with his brother Roscoe and his cousin Harry Roscoe (who would later become Professor of Chemistry at Owen's College, Manchester) in which they used a wooden balance with a fair amount of precision. His cousin Harry Roscoe recollects in his autobiography the "delights" of making "fireworks for the 5th November" (*PC* 1:7, Black quoting Harry Roscoe). It is tempting to think of Jevons's parental

---

[8] The Mechanics' Institutes find their basis in John Anderson's "Anti-Toga class" at Glasgow University, an experimental course on natural philosophy. Anderson deliberately allowed the general public to attend the lectures which were given using experiments, models, and little formal mathematics so that even a labourer could understand them. See Katoh (1989) for a short and helpful overview on the emergence of the Mechanics' Institutes as a form of adult education. Inkster (1975) and Shapin and Barnes (1977) emphasise the political role of these institutes. Their thesis is critically examined in Watson (1987). On the educational effectiveness of these institutes, see Stephens and Gordon (1972) and, more positively, Inkster (1975).

home as "crammed with demonstration equipment if not with experimental equipment".[9] Jevons became even better acquainted with the secrets of the balance when he trained as a gold assayer under the guidance of his Professor of Chemistry at London University College, Thomas Graham. His daily use of the balance as gold assayer in Sydney meant its principles became part of Jevons's second nature, and it is not surprising that he framed his empirical and theoretical work in accordance with them. The balance, for Jevons, was not just a metaphor; it was a genuine means to disclose the mechanics of both the physical and, as we will see, the mental world.

It was therefore natural that Jevons be asked to contribute several entries to the *Dictionary of Chemistry and the Other Allied Branches of the Sciences* (1868) on, amongst others, the topics of the balance and gold assaying during a period when dictionaries had become an important aid in the diffusion of scientific knowledge (Layton 1965; Yeo 2001). From the exposition of Jevons's entry on the balance, we acquire an extremely rich and detailed idea not only of the balance itself, but also of the intricacies of its use and the precautions that should be taken into account to arrive at significant results. The reader is struck by the effort Jevons made to spell out all possible difficulties in making an accurate measurement with a balance and how to circumvent them. In this respect, his entry was an effort to explicate tacit knowledge and impart practical guidance in using the balance.

Jevons's entry contains a description of the geometry of the balance, a description of the actual instrument, and how it should be used with care in practice. His geometrical account nicely captures the aim of such dictionaries to convey useful knowledge without troubling readers with notations they may not understand.[10] One of his drawings (Figure 10-1) gives a detailed geometry of the balance, showing how the different forces acting on the balance were interrelated. It is easy to see that the geometry of the balance is identical to that of a lever. Figure 10-2 shows how the effect of an additional weight, p, added to a balance at rest may be understood by conceiving of the balance as a compound pendulum, where the greatest velocity of the beam (proportional to $[\theta]$) gives an indication of p.

---

[9] As Ian Inkster suggested to me in private correspondence of 30 January 2004.

[10] Even though the secondary literature Jevons refers to makes use of the principle of virtual velocities, which is mentioned in *The English Cyclopaedia* of 1861 as "perhaps the most important generalisation in Mechanics", Jevons does not use this principle in his dictionary entry. Jevons did rely on this principle in the *Theory*.

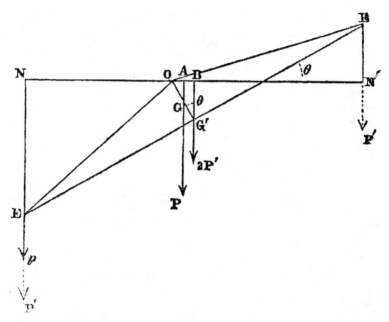

10-1. Jevons's drawing of the geometry of the balance, in entry on 'Balance', *A Dictionary of Chemistry and the Allied Branches of the Other Sciences*, 1863, 1:481–91, p. 487. Courtesy of University Library Leiden.

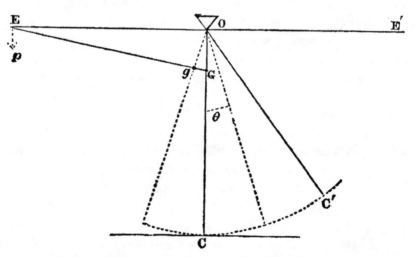

10-2. Jevons's drawing of the balance as a compound pendulum, in entry on 'Balance', *A Dictionary of Chemistry and the Allied Branches of Other Sciences*, 1863, 1:481–91, p. 488. Courtesy of University Library Leiden.

THE BALANCE AS A MEASURING INSTRUMENT

Given its role in Lavoisier's "chemical revolution", it is no surprise that Jevons described the balance as "the chemist's most important instrument" (1863a, 481). As Sibum (1995, 74n4) notes, in Jevons's day, "precision" and "accuracy" related to different aspects of scientific instruments. "Precision" referred to the tools and their quality, whereas "accuracy" referred to the quality of the workmanship. Jevons discussed both these issues in his entries on the balance and gold assaying. An image of a precision balance, for the use of which great accuracy was required, accompanied his entry on gold assaying and is reproduced here (Figure 10-3). If we examine this image, we see that the balance is placed in what looks like an experimental setting. At some points in his entries, Jevons suggests that using the balance was the same as conducting an experiment (e.g., 482: "... when a weighing is actually being made ... retain [the planes on the edges] in the exact positions proper for a new experiment ... "). Such an experiment places high demands both on the quality of the instrument and on the accuracy of the weigher.

Jevons provided criteria for the best material for the balance, the weights used, and other technicalities concerning the construction of the instrument. The material composition of the balance, for example, should be such that as many disturbing causes as possible are excluded. These construction requirements were intimately linked with the balance's geometry. The geometry of the balance implied special requirements for the construction of the actual contrivance: "In its most perfect form ... it consists of a perforated brass beam, cast in a single piece, combining great strength and perfect inflexibility with comparatively small weight" (482). These requirements were not easily reconcilable in practice. Small weight of the balance, for example, could be obtained by the use of aluminium. However, aluminium was highly corrosive and flexible, properties which rendered aluminium unsuitable. In practice, the instrument inevitably fell short of the ideal requirements.[11] Other technicalities related to the adjustment possibilities of the beam or the edges. Screws – still known as precision instruments to this day – played an important role in adjusting the edges or the beam itself. The balance

---

[11] "All the instruments with which we perform our measurements are faulty" (PS 461). On the conflicting requirements of measurement instruments in relation to their mathematical ideal, see especially Boumans (2001). Attempts to combine conflicting attributes created a separate discipline and literature on instrument making. Jevons was well-read in this literature and refers to it throughout the *Principles*.

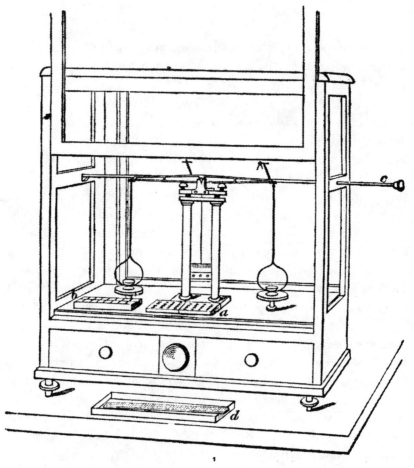

10-3. Jevons's drawing of a balance used in gold assaying, as Jevons added "exactly as in use", in entry on "Gold-Assay", *A Dictionary of Chemistry and the Allied Branches of Other Sciences*, 1864, 2:932–8. Courtesy of University Library Leiden.

should be enclosed in a "glass case, with convenient windows" to ensure that there are no "casual sources of mistake" (486).

Such casual sources of mistake related to inaccuracies on the part of the scientist or weigher and could not be known or corrected for in advance. Jevons gave the example of a "scrupulously exact gold-assayer led into serious mistakes by a small fly, which settled on his balance, unobserved at the time" (486). Even an accurate assayer could be misled by not taking proper care or inattention to some of the relevant details. Jevons wrote, "the casual sources of mistake are too many to mention" (486). To minimise these sources of inaccuracy, Jevons provided a list of "suggestions for the care of a balance" (486) which in fact urged the weigher to follow minutely established routines in handling the instrument so that, when in doubt, errors could be retraced.

Even when the technical layout of the balance matched the highest standards of precision attainable and the instrument was handled by a skilled weigher, sources of error remained. Some of these sources of error related to accuracy in a different and more modern sense, namely whether the scientist was actually measuring the target object or not. It is important that, in some such cases, the geometry of the instrument came to its aid; the formalism of the instrument rather than its material correlate served as a measuring instrument. The inequality of the arms of the beam is a case in point, "for the extreme edges can never be adjusted at perfectly equal distances from the centre edge" (490). As a consequence, one can never be sure the value found, however precise and reproducible, is the value searched for. The geometry of the balance gives in this case a straightforward precept of how to correct this error. Jevons referred to Gauss, who "by simply weighing the object alternately in one pan or the other" had made use of the geometrical average of both measurements to obtain faultless results. It is easy to show that one can obtain the true value of the required weight by following this procedure. Another such example was the insensibility of the arms to very small weights (a problem related to Figure 10-1: To turn the arm "some *definite* weight" was required. Both types of errors, Jevons argued, could be avoided by taking recourse to mean values instead of the read values (490). The geometry of the balance, rather than the material instrument itself, suggested how to average out irregular variations and to obtain the "true value".

We see that the use of the balance involved a complex interplay between the actual instrument, its geometry, the target of measurement, and its users. The balance imposed routines on its users, otherwise accuracy could not be guaranteed. Its geometry imposed demands on the materials used and on the construction of the apparatus, because otherwise precision in the results was unattainable. Its geometry related targets to average values; the average itself became the target of scientific inquiry.

These practical and analytical demands could not all be combined in practice (see also Boumans 2001). However, it was the very same geometry that placed such high demands on the construction (given the existing state of technology at that time) which also suggested solutions to measurement problems that could not be solved by merely following fixed routines and procedures. Finally, users needed considerable expertise and training. But even expert weighers could not rely on these routines alone. At various moments in the weighing process, their judgement also was required to attain precise and accurate results. As Jevons remarked in the *Principles*: "Measuring apparatus and mathematical theory should advance *pari passu*, and with just such precision as the theorist can anticipate results, the experimentalist should be able to compare them with experience" (*PS* 270). The balance served the same function for Jevons as it had for Galileo and Lavoisier: as an engine of discovery.[12]

Balancing Disturbing Causes: "A Serious Fall in the Value of Gold Ascertained"

We have seen that for Jevons the imperfection of the measuring instrument and the consequent occurrence of measurement errors were the "normal state of things". In fact, as we have seen earlier in relation to his experiments on the exertion of muscular force, he considered it even "one of the most embarrassing things" when "experimental results agree too closely" (*PS* 357–8). Jevons suggested in the *Principles* to eliminate "the multitude of small disturbing influences . . . by balancing them off against each other" (*PS* 357). That is to say, Jevons motivated the usual argument in statistics: that small independent disturbances or errors will cancel each other out on average by using the balance not as a real, but as a virtual, measuring instrument. The different methods of error reduction he discussed in Chapter XV of the *Principles* resemble his accounts of working with the mechanical balance.[13] Even when he attacked situations in his statistical work for which he acknowledged that causes were *interconnected*, he still argued that it was legitimate to treat them as "noxious" measurement errors that averaged out when as many causes as possible were included.[14] His famous gold study is the best case in point.

Historians of economics have depicted Jevons's gold study in line with contemporary quantity theory attempts to counter ideas, as propagated for example by Thomas Tooke, that an influx of gold would lead to an increase of wealth (Bordo 1975; Peart 1996). There is much to be said for this argument,

---

[12] See Wise (1989a,b).

[13] See especially Peart (1995a, 1996, 2001).

[14] Statisticians of the day might have considered this illegitimate. It offered Jevons, however, the possibility of circumventing the problem of multiple causation, which, as pointed out in Morgan (1997), could not be dealt with then. See also Aldrich (1987, 1992).

as Jevons was of the opinion that an influx of gold was comparable with "over-issuing and depreciating its own currency" by the government. And with Cairnes and Ruskin (*bien étonnés de se trouver ensemble*), he considered gold digging itself "almost a dead loss of labour . . . a wrong against the human race" (Jevons 1884, 67). His preliminary discussion of causes of economic fluctuations in his gold study conveyed to his readers that, in order to estimate the influence of the Californian and Australian gold discoveries on prices, a neutral benchmark was needed for comparison, freed from all disturbing causes. As Goodwin (1970, 410) explained, Jevons had "little to say about gold itself", and that was precisely his stronghold.

Jevons's study is remembered not so much for its remarks on gold as for its most important innovation: the use of index numbers to numerically assess a rise in prices (and hence a fall in the value of gold). Over the years, important studies have appeared addressing the technicalities of Jevons's index numbers and assessing the (il)legitimacy of their use. Astonishingly, the general setup of Jevons's measuring procedure escaped attention. Once we see the importance of the mechanical balance for Jevons's approach to the problem his most-discussed innovation in this context – the use of index numbers to prove his point – naturally follows. Jevons used the mechanical balance as a tool of investigation: first as thinking tool to restructure analysis of the causal influence of a gold influx on prices and, second, as a virtual, not a material, measuring instrument to attribute a number to the fall in the value of gold. In doing so, he restructured the thoughts of political economists and statisticians of his day and made index numbers relevant for computing a measurement. Numerical assessment replaced qualitative judgement.

When Jevons undertook the gold study, it was commonly considered impossible to give a numerical estimate of the influence of new gold discoveries on prices. Cairnes's views on the issue may serve as an example here. Precisely in relation to the influence of the "large influx [of gold] from Australia and California" on the value of gold, Cairnes (1857, 95) concluded in his *Lectures*:

> Now if Political Economy were an exact science, this question could be at once determined by calculating the effect of the causes assigned, and comparing the result of our calculation with the actual market price.

But because at that time political economy was not such an "exact science", Cairnes considered this calculation "impracticable". Even had accurate statistics been available, there were simply too many other causes involved to separate the effect of the gold influx. In line with received methodology, all these causes had to be assessed separately as possible contributors to the event.

Jevons began with the simple observation that "the comparative values of two articles are said to be altered when the proportion of the quantities usually exchanged in the market is altered". The ingenuity lay in the sequel. Drawing an analogy between an exchange on the market and the balancing of two weights at once dramatically simplified the problem faced by other authors (1884, 18):

> This alteration may arise from circumstances affecting the supply or de-
> mand of either article, just as a balance may be disturbed by an upward
> or downward force, applied to either arm. There is nothing in the simple
> motion to indicate from which side the change comes.

Jevons's recourse to the mechanical balance was more than drawing an analogy or even invoking a metaphor; it completely restructured the way one should think about the problem of multiple causation in price formation, just as the analytical properties of the balance structured the way students at the Mechanics' Institutes were trained to understand the laws governing material objects. There was no need to go into the causes of the separate changes in prices of the innumerable commodities involved, for the situation was simple: The price of gold was in the one pan and the prices of all other commodities were in the opposite. The mechanics of the balance provided an immediate connexion between a change on the one side of the beam and the other: "It is obvious, in short, that an alteration in any one article is shown in its rate of exchange with all other articles, so that the fact of an alteration may be ascertained with a continual approach to certainty" even though "there always remains the alternative of a concurrence of causes affecting all other articles" (19). The balance mechanism structured the way we should think about the cause of price changes in relation to gold.

Jevons only loosely referred to probability arguments since he assumed that everyone would agree that the odds were clearly against all the weights (prices) in one pan altering in the same direction; it was far more likely that all these different changes would average out. Thus, the cause of a movement of the beam must lie in the other pan, that is, in the factors affecting gold. The more commodities involved, the more confidence one could have in this kind of reasoning.

Jevons then used the analytical properties of the balance to compute a numerical estimate of the fall in the value of gold. To ascertain this, one needed to ascertain the general rise in prices based on the idea that, departing from the balance being initially in equilibrium, *all* or at least a preponderance of prices would have risen against the price of gold. At this point in the argument, an average was needed. But of what kind? Jevons's choice of the geometric mean to calculate the average change in the ratios of prices perhaps followed naturally from his use of the mechanical balance to structure his investigation for the balance measures ratios.[15]

Jevons's choice of the geometric mean to evaluate the fall in the value of gold has remained something of an enigma to this day. In contrast with the present day, Jevons did not interpret the choice of a mean value in terms of the distributional characteristics of the observations – an argument that was only explicitly made from Edgeworth's pioneering investigations in this topic later. Instead, Jevons thought in terms of the Law of Error and treated divergences accordingly – as errors in measurement – and he linked the law explicitly to measuring instruments. "Every measuring instrument and every form of experiment may have its own special law of error", but the "general Law of Error" was the best way of correcting for errors when "causes" were "unknown" (*PS* 374).[16] Laspeyres interpreted Jevons as making an index number argument and queried the use of a geometric mean in that context. Jevons specially linked his choice of the geometric mean to the balance in answer to Laspeyres's stated preference for the arithmetic mean:[17]

---

[15] At the turn of the nineteenth century, some controversy arose as to whether measuring a ratio could be considered as a measurement. For example, see Carter (1907). I owe this reference to Judy Klein.

[16] Aldrich (1992, 674) rightly points out that "the overall impression from [Jevons's] writing is that the use of the geometric mean was divorced from any consideration of the distribution of price changes", but this does not render his choice the result of a "jumble of reasons". In the nineteenth century, errors were considered to average out with zero mean due to the "Law of Error". It is only at the end of the nineteenth century, as Aldrich himself points out, and in the twentieth century that explicit recourse was taken to the distributional characteristics of observations. See especially Krüger et al. (1987), Morgan (1990), and Porter (1986). In relation to Jevons, see Stigler (1982), Aldrich (1987, 1992), Kim (1995), and Peart (1995a, 2001).

[17] Jevons passed over Laspeyres's argument for weighting the price changes in the arithmetic mean rather quickly. He had two other arguments for choosing the geometric mean. The first was that the geometric mean was to be preferred over the arithmetic or the harmonic (unweighted) averages, because it lay in between, an argument that – as Marcel Boumans pointed out to me – would be repeated by Fisher. The second argument was for convenience only. Jevons had a strong predilection for using logarithms, and this made the choice for the geometric mean the most natural.

[The geometric mean] seems likely to give in the most accurate manner such a general change in price as is due to a change in the part of gold. For any change in gold will affect all prices in an equal ratio; and if other disturbing causes may be considered proportional to the ratio of the change in price they produce in one or more commodities, then all the individual variations of prices will be correctly balanced off against each other in the geometric mean, and the true variation in the value of gold will be detected.

(Jevons 1884, 122)

From the *Principles*, it was clear that Jevons was well acquainted with the different ways in which the "Law of Error" was obtained. Gauss had argued that the best average was the arithmetical mean, yet Jevons's choice for the geometric mean shows that Jevons considered the Law of Error more in line with Quetelet, who thought of it as balancing errors. In that case, the geometric mean is the best choice. Thus, Jevons's argument for the geometric mean resembles Gauss's procedure for averaging out measurement errors when using a balance. For Jevons, averaging was balancing.

Jevons's "proof" for the fallen value of gold began with the average rise in the prices of thirty-nine commodities, and he subsequently enlarged the group of commodities to 118. Taking account of intricacies such as the commercial tide which could bias the outcome, Jevons's calculations led him to conclude that there had been a fall in the value of gold "*by about* $9\frac{1}{3}$ *per cent* " (54). This result obviously convinced Jevons that he did not have to worry too much about causes on the other side of the balance, for the fall in the value of gold was so considerable that Jevons hardly doubted the influence of the new gold influx.

In his gold study, Jevons relied on common arguments used in his own experimental practices. Since he had shown that prices had risen on average, he argued that this "*is and constitutes* the alteration of value of gold asserted to exist" (21). Notwithstanding remaining problems – of which he was fully aware – Jevons had no doubt that the result of his computations effectively established a fall in the value of gold and enabled him to give numerical evidence for its decline in value.

Many of Jevons's contemporaries missed the novelty of his approach to the issue of multiple causation and argued that the causes of the change in prices for all commodities should be investigated singly. As Hoover and Dowell (2001) argue, this more common method was akin to Mill's "Method of

Residues" in *Logic*. Cliffe Leslie was one of its proponents. Against Jevons's argument that "the average must, in all reasonable probability, represent some single influence acting on all commodities", Leslie argued: "But why not a plurality of causes" (quoted from Peart 2001). Leslie's approach diverged sharply from the setup of Jevons's enquiry. Jevons fully admitted that it would be possible to give causes for price changes in all individual cases. But if, on these grounds, one were to throw out the commodity in question, "the whole inquiry would be thrown into confusion by any such attempt ... the impartial balance of the inquiry" would be "overthrown" (58).[18] The reference to the impartial balance should be taken literally. If one changes the weights in the balance during the process, the whole outcome is thrown into disarray. This just proves that the investigator is an inaccurate weigher. His subjective judgement, rather than the "impartial" result of the balancing process, will decide the outcome.

Cairnes, in contrast to Leslie, acknowledged Jevons's accomplishment. He referred to it in a letter in the *Times* and used Jevons's results to substantiate his own conclusions in the same direction. But it is worth noting that, in correspondence with Jevons, he underlined the complete differences in methods used to arrive at the same results. Cairnes considered this an advantage, since the argument was strengthened when the results were obtained by completely dissimilar means. In the introduction to his *Essays in Political Economy* (1873), Cairnes denoted these studies as "applied economics", that is, as attempts to apply the theoretical principles of political economy to concrete economic phenomena. His studies into the effects of the gold discoveries are a case in point. Rather than starting from empirical materials, Cairnes approached the topic from a priori principles. He considered what the effect would be from an increase in the gold influx on trade and prices. In the original essays, statistical data did not play any formative role in the argument. If they were there at all, they served illustrative purposes, and it is typical for Cairnes's apriorism that statistical materials were added later on, sometimes only to illustrate and underline later developments. Cairnes's primary interest in these essays was theoretical rather than practical. He aimed to delineate the "modus operandi" – that is, the transmission

[18] To be able to make this argument, Jevons implicitly assumes uncorrelated price changes even though he knows this is not the case. This clearly made Jevons's argument flawed. See, for example, Aldrich (1987, 1992), Kim (1995), and Peart (1995a).

mechanism – of monetary shocks on the economy, not to estimate their numerical effects. Both Cairnes and Jevons were well-aware that they used "entirely distinct methods of inquiry" (*PC* 3:17–18). In this case, it gave Cairnes no reason to dismiss Jevons's results. Things were different when it came to the use of the balance as a tool of investigation in the *Theory*.

BALANCING PLEASURE AND PAIN

It was a widely held opinion in mid-nineteenth century that tools and methods, that could be so fruitfully applied to nature were inapplicable to the phenomena of the mind, including political economy. This has been a recurring theme in this book. Whewell, we have seen, had limited the sciences to the study of the natural world, but not the moral one, even though he himself pioneered the use of mathematics in political economy. John Stuart Mill's famous essay on method (1836) and *Logic* (1843) made political economy a science as respectable as the natural sciences, yet its tools and methods were thought to exclude experiments and mathematics. In short, political economy was primarily conceived as part of the moral or mental sciences, which made a marriage with the tools and methods of the natural sciences almost inconceivable.

By the time Jevons began to think about his new approach to political economy, this view had lost its status as a self-evident truth. We have seen how developments within psychophysiology and engineering mechanics created doubts over the categorical distinction between the phenomena of mind and matter. Physiologists such as William Carpenter argued for the so-called principle of the correlation of force, in which motives were considered as forces, just as forces work on matter. Similarly, the idea that human labour could be examined in the very same terms as the work performed by inanimate machines gained wide currency. The decisive contribution of Richard Jennings to Jevons's thought was how to consider human behaviour in terms of functional form. Jevons wrote his new theory of exchange against this background.

In the *Theory*, Jevons pointed at the "vague notion" that had existed among political economists, "that the conditions of exchange may be expressed in the form of an equation" (*TPE1* 101–2). Yet it was not just an equation, as he pointed out against Mill's claim that "the proper mathematical analogy is that of an *equation*" (Jevons quoting Mill, *PS* 102). Mill "failed to reach the root of the matter" (102). Thus, thinking of supply and demand only expressed the truism that supply and demand should equal if any exchange was to take place at all. The proper analogy, Jevons argued in his early mathematical paper to the BAAS, was the balance. Individuals balanced utilities to the point of equilibrium, at which point exchange would take place. The analogy of exchange with the balancing of utilities is clearly expressed in the early version of the theory he presented to the BAAS:

> Whether the exchange will take place or not can only be ascertained by estimating the utility of the objects on either side, which is done by integrating the appropriate functions of utility up to the quantity of each object as limits. A balance of utility on both sides will lead to an exchange.
>
> (Jevons 1866, 284)

The behavioural adjustments of individuals was itself a balancing process that Jevons analysed by means of functional equations. Here, of course, Jevons's utility theory took pride of place: "if we had the functions of utility determined, it would be possible to throw them into a form clearly expressing the equivalence of supply and demand", thus making the laws of supply and demand the "result of what seems to me the true theory of value or exchange" (*TPE1* 103).

For Jevons, the laws of supply and demand were founded on the "laws of human enjoyment", whose relevance Mill denied for the explanation of market exchange, and these laws obeyed the mechanism of the balance, leading to the surface event of exchange. Jevons found these laws, as he said in his *Brief Account* and repeated in the *Theory*, in Bentham's "springs of human action" – our feelings of pleasure and pain. In the *Theory*, Jevons wrote that Bentham had "thoroughly" understood the mathematical character of the subject and quoted his description of how to estimate the "tendency of an action": "Sum up all the values of all the pleasures on the one side, and those of all the pains on the other. The balance, if it be on the side of pleasure, will give the good tendency of the act ... with respect to the interests of that individual person; if on the side of pain, the bad tendency of it upon the whole" (*TPE1* 12, quoting Bentham). However, Jevons's rendering of pleasures and pains into functional form entailed a far stronger analogy with a mechanical balance than the just-quoted fragment of Bentham. The difference resides in a description of procedures that enforce a mechanism, or a description of the geometry of the balance that entails a mechanism.

Let me illustrate this difference by taking recourse to Benjamin Franklin's so-called *Moral Algebra*, a procedure that strongly resembles Bentham's balancing procedure. In the *Theory*, Jevons alluded to Franklin's procedure in his own description of pleasure and pain as positive and negative quantities (*TPE1* 38–9): "The algebraic sum of a series of pleasures and pains will be obtained by adding the pleasures together and the pains together, and then striking the balance by subtracting the smaller amount from the greater". Jevons knew of Franklin's procedure from Alexander Bain's *The Emotions and the Will* (1859). In a letter to Joseph Priestley, quoted in Bain, Franklin described his method of deciding in matters of great difficulty by making up a balance sheet of arguments:

> To get over this [the uncertainty that perplexes us], my way is, to divide half a sheet of paper by a line into two columns; writing over the one *pro*, and over the other *con*; then, during three or four days' consideration, I put down, under the different heads, short hints of the different motives, that at different times occur to me, *for* or *against* the measure. When I have thus got them altogether in one view, I endeavour to estimate their respective weights; and when I find two (one on each side) that seem equal, I strike them both out. If I find the reason *pro* equal to some *two* reasons *con*, I strike out the *three*. If I judge some two reasons *con* equal to some *three* reasons *pro*, I strike out the *five*; and, thus proceeding, I find out where the balance lies; and if, after a day or two of further consideration, nothing new that is of importance occurs on either side, I come to a determination accordingly. And though the weights of reasons cannot be taken with the precision of algebraic quantities, yet, when each is thus considered separately and comparatively, and the whole lies before me, I think I can judge better, and am less liable to take a false step; and, in fact, I have found great advantage from this kind of equation, in what may be termed *moral* or *prudential algebra*.
>
> (Franklin quoted from Bain 1859, 463)

Franklin's balancing procedure is similar to the procedure of a weigher when making measurements with a balance. The care of the weigher and his trust in the procedure enable him to improve his judgement. Once he has decided on the weights for the different arguments, the decision follows mechanically, that is, as a matter of routine; no further judgement is involved. Franklin's procedure may be a useful routine, but it lacks the mechanics of a material balance. A routine only makes for a mechanism if people rigorously adhere to it. It is to be compared with the routines of the factory system – or of Bentham's panopticon – that enforce mechanical conduct upon individuals but does not rob them of their capacity to break the rules. As John Stuart Mill rightly perceived, we only adhere to the rules "if we wish", thus breaking the spell of the coldly mechanical Benthamite take on the individual – mankind does not of necessity behave like a machine.

When we turn to a description of a balance by means of its geometry, there is no such possibility to break the rules – a weigher may diverge from his rules and routines, but the balance cannot escape its geometry. Franklin provided a prescriptive routine to aid judgement, not a mechanism that establishes equilibrium in accordance with mechanical principles. Franklin's balance sheet without the prescriptive routine may contain numbers, but that does not make it suitable for applying the geometry of the balance – let alone the calculus – to demonstrate its properties.

To provide for a mechanism, it is not sufficient to consider feelings of pleasure and pain, like Bentham, as quantities, capable of *more or less*, and therefore susceptible to "scientific" – that is, mathematical – treatment. Rather, pleasure and pain have to be considered not just as numbers, but as forces that move the will automatically, just like forces that move the balance (Figure 10-1).

Reading the *Theory*, one perceives a tension between Jevons's narrative, describing the individual's balancing act in judgmental terms, as when he talks about the mind "hesitating" and being "perplexed in making a choice of great importance" (*TPE1* 19–20). There is no place for hesitation or perplexion in Jevons's functional equations. Not incidentally, Jevons interchangeably denoted feelings of pleasure and pain as motives or forces. This marks a substantial difference. In Jevons's mathematical rendering of pleasures and pains, individuals do not act according to an array of different motives that each have to be judged as to their weight, but on forces that automatically move them into one direction or the other. In fact, the associationist term "feelings" served to blur the distinction between motives and forces, holding a middle ground between "physical pleasure or pain" and "mental and moral feelings of several degrees of elevation". When Jevons, in his 1879 criticism of Mill's utilitarianism, referred to Bentham's procedure to estimate the "values of pleasures and pains", he adds that Bentham "obviously" meant by "*values* the quantities or forces" (*PL* 276). Jevons's mathematical rendering

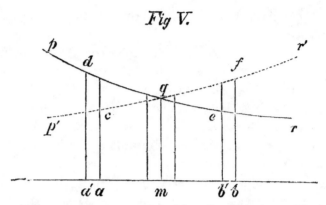

10-4. Jevons's diagrammatic representation of the utility adjustments of one individual (or trading body) to its optimum at *m*. The vertical axis (not drawn) depicts utility, the horizontal two different commodities, apparently measured in the same quantities. The two curves represent the utility functions for the respective goods, where the dotted one (*p'qr'*) is superposed and inverted on the other (*pqr*). *The Theory of Political Economy*, 1871, p. 97. The ratio of exchange is fixed on 1:1. Courtesy of Palgrave/Macmillan Press.

of pleasures and pains framed the "laws of human enjoyment" in terms of man's physiology – as natural forces instead of motives.[19]

Jevons gave the following graphical illustration of how the functions describing these forces were interrelated for one person (Figure 10-4). In the diagram, two utility curves are superposed and inverted upon one another; utility is measured on the vertical axis, commodities on the horizontal. Jevons showed how this person would make a net gain in utility by extending trade from *a''* in the direction of *m*, and would lose in utility when trading beyond that point. Hence, there automatically emerges an equilibrium for this individual at *m*. Jevons's balancing model thus moved from balancing disturbing causes (as in his gold study) to optimising outcomes in an equilibrium state. This balancing model, stemming from mechanics, was taken to represent the individual's balancing of pleasures and pains at the margin. In making this analogy between the balancing of feelings and the balancing of a material balance – which from a modern perspective may seem completely trivial – the distinction between the laws of mind and matter that had haunted Victorian discourse evaporated. Human deliberation and choice were pictured mechanically.

[19] Warke (2000) recently examined, from a slightly different perspective than is pursued here, the mathematical fitness of Jevons's rendering of Bentham's felicific calculus.

For Jevons, the "laws of human wants" in which "the basis of economy" was to be sought, became grounded in mankind's "chemical and physiological conditions" (*TPE1* 158). His own experiments on the exertion of muscular force convinced him that he was on the right track for his theory of labour. His reading into psychophysiology was also an important source, most notably Jennings's *Natural Elements*. From these sources, Jevons derived the idea that additional increments of commodity would lead to ever-smaller gains in utility, an idea that was reflected in the form of the curves in the diagram. There was but one solution to them – at the point where the final degrees of utilities of both commodities "balanced".

The verbal story one may tell about Jevons's diagram, and that Jevons told about it, may be about individuals freely adjusting their behaviour out of self-interest.[20] Yet the diagram tells another and stronger story, as Jevons extensively clarified in the second edition by comparing his equation of exchange with the equilibrium of the lever. Jevons analysed the laws of supply and demand as the balancing of moments. There is no unspecified use of the "laws of supply and demand" as there were in many of the contemporary newspapers and periodicals. There is a specified description of optimising behaviour in functional form. The diagram depicts a genuine mechanism explaining behavioural adjustment to an optimal state – a "*mechanics of utility and self-interest*" – in contrast with authors such as Mill who made reference to the laws of supply and demand without providing a mechanism explaining their workings. Jevons described our will, in consequence, with some justness as a "pendulum" moved by pleasure and pain, "and its oscillations are minutely registered in all the price lists of the markets" (*TPE1* 14).

It is well-known that Jevons's mechanics only worked for a fixed ratio of exchange. In his famous letters on Jevons's marginal utility theory, Fleeming Jenkin argued that he saw "no motive power" moving two individuals towards an equilibrium rate of exchange, and he challenged Jevons to show the opposite (*PC* 3:167–78). Jevons's explicit analogy of the equation of exchange with the theory of the lever implicitly makes clear Jenkin's problem. If the ratio of exchange is not fixed, the fulcrum is not fixed either, and the balance becomes a defective instrument. But Jenkin mistook Jevons's diagrams to treat two different individuals, whereas Jevons's intent was to

---

[20] We needed Jevons's explanations of his cloud images to understand them as representing "real" clouds.

picture the gains and losses of utility for one individual only. Already in his *Brief Account*, Jevons consistently argued on the basis of his so-called law of indifference or law of one price. That is, an individual balanced gains and losses in utility on the basis of a uniform price in the market.[21]

CONCLUSIONS

In the introduction to the *Theory*, Jevons approvingly quoted Augustus De Morgan, his teacher in mathematics at University College London:

> Had it not been for the simple contrivance of the balance, which we are well assured (how, it matters not here) enables us to poise equal weights against one another, that is, to detect equality and inequality, and thence to ascertain how many times the greater contains the less, we might not to this day have had much clearer ideas on the subject of weight, as a magnitude, than we have on those of talent, prudence, or self-denial, looked at in the same light. All who are ever so little of geometers will . . . remember the steps by which this vagueness became clearness and precision.
>
> (*TPE1* 11, quoting De Morgan)

It is perhaps not surprising that Jevons, who was a chemist, gold assayer, and natural philosopher by training, made the balance his most important tool of research. It *is* surprising, I think, that this simple fact has escaped the attention of historians of economics for so long, probably because economists do not think of their subject as an "allied branch" of chemistry, as Cairnes had plainly stated. Jevons did. In this chapter, we have seen how Jevons used the balance as a tool of investigation to impose clarity and precision on economics. The result can truly be termed a revolution.

In his gold study, Jevons used the balance as a thinking and calculating tool to measure a fall in the value of gold and to make an inference as to its cause as well. Thinking with the balance restructured the way one might conceive of the causal influence of the new gold influx on prices and focussed attention on the rise or fall in the average level of prices as a numerical indicator for the amount in which gold had fallen in value. In

---

[21] Jevons made additional assumptions about the infinite divisibility of commodities, without which the assumption of a uniform price would be of itself insufficient to establish a trade. For recent detailed analyses of these conditions, of the wider context of Jevons's theory of exchange, and on his attempts to redress the inherent difficulties it encountered, see White (2001).

his *Theory of Political Economy*, Jevons used the principles of the balance to reconstruct the process of human deliberation. He was thus able to relate the marginal utility considerations of individuals with exchange on the market. The balance restructured economists' thinking about the laws of supply and demand: By connecting the decisions of individuals to exchange to the geometry of a simple machine, Jevons provided in outline form an equilibrating mechanism for market exchange resting on what we nowadays would call a preference ordering. These accomplishments fundamentally changed the outlook of economics on both the theoretical and practical planes. Following Jevons's work, it became feasible to ask for numerical estimates for empirical questions. It became equally feasible to consider human deliberation in relation to price formation in terms of the calculus.

Jevons's approach was extremely successful in the case of the gold study and widely approved. To understand mental deliberation in terms of the mechanism of a balance, however, required a shift in perspective that many of Jevons's contemporary economists were not prepared to make. An anonymous reviewer of the *Theory*[22] quickly spotted that the novelty of the book rested not primarily on Jevons's use of mathematics, but on his persistent comparison of man with an instrument:

> In what then, does Mr. Jevons's originality consist? First, in the fact that he approaches the subject from a new point of view; and, secondly, that this method enables him to express his conclusions in mathematical symbols. To explain the first statement we may remark that, for scientific purposes, human society may be considered as a vast piece of machinery, in which the actions of the various parts is determined by the various forces which affect the will. Each man is regarded as an instrument moved by pain and pleasure; and the arrangements of society at large are determined by the aggregate impulses of all its individual members.
>
> (*PC* 7:152–3)

---

[22] In the *Saturday Review* of 11 November 1871, possibly written by the mathematician George Wirgman Hemming, fellow of St John's College, Cambridge. Better-acquainted with Jevons's mode of reasoning than might be expected from someone like Cairnes, the reviewer was more perceptive of Jevons's accomplishment, even though he was in general quite sceptical about Jevons's undertaking in the *Theory*.

ELEVEN

~

THE IMAGE OF ECONOMICS

BRIDGING THE NATURAL AND THE SOCIAL

In his 1889 address to section F of the British Association for the Advancement of Science (BAAS), Francis Ysidro Edgeworth addressed the usefulness of "the application of mathematics to political economy". The subject
was prompted by emerging debates over the use and usefulness of the new
tools and methods Jevons's work promised to economics. Edgeworth explained he would not "dwell" on the substance of Jevons's new theory, of
which the "cardinal article" was his theory of exchange in terms of final utility. This "economic kernel... divested of its mathematical shell" had been
well-treated by economists like Sidgwick, Marshall, and others. Edgeworth's
"object" was "to consider the use of that shell: whether it is to be regarded
as a protection or an encumbrance".

As might be expected, Edgeworth's assessment of the use of mathematics
in economics was highly positive. It took Sidgwick, for example, "a good
many words" to explain the effects of a tariff on international trade benefits. Edgeworth presented mathematics as a shorthand language, a more
efficient language, and diagrams served as a similar example: "the truth in
its generality is more clearly conveyed by the aid of diagrams" (*Peart* 2003
4:143). He continued:

> There seems to be a natural affinity between the phenomena of supply and
> demand and some of the fundamental conceptions of mathematics, such
> as the relation between a function and a variable, between the ordinate of a
> curve and the corresponding abscissa, and the first principles of the differ-
> ential calculus, especially in its application to the determination of *maxima*
> and *minima*. The principle of Equilibrium is almost as dominant in what

Jevons called the mechanics of utility as in natural philosophy itself. In so many instances does mathematical science supply to political economy what Whewell would have called "appropriate and clear" conceptions.

Edgeworth's summary labelling of the "natural affinity" between economic concepts and "the fundamental concepts of mathematics" conceals a century of struggles over the appropriate method in economics. The description of algebra and geometry, "the ordinary language in political economy", as a mere shorthand for a more elaborate verbal phrasing ignored that predecessors like Mill and Cairnes, and contemporaries like Henry Sidgwick, did not perceive this language as the "ordinary one" for economics at all. For those economists there was no "natural affinity" between economic phenomena like supply and demand and diagrams or mathematics. The very attitude towards explanation in the moral sciences – and what role instruments like graphs, diagrams, and mathematics could play in them – had to be changed to make such tools acceptable. To see the use of mathematics as "natural" meant to think differently about historical and social explanation, and to think differently about the categorical distinction between the phenomena of mind and matter, that had haunted Victorian discourse.

Edgeworth tacitly brought in the missing element to make mathematics the "ordinary language" of economics, that is Jevons's recourse to the "mechanics of utility". Jevons's mechanics of utility bridged the gap between the natural and the social, to use Michael White's phrasing. Turning economics into social mechanics was based on, and biased by, the use of specific mechanical analogies, and their mathematics.

Mathematics was not just a shorthand language for what could also be said in the language of the businessmen, as Marshall famously seems to have had it.[1] Edgeworth reviewed a great many examples to show that mathematics is more than a language. Using mathematics, it "is hardly possible to keep to what may be called the simplest type of supply and demand". Using mathematics, economists could, and did, proceed to other more complex cases. Weintraub (2002) recently wrote that Edgeworth "conceives of mathematics as the intellectual structure in which physical reasoning may be developed". Thinking about human deliberation as a mechanical balancing

---

[1] On Marshall's attitude towards mathematics, see especially Weintraub (2002, Chapter 1).

act, economists like Jevons or Edgeworth "naturally" took this message to economics.

MECHANICAL DREAMS

This brings me to the more general issue of the use of mechanical analogies, or metaphors, in economics. It may be argued that mechanical analogies had long been used in social explanations. True enough, but they never played the constructive and structuring role they had in Jevons's work. Jevons's approach to economics and to science is fundamentally inscribed in a culture of scientific instruments and their constructive role for theory and evidence. Dugald Stewart, the great summariser of Scottish Enlightenment philosophy, considered mechanical analogies to serve, like poetic metaphors, a distinctly different function than to unravel the laws governing society. He offered Smith's well-known comparison of society with a grand machine in *The Theory of Moral Sentiments* (*TMS* 316) as an example:

> Human society, when we contemplate it in a certain abstract and philo-sophical light, appears like a great, an immense machine, whose regular and harmonious movements produce a thousand agreeable effects. As in any other beautiful and noble machine that was the production of human art, whatever tended to render its movements more smooth and easy, would derive a beauty from its effect, and, on the contrary, whatever tended to obstruct them would displease upon that account: so virtue, which is, as it were, the fine polish to the wheels of society, necessarily pleases; while vice, like the vile rust, which makes them jar and grate upon one another, is as necessarily offensive.

The issue at stake is to what extent a scientist is willing to take on the commitments implied in a metaphor. Following Dugald Stewart, I would maintain that these commitments in Smith's case did not go very far. Smith considered himself as pursuing the same rigor in his moral philosophy as was pursued by Newton in the *Principia*; but, in those days, it was common among the literati to claim that one was a Newtonian. In practice, this related more to a commitment to a blend of Baconianism and Newton's famous *regulae philosophandi*, that is, a commitment to an inductive mode of enquiry, than to a commitment to the specific tools and instruments Newton used in his investigations. The *Theory of Moral Sentiments* is a case in point. Reading the book, we see the importance our faculty of judgement and our capacity of self-command play in the formation of a virtuous character. This, how-ever, did not prohibit Smith from comparing society with a machine. Smith did not consider his comparison of society with a machine in opposition to notions such as self-command, but it obviously was not his intention to talk about the virtue of a gear as having the same meaning as the virtue of an individual agent.

Smith's purpose was not to dig into the mechanical principles regulating his grand machine and to transpose them, "word-for-word", to human so-ciety. At no point was the *Theory of Moral Sentiments* designed as an enquiry into the *mechanical principles* regulating society. Rather, it was a dialogue on virtue.[2] The metaphor of a machine did not relate to the explanatory princi-ples of the formation of society, nor did it serve any constructive role in his theory of the moral sentiments. It only illustrated the sense of harmony indi-viduals perceived either in looking at a perfect and well-contrived machine or the inner sense of harmony felt when perfecting their own moral sen-sibilities. Indeed, Smith criticised philosophers such as Hobbes, who were satisfied with abstract comparisons of machines and society, ignoring the role played by notions as sympathy and self-command in individual moral conduct (see Griswold 1999, 53, also 152; Montes 2002). Society was not an air pump, nor was the human individual an hydraulic machine or a gear.[3]

In Victorian Britain, this rejection of any substantial comparison of man and machines was shared, as I have argued in this book, by two of the most violent opponents on the methods of the sciences in general and of political economy in particular: John Stuart Mill and William Whewell. Both considered the phenomena of the moral sciences (including political economy) distinct from those of the natural sciences, even though Whewell never successfully got this conviction straight with his simultaneous claim for an inductive method of political economy. Because of this conviction, his *Bridgewater Treatise* (1833) set clear limits to "mechanical philosophy". These limits were no longer respected by Jevons or his successors.

---

[2] See especially Vivienne Brown (1994). Also Montes (2002).

[3] The argument here spills over to *The Wealth of Nations* itself, for one of the virtues in which judgement and self-command were of utmost importance was self-interest, *the* explanatory motive behind social harmony in a market society. Whatever type of explanation we can find for social harmony in Smith's works (and it is not my purpose to say anything definite about it in this book), it is distinctly *not* a mechanical one. For a recent argument on this issue, see Griswold (1999, especially 359–60).

282 ~ WILLIAM STANLEY JEVONS AND THE MAKING OF MODERN ECONOMICS

The importance of mechanical analogies in economics is of course a major topic in Philip Mirowski's recent *Machine Dreams* and in his earlier work as well. It pertains to the image of economics as a science, and it is therefore understandable that comments on Mirowski's earlier work centred on what the commitment to a metaphor, or analogy, entails. As Kevin Hoover (1991, 142) stated: "A central problem in Mirowski's view of history and method is that metaphors are all important, yet there is no explanation of their mode of influence" (Hoover 1991, 142). Like Dugald Stewart, he illustrates this by wondering about the different uses of metaphors in science and poetry: "If my love is like a summer's breeze, I still have no reason to think that an anemometer would help to gauge the intensity of her devotion". But Hoover was not quite justified in his criticism, because Mirowski does give an account of how analogies function in science.

Mirowski points at the "explanatory structures" (Mirowski 1989, 272) implied in (mechanical) analogies and the commitments of the scientist to them. He rightly emphasises that metaphors *constrain* the researcher. They impose an "analytical regimen" (1988, 19), and he describes this regimen as being committed to a "word-for-word" mapping of the metaphor to the subject under study. Mechanical metaphors function like a straitjacket, or what Hoover (1991, 142) describes as the "*metaphorical* imperative: to use a metaphor is to commit oneself to the complete mapping of that metaphor onto the subject at hand". What Mirowski's account of analogies as a "straitjacket" ignores is their positive side: They may also serve as constructive and structuring devices in the search for regularities in the natural and social realms – they not only restrain, but also serve as engines of discovery. Mechanical analogies have both these sides, as may transpire from my account of Jevons, but also may be briefly illustrated for other economists as well.

Mary Morgan (1999) examined recently how Irving Fisher used different models to investigate the equation of exchange and the issue of bimetallism. For the first, one of Fisher's models was a steelyard. For the second, Fisher used a system of connected reservoirs of fluids. Morgan demonstrates how such comparisons guided Fisher to pose further research questions. To use the steelyard to understand the equation of exchange, for example, brings in dynamic principles of adjustment to equilibrium which can be compared with the oscillating process of a pendulum. Such an adjustment process cannot possibly be read from an algebraic rendering of the equation of exchange. Morgan also discusses the negative drawbacks of making such analogies. In a comparison with the equation of exchange, one may have good grounds for excluding certain features of a mechanical balance which may, however, inevitably slip in. The point is to what extent the researcher feels committed to pursuing the analogy in full. Such an account may serve as an example of how an analogy may provide several levels of commitment to it. It shows how an analogy constrains and structures the enquiry and, further, how it may lead to subsequent research questions. Mechanical analogies are not merely straitjackets; they do have their positive heuristics.

The commitment to an analogy is, in practice, a matter of gradation and will depend on the reasons the economist has to either go with or reject its implications. Using such analogies is, in its turn, embedded in a further network of commitments as to the type of questions asked and answers received. But if one does not consider it apt on a *prima facie* basis to compare human behaviour or economic processes to a mechanism, as it was the case with economists before Jevons, it is not very likely that some questions will be posed, such as: What is the functional form of the preference ordering for luxuries of an Indian beggar as compared with that of Bill Gates? What form has the production function of a capital-intensive industry as compared with a labour-intensive one? How can we model discretionary choices? What sort of empirical data do we need to give numerical values to such functions? What dynamic process can a business cycle be compared with? Nor will it make much sense to scrutinise the data; to plot them in graphs, "tinting them neatly with delicate colours" (Keynes [1936] 1988, 66); or to take moving averages or construct index numbers with the purpose of finding an indication in the form of the movement of these data or data constructs of the sort of mechanism that might explain them.

These types of questions were alien to most economists before Jevons, but they became "natural" to ask in the twentieth century. Look once again at the plate of engravings accompanying the lemma in *Chambers' Cyclopaedia* (Figure 1-2). In effect, this plate offers a logic of machines and mechanical structures. If an economist, with modern eyes, contemplates these "simple machines", some of them appear quite familiar. Take, for example, Figures 59 and 60 on the bottom row of this plate, showing Simon Stevin's inclined plane and geometry.

Herbert Simon used Stevin's vignette to illustrate how complexity might result from the working of simple mechanical principles. Herbert Simon concluded: "This is the task of natural science: to show that the wonderful is not incomprehensible, to show how it can be comprehended – but not to destroy wonder" (1969, 2). Nature is compared with a construct, a contrivance, an artifice. Its logic is the logic of a machine. Simon outlined a similar program with respect to human behaviour and "the most interesting of all artificial systems, the human mind". Human behaviour, human thinking, and the human mind might be understood by comparing them with computers and understanding the "simple general laws" governing them (22). True enough, Herbert Simon did not use the inclined plane but a string of transistors as a structuring tool of enquiry, and his program is much more complex than can be done justice to in one sentence (see Mirowski 2002; Sent 2000). But, it is undeniable that the analogy with a string of transistors helped him to frame his research into the organising principles of mind and society.

Other figures we see in the plate are the pendulum and friction (Figure 1-2, Figures 36–38). The pendulum was used by Tinbergen to explain and understand business cycles. In his inaugural lecture (1933), he programmatically stated that "the phenomena that play a role in the business-cycle" could be compared with the oscillations of the pendulum. "Such an oscillation is well-known under the name of harmonic oscillation, that occurs with pendulums, swings, elastic swings, etc." (1933, 14–15, translated in Boumans 1992, 73).[4] To understand the business cycle, Ragnar Frisch considered "for simplicity an oscillating pendulum whose movement is hampered by friction" (1933, p. 199). Once again, look in Chambers' plate at Figure 35, the figure of the steelyard that was used by Fisher to learn about the properties of the equation of exchange. It is significant that Jan Tinbergen started off depicting his first econometric model (of The Netherlands) as a mechanism, and wavered for quite some time between the notions of a "model" and a "mechanism" to switch to a model in the end (see Boumans, 2005).

In all these examples, the comparison of an economic, social, or mental system with a mechanical contrivance, that is, a machine that functions according to known mechanical principles, plays a crucial role. This does not mean these authors all believed their object of study genuinely *was* a steelyard, a pendulum, or a string of transistors, just as it is absurd to

---

[4] Marcel Boumans (1992) argues that Tinbergen's use of the analogy of business cycles with a pendulum in harmonic oscillation concerned its formalism, and was therefore not a wholesale adoption of a specific theory in physics. It was "a case of *limited* physics transfer".

suggest that Jevons believed that the human mind consisted of a set of wooden levers. Nor do I mean to say that all mechanical analogies should be with simple machines instead of more complicated ones, like the steam engine, the automobile, or the computer. Rather, such comparisons involve an *epistemological* claim; to understand society, the economy, or the mind in analogy with a mechanical contrivance gives a mode of intelligibility. It helps the economist to "look under the hood". In his famous article on the measurement of utility, Frisch referred to this way of understanding society as the realisation of the "dream of Jevons". Mechanical dreams lay at the root of modern economics.

ECONOMICS AS A NATURAL SCIENCE

It would be stretching the narrative of this book too far to claim that all economics since Jevons made similar use of mechanical analogies to understand man and society. Relegating psychophysiology outside the domain of economic discourse, while maintaining the instruments that were introduced with its help, *rationality* – not the mechanics of pleasure and pain – became the totem of twentieth-century economics. Jevons's own work in logic suggests why it was so easy to shift from mechanics to rationality. Logic, the embodiment of rationality *par excellence*, served as the means of transport.[5]

In Jevons's approach to the sciences, logic was tied in with mechanics and with his general views on induction. There is no doubt that Jevons's argument for the essential uniformity of the method of the sciences is one of the dominant themes in the *Principles of Science*. In that book, the Logical Machine, itself a complex of pulleys and levers, structured Jevons's thinking about foundational questions on the nature of inductive inferences in the sciences and made him argue against some of the accepted theories on the subject, most notably those of John Stuart Mill. Jevons did not only use the Logical Machine to unravel the intricacies of induction, however, but he also considered it as an instrument that mimicked our mental organisation. It made the distinction between the phenomena of mind and matter scientifically flawed and obsolete.

---

[5] This is how the marginalist revolution was reinterpreted by Charles Sanders Peirce in the Cambridge Scientific Club, as becomes clear from important recent research by James Wible (2003). See also Peirce ([1887] 1997) on Jevons's Logical Machine.

Whereas Mill granted political economists a separate and privileged route to truth by the use of introspection, this procedure was denied its scientific credibility by Jevons. Even though he granted Mill and Cairnes in the second edition of the *Theory* the somewhat "peculiar position" of the political economist, because he could borrow "ready-made" laws from other sciences (like psychophysiology), these laws still served as hypotheses in need of verification. They were never granted the introspective certainty they had with Mill and Cairnes. In clear contrast with Mill, all science was hypothetical. "In the writings of some recent philosophers, especially of Auguste Comte, and in some degree John Stuart Mill, there is an erroneous and hurtful tendency to represent our knowledge as assuming an approximate complete character" (*PS* 752). All scientific investigation consisted, for Jevons, in the "marriage of hypothesis and experiment" (504). Analogies served as the heuristic instruments to generate hypotheses.

Jevons's recourse to machines as engines of discovery in science challenged the boundaries between the moral and physical sciences that were cherished by John Stuart Mill, and challenged as well the sort of evidence that economists could take recourse to in support of their theoretical views. Using mechanical analogies, Jevons aimed at finding mathematical expressions for his quantitative data, attempting to explain their general form. In the *Principles*, Jevons explicitly argued that this was the format for all of the sciences. There was no one way from theory to data, nor did the opposite hold; statistical data might suggest the range of functions that came into consideration to explain the phenomena, while theory might dictate the admissible form of the functions from its side.

Granted there are no boundaries between the sciences, it is hard arguing against the use of the tools and the instruments of the natural sciences in the moral ones. The complexity of the subject, the multifarious causes that produce a single social fact, may make inconceivable how such instruments are to be applied in the mental and social realms, but this is no longer a matter of principle. What could be done in astronomy or meteorology could be done in economics as well. Political economy was, for Jevons, "a kind of physical astronomy investigating the mutual perturbations of individuals" (*PS* 760). For Jevons, De Morgan's suggestion was the relevant one: to consider any subject of investigation, natural, mental, or social, as a "complicated apparatus"; as a pendulum, a balance or a compound of such simple machines. This typifies Jevons's approach not only to the laws of the mind (in his work on formal logic), but also to his approach to the laws of the market. Jevons's investigations in logic and in economics stem from a common source in which mechanical contrivances provide the mode of intelligibility.

There can be no doubt that using mechanical analogies as aids in understanding was far easier for those who had practical as well as theoretical knowledge of the workings of such machines, than for those who lacked such detailed knowledge. Indeed, the man–machine analogies that permeated the Victorian Age were cherished by those whom we nowadays would call engineers. But they proved an insurmountable gulf to contemporaries like Mill or Cairnes. If it was not even obvious to someone like William Whewell to think of the providential order in nature mechanically, how strange it must have been for Mill and Cairnes, who had no background in the sciences, to consider mechanical contrivances like Jevons's Logical Machine, or Babbage's calculating engines, as in some way representing properties of the mind or of society. It is one thing to think of the mind as obeying causal laws (as did Mill and Cairnes); it is another thing entirely to consider the mind as nothing more than an extremely complex mechanical contrivance.

How great a leap it must have actually been for someone in the Victorian Age to consider a mere wooden construct, this so-called Logical Machine, or the fancy of a more complex one, as capturing the very laws of the mind! Jevons was not blinded to the fears of these sceptics of science – quite by contrast, they were a great source of worry. "Theologians have dreaded the establishment of the theories of Darwin and Huxley and Spencer, as if they thought that those theories could explain everything upon the purest mechanical and material principles, and exclude all notions of design" (*PS* 764). "Materialism", this "coming religion", seemed a "resignation to the nonentity of human will". Jevons acknowledged such "secret feelings of fear which the constant advance of scientific investigation excites in the minds of many" (736). But he did not share them. Just the hypothetical character of science made it impossible to exclude the hypotheses of free will and a Divine Creator, or to "deny the existence of things because they cannot be weighed and measured" (768).

Yet, it is no incidence that Jevons only speculated on writing a *Bridgewater Treatise* and never wrote one. Even when his religious convictions may have moved in opposite directions, his scientific spirits were those of Babbage or Huxley, who saw no limits to mechanical philosophy, rather than those of Mill or Whewell. For Jevons to make mechanical analogies was part and parcel of scientific practice, and he applied it to all different branches of the sciences. The emergence of psychophysiology, the shaping of the physical concept of work, and the emergence of formal logic all contributed to Jevons's conviction that in searching for the laws of political economy, the economist should delve into the physical "groundwork" of man. Nowadays, we may think of the attempts of phrenologists to locate sexual instinct, maternal behaviour, carnivorous instinct, and verbal memory (to name but a few) at specific centres of the brain as extravagant and open to ridicule (Young 1970, 23). The phrenological movement was condemned by John Stuart Mill in similar terms. Yet, the phrenologists' approach to the brain is not that different from the ones which are becoming increasingly popular and practiced today.[6] Jevons would certainly have been less amazed than Mill by recent attempts of behavioural and experimental economists, including Nobel laureate Vernon Smith, to explain choice processes by identifying activity in specific regions of the brain.[7]

The first edition of the *Theory* stated the case for economics clearly and distinctly: "A few of the simplest principles or axioms concerning the nature of the human mind must be taken as its first starting-point, just as the vast theories of mechanical science are founded upon a few simple laws of motion" (*TPE1* 24). By considering the analogy of a mechanical balance with the deliberations of the mind, Jevons was able to tie the mechanics of human deliberation to the laws of exchange. Psychophysiology provided the form of the utility relation. Loosely relying on its findings, Jevons thus provided a mechanism suggesting that there were no missing links between the utilities individuals attributed to different quantities of commodities and the acts of exchange in which these individuals engaged. Jevons's gold study also concurs with the image of a scientist using the principles of a mechanical contrivance, the balance, to come to grips with an extremely complex social reality.

---

[6] The location of the Centre of Broca, the centre of speech, halfway during the nineteenth century was the first concrete evidence that it was not that farfetched after all to search for a neurophysiological basis for mental processes.

[7] See, for example, McCabe et al. (2001), Camerer (2003), and entry on "experimental methods in (Neuro)Economics" in Nadel (2003). It is interesting to note that some of these new developments start from Hayek's *Sensory Order*, a book that was written in an explicit defence of introspection and in opposition to the physiological reductionism of Otto Neurath. See Caldwell (2003, Chapter 12). I would like to thank Bruce Caldwell for giving me a preview in his book.

At various places, we have looked in more detail at these and other examples. In his study on the exertion of muscular force and his approach to the King Davenant table of price and quantity data on corn, Jevons used empirical, experimentally acquired (as in the first case) or allegedly statistical data (as in the case of the King Davenant table) to find functional relations. Jevons's search for functional form was in both cases informed by assumptions that could be traced back to psychophysiology as Jevons knew it or straightforwardly to engineering mechanics.

Jevons, thus, showed economists, and social scientists more generally, that the methodological challenges faced by them were not in principle insoluble and not all that different from those facing the natural scientist. Economists did not need a privileged route to truth, as had once been claimed by Mill. They could use the same tools and instruments as any natural scientist, if only they knew how to use them and how to adapt them for the specific questions at hand. As a consequence, the image of economics, that is, its tools and methods of investigation, changed distinctly and irrevocably. In the *Theory*, Jevons referred back to Adam Smith's days, in which electricity was considered immeasurable. Jevons's sympathy clearly lay with those scientists who had slowly turned what was considered unknowable into something that could be measured with a considerable amount of precision. It was the same in economics: "those who despair are almost invariably those who have never tried to succeed . . . the popular opinions on the extension of mathematical theory tends to deter any man from attempting tasks which, however difficult, ought, some day, to be achieved" (*TPE1* 9).

In many of the sciences, a "satisfactory explanation" nowadays "requires providing a description of a mechanism" (Machamer et al. 2000, 1). Economics is certainly no exception. Robert Lucas (1988) even describes economic theory as "an explicit set of instructions for building . . . a mechanical imitation system". We hear the echo of William Thomson in these words, as we now may hear that of Jevons. To this day, mind-machine analogies remain problematic, perhaps because of the uncanny experience of doubling and death that invariably accompany them (Mirowski 2002; Wood 2002). Surely, there is circularity in any claim that machines represent the world, and Jevons's machine dreams were haunted by it. Yet, he set this circularity to work to solve concrete problems, sometimes with positive results. For the nonscientist, mimicking a cello player by using a robot can hardly be regarded as an aid in understanding how the genius of Casals transformed the scores of Bach's Suites into great works of art. Yet, such research is currently common practice and sets the standards of intelligibility. It has been my argument that Jevons introduced this mode of research in economics. Jevons's achievement was that he thoroughly reconsidered the relation between evidence and theories, and between man and machines. This did not make political economy just like the natural sciences – it made it a natural science in all things.

Bibliography

Primary Sources

Manuscripts

Augustus De Morgan Papers: University of London Library, Senate House.
Correspondence of William Stanley Jevons with G. H. Lewes: The Beinecke Rare Book and Manuscript Library, Yale University Library.
Jevons Archive. John Rylands Library, Manchester University.
Herschel-Jevons Correspondence. Archives of the Royal Society, London.
Sidgwick Papers, Wren Library, Trinity College, Cambridge.
Whewell Papers, Wren Library, Trinity College, Cambridge.

Published Materials

Atwood, George. 1784. *A Treatise on the Rectilinear Motion and Rotation of Bodies: With a Description of Original Experiments Relative to the Subject.* Cambridge: J. & J. Merrill.

Babbage, Charles. 1830. *Reflections on the Decline of Science in England, and on Some of Its Causes.* London: B. Fellowes.

[1835] 1963. *On the Economy of Machinery and Manufactures.* New York: Augustus M. Kelley.

1989. *The Works of Charles Babbage.* Edited by M. Campbell-Kelly and P. M. Roget. London: William Pickering.

Bain, Alexander. 1855. *The Senses and the Intellect.* London: John W. Parker and Son.

1859. *The Emotions and the Will.* London: John W. Parker and Son.

1867. On the Correlation of Force in Its Bearing on Mind. *Macmillan's Magazine.* **95**: 372–383.

1868. *The Senses and the Intellect.* London: Longmans Green and Co.

1882. *John Stuart Mill: A Criticism with Personal Recollections.* London: Longmans Green and Co.

1893. The Respective Spheres and Mutual Helps of Introspection and Psycho-Physical Experiment in Psychology. *Mind.* **2**: 42–53.

Barratt, Alfred. [1869] 1991. *Physical Ethics, or, the Science of Action*. Bristol: Thoemmes.

——. 1877. The "Suppression" of Egoism. *Mind*. **2**.6: 167–186.

Bastian, H. Charlton. 1869a. On the Physiology of Thinking. *The Fortnightly Review*. **15**: 57–71.

——. 1869b. On the "Muscular Sense" and on the Physiology of Thinking. *The British Medical Journal*. **15**: 394–396.

——. 1869c. Remarks on the "Muscular Sense" and on the Physiology of Thinking. *The British Medical Journal*. **15**: 437–439.

Belsham, Thomas. [1789] 1996. *An Introduction to the Principles of Morals and Legislation*. Oxford: Clarendon.

——. 1801. *Elements of the Philosophy of the Mind, and of Moral Philosophy: To Which Is Prefixed a Compendium of Logic*. London: J. Johnson St. Paul's Churchyard.

Bentham, Jeremy. 1995. *The Panopticon Writings*. Edited by M. Boézoviéc. London: Verso.

Boerhaave, Hermanni. [1703] 1964. *De usu ratiocinii mechanici in medicina: oratio habita in auditorio magno XXIV. Septembris. MDCCIII*. [S.l.: s.n.].

Boole George. 1847. *The Mathematical Analysis of Logic: Being an Essay towards a Calculus of Deductive Reasoning*. Cambridge: Macmillan Barclay & Macmillan.

——. [1854] 1958. *An Investigation of the Laws of Thought*. New York: Dover.

Bowring, John. 1843. *The Works of Jeremy Bentham*. Edinburgh: William Tait.

Cairnes, John Elliot. 1857. *The Character and Logical Method of Political Economy*. London: Longman Brown Green Longmans and Roberts.

——. 1862. *The Slave Power*. New York: Carleton.

——. [1873] 1965. *Essays in Political Economy*. New York: Augustus M. Kelly.

——. [1875] 1965. *The Character and Logical Method of Political Economy*. New York: Kelley.

Carpenter, William B. 1852. On the Relation of Mind and Matter. *British and Foreign Medico-chirurgical Review*. **10**. Oct.: 506–518.

——. 1855. *Principles of Human Physiology*, 5th edition. London: Churchill.

——. 1875. On the Doctrine of Human Automatism. *The Contemporary Review*. **25**: 397–416.

Chambers, Ephraim. 1741. *Cyclopaedia or, an Universal Dictionary of Arts and Sciences*. 2 Vols. London: D. Midwinter, M. Senex, R. Gosling, et al.

Comte, Auguste. 1975. *Cours de Philosophie Positive*. 2 Vols. Paris: Hernan.

De Morgan, Augustus. 1842. *The Differential and Integral Calculus*. London: Baldwin.

——. 1847. *Formal Logic, or, The Calculus of Inference, Necessary and Probable*. London: Taylor & Walton.

——. 1850. On the Symbols of Logic, The Theory of the Syllogism and in Particular of the Copula and the Application of the Theory of Probabilities to Some Questions of Evidence. *Transactions of the Cambridge Philosophical Society*. **9**: 79–127.

——. 1854. Account of a Correspondence between Mr. George Barrett and Mr. Francis Baily. *The Assurance Magazine, and Journal of the Institute of Actuaries*. 185–199.

——. 1860. *Syllabus of a Proposed System of Logic*. London: Walton & Maberly.

De Morgan, Sophia. 1882. *Memoir of Augustus De Morgan*. London: Longmans Green and Co.

Dickens, Charles. 1994. *Hard Times*. London: Everyman.

Edgeworth, Francis Ysidro. 1876. Mr. Matthew Arnold on Bishop Butler's Doctrine of Self-Love. *Mind*. **1**.4: 570–571.

1877. *New and Old Methods of Ethics, or "Physical Ethics" and "Methods of Ethics"*. Oxford: James Parker & Co.

1879. The Hedonic Calculus. *Mind*. **4**: 349–409.

[1881] 1967. *Mathematical Psychics. An Essay on the Application of Mathematics to the Moral Sciences*. New York: Augustus M. Kelly.

1994. *Edgeworth on Chance, Economic Hazard, and Statistics*. Edited by P. Mirowski. Lanham, MD: Rowman & Littlefield.

Frisch, Ragnar. 1933. Propagation Problems and Impulse Problems in Dynamic Economics. In: *Economic Essays in Honour of Gustav Cassel*. pp. 171–205. London: Allan & Unwin.

Grove, W. R. 1846. *On the Correlation of Physical Forces*. London: Highley.

Guy, William A. 1879. On Tabular Analysis. *Journal of the Statistical Society of London*. **42**.3: 644–662.

Hall, Marshall. 1837. *Memoirs on the Nervous System*. London.

Hamilton, Sir William. 1829. M. Cousin's *Course of Philosophy*. *Edinburgh Review*.

1833. Logic. In Reference to the Recent English Treatises on that Science. *Edinburgh Review*. **66**(April): 194–238.

Hartley, David. [1746] 1967. *Various Conjectures on the Perception, Notion, and Generation of Ideas (1746)*. Edited by M. Kallich. New York: Kraus.

[1749] 1967. *Observations on Man, His Frame, His Duty, and His Expectations*. Hildesheim: Georg Olms.

Haughton, Samuel. 1870. On the Natural Laws of Muscular Exertion. *Nature*. **2**: 324–325.

1871. On the Natural Laws of Muscular Exertion II. *Nature*. **3**: 289–293.

1873. *Principles of Animal Mechanics*. London.

Heath, D. D. 1868. Professor Bain on the Doctrine of the Correlation of Force and Its Bearing on Mind. *The Contemporary Review*. **8**: 57–78.

Helmholtz, Hermann von. 1995. *Science and Culture: Popular and Philosophical Essays*. Edited by D. Cahan. Chicago: University of Chicago Press.

Herschel, John F. W. 1861. *Meteorology*. Edinburgh.

Howard, Luke. 1803. On the Modification of Clouds and on the Principles of their Production, Suspension, and Destruction. *Journal of Natural Philosophy, Chemistry, and the Arts*. **17**: 3–32.

1812. The Natural History of Clouds. *Journal of Natural Philosophy, Chemistry and the Arts*. **30**: 35–62.

Hume, David. [1739] 1975. *A Treatise of Human Nature*. Oxford: Clarendon.

Hutcheson, Francis. 1725. *An Inquiry into the Original of Our Ideas of Beauty and Virtue*. London: Darby Bettesworth &c.

Huxley, Thomas. 1874. On the Hypothesis that Animals are Automata. *Fortnightly Review*. **16**: 555–580.

Inoue, Takutoshi. 2002. *W. Stanley Jevons: Collected Reviews and Obituaries*. 2 Vols. Bristol: Thoemmes.

James, William. 1884. On Some Omissions of Introspective Psychology. *Mind*. **9**.33: 1–26.

Jenkin, Fleeming. 1887. *Papers Literary, Scientific, &c.* 2 Vols. London: Longmans Green and Co.

Jennings, Richard. [1855] 1969. *Natural Elements of Political Economy.* New York: Augustus M. Kelley.

Jevons, Harriet A. 1886. *Letters and Journal of William Stanley Jevons.* London: Macmillan.

Jevons, W. Stanley. 1857. On the Cirrous Form of Cloud. *London, Edinburgh and Dublin Philosophical Magazine and Journal of Science.* **14**.90: 22–35.

1858a. On Clouds; Their Various Forms, and Producing Causes. *Sydney Magazine of Science and Art.* **1**.8: 163–176.

1858b. On the Forms of Clouds. *London, Edinburgh and Dublin Philosophical Magazine and Journal of Science.* **15**.100: 241–255.

1859. Some Data Concerning the Climate of Australia and New Zealand. In: *Waugh's Australian Almanac for the Year 1859.* pp. 47–98. Sydney: Waugh.

1863a. Balance. In: *Dictionary of Chemistry and the Allied Branches of the Other Sciences.* Edited by H. Watts. Vol. 1. pp. 481–491. London: Longman Green Longman Roberts and Green.

1863b. *A Serious Fall in the Value of Gold Ascertained, and Its Social Effects Set Forth, With Two Diagrams.* London: Stanford.

1864. Gold-Assay. In: *Dictionary of Chemistry and the Allied Branches of the Other Sciences.* Edited by H. Watts. Vol. 2. pp. 932–938. Longman Green Longman Roberts and Green.

1865. *The Coal Question: An Inquiry Concerning the Progress of the Nation, and the Probable Exhaustion of Our Coal-mines.* London: Macmillan.

[1865] 1884. On the Variation of Prices and the Value of the Currency since 1782. In: *Investigations in Currency and Finance.* Edited by H. Foxwell. pp. 119–150. London: Macmillan.

1866. Brief Account of a General Mathematical Theory of Political Economy. *Journal of the Statistical Society of London.* **29**: 282–287.

1867a. Sir. B. C. Brodie's Chemical Symbols. *Laboratory.* **1**: 220.

1867b. Calculus of Chemical Operations. *Laboratory.* **1**: 256–257.

1870a. Opening Address of the President of Section F. *Journal of the Statistical Society of London.* **33**.3: 309–326.

1870b. On the Natural Laws of Muscular Exertion. *Nature.* **2**: 158–160.

1870c. *Elementary Lessons in Logic: Deductive and Inductive: With Copious Questions and Examples and a Vocabulary of Logical Terms.* London: Macmillan.

1871. *The Theory of Political Economy.* London: Macmillan.

1871a. The Power of Numerical Discrimination. *Nature.* **3**: 281–282.

1871b. Helmholtz on the Axioms of Geometry. *Nature.* **4**: 481–482.

[1874] 1958. *The Principles of Science: A Treatise on Logic and Scientific Method.* New York: Dover.

1875. Comte's Philosophy. *Nature.* **12**: 491–492.

1876. Boole. In: *Encyclopedia Britannica,* 9th Edition. pp. 47–48.

1877a. De Morgan. In: *Encyclopedia Britannica,* 9th Edition. pp. 64–67.

1877b. Cram. *Mind.* **2**: 193–207.

1878a. On the Movement of Microscopic Particles Suspended in Liquids. *Quarterly Journal of Science.* **15 o.s., 8 n.s.**: 167–186.

1878b. Remarks on the Statistical Use of the Arithmometer. *Journal of the Statistical Society of London.* **41**: 597–601.

[1879] 1970. *The Theory of Political Economy.* Edited by R. D. C. Black. Harmondsworth: Penguin.

1879. Remarks on W. A. Guy's paper "On Tabular Analysis", read before the Statistical Society of London. *Journal of the Statistical Society of London.* **42**: 657–660.

[1882] 1968. *The State in Relation to Labour.* New York: Augustus M. Kelley.

1882. The Solar-Commercial Cycle. *Nature.* **26**: 226–228.

1883. *Methods of Social Reform.* London: Macmillan.

1884. *Investigations in Currency and Finance.* London: Macmillan.

[1890] 1971. *Pure Logic and Other Minor Works.* New York: Burt Franklin.

1905. *The Principles of Economics and Other Papers.* London: Macmillan.

1972–1981. *Papers and Correspondence.* Vols. 1–7. Edited by R. D. C. Black and R. Könekamp. London: Macmillan.

Jones, Richard. [1831] 1964. *An Essay on the Distribution of Wealth and on the Sources of Taxation.* New York: Kelley.

[1859] 1964. *Literary Remains Consisting of Lectures & Tracts on Political Economy.* Edited by W. Whewell. New York: Kelley.

JSSL. 1838. Introduction. *Journal of the Statistical Society of London.* **1.1**: 1–5.

Juglar, Clément. [1862] 1889. *Des crises commerciales et de leur retour périodique en France, en Angleterre et aux États-Unis.* Paris: Guillaumin.

Laycock, Thomas. 1845. On the Reflex Function of the Brain. *British and Foreign Medical Journal.* **19**: 298–311.

1860. *Mind and Brain: or, the Correlations of Conciousness and Organisation: With Their Applications to Philosophy, Zoology, Physiology, Mental Pathology, and the Practice of Medicine.* London: Simpkin Marshall and Co.

LDP 1865. *Liverpool Daily Post* of 3 October 1865.

Lewes, George Henry. 1874. Imaginary Geometry and the Truth of Axioms. *Fortnightly Review.* **16 n.s.** July: 192–200.

1995. *The Letters of George Henry Lewes.* Edited by W. Baker. Victoria: University of Victoria.

Locke, John. 1978. *An Essay Concerning Human Understanding.* London: Dent.

Marshall, Alfred. 1885. On the Graphic Method of Statistics. *Journal of the Statistical Society of London.* **Jubilee Issue**: 251–260.

Martineau, James. 1872. The Place of Mind in Nature and Intuition in Man. *The Contemporary Review.* **19**: 606–623.

[1885] 1901. *Types of Ethical Theory.* 2 Vols. Oxford: Clarendon.

Marx, Karl. 1969. *Theories of Surplus Value.* London: Lawrence and Wishart.

Mill, James. 1802a. Elements of the Philosophy of the Mind, and of Moral Philosophy. To Which is Prefixed a Compendium of Logic. By Thomas Belsham. *The Anti-Jacobin Review and Magazine.* **12**: 1–13.

1802b. Thomson's System of Chemistry. *The Anti-Jacobin Review and Magazine.* **12**: 161–170.

[1869] 1982. *Analysis of the Phenomena of the Human Mind.* Hildesheim: Georg Olms.

Mill, John Stuart. 1850. The Negro Question. *Littell's Living Age*. **24**: 465–469 (appeared originally in *Fraser's Magazine* 1850).

    1963. *Collected Works of John Stuart Mill*. 33 Vols. Edited by J. M. Robson. Toronto: University of Toronto Press.

Mouat, Frederic J. 1885. History of the Statistical Society of London. *Journal of the Statistical Society of London*. **Jubilee Issue**: 14–62.

Newmarch, William. 1869. Inaugural Address on the Progress and Present Condition of Statistical Inquiry. *Journal of the Statistical Society of London*. **32**.4: 359–390.

    1871. Address as President of the Economy and Trade Department, Social Science Association at Leeds, 10th October, 1871. *Journal of the Statistical Society of London*. **43**.4: 476–498.

Peirce, Charles S. [1887] 1997. Logical Machines. *Modern Logic*. **7**: 71–77.

Playfair, William. 1796. *A Real Statement of the Finances and Resources of Great Britain*. London: Whittingham.

Priestley, Joseph. 1765. *A Chart of Biography*. London: J. Johnson.

    1775. *Hartley's Theory of the Human Mind, on the Principle of the Association of Ideas; with Essays Relating to the Subject of It*. London: J. Johnson.

    [1777] 1976. *Disquisitions Relating to Matter and Spirit*. London: Garland.

    [1778] 1978. *A Free Discussion of the Doctrines of Materialism and Philosophical Necessity*. London: Garland.

    1778. *Miscellaneous Observations Relating to Education*. Bath: Cruttwell.

Raffaelli, Tiziano. 1994. *Alfred Marshall's Early Philosophical Writings*. In: *Research in the History of Economic Thought and Methodology*. Edited by W. Samuels. London and New York: Routledge. Archival Supplement 4.

Reid, Thomas. 1967. *Philosophical Works*. 2 Vols. Hildesheim: Georg Olms.

Ruskin, John. [1830] 1990. *A Tour to the Lakes in Cumberland: John Ruskin's Diary for 1830*. Aldershot: Scholar.

    1854. *Lectures on Architecture and Painting*. London: George Routledge & Sons.

    1903–1912. *The Works of John Ruskin*, 39 Vols. London: Allen.

    1985. *Unto This Last and Other Writings*. Harmondsworth: Penguin.

    1995. *Selected Writings*. London: Everyman.

    1996. *Lectures on Art*. New York: Routledge.

Senior, Nassau W. 1860. Opening Address of the President of Section F of the British Association for the Advancement of Science. *Journal of the Statistical Society of London*. **23**: 357–361.

    1965. *An Outline of the Science of Political Economy*. New York: Kelley.

Sidgwick, Henry. 1873. Review of Mr. Spencer's "Principles of Psychology". *The Spectator*. 798–799.

    [1874] 1962. *The Methods of Ethics*. London: Macmillan.

    [1883] 1996. *The Principles of Political Economy*. Bristol: Thoemmes.

    1996. *The Methods of Ethics*. Bristol: Thoemmes.

Smith, Adam. [1759] 1976. *The Theory of Moral Sentiments*. Oxford: Oxford University Press.

    [1776] 1976. *An Inquiry into the Nature and Causes of the Wealth of Nations*, Vols. 1 & 2. Oxford: Clarendon.

Sonnenschein, Hugo. 1883. *On Jevons' Logical Machine*. New York: Arno.

————. 1883. On Jevons Logical Machine. *Proceedings of the Birmingham Philosophical Society*. IV, Part I: 72–84.

Statistical Society of London. 1851. Minutes of the Seventeenth Annual Meeting of the Statistical Society of London. *Journal of the Statistical Society of London*. **14**.2: 97–108.

Stevin, Simon. 1586. *De Beghinselen der Weeghconst*. Leyden: in de Druckerye van Chr. Plantijn by Françoys van Raphelinghen.

Stewart, Dugald. 1994. *The Collected Works of Dugald Stewart*. 11 Vols. Edited by W. Hamilton and K. Haakonssen. Bristol: Thoemmes.

Stewart, Dugald and John Playfair. 1975. *Dissertations on the Progress of Knowledge*. New York: Arno.

Sully, James. 1874. *Sensation and Intuition: Studies in Psychology and Aesthetics*. London: King.

Tait, Peter Guthrie. 1870. Energy, and Prof. Bain's Logic. *Nature*. **1 Dec.**: 89–90.

Taylor, William Cooke. 1835. Objects and Advantages of Statistical Science. *The Foreign Quarterly Review*. **16**: 205–229.

————. [1841] 1968. *Notes of a Tour in the Manufacturing Districts of Lancashire*. New York: Augustus M. Kelley.

Todhunter, Isaac. [1876] 2001. *William Whewell: An Account of His Writings, with Selections from His Literary and Scientific Correspondence*. 2 Vols. Edited by R. Yeo. Bristol: Thoemmes.

Tyndall, John. 1874. *Address Delivered before the British Association Assembled at Belfast: With Additions*. London: Longmans Green and Co.

Ure, Andrew. 1835. *The Philosophy of Manufactures or An Exposition of the Scientific, Moral, and Commercial Economy of the Factory System*. London: Knight.

Watts, Henry. 1868. *A Dictionary of Chemistry and the Allied Branches of Other Sciences*. London: Longmans Green & Co.

West, Edward F. 1826. *The Price of Corn and the Wages of Labour*. London: J. Hatchard.

Whewell, William. 1830. Mathematical Exposition of Some Doctrines of Political Economy. *Transactions of the Cambridge Philosophical Society*. **3**: 191–230.

————. 1833. *Astronomy and General Physics, Considered with Reference to Natural Theology*. London: Pickering.

————. 1837. Letter to Charles Babbage. *Athenaeum*.

————. 1838. Description of a New Tide-Gauge, Constructed by Mr. T. G. Bunt, and Erected on the Eastern Bank of the River Avon, in front of the Hotwell House, Bristol, 1837. *Philosophical Transactions of the Royal Society of London*. **128**: 249–251.

————. [1847] 1967. *The Philosophy of the Inductive Sciences*. London: Frank Cass.

————. [1860] 1971. *On the Philosophy of Discovery*. New York: Burt Franklin.

————. [1862] 1967. *Six Lectures on Political Economy*. New York: Kelley.

————. 2001. *Collected Works of William Whewell*. Edited by R. Yeo. Bristol: Thoemmes.

Wicksteed, Philip H. 1905. Jevons's Economic Work. *The Economic Journal*. **5**: 432–436.

1949. *The Common Sense of Political Economy and Selected Papers and Reviews on Economic Theory*. Edited by L. Robbins. London: Routledge.
Wordsworth, William. 1969. *The Prelude or Growth of a Poet's Mind (Text of 1805)*. Oxford: Oxford University Press.

Secondary Sources

Akl, Selim G. 1980. *Professor Jevons and His Logical Machine*. Oxford Science Museum.
Aldrich, John. 1987. Jevons as Statistician: The Role of Probability. *The Manchester School*. **55**: 233–256.
1992. Probability and Depreciation: A History of the Stochastic Approach to Index Numbers. *History of Political Economy*. **24**.3: 657–687.
Anderson, Katharine. 2003. Looking at the Sky: The Visual Context of Victorian Meteorology. *British Journal for the History of Science*. **36**.130: 301–332.
Ankersmit, F. R. 1988. Historical Representation. *History and Theory*. **27**.3: 205–228.
2001. *Historical Representation*. Stanford, CA.: Stanford University Press.
Arnon, Arnie. 1990. What Thomas Tooke (and Ricardo) Could Have Known Had They Constructed Price Indexes. In: *Perspectives on the History of Economic Thought*. Edited by D. E. Moggridge. pp. 1–20. Aldershot: Edward Elgar.
1991. *William Tooke*. Aldershot: Edward Elgar.
Ashfield, Andrew and Peter De Bolla. 1996. *The Sublime: A Reader in British Eighteenth-Century Aesthetic Theory*. Cambridge: Cambridge University Press.
Ashworth, William J. 1996. Memory, Efficiency, and Symbolic Analysis: Charles Babbage, John Herschel, and the Industrial Mind. *Isis*. **87**.4: 629–653.
1998. "System of Terror": Samuel Bentham, Accountability and Dockyard Reform during the Napoleonic Wars. *Social History*. **23**.1: 63–79.
Bailer-Jones, Daniela M. 2002. *It Is Still Mechanisms That Make Us Understand*: Mimeo.
Balisciano, Márcia and Steven Medema. 1999. Positive Science, Normative Man: Lionel Robbins and the Political Economy of Art. *History of Political Economy*. **31**, Annual Supplement: 256–284.
Barber, William J. 1975. *British Economic Thought and India, 1600–1858: A Study in the History of Development Economics*. Oxford: Clarendon.
Barfoot, Michael. 1983. *James Gregory (1753–1821) and Scottish Scientific Metaphysics, 1750–1800*. PhD Thesis: University of Edinburgh.
Batchelor, John. 2000. *John Ruskin: No Wealth But Life*. London: Chatto & Windus.
Becher, Harvey W. 1980. Woodhouse, Babbage, Peacock, and Modern Algebra. *Historia Mathematica*. **7**: 389–400.
1981. William Whewell and Cambridge Mathematics. *Historical Studies in the Physical Sciences*. **11**.1: 1–48.
1992. The Whewell Story. *Annals of Science*. **49**: 377–384.
Beer, Gillian. 1996. *Open Fields: Science in Cultural Encounter*. Oxford: Clarendon.
Bellot, H. Hale. 1929. *University College, London, 1826–1926*. London: University of London Press.

Beniger, James and Dorothy L. Robyn. 1978. Quantitative Graphs in Statistics: A Brief History. *American Statistician*. **32**: 1–11.

Benjamin, Walter. 1978. Über den Begriff der Geschichte. In: *Gesammelte Schriften 1.2*. Edited by W. Tiedemann. Frankfurt: Suhrkamp.

Bensaude–Vincent, Bernadette. 1992. The Balance: Between Chemistry and Politics. *The Eighteenth Century*. **33**.3: 217–237.

Benschop, Ruth. 1998. What is a Tachistoscope? Historical Explorations of an Instrument. *Science in Context*. **11**.1: 23–50.

Benschop, Ruth and Douwe Draaisma. 2000. In Pursuit of Precision: The Callibration of Minds and Machines in Late Nineteenth-Century Psychology. *Annals of Science*. **57**: 1–25.

Berg, Maxine. 1980. *The Machinery Question and the Making of Political Economy 1815–1848*. Cambridge: Cambridge University Press.

1994. *The Age of Manufactures 1700–1820: Industry, Innovation and Work in Britain*. London & New York: Routledge.

Bergson, Henri. 1889. *Essai sur les données immédiates de la conscience*. Paris: Alcan.

1959. *Oeuvres*. Paris: Presses Universitaires de France.

Black, R. D. Collison. 1972a. Jevons, Bentham, and De Morgan. *Economica*. **39**: 119–134.

1972b. W. S. Jevons and the Foundation of Modern Economics. *History of Political Economy*. **4**: 364–378.

1990. Jevons, Marshall and the Utilitarian Tradition. *Scottish Journal of Political Economy*. **37**.1: 5–17.

Black, R. D. Collison, Coats, Alfred W., and Craufurd D. W. Goodwin. 1973. *The Marginalist Revolution in Economics: Interpretation and Evaluation*. Durham: Duke University Press.

Blaug, Mark. 1976. *Ricardian Economics: A Historical Study*. Westport, CT: Greenwood.

1985. *Economic Theory in Retrospect*. Cambridge: Cambridge University Press.

1992. *The Methodology of Economics, or How Economists Explain*. Cambridge: Cambridge University Press.

Bogaard, Adrienne van den. 1998. *Configuring the Economy: The Emergence of a Modelling Practice in the Netherlands, 1920–1955*: University of Amsterdam.

Bogen, James and James Woodward. 1988. Saving the Phenomena. *The Philosophical Review*. **97**. July: 303–352.

Bordo, Michael D. 1975. John E. Cairnes on the Effects of the Australian Gold Discoveries 1851–73: An Early Application of the Methodology of Positive Economics. *History of Political Economy*. **7**.3: 337–359.

Boring, Edwin G. 1950. *A History of Experimental Psychology*. New York: Appleton.

Bostaph, Sam and Y. N. Shieh. 1986. W. S. Jevons and Lardner's Railway Economy. In: *William Stanley Jevons – Critical Assessments*. Edited by J. C. Wood. pp. 316–332. London and New York: Routledge.

Boumans, Marcel. 1992. *A Case of Limited Physics Transfer: Jan Tinbergen's Resources for Re-shaping Economics*: University of Amsterdam.

2001. Fisher's Instrumental Approach to Index Numbers. *History of Political Economy*. **33**. Annual Supplement: 313–344.

2005. *How Economists Model the World into Numbers*. London and New York: Routledge.

Boumans, Marcel J. and Mary S. Morgan. 2004. The Secrets Hidden by Two-Dimensionality Modelling the Economy as a Hydraulic System. In: *Displaying the Third Dimension: Models in the Science, Technology and Medicine*. Edited by S. D. Shadarevian and N. Hopwood. Stanford: Stanford University Press.

Bower, George Spencer. 1881. *Hartley and James Mill*. London: Sampson Low Marston Searle and Rivington.

Bowley, Arthur L. 1901. *Elements of Statistics*. London: King.

Brock, W. H. 1967. *The Atomic Debates: Brodie and the Rejection of the Atomic Theory*. Leicester: Leicester University Press.

Bromley, A. G. 1987. The Evolution of Babbage's Calculating Engines. *Annals of the History of Computing*. **9**: 113–136.

Brown, Vivienne. 1994. *Adam Smith's Discourse: Canonicity, Commerce and Conscience*. London and New York: Routledge.

Brownlie, A. D. and M. F. Lloyd Prichard. 1963. Professor Fleeming Jenkin, 1833–1885, Pioneer in Engineering and Political Economy. *Oxford Economic Papers*. **15**.3: 204–216.

Bryson, Gladys. 1945. *Man and Society: The Scottish Inquiry of the Eighteenth Century*. Princeton, NJ: Princeton University Press.

Buck, G. H. and S. M. Hunka. 1999. W. Stanley Jevons, Allan Marquand, and the Origins of Digital Computing. *IEEE Annals of the History of Computing*. **21**.4: 21–27.

Burke, I. [1955] 1988. Australia's First Pictorialist. In: *William Stanley Jevons: Critical Assessments*, 3 Vols. Edited by J. C. Wood. pp. 188–196. London and New York: Routledge.

Cahan, David. 1994. *Hermann von Helmholtz and the Foundations of Nineteenth-Century Science*. Berkeley: University of California Press.

Caldwell, Bruce. 2003. *Hayek's Challenge: An Intellectual Biography of F. A. Hayek*. Chicago: Chicago University Press.

Camerer, C. F. 2003. Strategizing in the Brain. *Science*. **300**.5626: 1673–1674.

Campbell, R. H. and Andrew S. Skinner. 1982. *The Origins and Nature of the Scottish Enlightenment*. Edinburgh: Donald.

Cannon, Susan Faye. 1978. *Science in Culture: The Early Victorian Period*. New York: Science History Publications.

Cannon, Walter F. 1964a. Scientists and Broad Churchmen: Early Victorian Intellectual Network. *Journal of British Studies*. **4**.1: 65.

1964b. The Normative Role of Science in Early Victorian Thought. *Journal of the History of Ideas*. **25**.4: 487.

Carmichael, Colin. 1950. *Kent's Mechanical Engineers Handbook, Vol. 1: Design and Production Volume*. New York, London and Sydney: John Wiley and Sons.

Carr, David. 1986. *Time, Narrative, and History*. Bloomington: Indiana University Press.

Carter, T. N. 1907. The Concept of an Economic Quantity. *Quarterly Journal of Economics*. **21**. May: 427–448.

Cartwright, David Edgar. 1999. *Tides: A Scientific History*. Cambridge: Cambridge University Press.

Cartwright, Nancy. 1983. *How the Laws of Physics Lie*. Oxford: Clarendon.

1989. *Nature's Capacities and Their Measurement*. Oxford: Clarendon.

1999. *The Dappled World: A Study of the Boundaries of Science*. Cambridge: Cambridge University Press.

Chaigneau, Nicolas 1996. *Utilitarisme et Psychophysique dans les New and Old Methods of Ethics d'Edgeworth*. Lille, mimeo.

1997. *Contrat et Utilité. Origines et Fondements de la Théorie de l'Échange de Francis Ysidro Edgeworth*. Paris: Université de Paris I Panthéon-Sorbonne, PhD Thesis.

2002. Jevons, Edgeworth et les "Sensations Subtiles du Coeur Humain": l'Influence de la Psychophysiologie sur L'Economie Marginaliste. *Revue d'Histoire des Sciences Humaines*. **1**.7: 13–40.

Chandler, George. 1953. *William Roscoe of Liverpool*. London: Batsford.

Chang, Hasok. 2001. Spirit, Air, and Quicksilver: The Search for the "Real" Scale of Temperature. *Historical Studies in the Physical and Biological Sciences*. **31**.2: 249–284.

Checkland, S. G. 1949. The Propagation of Ricardian Economics in England. *Economica*. **16**: 40–52.

[1951] 1988. Economic Opinion in England as Jevons Found It. In: *William Stanley Jevons: Critical Assessments*, 3 Vols. Edited by J. C. Wood. pp. 125–145. London and New York: Routledge.

Cianci, John and Peter Nicholls. 2001. *Ruskin and Modernism*. Basingstoke: Palgrave.

Clark, B. and J. B. Foster. 2001. William Stanley Jevons and The Coal Question – An Introduction to Jevons's "Of the Economy of Fuel". *Organization & Environment*. **14**.1: 93–98.

Clercq, Peter de. 1997. *The Leiden Cabinet of Physics: A Descriptive Catalogue*. Leiden: Museum Boerhaave.

Coleman, William O. 1996. How Theory Came to English Classical Economics. *Scottish Journal of Political Economy*. **43**.2: 207–228.

Collins, Harry. 1990. *Artificial Experts*. Cambridge: MIT Press.

Comim, Flavio V. 1998. Jevons and Menger Re-homogenized? Jaffé after 20 Years: A Comment on Peart. *American Journal of Economics and Sociology*. **57**.3: 341–344.

Costigan-Eaves, Patricia and Michael Macdonald-Ross. 1990. William Playfair (1759–1823). *Statistical Science*. **5**.3: 318–326.

Cowles, Thomas. 1937. Malthus, Darwin, and Bagehot: A Study in the Transference of a Concept. *Isis*. **26**.2: 341–348.

Creedy, John. 1986. On the King Davenant "Law" of Demand. *Scottish Journal of Political Economy*. **33**.3: 193–212.

1992. *Demand and Exchange in Economic Analysis: A History from Cournot to Marshall*. Aldershot: Edward Elgar.

Cullen, M. 1975. *The Statistical Movement in Early Victorian Britain: The Foundation of Economic Research*. Hassocks: Harvester.

Danziger, Kurt. 1990. *Constructing the Subject: Historical Origins of Psychological Research*. Cambridge: Cambridge University Press.

1997. *Naming the Mind: How Psychology Found Its Language*. London: Sage.

1982. Mid-Nineteenth-Century British Psycho-Physiology: A Neglected Chapter in the History of Psychology. In: *The Problematic Science: Psychology in Nineteenth Century Thought*. Edited by W. R. Woodward and M. G. Ash. New York: Praeger.

Daston, Lorraine J. 1978. British Responses to Psycho-Physiology, 1860–1900. *Isis*. **69**.247: 192–208.

1982. The Theory of Will versus the Science of Mind. In: *The Problematic Science: Psychology in Nineteenth Century Thought*. Edited by W. Woodward and M. G. Ash. pp. 88–115. New York: Praeger.

1994. Enlightenment Calculations. *Critical Inquiry*. **21**: 182–102.

Daston, Lorraine J. and Peter Galison. 1992. The Image of Objectivity. *Representations*. **40**. Fall: 81–128.

Davies, J. Llewelyn. 1904. *The Working Men's College 1854–1904*. London: Macmillan.

Davis, John B. 2003. *The Theory of the Individual in Economics: Identity and Value*. London and New York: Routledge.

De Marchi, Neil B. 1972. Mill and Cairnes and the Emergence of Marginalism in England. *History of Political Economy*. **4**.3: 344–363.

1973. The Noxious Influence of Authority: A Correction of Jevons' Charge. *The Journal of Law & Economics*. **16**.1: 179–189.

1986. Mill's Unrevised Philosophy of Economics: A Comment on Hausman. *Philosophy of Science*. **53**: 89–100.

2002. Putting Evidence in Its Place: John Mill's Early Struggles with "Facts in the Concrete". In: *Fact or Fiction*. Edited by U. Mäki. pp. 304–328. Cambridge: Cambridge University Press.

De Marchi, Neil B. and Hans J. Van Miegroet. 1999. Ingenuity, Preference, and the Pricing of Pictures. The Smith-Reynolds Connection. In: *Economic Engagements with Art*. Edited by N. B. De Marchi and C. D. W. Goodwin. pp. 379–412. Durham, NC: Duke University Press.

Debru, Claude. 2001. Helmholtz and the Psychophysiology of Time. *Science in Context*. **14**.3: 471–492.

Desrosières, Alain. 1993. *La Politique des Grands Nombres: Histoire de la Raison Statistique*. Paris: La Découverte.

Diagne, Souleymane Bachir. 1989. *Boole, l'Oiseau de Nuit en Plein Jour; un Savant, une Époque*. Paris: Belin.

Dijksterhuis, E. J. 1950. *De Mechanisering van het Wereldbeeld*. Amsterdam: Meulenhoff.

Dodd, T. 1988. *A Note on Jevons Logical Piano*. Oxford Science Museum. Mimeo.

Donoghue, Mark. 1998. John Elliot Cairnes and the "Rehabilitation" of the Classical Wage Fund Doctrine. *The Manchester School of Economic and Social Studies*. **66**: 396–417.

Dubbey, J. M. 1978. *The Mathematical Work of Charles Babbage*. Cambridge: Cambridge University Press.

Duhem, Pierre. 1906. *La Théorie Physique: Son Object et Sa Structure*. Paris: Chevalier & Rivière.

1981. *The Aim and Structure of Physical Theory*. New York: Atheneum.

Durand-Richard. 2000. Logic versus Algebra. In: *A Boole Anthology*. Edited by J. Gasser. pp. 139–166. Dordrecht: Kluwer.

Eatwell, John, Murray Milgate, et al. 1998. *The New Palgrave: A Dictionary of Economics*. London and New York: Macmillan.

Ekelund, Robert B., Jr. and F. Hébert Robert. 1999. *Secret Origins of Modern Microeconomics: Dupuit and the Engineers*. Chicago and London: Chicago University Press.

Ekelund, Robert B., Jr. and Mark Thornton. 2001. William T. Thornton and Nineteenth Century Economic Policy: A Review Essay. *Journal of the History of Economic Thought*. **23**.4: 513–531.

Elster, Jon. 1999. *Alchemies of the Mind: Rationality and the Emotions*. Cambridge: Cambridge University Press.

Emerson, Roger L. 1988. Science and the Origins and Concerns of the Scottish Enlightenment. *History of Science*. **26**.4.

Emerson, Sheila. 1993. *Ruskin: The Genesis of Invention*. Cambridge: Cambridge University Press.

Enros, Philip. 1983. The Analytical Society (1812-1813): The Precursor of the Renewal of Cambridge Mathematics. *Historia Mathematica*. **10**: 24–47.

Feldhay, Rivka. 1994. Narrative Constraints on Historical Writing: The Case of the Scientific Revolution. *Science in Context*. **7**.1: 7–24.

Fisch, Menachem. 1991. *William Whewell: Philosopher of Science*. Oxford: Clarendon.

   1994. "The Emergency Which Has Arrived": The Problematic History of 19th-Century British Algebra – A Programmatic Outline. *British Journal for the History of Science*. **27**.94: 247–276.

Fisch, Menachem and Simon Schaffer. 1991. *William Whewell: A Composite Portrait*. Oxford: Clarendon.

Fisher, Irving. 1892. *Mathematical Investigations in the Theory of Value and Prices, Transactions of the Connecticut Academy*, Vol. IX. New Haven: Yale University Press.

Fogel, Robert William and Stanley L. Engerman. 1974. *Time on the Cross: The Economics of American Negro Slavery*. Boston: Little Brown.

Fontaine, Philippe. 1998. Menger, Jevons, and Walras Un-homogenized, De-homogenized, and Homogenized: A Comment on Peart. *American Journal of Economics and Sociology*. **57**.3: 333–339.

Forget, Evelyn L. 1989. J. S. Mill and J. E. Cairnes on Natural Value: The Role of Expectations in Late-Classical Thought. *History of Political Economy*. **21**: 103.

Forster, Paul. 1997. Kant, Boole and Peirce's Early Metaphysics. *Synthese*. **113**: 43–70.

Friedman, Milton. 1953. The Methodology of Positive Economics. In: *Essays in Positive Economics*. pp. 3–43. Chicago: Chicago University Press.

Frisch, Ragnar. [1926] 1971. On a Problem in Pure Economics. In: *Preferences, Utility, and Demand*. Edited by J. S. Chipman. New York: Harcourt Brace Jovanovich.

   1933. Propagation Problems and Impulse Problems in Dynamic Economics. In: *Economic Essays in Honour of Gustav Cassel*. pp. 171–205. London: Allan and Unwin.

Funkhouser, H. Gray. 1935. Playfair and His Charts. *Economic History: A Supplement to the Economic Journal*. 103–109.

1938. Historical Development of the Graphical Representation of Statistical Data. *Osiris*. **3f**: 269–404.

Gagnier, Regenia. 1993. "On the Insatiability of Human Wants: Economic and Aesthetic Man. *Victorian Studies*. **36**.2: 125–153.

2000. *The Insatiability of Human Wants: Economics and Aesthetics in Market Society*. Chicago: University of Chicago Press.

Galison, Peter. 1997. *Image and Logic: A Material Culture of Microphysics*. Chicago: University of Chicago Press.

1998. Judgment against Objectivity. In: *Picturing Science, Producing Art*. Edited by C. A. Jones and P. Galison. pp. 327–359. London and New York: Routledge.

Galison, Peter and Alexi Assmus. 1989. Artificial Clouds, Real Particles. In: *The Uses of Experiment*. Edited by D. Gooding, T. Pinch and S. Schaffer. Cambridge: Cambridge University Press.

Galison, Peter, David J. Stump, et al. 1996. *The Disunity of Science: Boundaries, Contexts, and Power*. Stanford: Stanford University Press.

Garber, Elisabeth. 1999. *The Language of Physics: The Calculus and the Development of Theoretical Physics in Europe, 1750–1914*. Boston, Basel and Berlin: Birkhäuser.

Gardner, M. 1958. *Logic Machines and Diagrams*. New York: McGraw-Hill.

Gasser, James. 2000. *A Boole Anthology: Recent and Classical Studies in the Logic of George Boole*. Dordrecht: Kluwer.

Geddes, Patrick. 1884. *Ruskin: Economist*. Edinburgh: William Brown.

Golby, J. M. and A. W. Purdue. 1984. *The Civilisation of the Crowd, Popular Culture in England 1750–1900*. London: Batsford Academic and Educational.

Goldman, Lawrence. 1983. The Origins of British "Social Science": Political Economy, Natural Science and Statistics, 1830–1835. *The Historical Journal*. **26**.3: 587–616.

Goldstine, H. H. 1972. *The Computer from Pascal to von Neumann*. Princeton: Princeton University Press.

Golinski, Jan. 1994. Precision Instruments and the Demonstrative Order of Proof in Lavoisier's Chemistry. *Osiris: Studies on the History and Philosophy of Science, and on the History of Learning and Culture*. **9**: 30–47.

Gooding, David, Trevor Pinch, and Simon Schaffer. 1989. *The Uses of Experiment: Studies in the Natural Sciences*. Cambridge: Cambridge University Press.

Goodwin, Craufurd D. 1970. British Economists and Australian Gold. *The Journal of Economic History*. **30**.2: 405–426.

Grampp, William D. 1970. "Edward West Reconsidered". *History of Political Economy*. **2**.2: 316–343.

Grattan-Guinness, Ivor. 1990a. *Convolutions in French Mathematics: 1800–1840*. Basel, Boston, and Berlin: Birkhäuser.

1990b. The Varieties of Mechanics by 1800. *Historia Mathematica*. **17**: 313–338.

1990c. Work for the Hairdressers: The Production of de Prony's Logarithmic and Trigonometric Tables. *Annals of the History of Computing*. **12**.3: 177–185.

1991. The Correspondence between George Boole and Stanley Jevons, 1863–1864. *History and Philosophy of Logic*. **12**: 15–35.

1992. Charles Babbage as an Algorithmic Thinker. *IEEE Annals of the History of Computing*. **14**.3: 34–48.

2002. "In Some Parts Rather Rough": A Recently Discovered Manuscript Version of William Stanley Jevons's "General Mathematical Theory of Political Economy" (1862). *History of Political Economy*. **34**.4: 685–726.

Grattan-Guinness, Ivor and Gerard Bornet. 1997. *George Boole : Selected Manuscripts on Logic and Its Philosophy*. Basel: Birkhäuser.

Griswold, Charles L. 1999. *Adam Smith and the Virtues of the Enlightenment*. Cambridge: Cambridge University Press.

Hacking, Ian. 1975. *The Emergence of Probability*. London: Cambridge University Press.

1983. *Representing and Intervening*. Cambridge: Cambridge University Press.

Hackney, Melissa. 1998. *The Decisive Role of Art in Defining Victorian Manchester's Social Divisions and Cultural Status*. BA Thesis, University of Manchester.

Hailperin, T. 1981. Boole's Algebra Isn't Boolean Algebra. *Mathematics Magazine*. **54**: 172–184.

Halévy, Elie. [1901] 1995. *La Formation du Radicalisme Philosophique*. 3 Vols. Paris: Presses Universitaires de France.

Hall, Vance M. D. 1979. The Contribution of the Physiologist, William Benjamin Carpenter (1813–1885), to the Development of the Principles of the Correlation of Forces and the Conservation of Energy. *Medical History*. **23**: 129–155.

Hamblyn, Richard. 2001. *The Invention of Clouds: How an Amateur Meteorologist Forged the Language of the Skies*. New York: Farrar Straus and Giroux.

Hands, D. Wade. 2001. *Reflection without Rules: Economic Methodology and Contemporary Science Theory*. Cambridge: Cambridge University Press.

Hankins, Thomas L. 1999. Blood, Dirt, and Nomograms: A Particular History of Graphs. *Isis*. **90**: 50–80.

Hanson, Norwood Russell. 1965. *Patterns of Discovery: An Inquiry into the Conceptual Foundations of Science*. Cambridge: Cambridge University Press.

Harley, Robert. 1879. The Stanhope Demonstrator: An Instrument for Performing Logical Operations. *Mind*. **4**: 192–210.

Hartman, Geoffrey H. 1970. History-Writing as Answerable Style. *New Literary History*. **2**.1: 73–83.

Haskell, Thomas L. 1993. Persons as Uncaused Causes: John Stuart Mill, the Spirit of Capitalism, the "Invention" of Formalism. In: *The Culture of the Market: Historical Essays*. Edited by T. Haskell, L. I. Teichgraeber, and F. Richard. pp. 441–502. Cambridge: Cambridge University Press.

Hausman, Daniel M. 1981. John Stuart Mill's Philosophy of Economics. *Philosophy of Science*. **48**: 363–385.

1992. *The Inexact and Separate Science of Economics*. Cambridge: Cambridge University Press.

Hébert, R. F. 1998. Jevons and Menger Re-Homogenized: Who is the Real "Odd Man Out"? A Comment on Peart. *American Journal of Economics and Sociology*. **57**.3: 327–332.

Heertje, Arnold. [1982] 1988. An Important Letter from W. S. Jevons to L. Walras. In: *William Stanley Jevons: Critical Assessments*, 3 Vols. Edited by J. C. Wood. pp. 261–265. London and New York: Routledge.

Heffernan, James A. W. 1984. *The Re-Creation of Landscape: A Study of Wordsworth, Coleridge, Constable, and Turner.* Hanover and London: University Press of New England.

Heidelberger, Michael. 1993. *Die Innere Seite der Natur: Gustav Theodor Fechners wissenschaftlich-philosophische Weltauffassung,* 2 Vols. Frankfurt a.M.: Klostermann.

Henderson, James P. 1996. *Early Mathematical Economics: William Whewell and the British Case.* Lanham, MD: Rowman & Littlefield.

Hesse, Mary B. 1970. *Models and Analogies in Science.* Notre Dame: University of Notre Dame Press.

1974. *The Structure of Scientific Inference.* London and New York: Macmillan.

Hewison, Robert. 1976. *John Ruskin: the Argument of the Eye.* Princeton: Princeton University Press.

Hilton, Tim. 1985. *John Ruskin: The Early Years 1819–1859.* New Haven: Yale University Press.

2000. *John Ruskin: The Later Years.* New Haven: Yale University Press.

Hilts, Victor L. 1978. Aliis Exterendum, or, the Origins of the Statistical Society of London. *Isis.* **69**.1: 21–43.

Hirsch, Abraham. 1978. J. E. Cairnes' Methodology in Theory and Practice. *History of Political Economy.* **10**.2: 322–331.

1992. John Stuart Mill on Verification and the Business of Science. *History of Political Economy.* **24** 843–866.

Hollander, Samuel. 1983. William Whewell and John Stuart Mill on the Methodology of Political Economy. *Studies in History and Philosophy of Science.* **14**.2: 127–168.

Hollander, Samuel and Sandra Peart. 1999. John Stuart Mill's Method in Principle and Practice: A Review of the Evidence. *Journal of the History of Economic Thought.* **21**.4: 369–397.

Holmes, Frederic L. 2000. The Evolution of Lavoisier's Chemical Apparatus. In: *Instruments and Experimentation in the History of Chemistry.* Edited by F. L. Holmes and T. H. Levere. pp. 137–152. Cambridge: MIT Press.

Holmes, Frederic L. and Kathryn M. Olesko. 1995. The Images of Precision: Helmholtz and the Graphical Method in Physiology. In: *The Values of Precision.* Edited by M. N. Wise. pp. 198–221. Princeton: Princeton University Press.

Hont, Istvan and Michael Ignatieff. 1983. *Wealth and Virtue: The Shaping of Political Economy in the Scottish Enlightenment.* Cambridge: Cambridge University Press.

Hoover, Kevin D. 1991. Mirowski's Screed: A Review of Philip Mirowski's *More Heat than Light. Methodus.* **3**.1: 139–145.

Hoover, Kevin D. and Michael E. Dowell. 2001. Measuring Causes: Episodes in the Quantitative Assessment of the Value of Money. *History of Political Economy.* **33**. Annual Supplement: 137–161.

Horkheimer, Max and Theodor W. Adorno. [1947] 1986. *Dialektik der Aufklärung.* Frankfurt a.M.: S. Fischer.

Houghton, Walter E. and Jean Harris Slingerland. 1966. *The Wellesley Index to Victorian Periodicals, 1824–1900: Tables of Contents and Identification of Contributors with Bibliographies of Their Articles and Stories.* London and New York: Routledge.

Howey, R. S. 1960. *The Rise of the Marginal Utility School 1870–1889*. Lawrence, KS: University of Kansas Press.

Hutchison, Terence W. [1982] 1988. The Politics and Philosophy in Jevons's Political Economy. In: *William Stanley Jevons: Critical Assessments*, 3 Vols. Edited by J. C. Wood. pp. 383–395. London and New York: Routledge.

Hyman, Anthony. 1985. *Science and Reform: Selected Works of Charles Babbage*. Cambridge: Cambridge University Press.

1989. *Science and Reform: Selected Works of Charles Babbage*. Cambridge: Cambridge University Press.

Inkster, Ian. 1975. Science and the Mechanics Institutes, 1820–1850: The Case of Sheffield. *Annals of Science*. **32**: 451–474.

Inoue, Takutoshi and Michael V. White. 1993. Bibliography of Published Works by W. S. Jevons. *Journal of the History of Economic Thought*. **15**: 122–147.

Israel, Jonathan I. 2001. *Radical Enlightenment: Philosophy and the Making of Modernity, 1650–1750*. Oxford: Oxford University Press.

Jacyna, L. S. 1981. The Physiology of Mind, The Unity of Nature, and the Moral Order in Victorian Thought. *British Journal for the History of Science*. **14**.2: 109–132.

1983. Immanence or Transcendence: Theories of Life and Organization in Britain, 1790–1835. *Isis*. **74**: 311–329.

1994. *Philosophic Whigs: Medicine, Science and Citizenship in Edinburgh, 1789–1848*. London and New York: Routledge.

Jaffé, William. 1976. Menger, Jevons and Walras De-Homogenized. *Economic Inquiry*. **14**.4: 511–524.

Johnston, Stephen. 1997. Making the Arithmometer Count. *Bulletin of the Scientific Instrument Society*. **52**: 12–21.

Katoh, Shoji. 1989. Mechanics Institutes in Great Britain to the 1850s. *Journal of Educational Administration and History*. **21**.2: 1–7.

Keynes, John Maynard. [1936] 1988. William Stanley Jevons 1835–1882: A Centenary Allocution on His Life and Work as Economist and Statistician. In: *William Stanley Jevons: Critical Assessments*. Edited by J. C. Wood. pp. 50–93. London and New York: Routledge.

Kidd, A. J. and K. W. Roberts. 1985. *City, Class and Culture: Studies of Cultural Production and Social Policy in Victorian Manchester*. Manchester: Manchester University Press.

Kim, Jinbang. 1995. Jevons versus Cairnes on Exact Economic Laws. In: *Measurement, Quantification and Economic Analysis: Numeracy in Economics*. Edited by I. H. Rima. pp. 140–156. London and New York: Routledge.

Klamer, Arjo. 1990. The Textbook Presentation of Economic Discourse. In: *Economics as Discourse*. Edited by W. Samuels. pp. 129–154. Boston: Kluwer.

Klein, Judy L. 1995. The Method of Diagrams and the Black Arts of Inductive Economics. In: *Measurement, Quantification and Economic Analysis: Numeracy in Economics*. Edited by Ingrid H. Rima. pp. 98–139. London and New York: Routledge.

1997. *Statistical Visions in Time: A History of Time Series Analysis 1662–1938*. Cambridge: Cambridge University Press.

2001. Reflections from the Age of Economic Measurement. *History of Political Economy*. **33**. Annual Supplement: 111–136.

Klein, Judy L. and Mary S. Morgan. 2001. *The Age of Economic Measurement (Annual Supplement to History of Political Economy,* Vol. 33). Durham, NC: Duke University Press.

Klein, Ursula. 1999. Techniques of Modelling and Paper-Tools in Classical Chemistry. In: *Models as Mediators.* Edited by M. S. Morgan and M. Morrison. Cambridge: Cambridge University Press.

——— 2001. Paper Tools in Experimental Cultures. *Studies in History and Philosophy of Science Part A.* **32.**2: 265–302.

Klever, Wim. 1994. Herman Boerhaave (1668–1738) oder Spinozismus als rein mechanische Wissenschaft des Menschen. In: *Spinoza in der europäischen Geistesgeschichte.* Edited by H. Delf and J. H. Schoeps. pp. 75–93. Berlin: Hentrich.

Kneale, W. and M. Kneale. 1971. *The Development of Logic.* Oxford: Clarendon.

Könekamp, Rosamund. [1962] 1988. William Stanley Jevons (1835–1882): Some Biographical Notes. In: *William Stanley Jevons: Critical Assessments.* Edited by J. C. Wood. pp. 233–250. London and New York: Routledge.

Krüger, Lorenz, Lorraine Daston, Michael Heidelberger, Gerd Gigerenzer, and Mary Morgan. 1987. *The Probabilistic Revolution.* 2 Vols. Cambridge: MIT Press.

La Nauze, J. L. [1941] 1988. Jevons in Australia. In: *William Stanley Jevons: Critical Assessments.* Edited by J. C. Wood. pp. 109–124. London and New York: Routledge.

Lawrence, Christopher. 1979. The Nervous System and Society in the Scottish Enlightenment. In: *Natural Order: Historical Studies of Scientific Culture.* Edited by S. Steven and B. Barry. pp. 19–40. Beverly Hills and London: Sage.

Layton, David. 1965. Diction and Dictionaries in the Diffusion of Scientific Knowledge: An Aspect of the History of the Popularization of Science in Great Britain. *British Journal for the History of Science.* **2.**7: 221–234.

Letsky, Erna. 1979. *Franz Joseph Gall: 1758–1828, Naturforscher und Anthropologe; Ausgewählte Texte.* Bern: Huber.

Levere, Trevor. 1990. *Lavoisier. In Nature, Experiment, and the Sciences.* Dordrecht, Boston and London: Kluwer.

——— 1994. *Chemists and Chemistry in Nature and Society: 1770–1878.* Aldershot: Ashgate.

Levi Mortera, Emanuele. 2001. Dugald Stewart: Science, Methodology and Political Economy. Paper read to *ECSSS/IASSS Conference "Political Economy and Eighteenth Century Scottish Culture", George Mason University,* 10–12 June 2001.

Levy, David. 2000. *Poets Come Bringing Death to Friends of the Dismal Science.* George Mason University. Mimeo.

Levy, David and Sandra J. Peart 2001–2002. *The Secret History of the Dismal Science.* http://www.econlib.org/library/Colums/LevyPeartdismal6.html.

Lewin, Shira. 1996. Economics and Psychology: Lessons for Our Own Day from the Early Twentieth Century. *The Journal of Economic Literature.* **34.**3: 1293–1323.

Lindeboom, G. A. 1968. *Herman Boerhaave.* London: Methuen.

Lucas, Robert. 1988. On the Mechanics of Economic Development. *Journal of Monetary Economics.* **22.**1: 3–42.

Lyotard, Jean-François. 1991. *Leçons sur l'Analytique du Sublime: (Kant, Critique de la Faculté de Juger,* §§23–29). Paris: Galilée.

Maas, Harro. 1999a. Mechanical Rationality: Jevons and the Making of Economic Man. *Studies in History and Philosophy of Science.* **30.**4: 587–619.

1999b. Pacifying the Workman: Ruskin and Jevons on Labour and Popular Culture. *History of Political Economy*. **31**. Annual Supplement: 85–120.

1999c. Of Clouds and Statistics: Inferring Causal Structures from the Data. In: *Research Memoranda in History and Methodology of Economics 99–2*. Amsterdam: University of Amsterdam.

2001. An Instrument Can Make a Science: Jevons's Balancing Acts in Economics. *History of Political Economy*. **33**: 277–302.

2003. Where Mechanism Ends: Thomas Reid on the Moral and the Animal Oeconomy. *History of Political Economy*. **35**, Annual Supplement: 338–360.

Maas, Harro and Morgan, Mary. 2002. Timing History: The Introduction of Graphical Analysis in 19th Century British Economics. *Revue d'Histoire des Sciences Humaines*. **7**: 97–127.

MacHale, Desmond. 1985. *George Boole : His Life and Work*. Dublin: Boole.

Machamer, Peter. 1998. Galileo's Machines, His Mathematics, and His Experiments. In: *The Cambridge Companion to Galileo*. Edited by P. Machamer. pp. 53–79. Cambridge: Cambridge University Press.

Machamer, Peter, Lindley Darden, et al. 2000. Thinking about Mechanisms. *Philosophy of Science*. **67**: 1–25.

Maclennan, Barbara. 1972. Jevons's Philosophy of Science. *The Manchester School*. **40**: 53–71.

Maloney, John. 1976. Marshall, Cunningham, and the Emerging Economics Profession. *The Economic History Review*. **29**.3: 440–451.

Mays, Wolfe. [1962] 1988. Jevons's Conception of Scientific Method. In: *William Stanley Jevons: Critical Assessments*. Edited by J. C. Wood. pp. 212–232. London and New York: Routledge.

Mays, Wolfe and D. P. Henry. [1953] 1988. Jevons and Logic. In: *William Stanley Jevons – Critical Assessments*. Edited by J. C. Wood. pp. 167–187. London and New York: Routledge.

McCabe, Kevin, Daniel Houser, et al. 2001. A Functional Imaging Study of Cooperation in Two-Person Reciprocal Exchange. *Proceedings of the National Academy of Sciences of the United States of America*. **98**.20: 11832–11835.

McCallum, D. M., and J. B. Smith. 1951. Mechanized Reasoning: Logical Computers and Their Design. *Electronic Engineering*. **23**.278: 126–133.

McCloskey, Deirdre. 2001. *Measurement and Meaning in Economics: The Essential Deirdre McCloskey*. Edited by S. T. Ziliak. Cheltenham: Edward Elgar.

McCosh, James. [1875] 1990. *The Scottish Philosophy, Biographical, Expository, Critical, from Hutcheson to Hamilton*. Bristol: Thoemmes.

McNiven, Peter. 1983. Hand-List of the Jevons Archives in the John Rylands University Library. *Bulletin of the John Rylands University Library*. **66**: 213–55.

McReynolds, Paul. 1968. The Motivational Psychology of Jeremy Bentham: I. Background and General Approach. *Journal of the History of the Behavioral Sciences*. **4**: 230–244.

1968. Vol. 1. The Motivational Psychology of Jeremy Bentham. *Journal of the History of the Behavioral Sciences*. **4**: 349–364.

Ménard, Claude. 1980. Three Forms of Resistance to Statistics: Say, Cournot, Walras. *History of Political Economy*. **12**.4: 524–541.

Mink, Louis O. 1970. History and Fiction as Modes of Comprehension. *New Literary History*. **1**.3: 541–558.

Mirowski, Philip. [1984] 1988. Macroeconomic Instability and the Natural Processes in Early Neoclassical Economics. In: *William Stanley Jevons: Critical Assessments*. Edited by J. C. Wood. pp. 283–293. London and New York: Routledge.

  1988. Physics and the "Marginalist Revolution". In: *Against Mechanism: Protecting Economics from Science*. pp. 11–30. Lanham, MD: Rowman & Littlefield.

  1989. *More Heat than Light: Economics as Social Physics, Physics as Nature's Economics*. Cambridge: Cambridge University Press.

  1994. *Natural Images in Economic Thought: "Markets Read in Tooth & Claw"*. Cambridge: Cambridge University Press.

  2002. *Machine Dreams: Economics Becomes a Cyborg Science*. Cambridge: Cambridge University Press.

Montes, Leonidas. 2002. *Philosophical and Methodological Underpinnings of Adam Smith's Political Economy: A Critical Reconstruction of Some Central Components*. PhD Thesis, University of Cambridge.

Morgan, Mary S. 1990. *The History of Econometric Ideas*. Cambridge: Cambridge University Press.

  1997. Searching for Causal Relations in Economic Statistics: Reflections from History. In: *Causality in Crisis? Statistical Methods and the Search for Causal Knowledge in the Social Sciences*. Edited by R. M. Vaughn and S. P. Turner. pp. 47–80. Notre Dame: University of Notre Dame Press.

  1999. Learning from Models. In: *Models as Mediators*. Edited by M. Morrison and M. S. Morgan. pp. 347–388. Cambridge: Cambridge University Press.

  2000. Explanatory Strategies for Monetary Policy Analysis. In: *Macroeconomics and the Real World: Vol. I, Models, Evidence, and Techniques*. Edited by R. E. Backhouse and A. Salanti. pp. 141–153. Oxford: Oxford University Press.

  2001. Models, Stories and the Economic World. *Journal of Economic Methodology*. **8**.3: 361–384.

Morgan, Mary S. and Margaret Morrison. 1999. *Models as Mediators*. Cambridge: Cambridge University Press.

Morrell, Jack and Arnold Thackray. 1981. *Gentlemen of Science: Early Years of the British Association for the Advancement of Science*. Oxford: Clarendon.

Morris, Susan W. 1994. Fleeming Jenkin and The Origin of Species: A Reassessment. *British Journal for the History of Science*. **27**: 313–343.

Morrison, P. and E. Morrison. 1961. *Charles Babbage and His Calculating Engines*. New York: Dover.

Moseley, Maboth. 1964. *Irascible Genius: The Life of Charles Babbage*. Chicago: Regnery.

Mosselmans, Bert. 1998. William Stanley Jevons and the Extent of Meaning in Logic and Economics. *History and Philosophy of Logic*. **19**: 83–99.

Mosselmans, Bert and Ernst Mathijs. 1999. Jevons's Music Manuscript and the Political Economy of Music. In: *Economic Engagements with Arts*. Edited by N. De Marchi and C. D. W. Goodwin. pp. 121–156. Durham, NC: Duke University Press.

Mumford, Lewis. 1946. *Technics and Civilization*. London and New York: Routledge.

Murray, David J. 1993. A Perspective for Viewing the History of Psychophysics. *Behavioural and Brain Sciences*. **16**: 115–186.

Nadel, Lynn. 2003. *Encyclopedia of Cognitive Science*. London: Macmillan.

Newman, William R. 2000. Alchemy, Assaying, and Experiment. In: *Instruments and Experimentation in the History of Chemistry*. Edited by F. L. Holmes and T. H. Levere. pp. 35–54. Cambridge: MIT Press.

Nicholls, Neville. 1998. William Stanley Jevons and the Climate of Australia. *Australian Meteorological Magazine*. **47**: 285–93.

Nikolow, Sybilla. 1999. Die Versinnlichung von Staatskräften: Statistische Karten um 1800. *Traverse*. **6**.3: 63–82.

———. 2001. A. F. W. Crome's Measurements of the Strength of the State Statistical Representations in Central Europe Around 1800. *History of Political Economy*. **33**. Annual Supplement: 23–56.

Paetzold, Heinz. 1974. *Neomarxistische Ästhetik*. Düsseldorf: Schwann.

Parssinen, T. M. 1974. Popular Science and Society: The Phrenology Movement in Early Victorian Britain. *Journal of Social History*. **8**.1: 1–20.

Peart, Sandra J. 1990. The Population Mechanism in Jevons, W. S. Applied Economics. *Manchester School of Economic and Social Studies*. **58**.1: 32–53.

———. 1993. W. S. Jevons's Methodology of Economics: Some Implications of the Procedures for "Inductive Quantification." *History of Political Economy*. **25**.3: 435–460.

———. 1995a. "Disturbing Causes", "Noxious Errors", and the Theory-Practice Distinction in the Economics of J. S. Mill and W. S. Jevons. *Canadian Journal of Economics*. **28**.4b: 1194–1211.

———. 1995b. Measurement in Utility Calculations: The Utilitarian Perspective. In: *Numeracy in Economics*. Edited by H. R. Ingrid. pp. 63–86. London and New York: Routledge.

———. 1996. *The Economics of W. S. Jevons*. London and New York: Routledge.

———. 1998. Jevons and Menger Re-homogenized?: Jaffé after 20 Years. *American Journal of Economics and Sociology*. **57**.3: 307–325.

———. 2001. "Facts Carefully Marshalled" in the Empirical Studies of William Stanley Jevons. *History of Political Economy*. **33**. Annual Supplement: 252–276.

———. 2003. *W. S. Jevons: Critical Responses*. 4 Vols. London and New York: Routledge.

Peckhaus, Volker. 2000. Was George Boole Really the "Father" of Modern Logic? In: *A Boole Anthology*. Edited by J. Gasser. pp. 271–285. Dordrecht: Kluwer.

Pocock, J. G. A. 1975. *The Machiavellian Moment: Florentine Political Thought and the Atlantic Republican Tradition*. Princeton: Princeton University Press.

Pointon, Marcia. 1999. Dealer in Magic: James Cox's Jewelry Museum and the Economics of Luxurious Spectacle in Late-Eighteenth-Century London. *History of Political Economy*. **31**. Annual Supplement: 423–451.

Pollard, Sidney. 1963. Factory Discipline in the Industrial Revolution. *The Economic History Review*. **16**.2: 254–271.

Porter, Theodore M. 1986. *The Rise of Statistical Thinking 1820–1900*. Princeton: Princeton University Press.

———. 1994. Making Things Quantitative. *Science in Context*. **7**.3: 389–407.

1995. *Trust in Numbers: The Pursuit of Objectivity in Science and Public Life.* Princeton: Princeton University Press.

2001. Economics and the History of Measurement. *History of Political Economy.* **33**. Annual Supplement: 4–22.

Pycior, Helena M. 1981. George Peacock and the British Origins of Symbolic Algebra. *Historia Mathematica.* **8**: 23–45.

1983. Augustus De Morgan's Algebraic Work: The Three Stages. *Isis.* **74**: 211–226.

1984. Internalism, Externalism, and Beyond: 19th Century British Algebra. *Historia Mathematica.* **11**: 424–441.

Rabinbach, Anson. 1992. *The Human Motor: Energy, Fatigue, and the Origins of Modernity.* New York: Basic Books.

Raffaelli, Tiziano. 1991. The Analysis of the Human Mind in the Early Marshallian Manuscripts. *Quaderni di Storia dell'Economia Politica.* **9**: 29–58.

2003. *Marshall's Evolutionary Economics.* London and New York: Routledge.

Rashid, Salim. 1977. William Whewell and Early Mathematical Economics. *The Manchester School.* **45**.4: 381–392.

1979. Richard Jones and Baconian Historicism at Cambridge. *Journal of Economic Issues.* **13**.1: 159–173.

1981. Political Economy and Geology in the Early Nineteenth Century: Similarities and Contrasts. *History of Political Economy.* **13**.4: 726.

1985. Dugald Stewart, "Baconian" Methodology, and Political Economy. *Journal of the History of Ideas.* **46**.2: 245–257.

Rice, Adrian. 1996a. Mathematics in the Metropolis: A Survey of Victorian London. *Historia Mathematica.* **23**.4: 376–417.

1996b. Augustus De Morgan: Historian of Science. *History of Science.* **34**.104: 201–240.

1999. What Makes a Great Mathematics Teacher? The Case of Augustus De Morgan. *The American Mathematic Monthly.* **106**.6: 534–552.

Rice, Adrian C., Robin J. Wilson, et al. 1995. From Student Club to National Society: The Founding of the London Mathematical Society in 186. *Historia Mathematica.* **22**.4: 402–421.

Richards, Joan. 1980. The Art and Science of British Algebra: A Study in the Perception of Mathematical Truth. *Historia Mathematica.* **7**: 343–65.

1987. Augustus De Morgan, the History of Mathematics, and the Foundations of Algebra. *Isis.* **78**.1: 6–30.

1991. Rigor and Clarity: Foundations of Mathematics in France and England, 1800–1840. *Science in Context.* **4**.2: 297–319.

2002. "In a Rational World All Radicals Would be Exterminated": Mathematics, Logic, and Secular Thinking in Augustus De Morgan's England. *Science in Context.* **15**.1: 137–164.

Robbins, Lionel. [1936] 1988. The Place of Jevons in the History of Economic Thought. In: *William Stanley Jevons: Critical Assessments.* Edited by J. C. Wood. pp. 94–108. London and New York: Routledge.

Robertson, R. M. [1951] 1988. Jevons and His Precursors. In: *William Stanley Jevons: Critical Assessments.* Edited by J. C. Wood. pp. 146–166. London and New York: Routledge.

Romano, Richard M. 1982. The Economic Ideas of Charles Babbage. *History of Political Economy*. **14**.3: 385–405.

Rosenberg, Nathan. 1965. Adam Smith on the Division of Labour: Two Views or One? *Economica*. **32**.125: 127–139.

1994. *Exploring the Black Box: Technology, Economics, and History.* Cambridge: Cambridge University Press.

Royston, Erica. 1956. Studies in the History of Probability and Statistics: III. A Note on the History of the Graphical Presentation of Data. *Biometrika*. **43**.3/4: 241–247.

Russell, Terence M. 1997. *Ephraim Chambers Cyclopaedia.* Aldershot: Ashgate.

Ryan, Alan. 1974. *John Stuart Mill.* London and New York: Routledge.

Rylance, Rick. 2000. *Victorian Psychology and British Culture, 1850–1880.* Oxford: Oxford University Press.

Sánchez Valencia, Victor. 2001. An Athenaeum Curiosity: De Morgan's Reviews of Boole and Jevons. *History and Philosophy of Logic*. **22**.2: 75–79.

Sandori, Paul. 1982. *The Logic of Machines and Structures.* New York: John Wiley & Sons.

Schabas, Margaret. [1984] 1988. The "Worldly Philosophy" of William Stanley Jevons. In: *William Stanley Jevons: Critical Assessments.* Edited by J. C. Wood. pp. 401–418. London and New York: Routledge.

1989. Alfred Marshall, W. Stanley Jevons, and the Mathematization of Economics. *Isis*. **80**: 60–73.

1990. *A World Ruled by Number: William Stanley Jevons and the Rise of Mathematical Economics.* Princeton: Princeton University Press.

1997. Victorian Economics and the Science of the Mind. In: *Victorian Science in Context.* Edited by B. Lightman. pp. 72–93. Chicago: Chicago University Press.

Schaffer, Simon. 1990. States of Mind: Enlightenment and Natural Philosophy. In: *The Languages of Psyche: Mind and Body in Enlightenment Thought.* Edited by G. S. Rousseau. pp. 233–290. Berkeley: University of California Press.

1994a. Babbage's Intelligence: Calculating Engines and the Factory System. *Critical Inquiry*. **21**: 203–227.

1994b. Machine Philosophy: Demonstration Devices in Georgian Mechanics. *Osiris*. **9**: 157–182.

1996. Babbage's Dancer and the Impresarios of Mechanism. In: *Cultural Babbage, Technology, Time and Invention.* Edited by F. Spufford and J. S. Uglow. pp. 52–80. London: Faber & Faber.

1997. Babbage's Dancer and the Impresarios of Mechanism. In: *Cultural Babbage, Technology, Time and Invention.* Edited by F. Spufford and J. S. Uglow. pp. 52–80. London: Faber & Faber.

Schmitt, Raymond W. 1995. The Salt Finger Experiments of Jevons (1857) and Rayleigh (1880). *Journal of Physical Oceanography*. **25**.1: 8–17.

Schneewind, J. B. 1977. *Sidgwick's Ethics and Victorian Moral Philosophy.* Oxford: Clarendon.

Schofield, Robert E. 1970. *Mechanism and Materialism: British Natural Philosophy in an Age of Reason.* Princeton: Princeton University Press.

Secord, Anne. 2003. "Be What You Would Seem to Be": Samuel Smiles, Thomas Edward, and the Making of a Working-Class Scientific Hero. *Science in Context*. **16**: 147–173.

Sent, Esther-Mirjam. 2000. Herbert A. Simon as a Cyborg Scientist. *Perspectives on Science*. **8**.4: 380–406.

Shapin, Steven. 1979. Homo Phrenologicus: Anthropological Perspectives on an Historical Problem. In: *Natural Order: Historical Studies of Scientific Culture*. Edited by S. Shapin and B. Barnes. pp. 41–72. London: Sage.

Shapin, Steven and Barry Barnes. 1977. Science, Nature and Control: Interpreting Mechanics Institutes. *Social Studies of Science*. **7**: 31–74.

Sheenan, R. G. and R. Grieves. [1982] 1988. Sunspots and Cycles: A Test of Causation. In: *William Stanley Jevons: Critical Assessments*. Edited by J. C. Wood. pp. 189–192. London and New York: Routledge.

Sher, Richard. 2000. Science and Medicine in the Scottish Enlightenment. In: *The Scottish Enlightenment: Essays in Reinterpretation*. Edited by P. B. Wood. pp. 99–156. Rochester: University of Rochester Press.

Sibum, Heinz Otto. 1995. Reworking the Mechanical Value of Heat: Instruments of Precision and Gestures of Accuracy in Early Victorian England. *Studies in History and Philosophy of Science*. **26**.1: 73–106.

Sigot, N. 2002. Jevons's Debt to Bentham: Mathematical Economy, Morals and Psychology. *The Manchester School*. **70**.2: 262–278.

Simon, Herbert. 1969. Understanding the Natural and the Artificial Worlds. In: *The Sciences of the Artificial*. pp. 1–22. Cambridge: Cambridge University Press.

Smith, C. U. M. 1997. Worlds in Collision: Owen and Huxley on the Brain. *Science in Context*. **10**.2: 343–366.

Smith, Crosbie. 1980. Engineering the Universe: William Thomson and Fleeming Jenkin on the Nature of Matter. *Annals of Science*. **37**.4: 387–415.

Smith, Crosbie and M. Norton Wise. 1989. *Energy and Empire: A Biographical Study of Lord Kelvin*. Cambridge: Cambridge University Press.

Smith, G. C. 1982. *The Boole–De Morgan Correspondence (1842–1864)*. Oxford: Clarendon.

Smith, Lindsay. 1995. *Victorian Photography, Painting, and Poetry: The Enigma of Visibility in Ruskin, Morris, and the Pre-Raphaelites*. Cambridge: Cambridge University Press.

Smith, Roger. 1973. The Background of Physiological Psychology in Natural Philosophy. *History of Science*. **11**.2: 75–123.

Stamhuis, Ida. 1989. *Cijfers en Aequaties en Kennis der Staatskrachten: Statistiek in Nederland in de Negentiende Eeuw*. Amsterdam-Atlanta: Rodopi.

Standage, Tom. 2002. *The Mechanical Turk: The True Story of the Chess-Playing Machine that Fooled the World*. London: Allen Lane.

Stephens, Michael D. and W. Roderick Gordon. 1972. Science, the Working Classes and Mechanics Institutes. *Annals of Science*. **29**.4: 349–360.

Stewart, M. A. 1990. *Studies in the Philosophy of the Scottish Enlightenment*. Oxford: Clarendon.

Stigler, George. [1983] 1988. Review of Papers and Correspondence of William Stanley Jevons. In: *William Stanley Jevons – Critical Assessments*. Edited by J. C. Wood. pp. 277–279. London and New York: Routledge.

Stigler, Stephen M. 1982. Jevons as Statistician. *The Manchester School*. **50**: 354–365.
     1994. Jevons on the King Davenant Law of Demand: A Simple Resolution of a Historical Puzzle. *History of Political Economy*. **26**: 185–191.
Swade, Doron. 1991. *Charles Babbage and His Calculating Engines*. London: Science Museum.
     1996. "It Will Not Slice a Pineapple": Babbage, Miracles and Machines. In: *Cultural Babbage, Technology, Time and Invention*. Edited by F. Spufford and J. S. Uglow. pp. 34–51. London: Faber & Faber.
     2000. *The Cogwheel Brain: Charles Babbage and the Quest to Build the First Computer*. London: Little, Brown and Company.
Swijtink, Zeno G. 1987. The Objectification of Observation: Measurement and Statistical Methods in the Nineteenth Century. In: *The Probabilistic Revolution*. Edited by L. Krüger et al . Vol. 1. pp. 261–286. Cambridge: MIT Press.
Thompson, E. P. 1968. *The Making of the English Working Class*. Harmondsworth: Penguin.
     1978. *The Poverty of Theory and Other Essays*. London: Merlin.
Thomson, William. [1884] 1987. *Kelvin's Baltimore Lectures and Modern Theoretical Physics: Historical and Philosophical Perspectives*. Edited by R. Kargon and P. Achinstein. Cambridge: MIT Press.
Trevor-Roper, Hugh (Lord Dacre). 1977. The Scottish Enlightenment. *Blackwood's Edinburgh Magazine*. **322**.1945: 371.
Tufte, Edward R. 1983. *The Visual Display of Quantitative Information*. Cheshire: Graphics.
     1997. *Visual Explanations: Images and Quantities, Evidence and Narrative*. Cheshire: Graphics.
Turner, G. L. and T. H. Levere, 1973. *Martinus Van Marum: Life and Work. Vol. 4. Van Marum's Scientific Instruments in Teyler's Museum*. Leiden: Noordhoff.
Twyman, Michael. 1986. Articulating Graphic Language: A Historical Perspective. In: *Toward a New Understanding of Literacy*. Edited by M. E. Wrolstad and D. F. Fisher. pp. 188–251. New York: Praeger.
Uglow, Jennifer S. 2002. *The Lunar Men: The Friends Who Made the Future, 1730–1810*. London: Faber & Faber.
Underwood, E. Ashworth. 1977. *Boerhaave's Men at Leyden and After*. Edinburgh: Edinburgh University Press.
Vass, Pamela. 1999. Rediscovering Thomas Fowler (1777–1843): Mathematician and Inventor. *Report and Transactions of the Devonshire Association for the Advancement of Science, Literature and Art*. **131**: 11–25.
Vassallo, Nicla. 1997. Analysis versus Laws: Boole's Explanatory Psychologism versus His Explanatory Anti-Psychologism. *History and Philosophy of Logic*. **18**: 151–163.
     2000. Psychologism in Logic: Some Similarities between Boole and Frege. In: *A Boole Anthology: Recent and Classical Studies in the Logic of George Boole*. Edited by J. Gasser. Dordrecht: Kluwer.
Vatin, François. 1993. *Le Travail: Economie et Physique*. Paris: Presses Universitaires de France.
     1996. Du Travail à la Fatigue: Genèse et Échec de la Psycho-Physiologie du Travail. *Bulletin de Psychologie*. **49**.425: 520–529.

Veblen Thorstein, B. [1904] 1975. *The Theory of Business Enterprise*. New York: Augustus M. Kelley.

Velthuis, Olav. 2002. *Talking Prices*. PhD Thesis, Erasmus University.

Vint, John. 1994. *Capital and Wages: A Lakatosian History of the Wages Fund Doctrine*. Aldershot: Edward Elgar.

Warke, Tom. 2000. Mathematical Fitness in the Evolution of the Utility Concept from Bentham to Jevons to Marshall. *Journal of the History of Economic Thought*. **22**.1: 5–27.

Warren, Howard C. [1921] 1967. *A History of the Association Psychology*. New York: Johnson Reprint.

Warwick, Andrew. 1995. The Laboratory of Theory or What's Exact About the Exact Sciences? In: *The Values of Precision*. Edited by M. N. Wise. pp. 311–351. Princeton: Princeton University Press.

Watson, Michael I. 1987. The Origins of the Mechanics Institutes of North Yorkshire. *Journal of Educational Administration and History*. **19**. 2: 12–25.

Weintraub, Roy. 2002. *How Economics Became a Mathematical Science*. Durham, NC: Duke University Press.

Wess, J. 1997. The Logic Demonstrators of the 3rd Earl Stanhope (1753–1816). *Annals of Science*. **54**.4: 375–395.

West, Edwin G. 1996. Adam Smith on the Cultural Effects of Specialization: Splenetics versus Economics. *History of Political Economy*. **28**.1: 83–105.

Westergaard, H. 1916. *Scope and Method of Statistics*. [S.l.]: American Management Association, no. 115.

White, A. 1988. Class, Culture and Control: the Sheffield Athenaeum Movement and the Middle Class 1847–64. In: *The Culture of Capital: Art, Power and the Nineteenth Century Middle Class*. Edited by S. J. and J. Wolff. Manchester: Manchester University Press.

White, Hayden. 1975. *Metahistory: the Historical Imagination in Nineteenth-Century Europe*. Baltimore: Johns Hopkins University Press.

White, Michael V. [1982] 1988. Jevons in Australia: A Reassessment. In: *William Stanley Jevons: Critical Assessments*. Edited by J. C. Wood. pp. 329–350. London and New York: Routledge.

1989. Why Are There No Supply and Demand Curves in Jevons. *History of Political Economy*. **21**.3: 425–456.

1991a. Frightening the Landed Fogies: Parliamentary Politics. *The Coal Question*, *Utilitas*. **3**.2: 289–302.

1991b. Jevons on Utility, Exchange, and Demand Theory: Comment. *The Manchester School*. **59**.1: 80–83.

1991c. Jevons's "Blunder" Concerning Value and Distribution: An Explanation. *Cambridge Journal of Economics*. **15**: 149–160.

1991d. Where Did Jevons' Energy Come From? *History of Economics Review*. **15**: 60–72.

1992. Diamonds Are Forever(?): Nassau Senior and Utility Theory. *The Manchester School*. **60**.1: 64–78.

1993. The Irish Factor in Jevons's Statistics: A Note. *History of Economics Review*. **19**.Winter: 79–85.

1994a. The Moment of Richard Jennings: The Production of Jevons's Marginalist Economic Agent. In: *Natural Images in Economic Thought: "Markets Read in Thooth and Claw"*. Edited by P. Mirowski. Cambridge: Cambridge University Press.

1994b. "That God-Forgotten Thornton": Exorcising Higgling after On Labour. *History of Political Economy*. **26**. Annual Supplement: 149–183.

1994c. Bridging the Natural and the Social: Science and Character in Jevons's Political Economy. *Economic Inquiry*. **32**.2: 429–444.

1994d. Following Strange Gods: Women in Jevons's Political Economy. In: *Feminism and Political Economy in Victorian England*. Edited by G. Peter. pp. 46–78. Aldershot: Edward Elgar.

1994e. Jevons and the Population Mechanism – Comment. *The Manchester School*. **62**.1: 97–102.

1994f. A Five Per Cent Racist? Rejoinder to Professor Hutchison. *History of Economics Review*. **21**. Winter: 71–86.

1995. *Perpetual Motion and Change: Statics and Dynamics in the Political Economy of W. S. Jevons*: Mimeo.

1996. No Matter of Regret: The Cambridge Critique(s) of Jevons's 'Hedonics'. In: *Economics and Ethics?* Edited by P. Groenewegen. pp. 103–120. London and New York: Routledge.

1999. Obscure Objects of Desire? Nineteenth-Century British Economists and the Price(s) of "Rare Art". *History of Political Economy*. **31**. Annual Supplement: 57–84.

2001. Indeterminacy in Exchange: Disinterring Jevons's Trading Bodies. *The Manchester School*. **69**.2: 208–226.

2004a. "A Grin Without a Cat": W. S. Jevons' Elusive Equilibrium. In: *History and Political Economy. Essays in Honour of P. D. Groenewegen*. Edited by T. Aspromourgos and J. Lodewijks. London and New York: Routledge.

2004b. In the Lobby of the Energy Hotel: W. S. Jevons' Formulation of the Post-Classical Economic Problem. *History of Political Economy*. **36**.2: 227–271.

Wible, James R. 2003. The Cambridge Scientific Club, the Pragmatism of the Metaphysical Club, and the Mathematical Political Economy of Charles Sanders Peirce in the 1870s: Mimeo.

Wilkes, M. V. 1990. Herschel, Peacock, Babbage and the Development of the Cambridge Curriculum. *Notes and Records of the Royal Society of London* **44**: 205–219.

Williams, Michael R. 1985. *A History of Computing Technology*. Englewood Cliffs, NJ: Prentice-Hall.

Winter, Alison. 1998. *Mesmerized: Powers of Mind in Victorian Britain*. Chicago: University of Chicago Press.

Wise, M. Norton. 1993. Mediations: Enlightenment Balancing Acts, or the Technology of Rationalism. In: *World Changes: Thomas Kuhn and the Nature of Science*. Edited by P. Horwich. pp. 207–256. Cambridge: MIT Press.

Wise, M. Norton (and Crosbie Smith). 1989a. Work and Waste – Political Economy and Natural Philosophy in Nineteenth-Century Britain. *History of Science*. **27**.3: 263–301.

1989b. Work and Waste – Political Economy and Natural Philosophy in Nineteenth Century Britain. *History of Science*. **27**.4: 391–449.

1990. Work and Waste – Political Economy and Natural Philosophy in Nineteenth Century Britain. *History of Science*. **28**.3: 221–261.

Wood, Gaby. 2002. *Edison's Eve: A Magical History of the Quest for Mechanical Life*. New York: Knopf.

Wood, John Cunningham. 1988. *William Stanley Jevons: Critical Assessments*. 3 Vols. London and New York: Routledge.

Wood, Paul. 1990. The Natural History of Man in the Scottish Enlightenment. *History of Science*. **28**.1: 89–123.

1995. *Thomas Reid on the Animate Creation*. Edinburgh: Edinburgh University Press.

2000a. "Dugald Stewart and the Invention of 'The Scottish Enlightenment'". In: *The Scottish Enlightenment: Essays in Reinterpretation*. Edited by P. Wood. pp. 1–37. Rochester, NY: University of Rochester Press.

2000b. *The Scottish Enlightenment: Essays in Reinterpretation*. Rochester, NY: University of Rochester Press.

Woodward, James. 2000. *Experimentation, Causal Inference, and Instrumental Realism*. Mimeo.

Woodward, William R. and Mitchell G. Ash. 1982. *The Problematic Science: Psychology in Nineteenth-Century Thought*. New York: Praeger.

Wright, John P. 1990. Metaphysics and Physiology. In: *Studies in the Philosophy of the Scottish Enlightenment*. Edited by M. A. Stewart. pp. 251–301. Oxford: Clarendon.

2000. Materialism and the Life Soul in Eighteenth-Century Scottish Physiology. In: *The Scottish Enlightenment: Essays in Reinterpretation*. Edited by P. B. Wood. pp. 177–198. Rochester: University of Rochester Press.

Yeo, Richard. 1993. *Defining Science: William Whewell, Natural Knowledge, and Public Debate in Early Victorian Britain*. Cambridge: Cambridge University Press.

2001. *Encyclopaedic Visions: Scientific Dictionaries and Enlightenment Culture*. Cambridge: Cambridge University Press.

Yolton, John W. 1984. *Thinking Matter: Materialism in Eighteenth-Century Britain*. Oxford: Basil Blackwell.

Young, Robert M. 1968. The Functions of the Brain: Gall to Ferrier (1808–1886). *Isis*. **59**.198: 251–268.

1970. *Mind, Brain and Adaptation in the Nineteenth Century: Cerebral Localization and Its Biological Context from Gall to Ferrier*. Oxford: Clarendon.

INDEX

Philosophical radicalism, 27, 45, 46, 51, 122, 157
  its agnosticism, 45
  a threat to English society, 46. *See also* Ricardian economics
Poor Law committee, 68
Popular amusement, 214
  a means of controlling the workmen, 210
Porter, Theodore, 44, 104, 223
Potter, Richard, 31
Pouillet, 93
Precision, 109, 255, 257, 261, 263. *See also* accuracy
Pricing of art, 192
Priestley, Joseph, 38, 112, 120, 129, 156, 157, 163, 225, 272
  his *Chart of Biography*, 221–223, 225, 226
Principle of least action, 202, 203, 206
The Principles of Science (Jevons), 5, 7, 8, 32–34, 124, 131, 141, 142, 144, 149, 174, 180, 203, 234, 235, 237, 239–241, 243, 254, 255, 261, 264, 268, 285, 286
Principles of the lever, 105, 132, 275. *See also* balance
Probability, 107, 266
Probability theory, 116, 145
Prony, Gaspard de, 100, 101, 147, 186
Protectionism, 252
Proust, Marcel, 221
Providence, 38, 45–47, 49, 57, 106, 108, 122, 287. *See also* Babbage, Charles; Jevons, William Stanley; Whewell, William
Psychological method, 168, 169
Psychologism. *See* Boole, George
Psycho-physics, 155, 167, 168, 169, 173
Psychophysiology, 10, 12, 23, 24, 25, 152, 153, 155, 162, 164, 165, 169, 172, 177, 178, 180, 270, 275, 285, 286, 288, 289
Pycior, Helena, 111

Quantification of the predicate, 115, 116, 118. *See also* De Morgan, Augustus; Hamilton, Sir William

Quantity theory of money, 25, 264, 269, 270
Queen's College, Liverpool, 33, 96, 124, 182, 213
Quetelet, Adolphe, 65, 68, 155, 175, 176, 268
Quincy, 14

Rabinbach, Anson, 163
Race (racism), 208, 214
Raffaelli, Tiziano, 157
Raleigh, Lord. *See* Strutt, John William
Raleigh-Taylor instability, 94
Ratio of utility, 31, 172
Rational explanations, 203
Rational formula, 234–236
Rationality, 285
  and logic, 285
Ratio of exchange, 275
Rational recreations, 163
Reaction time measurement, 169
Reasoning machine(s). *See* Logical machine. *See also* Calculating machines
Reflection. *See* Introspection
Reflex action, 162, 164–166
Reflex theory, 163
Regulae philosophandi (Newton), 149, 280
Reid, Thomas, 11, 37, 120, 157, 158, 160, 161
Res cogitans, 163
Res extensa, 163
Ricardian economics, 5, 38, 43, 44, 46, 50, 61, 63, 64, 68, 69, 71, 106, 156, 252
  its alleged use of the inductive method, 50
  contrasted with the "ethical school" of Malthus & Jones, 50. *See also* Jevons, William Stanley; Jones, Richard; McCulloch, John; Mill, John Stuart; Whewell, William
Ricardian rent scheme. *See* Tenure systems
Ricardians, 5, 46–48, 50, 51, 58, 60, 64, 65, 69
Ricardo, David, 2, 5, 34, 47, 49, 50, 151, 205, 238
Rice, Adrian, 23, 31
Richards, Joan, 147
Robbins, Lionel, 3, 4, 9, 192

Robertson, Croom, 32, 122, 149, 152, 153
Robertson, John, 37
Roscoe, Harry, 28, 33, 80, 182, 258
Roscoe, Mary-Ann, 26
Roscoe, William, 26
Routine labour, 185, 194
  and modern science, 149, 150
  and reasoning, 131, 138, 146–149
Royal Society, 101, 102, 130, 131, 148, 218, 232
Royal Statistical Society. *See* Statistical Society of London
Rusholme Town Hall, Manchester, 182
Ruskin, John, 77, 78, 88, 181–184, 189–196, 199, 212–216, 265
Russell, Bertrand, 22

Salt-fingers in the ocean, 79
Sánchez Valencia, Victor, 32
Saving the phenomena, 54, 57, 58, 61, 62
Schabas, Margaret, 5–7, 11, 30–32, 180, 256
Schaffer, Simon, 21, 105, 107, 130, 141
Schmitt, Raynold, 82, 83, 94
Schumpeter, Joseph A., 4
Science Museum London, 102–104
Science of operations, 23, 112, 117, 119
Scientific discovery, 123
Scottish Enlightenment, 37, 38, 120, 163, 280
Secession movement (and American Civil War), 252
Section F of the BAAS, 4, 31, 64, 68, 69, 183, 233, 247, 254, 278
Sedgwick, Adam, 65, 66
Self-acting inventions, 197, 198
Self-command, 280, 281
Senior, Nassau, 37, 51, 68, 69, 170, 171, 173, 205
Sensory-motor system, 164
A Serious Fall in the Value of Gold Ascertained, and Its Social Effects Set forth, with Two Diagrams (Jevons), 33, 97, 245, 257, 264
Shannon, C.E., 136
Shaw, Bernard, 34